The Writer's Craft

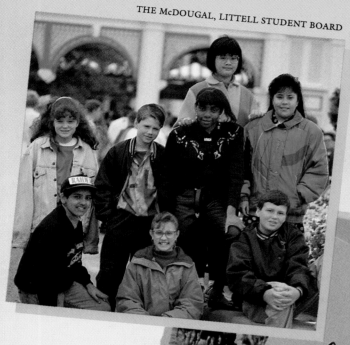

THE McDOUGAL, LITTELL STUDENT BOARD

Dear Pat,
We pitched our tent a few yards from a stream, and yesterday I saw two deer come down to get water. Birds like the ones in the photo are all around our campsite. They wake me up at 5:00 in the morning!
Chris

The Writer's Craft

SENIOR AUTHOR

SHERIDAN BLAU
University of California at Santa Barbara

CONSULTING AUTHOR

PETER ELBOW
University of Massachusetts at Amherst

SPECIAL CONTRIBUTING AUTHORS

Don Killgallon
Baltimore County Public Schools

Rebekah Caplan
Oakland Unified School District

SENIOR CONSULTANTS

Arthur Applebee
State University of New York at Albany

Judith Langer
State University of New York at Albany

McDougal Littell
A HOUGHTON MIFFLIN COMPANY
Evanston, Illinois · Boston · Dallas

SENIOR AUTHOR

Sheridan Blau, Senior Lecturer in English and Education and former Director of Composition, University of California at Santa Barbara; Director, South Coast Writing Project; Director, Literature Institute for Teachers

The Senior Author, in collaboration with the Consulting Author, helped establish the theoretical framework of the program and the pedagogical design of the Workshop prototype. In addition, he guided the development of the spiral of writing assignments, served as author of the literary Workshops, and reviewed completed Writer's Workshops to ensure consistency with current research and the philosophy of the series.

CONSULTING AUTHOR

Peter Elbow, Professor of English, University of Massachusetts at Amherst; Fellow, Bard Center for Writing and Thinking

The Consulting Author, in collaboration with the Senior Author, helped establish the theoretical framework for the series and the pedagogical design of the Writer's Workshops. He also reviewed Writer's Workshops and designated Writing Handbook lessons for consistency with current research and the philosophy of the series.

SPECIAL CONTRIBUTING AUTHORS

Don Killgallon, English Chairman, Educational Consultant, Baltimore County Public Schools. Mr. Killgallon conceptualized, designed, and wrote all of the features on sentence composing.

Rebekah Caplan, Coordinator, English Language Arts K–12, Oakland Unified School District, Oakland, CA; Teacher-Consultant, Bay Area Writing Project, University of California at Berkeley. Ms. Caplan developed the strategy of "Show, Don't Tell," first introduced in the book *Writers in Training,* published by Dale Seymour Publications. She also wrote the Handbook lessons and Sketchbook features for this series that deal with that concept.

SENIOR CONSULTANTS

These consultants reviewed the completed prototype to ensure consistency with current research and continuity within the series.

Arthur N. Applebee, Professor of Education, State University of New York at Albany; Director, Center for the Learning and Teaching of Literature; Senior Fellow, Center for Writing and Literacy

Judith A. Langer, Professor of Education, State University of New York at Albany; Co-director, Center for the Learning and Teaching of Literature; Senior Fellow, Center for Writing and Literacy

MULTICULTURAL ADVISORS

The multicultural advisors reviewed the literary selections for appropriate content and made suggestions for teaching lessons in a multicultural classroom.

Andrea B. Bermúdez, Professor of Multicultural Education; Director, Research Center for Language and Culture, University of Houston —Clear Lake

Alice A. Kawazoe, Director of Curriculum and Staff Development, Oakland Unified School District, Oakland, CA

Sandra Mehojah, Project Coordinator, Office of Indian Education, Omaha Public Schools, Omaha, NE

Alexs D. Pate, Writer, Consultant, Lecturer, Macalester College and the University of Minnesota

STUDENT CONTRIBUTORS

The following students contributed their writing.

Alyce Arnick, Aurora, CO; Gil Atanasoff, Kenosha, WI; Jaime Carr, York, PA; Celeste Coleman, Clovis, CA; Kara DeCarolis, Golden, CO; Jason Edwards, Clovis, CA; Ben Everett, Charleston, IL; Doug Frieburg, Lisle, IL; Jeff Hayden, St. Louis, MO; Latoya Hunter, Mt. Vernon, NY; Alisa Monnier, Arlington Heights, IL; Jonathan Moskaitis, Easton, PA; Vanessa Ramirez, Santa Barbara, CA; Dave Smith, Brookfield, WI; Tim Stanley, Las Vegas, NV; Melissa Starr, Houston, TX; Anna Quiroz, Kenosha, WI

The following students reviewed selections to assess their appeal.

Joseph Blandford, Barrington, IL; Janet Cheung, Chicago, IL; Andrea Dobrowski, Kenilworth, IL; Stephen Malcom, Chicago, IL; Utíca Miller, Evanston, IL; Andrea Ramirez, Kenosha, WI; Joy Rathod, Chicago, IL; Debra Simmet, Zion, IL; Elizabeth Vargas, Chicago, IL

TEACHER CONSULTANTS

The following teachers served as advisors on the development of the Workshop prototype and/or reviewed completed Workshops.

Wanda Bamberg, Aldine Independent School District, Houston, TX

Karen Bollinger, Tower Heights Middle School, Centerville, OH

Barbara Ann Boulden, Issaquah Middle School, Issaquah, WA

Sherryl D. Broyles, Language Arts Specialist, Los Angeles Unified School District, Los Angeles, CA

Christine Bustle, Elmbrook Middle School, Elm Grove, WI

Denise M. Campbell, Eaglecrest School, Cherry Creek School District, Aurora, CO

Cheryl Cherry, Haven Middle School, Evanston, IL

Gracie Garza, L.B.J. Junior High School, Pharr, TX

Patricia Fitzsimmons Hunter, John F. Kennedy Middle School, Springfield, MA

Mary F. La Lane, Driftwood Middle School, Hollywood, FL

Barbara Lang, South Junior High School, Arlington Heights, IL

Harry Laub, Newark Board of Education, Newark, NJ

Sister Loretta Josepha, S.C., Sts. Peter and Paul School, Bronx, NY

Jacqueline McWilliams, Carnegie School, Chicago, IL

Joanna Martin, Thompson Junior High School, St. Charles, IL

Karen Perry, Kennedy Junior High School, Lisle, IL

Patricia A. Richardson, Resident Teacher-Trainer, Harold A. Wilson Professional Development School, Newark, NJ

Pauline Sahakian, Clovis Unified School District, Clovis, CA

Elaine Sherman, Curriculum Director, Clark County, Las Vegas, NV

Richard Wagner, Language Arts Curriculum Coordinator, Paradise Valley School District, Phoenix, AZ

Beth Yeager, McKinley Elementary School, Santa Barbara, CA

Printed in the United States of America.

ISBN 0–395-86370-8

3 4 5 6 7 8 9 10 – VJM – 01 00 99 98

Table of Contents

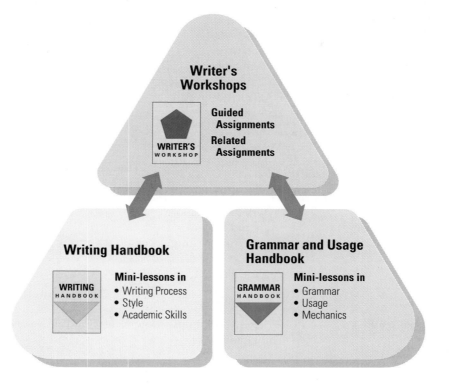

Writer's Workshops

WRITER'S WORKSHOP

Guided Assignments

Related Assignments

Writing Handbook

WRITING HANDBOOK

Mini-lessons in
- Writing Process
- Style
- Academic Skills

Grammar and Usage Handbook

GRAMMAR HANDBOOK

Mini-lessons in
- Grammar
- Usage
- Mechanics

You are special. You think and act in ways that are uniquely your own. This book recognizes the fact that you are an individual. On every page you will be encouraged to discover techniques best suited to your own personal writing style. Just as important, you will learn to think your way through every writing task.

In each of the Writer's Workshops, you will experiment with ideas and approaches as you are guided through a complete piece of writing. Cross-references to the Handbooks will allow you to find additional help when you need it. Then, as you write, you will discover what you think about yourself—and about the world around you.

Starting Points

For more in-depth treatment of each stage of the writing process, see the Writing Handbook Mini-lessons on pages 188–332.

Writer's Workshops

WRITER'S WORKSHOP 1
Personal and Expressive Writing

Observation and Description

Narrative and Literary Writing

Informative Writing: Explaining *How*

Persuasion

Responding to Literature

WRITER'S WORKSHOP 7

Informative Writing: Reports

Writing Handbook

MINI-LESSONS

Grammar and Usage Handbook

MINI-LESSONS

This Peruvian wall hanging illustrates the daily life of people in the mountains near Lima, Peru. The apple, carrot, potato, and prickly pear (fruit-bearing cactus) images represent some of the staples in the people's diet. They use the llamas to transport goods through mountains to the markets in Lima.

Starting Points

Do you write only when you have to? If so, you may be surprised to learn that writing isn't just a way of showing teachers what you know or telling your parents where you'll be after school. Writing is also an amazing tool that can help you in all kinds of everyday situations.

The Writer's Craft will help you discover all the possibilities of writing. It will show you how to use your pen or word processor to sort through your thoughts and feelings, to explore the answers to problems, and even to invent new worlds with words. All *you* have to do is read on—and start writing.

Getting Ready

Writing can help you with just about anything—from remembering the important details of a conversation to making sense of the changes going on inside you and around you. What's more, in the process of writing you can make all sorts of discoveries about yourself and the world—about what you know and what you might like to learn more about. Think for a minute about all the special purposes you can use writing for.

To Discover

Writing can help you discover what you think and feel. If you have a question or a problem, writing about it can lead you to an answer. If you have a feeling you can't quite pin down, putting that feeling into words can help you identify it. If you've had a confusing experience, writing about it may help you to make sense of it.

To Remember

Are there people, places, and experiences you never want to forget? memories you treasure? Writing in a journal about what you've seen, heard, tasted, touched, smelled, thought, and felt can capture these experiences on paper. Even when you've forgotten the events you've recorded, your writing will bring everything back to you. In this way, a journal can be your own personal time capsule. Years from now, it can give you gifts from the past.

To Explore and Invent

When you write, you can create your own world. You can go anywhere you want and do anything you want—anything you can imagine. You can explore ancient pyramids in Mexico or figure out what an eleven-year-old might do if he could pick up cellular-phone conversations on his braces. You can predict the future, change the past, invent a special gadget—even dance on the moon.

To Plan and Prepare

Putting your ideas on paper can help you plan what you'll do next Saturday afternoon or how you'll spend that money you've been earning by recycling cans. Jotting down a few key phrases or ideas can help you prepare for that all-important phone conversation with someone special. You can even use pen and paper to plan a party by making lists of the friends you want to invite and the foods you will serve. Writing is an ideal way to organize your thoughts.

To Learn

When you're reading or studying, do questions pop into your mind? Writing down those questions can remind you to look for the answers later. When you're reading a book or watching television, do you find yourself talking back to the characters? Why not write down your comments instead? Writing your reactions can help you tune in to what you're thinking and feeling.

Taking notes on what you're reading or hearing can also help you fix the information in your mind. If the information is confusing, writing it down can even help you make better sense of it. So whether you're covering a student council meeting for the school newspaper or listening to your grandfather talk about what life was like during the Great Depression, keep a pen and some paper handy.

Everyone has different moods. For example, sometimes you want to be alone, and at other times you want to be around people. In the same way, sometimes you'll want to write on your own, and at other times you'll prefer to write with others. This book gives you opportunities to do both.

Writing on Your Own

Whether you want to explore very personal thoughts and feelings or you just want to experiment with some new ideas and ways of expressing yourself, try writing on your own. In private writing you can take risks and say whatever is on your mind, because no one else ever has to read what you've written.

There are many ways to get started writing on your own. For instance, you might begin by writing in your journal or by freewriting. **Freewriting** is a way of exploring ideas or feelings by writing freely for a specific length of time. The activities in Handbooks 1 and 2 on pages 192–202 can also help you get started.

Writing with Others

You *may* choose to write alone and keep your writing to yourself. However, writing with others as well as sharing your writing can be very enjoyable, encouraging, and helpful. You and your classmates can help one another by

- brainstorming together to find topics
- listening to one another's ideas
- sharing ways you've solved writing problems
- responding, if you wish, to one another's work

Understanding the Writing Process

Every time you write, the experience is different. On one occasion, all your ideas might come out in a rush. Another time, you might need more help getting started. You might need to read, sketch, freewrite, or discuss your ideas with others. Most times you write, however, you will find yourself doing some or all of these activities: prewriting, drafting, revising, proofreading, publishing, presenting, and reflecting.

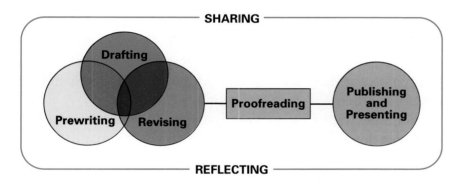

PREWRITE AND EXPLORE

Prewriting is what you do to find your topic and material for writing. You might draw pictures, talk with friends, freewrite, read, or daydream. You might even take a walk or rummage through a cluttered closet. Prewriting is whatever you do to figure out what you care about, what you think, what you know, and what you need to find out.

There may be times when you need to do very little prewriting before you draft. However, when you do want to explore your ideas to discover a topic or gather details, you may find the prewriting techniques in Handbooks 1–5 on pages 192–214 very helpful.

DRAFT AND DISCOVER

The process of **drafting** involves putting your ideas down on paper. It's a time for experimenting—for trying out ideas and seeing where they lead you. As you write, you may find that a new idea takes you in a surprising direction. That's all right. Just get everything down on paper. Later, you can go back and smooth out any rough spots.

After you finish a draft, it's a good idea to put your writing away for a while. Just a little time away from your work can help you see if there are words or ideas you want to change or develop further.

You may want to share your writing with your classmates—**peer readers.** Sharing the discoveries you've made during drafting helps you enjoy your writing and understand it better. Sometimes you will want to get responses to your writing. At other times you may just want to hear how your words sound. In any case, sharing your writing helps you see your work the way your readers do. You can then tell what's working and what needs changing.

REVISE YOUR WRITING

After drafting, you're ready to **revise,** or improve, what you've written. Usually the first step is taking a fresh look at your writing to see how it's working. Peer comments can help you with this. What you do next, though, depends on the kinds of improvements you decide to make. For example, to clear up a paragraph a reader found confusing, you might add information or rearrange your sentences. To make a description clearer, you might add transitions or replace some words with more vivid or specific ones. As you revise, you might also take new directions and make additional changes you hadn't thought of before.

PROOFREAD

Proofreading means carefully checking your writing and correcting any errors in grammar, usage, spelling, and punctuation. The symbols in Handbook 18, "Proofreading," on page 262 can help. After you've corrected any errors, you can make a final copy of your work.

PUBLISH, PRESENT, AND REFLECT

Although you've probably shown your writing to others as you've worked, **publishing and presenting** involves *formally* sharing your finished piece of writing with an audience. In this book you'll find many suggestions for publishing and presenting.

After you've finished your writing, it's helpful to think about what you've written and what you've learned about your topic and yourself as a writer. This kind of thinking, or **reflecting,** may involve asking yourself the following questions. How have my feelings about the subject changed since I started working on this piece? Did I write differently from the way I usually write? How? Why? What helped me to do a good job, and what got in my way?

Using This Book

Think of this book as your own personal writing coach, ready to offer you the advice, support, and direction you need to become a better writer. Like a good coach, *The Writer's Craft* tries to understand your needs, offers you helpful suggestions, and provides you with a variety of enjoyable and interesting opportunities for writing.

As you go through *The Writer's Craft,* you'll find that it is divided into three sections: **Writer's Workshops,** a **Writing Handbook,** and a **Grammar and Usage Handbook.**

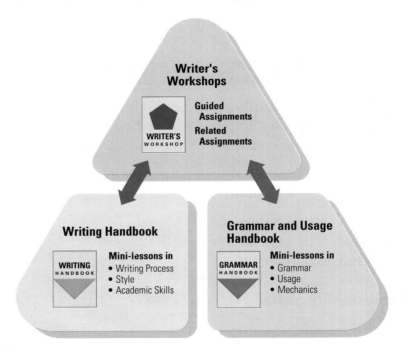

Writer's Workshops

WRITER'S
WORKSHOP

Guided Assignments
Related Assignments

Writing Handbook

WRITING
HANDBOOK

Mini-lessons in
• Writing Process
• Style
• Academic Skills

Grammar and Usage Handbook

GRAMMAR
HANDBOOK

Mini-lessons in
• Grammar
• Usage
• Mechanics

WRITER'S WORKSHOPS

The Writer's Workshops invite you to try many different kinds of writing—descriptions, stories, poems, jokes, family histories. Each Writer's Workshop consists of one Guided

Assignment and one Related Assignment. Special features that appear just before and after each Writer's Workshop—and in other places throughout *The Writer's Craft*—offer additional opportunities for writing.

Guided Assignments

Each Guided Assignment introduces you to a certain kind of writing—personal writing, writing to explain, writing about literature—and then guides you through the process of creating that kind of writing. Along the way, you get to see how a professional writer and another student have approached the same kind of writing assignment. As you work, **Problem Solving** notes in the margins point you to other parts of the book that can help you solve writing problems you may face.

Related Assignments

A Related Assignment follows each Guided Assignment. It gives you a chance to apply the skills you've just learned by experimenting with a related type of writing—a poem, perhaps, or a public-opinion survey. In the Related Assignments, you have the freedom to develop your writing in your own special way.

Additional Writing Opportunities

In addition to the workshops, throughout this book there are many other opportunities to write. For example, if you just want to play with your writing skills, you can turn to one of the Sketchbooks that appear before the workshops. These **Sketchbooks** offer "no-risk" writing warm-ups. To apply your writing skills to other school subjects or to find additional ideas to write about, you can flip to the **Springboards** at the end of each workshop. Springboards suggest interesting ways to use the writing skills you've learned.

Finally, if you like experimenting with words and phrases, you may like the **Sentence Composing** activities. In these activities you learn new ways to vary your sentences by imitating sentences written by professional writers. In the process you may discover your own personal style.

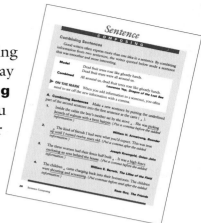

THE HANDBOOKS

The Writing Handbook and the Grammar and Usage Handbook offer the special help and practice you need to carry out the assignments in the workshops. Although Problem Solving notes in the workshops point out when certain handbook sections may be useful, you may also want to explore the handbooks on your own.

The Writing Handbook

This handbook is made up of mini-lessons that offer help and practice in everything from finding ideas and making your writing sound like you to using the library. Literary, professional, and student models show you how other writers use the skills and strategies you are learning. For example, the model on this page shows you how one author uses dialogue in his writing.

The Grammar and Usage Handbook

When you want a better understanding of how the English language works, the mini-lessons that make up this handbook can help. These lessons explain everything from the parts of speech to capitalization and punctuation. The page shown here, for example, teaches about adjectives.

Discovery Workshop

Maggie Sh...

Whenever you want to learn to do something new—whether it's planting a garden or painting a picture of one—you probably ask someone to show you how to do it. The Writer's Workshops in this book give you that kind of guidance. Each one tells you what form of writing you will work on and offers you suggestions on how to create that particular form.

One of the most wonderful things about writing, though, is that there isn't just one way to do it. In fact, when you let yourself write freely, writing can be a series of fascinating surprises.

In this Discovery Workshop, you'll have a chance to experience writing as an adventure. In addition, from the blue notes in the margins you'll learn how to use the sections and features of the Writer's Workshops that follow.

Writing to Discover

Where do you get your writing ideas? A journal entry gave Maggie Skeffington the idea to write about her first jump from a high board. As you read the different forms Maggie's writing took, look for similarities and differences between them. Why would she have written about the same experience in so many different ways?

> The *Starting from Literature* and *Reading a Student Model* boxes give you important information about the professional and student models.

July 14 — Jack, Ryan, Megan, and I went to their community pool today, and I conquered the high dive !! My first jump was because Jack and Ryan dared me to — but the headfirst dive was my idea. I don't know how I got the nerve to jump in the first place or why I let them embarrass me into it. I was so scared I was sick! But I did it. Then when the jump turned out to be so much fun I decided diving would be even better. I actually <u>dove</u> off the board.

High Dive

My heart is pounding
As I climb the metal steps.
Clank!
Clank!
Clank!
Icy water — Everything's spinning
Go back!
Hold on!
What a dumb dare.

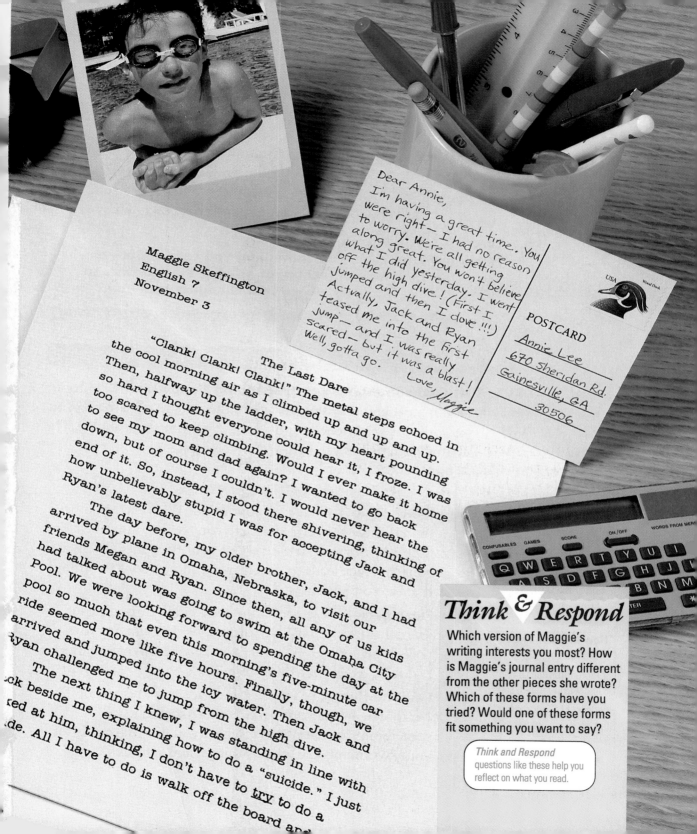

Dear Annie,
I'm having a great time. You were right— I had no reason to worry. We're all getting along great. You won't believe what I did yesterday. I went off the high dive! (First I jumped and then I dove !!!) Actually, Jack and Ryan teased me into the first jump— and I was really scared— but it was a blast! Well, gotta go.
Love, Maggie

POSTCARD

USA   Wood Duck

Annie Lee
670 Sheridan Rd.
Gainesville, GA
30506

Maggie Skeffington
English 7
November 3

The Last Dare

"Clank! Clank! Clank!" The metal steps echoed in the cool morning air as I climbed up and up and up. Then, halfway up the ladder, with my heart pounding so hard I thought everyone could hear it, I froze. I was too scared to keep climbing. Would I ever make it home to see my mom and dad again? I wanted to go back down, but of course I couldn't. I would never hear the end of it. So, instead, I stood there shivering, thinking of how unbelievably stupid I was for accepting Jack and Ryan's latest dare.

The day before, my older brother, Jack, and I had arrived by plane in Omaha, Nebraska, to visit our friends Megan and Ryan. Since then, all any of us kids had talked about was going to swim at the Omaha City Pool. We were looking forward to spending the day at the pool so much that even this morning's five-minute car ride seemed more like five hours. Finally, though, we arrived and jumped into the icy water. Then Jack and Ryan challenged me to jump from the high dive.

The next thing I knew, I was standing in line with [Ja]ck beside me, explaining how to do a "suicide." I just [star]ed at him, thinking, I don't have to try to do a [sui]cide. All I have to do is walk off the board an[d]

Think & Respond

Which version of Maggie's writing interests you most? How is Maggie's journal entry different from the other pieces she wrote? Which of these forms have you tried? Would one of these forms fit something you want to say?

Think and Respond questions like these help you reflect on what you read.

INVITATION
== TO ==
Write

Each time Maggie Skeffington wrote about her high-diving experience she made new discoveries. Some were about the experience. Others were about herself. Now you have the chance to make your own discoveries through writing.

Write to explore something you care about—an experience, a feeling, or an idea that matters to you. Then see where your thoughts lead you.

PREWRITE AND EXPLORE

1. Find something worth spending time with. The topics you'll most enjoy writing about are the ones that matter to you, so look for experiences and ideas you really care about. The following activities can help you find a topic.

Exploring Topics

PROBLEM
S O L V I N G

"How else can I find ideas?"

For more information on finding writing ideas, see

- Handbook 2, "Finding a Starting Point," pages 197–202

- **Freewriting**   What's on your mind? What have you been thinking about lately? What are you feeling right now? To find out, just start writing about your thoughts. Then, as your first idea leads to others, write more about the things that interest you most.

- **Flash back**   Take a few minutes to look through your journal entries or family photographs. Dig out any toys, collections, or souvenirs that you've saved. What memories and feelings do they bring to mind?

- **Favorite things**   Is there someplace you love to go? The beach? An amusement park? Is there someone or something that never fails to cheer you up? Make a list of your favorite people, places, things, and activities.

2. Explore your ideas.   Jot down the most interesting ones you've found. Then talk about them with others, or freewrite about one or two possibilities for a while.

One Student's Process

When Maggie was looking for writing ideas, a short poem she'd written reminded her of the time she conquered the high dive. She then did some freewriting to recall more about the experience.

> I remember that climb. My heart really was pounding hard. Worse, though, was that halfway up I just froze on the ladder. I was too scared to keep climbing, but I knew I couldn't go back. If I had, Ryan and Jack would never have let me hear the end of it. So I just stood there feeling terrified, wishing I hadn't taken their stupid dare.
>
> Talk about your dumb dares. That one was certainly at the top of the list. I'm never <u>ever</u> going to let myself be pushed into doing anything I'm that scared of doing again. I'm just glad everything worked out OK.

In One Student's Process, you'll see the prewriting, drafting, and revising done by a student writer like yourself. Your own writing process may be similar—or it may be very different.

3. Take stock.   Think about all the ideas you've just explored. Have you discovered one that you'd like to spend some time with? If not, look at some other journal entries or at some of the items you've paused over, or try more talking or freewriting.

4. Gather details.   Once you've found a topic you like, begin gathering details you can use to flesh out a draft. If you've done some freewriting, you may already have a lot of material. Otherwise, you can simply spend some time thinking about your topic or create lists or graphic organizers. For example, you might list the facts or background information you know about your topic. You might also list sensory details—how things looked, sounded, smelled, tasted, and felt.

PROBLEM
SOLVING

"How do I find details?"
For information on finding details, see
- Handbook 4, "Developing a Topic," pages 205–210

Writer's Choice   You can choose a form before drafting, or you can just begin writing and see what happens. However, even if you select a form before drafting, you can change your mind later.

Draft and Discover

1. Begin writing.   At this point all you need to do is get something down on paper. You don't need to know where your ideas will take you. Just begin writing and see what takes shape on the page. Let your ideas flow from your pen right onto the page without stopping to judge them.

2. Read what you've written.   Take a moment to look at your draft. Do you like what you see? Do you know what form you would like your writing to take? Have you given any thought to your personal goals for writing? Jotting down your answers to some of the following questions may help you figure out what you want to do next.

Questions to Ask Yourself	
Form and Organization	• What's a good way to present my ideas? Has my draft led me to a particular form of writing—such as a story, a poem, or a report?
	• What order should my ideas follow? What should my readers see first? next? last?
Development	• Have I included all of the most important details?
	• Have I gotten across the heart of what I want to say?
Personal Goals	• What do I want this writing to do?
	• Do I want to share this writing with an audience, or do I want to keep it private?

3. Consider sharing your writing. You don't *have* to share your writing. However, it can feel good to find out that someone else understands and likes what you've written. Furthermore, peer reactions can show you what is working in your draft and what you might need to add or change. If you do decide to share your draft, try asking your readers questions like these:

- What do you think my writing is about?
- What parts of my draft do you like best?
- What, if anything, do you want to know more about?

Peer reader comments in the margin show you the responses and suggestions that one student gave to another. When you feel ready, you can ask your own peer readers to give you feedback on your writing too.

One Student's Process

Maggie found herself writing the story of what happened on the high dive. Here is part of her first draft of that story, along with the peer comments she got on it.

> The sound of my feet pounding on the metal steps echoed in the morning air as I climbed. Then, halfway up, with my heart pounding, I froze. What I wanted was I wanted to go back down, but of course I couldn't. So, instead, I stood there feeling cold and thinking of how unbelievably stupid I was for accepting Jack and Ryan's latest dare.

Peer Reader Comments

I really like the part where you're frozen on the ladder.

Why did you want to go back down?

I've let myself be embarrassed into doing some pretty scary things too.

REVISE YOUR WRITING

1. Take a fresh look at your writing. Use your own ideas and your peer readers' comments to discover what's working in your draft and what you might want to change. Then decide on the improvements you want to make.

In this section you'll learn strategies for reworking your writing to make it as good as it can be.

2. Check your content and organization. Have you said everything you wanted to say? Is your material organized in a way that makes sense?

Marginal notes like these offer writing and grammar tips as well as suggestions for using a computer when you write.

One Student's Process

Here are some changes Maggie made to her draft. She would make even more changes later.

Clank! Clank! Clank!
The sound of my feet pounding on the metal

steps echoed in the morning air as I climbed.

Then, halfway up, with my heart pounding, I froze.

What I wanted was I wanted to go back down, but

of course I couldn't. So, instead, I stood there
I would never hear the end of it.

feeling cold and thinking of how unbelievably stupid

I was for accepting Jack and Ryan's latest dare.

I was too scared to keep climbing. Would I ever make it home to see my mom and dad again?

P R O O F R E A D

This section reminds you of all the little details you need to attend to before making a final copy of your draft.

Carefully check your writing and correct any errors in grammar, usage, spelling, and punctuation. The symbols on this chart can help you mark the changes you want to make.

Proofreading Symbols

∧ Add letters or words.	/ Make a capital letter lowercase.
⊙ Add a period.	⌐⌐ Begin a new paragraph.
≡ Capitalize a letter.	∼ Switch the positions of letters or words.
⌣ Close up space.	
⌄ Add a comma.	— or ⅋ Take out letters or words.

PUBLISH AND PRESENT

To share your work with others—your classmates, your teacher, or an even wider audience—try one or more of the following ideas.

Each workshop suggests a variety of ways for you to share your writing with a wide audience.

- **Plan a writing magazine.**   As a class, begin plans to publish writing you want to share with students in other classes. Such writing might include letters, movie reviews, journal entries, fiction, and even freewriting.
- **Go beyond the classroom.**   Take your work home to share it with family members and friends.
- **Market your manuscript.**   Submit your writing to a magazine that features student writing or to a school or community newspaper.

REFLECT ON YOUR WRITING

Reflecting on any experience can help you discover what you liked about it, what you learned from it, and what you want to do differently next time. So take some time now to think about the writing you've just completed, jotting down your answers to the following questions. Then, if you are using a portfolio, add your reflections to your portfolio as a note along with your finished piece.

After you complete each piece of writing, you'll have an opportunity to reflect on what you've learned about writing and about yourself.

- How did I discover what I wanted to say?
- How did I figure out what form I wanted to use?
- How do I feel about the piece I've written? What part of this piece am I most proud of?
- Which parts of the writing process were the most difficult for me?
- If I had this writing assignment to do over again, how might I do it differently?

One Student's Writing

Maggie Skeffington
English 7
November 3

The Last Dare

"Clank! Clank! Clank!" The metal steps echoed in the cool morning air as I climbed up and up and up. Then, halfway up the ladder, with my heart pounding so hard I thought everyone could hear it, I froze. I was too scared to keep climbing. Would I ever make it home to see my mom and dad again? I wanted to go back down, but of course I couldn't. I would never hear the end of it. So, instead, I stood there shivering, thinking of how unbelievably stupid I was for accepting Jack and Ryan's latest dare.

The day before, my older brother, Jack, and I had arrived by plane in Omaha, Nebraska, to visit our friends Megan and Ryan. Since then, all any of us kids had talked about was going to swim at the Omaha City Pool. We were looking forward to spending the day at the pool so much that even this morning's five-minute car ride seemed more like five hours. Finally, though, we arrived and jumped into the icy water. Then Jack and Ryan challenged me to jump from the high dive.

The next thing I knew, I was standing in line with Jack beside me, explaining how to do a "suicide." I just looked at him, thinking, I don't have to <u>try</u> to do a suicide. All I have to do is walk off the board and I'll be dead! The ground was too far away—and spinning. Then it was my turn.

"Come on! Hurry up!" My brother stood below me, screaming. I looked down, wanting to say something smart, but immediately realized that was a mistake. So I continued up, up THE STEPS TO DEATH.

"Clank! Clank! Clank!" All too soon I reached the tiny platform. With my heart pounding faster than ever, I stepped forward, and suddenly there was nothing under me.

For a moment I felt like one of those cartoon characters who has just stepped off a cliff and is still managing to hang in the air by pedaling his feet fast. Then, with my stomach churning, I began to fall.

Just when I was getting used to falling, "Boom!" I hit the water. Was this it? Was I dying? Sort of. I could hardly believe what was happening, but I was dying to do it again!

Of course, I was also still a little mad at myself for having gone through with something so terrifying just so that I wouldn't seem like a chicken. No more stupid dares, I promised myself. Then I got back in the high-dive line—this time to dive headfirst—but for <u>me</u>, because <u>I</u> wanted to dive, and not to prove anything to anyone else.

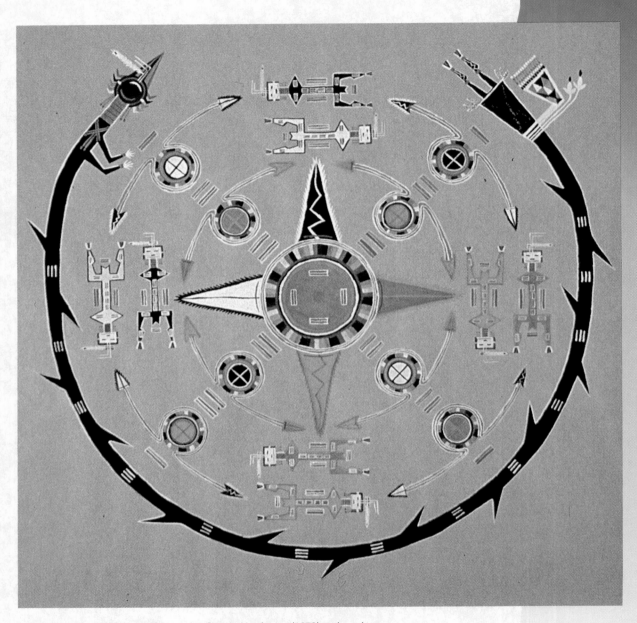

Big Star with Big Flies and Mountains Guarded by Arrows (1973), artist unknown.
Navajo artisans create sand paintings for religious ceremonies by sprinkling dry
pigments and other colored substances onto a flat surface. The outermost image
in this sand painting is a Rainbow Guardian in black flint armor. The Big Flies,
portrayed here with white faces, are important symbols in Navajo mythology.
The small circles represent the mountains that border Navajo homelands.

Writer's Workshops

Sketch Book

WRITING WARM-UPS

- Do any of these objects remind you of your childhood? Make a list of things you collected when you were younger, and freewrite about the memories they spark.

- What was the most important event in your life last year? What made it so important?

Show, Don't Tell

A writer keeps a journal to capture important thoughts, ideas, and feelings. Some writers expand journal entries into longer pieces of writing that *show* rather than *tell* their experiences. Try turning one of the *telling* sentences below into a *showing* paragraph.

- I don't know what I would do without my friends.
- I felt grown up.

26

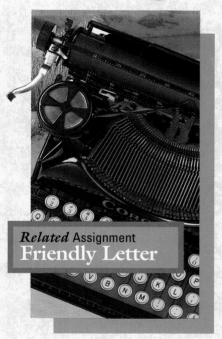

Personal and Expressive Writing

Guided Assignment
Writing from Your Journal

Related Assignment
Friendly Letter

Do you ever wish you could keep track of what you do every day—the places you go, things you see, conversations you have? Do you ever feel shy about telling someone how you feel? Keeping a journal may be the answer. You can discover what you think and how you feel by writing in this safe and private place.

In this workshop you'll keep a private journal. Then you'll learn how you can take an idea from your journal and turn it into a piece of writing to share with others. In a related assignment, you'll have a chance to write a letter to a friend or relative.

Writing from Your Journal

Starting from LITERATURE

Jean Fritz was born in Hankow, China. She lived there until she was twelve years old, when her family decided to move back to the United States. In *Homesick: My Own Story*, she writes about her last two years in China.

As you read this excerpt from Jean Fritz's autobiography, notice the way she shows how she felt about herself and her name. Have you ever had any of the thoughts or feelings Jean Fritz describes? How would you write about such feelings in a diary or journal?

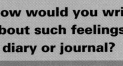

from

Homesick: My Own Story

by Jean Fritz

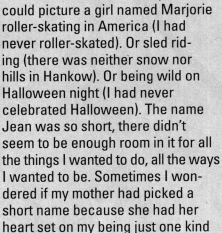

I always thought I would feel more American if I'd been named Marjorie. I could picture a girl named Marjorie roller-skating in America (I had never roller-skated). Or sled riding (there was neither snow nor hills in Hankow). Or being wild on Halloween night (I had never celebrated Halloween). The name Jean was so short, there didn't seem to be enough room in it for all the things I wanted to do, all the ways I wanted to be. Sometimes I wondered if my mother had picked a short name because she had her heart set on my being just one kind of person. Ever since she'd written in my autograph book, I was afraid that goodness was what she really wanted out of me.

"Be good, sweet child," she had written, "and let [those] who will, be clever."

Deep in my heart I knew that goodness didn't come natural to me. If I had to choose, I would rather be clever, but I didn't understand why anyone had to choose. I wasn't even sure that people could choose, although my mother was always saying that if they really tried, people could be whatever they wanted to be. But that was just more grown-up talk. As if wanting to be beautiful (like my mother) could make one bit of difference in my looks. As if trying to beat up Ian Forbes could do anything but land me in trouble. As for being good, I had to admit that I didn't always want to be. . . .

"I know what you can give me for Christmas," I told my mother.

"I've already bought your presents." My mother was writing letters at her little black lacquer desk and she didn't look up.

"This wouldn't cost a thing," I explained. "It would be easy."

"Well?" She still didn't look up.

"You could give me a new name. That's what I really want."

Now she did look up. She even put down her pen. "And what, may I ask, is the matter with the name you have?"

"I don't like it. Take it back." I put my arm around her neck because I didn't want her to feel bad about the mistake she'd made. "Give me the name Marjorie. Just write it on a gift card and put it in a box. You see how easy it would be."

My mother shook her head as if she couldn't understand how I'd got into the family. "I wouldn't name a cat Marjorie," she said.

Well, of course not! "Marjorie is not a cat's name," I yelled. And I stamped out of the room.

When I asked my father, he simply changed the subject. "I know one present you are getting for Christmas," he said, "that you've never even thought of."

He was a good subject-changer.

"Animal, vegetable, or mineral?" I asked.

"Vegetable."

"How heavy?"

"As heavy as a pound of butter." He'd give me no more clues, but of course I did give it a lot of thought between then and Christmas.

But I hadn't forgotten about Marjorie. . . .

Think & Respond

What do you think your name says about you? Do you have a nickname that suits you better? Why? How do you suppose this excerpt from Jean Fritz's autobiography is different from what she might have written in her journal?

One Student's Writing

Writers sometimes keep their journals and diaries private. At other times, though, writers want to share the experiences they've written about. Twelve-year-old Latoya Hunter revised and published the diary she kept during her first year in junior high school. As you read these excerpts from *The Diary of Latoya Hunter: My First Year in Junior High School*, ask yourself whether you have ever had the kinds of experiences Latoya writes about.

September 10, 1990
Dear Diary, It is hard to believe that this is the day I have anticipated and looked forward to for such a long time. . . . This may sound funny but somewhere in the back of my mind I thought the world would stop for my first day of J[unior] H[igh]. The day proved me wrong and I've grown to realize that nothing will be quite as I dreamed [it]. . . .

Diary, there isn't much of a welcoming committee at this school. However, there's a day eighth and ninth graders set out to show freshmen how they feel about us. They call it Freshman Day. It may sound sweet but it's not at all. What they set out to do is terrorize us. They really seem to want to hurt us. It's a tradition I guess. I hope with God's help that I'll be able to make it through without any broken bones. . . .

September 11, 1990
Dear Diary, I never thought I'd get desperate enough to say this but I envy you. . . . You don't have to go to J.H. and watch the clock, praying for dismissal time to come. You also don't have to go through a situation like sitting in a cafeteria watching others laughing and talking and you don't know anyone. To sit there and eat the food that is just terrible because there's nothing else to do.

You don't do any of those things. All you do is listen to pathetic twelve-year-olds like me tell you about it.

I guess you can tell how my day went. Diary, what am I going to do? My best friend left to go to another school. I wish she could be with me. We had so much fun together.

12

She moved right before summer started. She doesn't live anywhere close so it would be much easier if she stayed at the school closest to her. That's the only part of it that's easy. The hardest part is not being together. . . .

September 13, 1990
Dear Diary,   Is it strange for someone to <u>want</u> to get sick so they can't leave their house for a day? Well, I do and you know why—it's Freshman Day's eve and 'tis not the season to be jolly. The older kids are really trying to make us believe we're trespassing on their property. Well, it isn't theirs alone. If there is a special diary way of praying, pray I'll come home in one piece. I'll write to you tomorrow. If I survive.

September 14, 1990
Dear Diary,   I can't believe I'm here writing to you with no scratches or bruises. I actually made it! Something must have snapped in the minds of the older kids. Maybe they remembered when they were freshmen themselves because there were only a few fights today. . . .

In the morning, Mr. Gluck, the principal, announced that if anyone even thought of touching us it would mean suspension. Maybe that was why this Freshman Day was so much calmer. Whatever [the] reason why, I appreciate it.

Well Diary, what I assume was the worst week of J.H. is over. I hope things will get better next week. It has to. It can't get any worse . . . or can it?

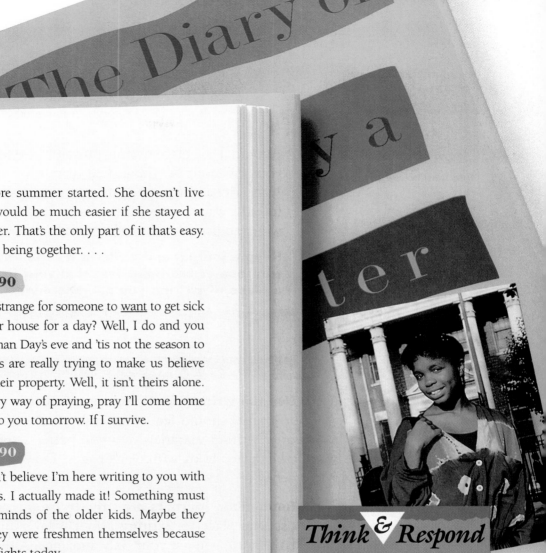

Think & Respond

Respond as a Reader

► Why do you think Latoya wrote about Freshman Day more than once?

► Why do you think Latoya calls her diary "you," as if it were a real person?

Respond as a Writer

► What do you think Latoya might have learned by keeping a diary?

► Latoya knew that other people would read her diary. How do you think that might have affected her writing?

INVITATION
TO
Write

A journal is a place where you can freely write for yourself about the things that matter to you most. Jean Fritz and Latoya Hunter are two writers who found a way to share such personal writing with a wider audience.

Keep a journal and write in it regularly. Then turn one or more entries from your journal into a piece of writing you can share with others.

KEEP A JOURNAL

1. Use the writing tools that are right for you.   Writing in your journal should feel comfortable and inviting, so use your favorite writing materials. Do you prefer a spiral or loose-leaf notebook or a book with blank pages? Do you like to use pencil or pen?

2. Remember, journals are private property.   Your journal is a special place for writing about what's important to you. What's more, you are your only audience. Although you might later choose to share parts of your journal with someone else, no one should read the parts you want to keep private.

3. Write in your journal.   Try to spend at least ten minutes each day freewriting in your journal. Remember, journal writing doesn't need to be planned, and it doesn't need to look polished. Therefore, you can start anywhere and write freely about whatever subjects are on your mind. On days when you're not sure what to write about, just start writing and see what happens.

Journal Writing Ideas

Topics	Questions	Idea Starters
Memories	• What happened in the past? • What do I remember about special places or events?	• a stuffed animal, a tape or CD, an autograph, a ticket stub
People	• Who's most important to me and why? • Whom do I most admire?	• photo albums, family, friends
Issues and Ideas	• What problems in the world or at home worry me? • How would I solve them?	• newspapers, magazines, TV, relationships at home
Daily Events	• What happened today? • What are my future plans and dreams?	• classes, conversations, after-school activities

 Writer's Choice   Do you want to fill your journal with only your personal writing? Do you want to use your journal as a kind of scrapbook and include drawings, snapshots, or clippings?

4. Be a reader of your own writing.   A journal is more than a place to write. Your journal is a wonderful book to read as well. It is the ever-changing story of *you.* Reread your writing each week and you'll discover what you've been thinking about most and how your thinking changes over time. You'll also see if you are expressing yourself clearly.

PREWRITE AND EXPLORE

1. Find a journal entry to turn into a finished piece. Your journal will have many entries about your experiences, thoughts, and feelings. Which entry or entries could be used as the basis for another piece of writing? Look for one or more of the following types of entries to find the best starting point for writing from your journal.

Writing
TIP

Some writers find it helpful to reflect on what they've written in their journals. Write an entry every couple of weeks about what you've been writing in your journal. This kind of reflective journal writing may help you learn more about yourself and your writing.

Exploring Topics

- **Feelings** Look through your journal for an entry in which you expressed the way you really felt about something. Did you write about a time when you were especially angry, sad, confused, or joyful?

- **Exclamation points** Did you write about something exciting that happened to you—a field trip, a day at the circus, your first concert? Find an entry about an event you'll want to remember years from now.

- **Common problems** Check your journal for an entry about a problem you faced and that other people might also face. Did you write about possible solutions? Would your solutions help others as well?

2. Do some freewriting about your entry or entries. First, ask yourself which parts of your journal writing are most worth sharing with others. Then, explore your ideas in writing. Don't recopy your journal; let your freewriting take you places you haven't yet explored.

Writing
═ TIP ═

Try using the questions *who, what, when, where, why,* and *how* to examine your topic. You could even show your answers on a chart in your journal.

One Student's Process

Many of Latoya Hunter's September diary entries focused on her fears about Freshman Day. If Latoya chose this subject idea to write about, she could start by exploring it through freewriting.

Freshman Day—still remember it like it was yesterday. I was nervous for days. I took the rumors the older kids spread about what they would do to us <u>so</u> seriously. It's funny to think about now tho. I thought it would be so much worse than it was! My imagination really went wild—it took over everything I did. In my mind, school felt like a scary place for a few days. Maybe I can do something with that idea.

DRAFT AND DISCOVER

1. Start drafting.   Use your journal and any freewriting you may have done to help you get started. Then write some more. You might begin by looking for bits of information you need to say more about. Also look for telling sentences you can turn into showing paragraphs.

2. Choose a form for your writing.   What direction is your writing starting to take? Have you been drafting a letter? a personal narrative? a poem? This chart shows you some forms your writing might take.

If my journal entry is about...	A possible form might be...
• a specific event	• story, skit, letter to a friend
• an intense feeling, memory, or experience	• poem, personal narrative, series of revised journal entries
• a social issue or world problem	• letter to the editor or to a politician

Notice that Jean Fritz focused on a specific memory and wrote a personal narrative.

3. Let yourself shine through.   The best writing comes straight from the heart, so be yourself. If you pretend to be someone you're not, your writing will sound phony and your readers may not believe what you say.

4. Think about your draft.   Once you've completed a draft, take a break. When you come back to your writing, you'll be able to review it with a fresh eye. Reread your piece and decide if you're ready to share it with one or more peer readers. Would you rather make some changes first, before you show your draft to someone else? The questions at the top of the next page will help you and your readers review your draft.

PROBLEM SOLVING

"How can I turn my notes into an interesting piece of writing?"

To help you present your ideas, see

• Handbook 12, "Show, Don't Tell," pages 239–242

PROBLEM SOLVING

"How can I make my writing sound like me?"

To help you develop your writing voice, see

• Handbook 21, "Personal Voice," pages 276–277

PROBLEM
S O L V I N G

"How can others help me write?"

For help in working with your peers, see

- Handbook 16, "Peer Response," pages 253–256

Questions for Yourself
- Why did I pick this idea to write about? What parts of my draft feel most important to me?
- What form is my writing taking? What other form might be worth trying?
- Have I included enough details for my readers to understand my ideas?

Questions for Your Peer Readers
- How does my writing make you feel? What parts of my writing were most interesting to you?
- What questions do you have about my subject?
- Does my writing sound like me? What doesn't sound natural?

Peer Reader Comments

I was scared before Freshman Day too. Can you add some details that would show how she felt?

I wonder what it would be like if you wrote the story from your own point of view. Do you think it might sound more like you?

One Student's Process

Latoya's diary entries about Freshman Day and her first awkward days in a new school make a terrific starting point for a short story. Here's part of a draft for that story. (A friend's responses are shown in the margin. What would you have said?)

She stood outside of her new school feeling small and afraid. The steps rose high in front of her. She took the flyer out of her pocket and read it again. It said Freshman Day is Tuesday. Freshmen beware. When the first bell sounded from inside, the kids in the upper grades rushed past her. Up the steps and through the double doors. She was afraid because she had heard about what was in store for the new kids. The warning was right there on the flyer. The final bell rang and jolted her out of her daydream.

REVISE YOUR WRITING

1. Judge your responses. Think about your own answers to the questions on page 36. Which of your peer readers' comments seem most helpful? What ideas do you now have about how to make your writing stronger?

2. Decide what changes to make. First, see if you want to try a new form. If not, look for more specific changes you can make. Do you need to reorder ideas, add details, or clarify any information?

 Paragraphs at Work When you're drafting about a personal feeling or experience, you may end up with one or two long paragraphs. As you revise, break your writing into paragraphs. Begin a new paragraph at these times:
- whenever there's a change in the action or setting
- whenever a new character begins to speak

PROBLEM

S O L V I N G

"How can I make my writing better?"

For information about revising your work, see

- Handbook 17, "Revising," pages 257–259

LINKING
GRAMMAR **AND** WRITING

Making Changes at the Best Time
When you work from your journal, translate notes to yourself into writing that others can understand. Turn abbreviations into words and brief fragments into sentences. Here are two revised lines from Latoya's journal.

Original

Cant believe Im here writing 2 U w/no scratches or anything I made it!

Revised

I can't believe I'm here writing to you with no scratches or bruises. I made it!

One Student's Process

Here's how Latoya might have revised her draft based on her reader's responses.

> I ˄ my   ˄ hugging my books
> ˄She stood outside of ~~her~~ new school ~~feeling~~
> ~~and looking back over my shoulder.~~
> ˄~~small and afraid.~~ The steps rose high in front of
> ~~me like a dangerous mountain peak.~~ I——my
> ~~her.~~ She took the flyer out of her pocket and read
>   ˄
> it again. ~~It said˄~~ "Freshman Day is Tuesday.
>   I" ¶
> Freshmen beware; When the warning bell sounded
>   the school,
> from inside, the kids in the upper grades rushed
>   me
> past ~~her.~~ Up the steps and through the double
>   What surprises were
> doors. ~~She was afraid˄because she had heard~~
>   us
> ~~about what was~~ in store for˄the new kids?

> Terror. Pain. The older kids seemed to want to
> hurt us. Our arms would be branded with an "F"
> for "freshman" in permanent ink so we'd always
> know our place.

PROOFREAD

1. Proofread your work. Correct mistakes you have made in grammar, spelling, punctuation, capitalization, and paragraphing.

2. Make a clean copy. Make any last-minute changes you want. Then make a clean copy or printout of your work.

PUBLISH AND PRESENT

- **Form a reader's circle.** Get together with several classmates and take turns reading your work aloud. After each piece has been read, discuss how it made you feel.

- **Make a journal sampler.** Collect everyone's writing in a loose-leaf notebook. As a class, decide on a title for your sampler and write a one-page introduction. You might even paste a photograph of your class on the cover.
- **Design a bulletin board.** Find photographs or make drawings that suit the subject or mood of your writing. Then post your work on a classroom bulletin board.

REFLECT ON YOUR WRITING

WRITER TO WRITER

I've recently done a lot of experiments with scrapbooks. I'll read in the newspaper something that reminds me of or has relation to something I've written. I'll cut out the picture or article and paste it in a scrapbook beside the words from my book.

William Burroughs, writer

1. Add your writing to your portfolio. How did it feel to share your writing with others? Think about the following questions. Then write a note to yourself in which you reflect on your writing. Clip it to your final draft.

- What am I learning about myself by keeping a journal?
- How did I change my original journal entry to get it ready to share with others?
- What was easiest about doing this kind of writing? What was hardest?
- How might keeping a journal help me with future writing assignments?

2. Explore additional writing ideas. See the suggestions for writing a friendly letter on pages 42–43 and Springboards on page 44.

FOR YOUR
PORTFOLIO

Friendly Letter

Starting from
LITERATURE

Everybody, even a professional writer, likes to get letters. However, not everybody likes to write them. When you write letters, do you have trouble thinking of things to say?

The well-known British scholar and author C. S. Lewis enjoyed exchanging letters with his god-daughter Sarah. As you read his letter, notice his casual tone, as if he were having a friendly conversation.

Magdalen College
Oxford
Feb 11th 1945

My dear Sarah—Please excuse me for not writing to you before to wish you a merry Christmas and a happy New Year and to thank you for your nice card which I liked very much; I think you have improved in drawing cats and these were very good, much better than I can do. I can only draw a cat from the back view like this I think it is rather cheating (don't you?) because it does not show the face, which is the difficult part to do. It is a funny thing that faces of people are easier to do than most animals' faces except perhaps elephants and owls. I wonder why that should be! The reason I have not written before is that we have had a dreadfully busy time with people being ill in the house and visitors and pipes getting frozen in the frost. All the same I like the frost (did you?): the woods looked really lovely with all the white on the trees, just like a picture to a story. But perhaps you were in London. I suppose it was not so nice there. We now have a Baby, about six weeks old, living in the house. It is a very quiet one and does not keep any of us awake at night. It is a boy. We still have our old big dog, he is eight years old. I think this is as much for a dog as fifty-six is for a man—you find this out by

finding what is seven times the dog's age. So he is getting rather gray and very slow and stately. He is great friends with the two cats, but if he sees a strange cat in the garden he goes for it at once. He seems to know at once whether it is a stranger or one of our own cats even if it is a long way off and looks just like one of them. His name is Bruce. The two cats are called Kitty-Koo and Pushkin. Kitty-Koo is old and black and very timid and gentle but Pushkin is gray and young and rather fierce. She does not know how to velvet her paws. She is not very nice to the old cat. I wonder how you are all getting on? Are you at school now and how do you like it? It must be about half way through term by now, I should think. Do you keep a "calendar" and cross off the days till the end of term? I am not going to post this till tomorrow because I want to put in a "book-token." You take it to a book-shop and they give you a book instead of it. This is for a kind of Christmas present, only it is very late. Now I have written you a letter you must write me one—that is, if you like writing letters but not otherwise. I used to like it once but I don't much now because I have so many to write, but my Brother does some of them for me on his type-writer which is a great help. Have you seen any snow-drops yet this year? I saw some two days ago. Give my love to the others—and to yourself

Your affectionate godfather
C. S. Lewis

Think & Respond

If you were Sarah, what things in the letter do you think you would have particularly enjoyed? Why? What details show that C. S. Lewis had Sarah's interests in mind?

INVITATION
TO
Write

Letter writing is a wonderful way to share your feelings with someone you care about. In today's world when everyone uses a telephone to stay in touch, a friendly letter is a special way to communicate.

Write a letter that shares with a reader something about yourself and your life.

KEEP IN TOUCH

1. Tell about yourself.   You might write to someone you know and share news and information that is important to you and that will interest your reader. Notice that many of the subjects C. S. Lewis writes about—the cat drawings, his old dog, the frost, the book-token—are things that will have meaning to Sarah.

2. Ask some questions.   Don't just write about yourself and your news. Also show an interest in your reader. What is happening in his or her life? Take your time and concentrate on writing interesting questions that call for more than just a yes or no answer. Remember that your questions give your reader a reason to write back.

3. What comes first?   Do you want to share your news first, or do you want to begin with questions you have? For example, you might write to an uncle who has always been interested in your sports activities to tell him about your last soccer match. A letter to a friend who recently moved might begin with questions about his or her new home.

4. Be yourself. A friendly letter is like one side of a conversation. Choose words that are comfortable and natural to you. Use your own writing voice. Be funny or serious, depending on your mood.

TAKE A FINAL LOOK

Even though a friendly letter is casual and informal, what you write should be clear and understandable. Keep these suggestions in mind as you look over your letter.

1. Read your letter to yourself. Have you included everything you planned to say? Does your writing sound like you?

2. Details matter. Look for errors in grammar, punctuation and spelling that may confuse a reader. Since friendly letters are often handwritten, you might want to be sure that your writing is neat and readable.

3. Letters follow a form. A friendly letter usually includes a date, a salutation or greeting, a body, a friendly closing, and sometimes a return address. For more information about letter forms see page 609.

Address your envelope carefully so that your letter gets to the right place. Include your own address as the return address.

PROBLEM
S O L V I N G

"What is my own writing voice?"

To write in a way that sounds like you, see

● Handbook 21, "Personal Voice," pages 276–277

Sarah Barrington
30 Forest Hills Avenue —— Return Address
Boston, MA 02130

Xavier Quiñones
286 Green Street
Marion, IL 62959

Spring boards

History

What do you think life was like for women living on the Western frontier during the 1800s? Take a new look at a period in history by reading a historical journal or a diary. Your librarian can help you locate a journal. Use the journal entries to create a story based on a person's life.

SOCIAL STUDIES

With your teacher's help, find and write to an international pen pal. Tell about a hobby, sport, or topic of interest to you. Ask your pen pal similar questions to learn about his or her interests.

Art

Look through art books to find a painting that especially interests you. Use your journal to jot down your feelings about the painting.

Literature

Have you ever wanted to talk to a character in a story? Try writing a letter instead. You might offer advice, share a secret, or ask a question.

Three Musicans (1921), Pablo Picasso.

Word Puzzles

If you have ever eaten a sausage, onion, mushroom, green pepper, olive, and pepperoni pizza, you probably know what this is:

> **everything**
> **pizza**

Since *everything* is sitting on top of *pizza,* this word puzzle says "pizza with everything on it."

Now see if you can figure out what popular phrase or expression each of these word puzzles says. Try inventing some of your own and sharing them with friends.

league

every   right   thing

R
G rosie I
N

T M
A   U
H   S
W   T

F   F
R   R
I   I
E   standing   E
N   miss   N
D   D
S   S

new leaf

wear
long

Sentence

Imitating Sentences

Life would be boring if you did the same things every day. Likewise, writing can be boring if you write every sentence the same way. You can learn new ways to vary your sentences by imitating sentences written by professional writers. Notice how each sentence in the description below is different.

Model A	The sword Dyrnwyn, blazing white with flame, leaped from Taran's hand and fell beyond his reach.
Model B	The Horned King stood over Taran.
Model C	With a cry, Eilonwy sprang at the antlered man.
Model D	Snarling, the giant Horned King tossed her aside.

Lloyd Alexander, *The Book of Three*

▶ **ON THE MARK**   Use commas to set off information that breaks up the flow of a sentence.

A. Chunking Sentence Parts   People read and write sentences in meaningful "chunks." That is, they break down sentences into groups of words that work together. Choose the sentence in each pair below that is divided into chunks of words that work together.

1. **a.** The sword / Dyrnwyn, blazing white with / flame, leaped from Taran's / hand and fell beyond his reach.
   b. The sword Dyrnwyn, / blazing white with flame, / leaped from Taran's hand / and fell beyond his reach.

2. **a.** The Horned / King stood over / Taran.
   b. The Horned King / stood / over Taran.

3. **a.** With a cry, / Eilonwy sprang / at the antlered man.
   b. With a / cry, Eilonwy sprang at the antlered / man.

4. **a.** Snarling, the / giant Horned / King tossed her aside.
   b. Snarling, / the giant Horned King / tossed her aside.

B. Identifying Imitations   Divide the sentences below into chunks. Then decide which sentences have chunks that match the models on page 46.

1. Choose the sentence that imitates Model A.

   a. Crashing over the rocks, the raft bounced and swirled as it sped through the rapids.

   b. My brother Bob, smiling broadly with pride, crossed over the finish line and waved to the crowd.

2. Choose the sentence that imitates Model B.

   a. The third baseman walked toward home plate.

   b. The dog and cat, usually enemies, became friends.

3. Choose the sentence that imitates Model C.

   a. In a flash, the horses bolted from the starting gate.

   b. The toddler peered up with a cute grin, charming everyone.

4. Choose the sentence that imitates Model D.

   a. As the game ended, the fans ran out onto the court.

   b. Diving, the shortstop snared the line drive.

C. Writing Imitations   Break each of the following model sentences from *The Book of Three* by Lloyd Alexander into meaningful chunks. Then write your own sentences made up of chunks that imitate the structure of the chunks in each model.

1. She unstrung the bow and picked up the arrows she had dropped.

2. To save his energy, he lay down on the straw and tried to relax.

3. He clambered easily to the top and perched there like an enormous crow, scanning the land in the direction they had traveled.

Grammar Refresher   To learn more about sentence parts and how they work together, see Handbook 34, "Understanding Sentences," pages 338–373.

THE FAR SIDE   By GARY LARSON

Chronicle Features, 1983

"Now now, Billy . . . How could you have seen a monster if you can't even describe him?"

- Write a description of a truly horrible monster.
- Tell about a dream you remember. Include as many details as you can recall.
- What is it like to be awake late at night? Describe what you feel, hear, see, smell, and taste, and also what you think about.

Show, Don't Tell

When you write about the world, instead of telling what you see, use details that show what you see—details that will bring a scene to life. Choose one of the telling sentences below and write a paragraph that shows the subject, using specific details.

- The crowd was interesting.
- Main Street is the center of activity in our town.

2

Observation and Description

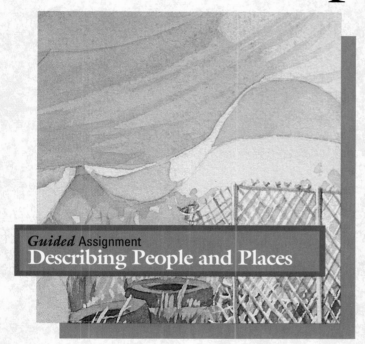

Guided Assignment
Describing People and Places

Related Assignment
Culture and Customs

Imagine a camera that captures not only how objects look but also how they sound, smell, taste, and feel. Impossible, right?

Wrong. You are that camera. What's more, the "pictures" you take don't have to remain trapped in your head. You can share everything you observe, feel, and think about a person, a place, or an object simply by writing a description of it.

In this workshop you will learn to observe and describe a person or place. In a related assignment, you'll see how the same skills can help you present the customs of a culture.

Describing People and Places

**Starting from
LITERATURE**

Imagine reading
this in a letter from a
friend: "We just moved
into a new apartment.
I hate the wallpaper,
but I guess I like the
view out my bedroom
window." Would you
be able to picture the
apartment or what your
friend sees out the win-
dow? Would you need
more details?

As you read Sandra
Cisneros's description
of a garden, see if you
can picture the garden.
Notice, too, the many
details that appeal to
your senses.

The Monkey Garden
FROM

BY SANDRA CISNEROS

The monkey doesn't live there anymore.
The monkey moved—to Kentucky—and
took his people with him. And I was glad
because I couldn't listen anymore to
his wild screaming at night, the twangy
yakkety-yak of the people who owned him.
The green metal cage, the porcelain table
top, the family that spoke like guitars.
Monkey, family, table. All gone.

And it was then we took over the garden we had been afraid to go into when
the monkey screamed and showed its
yellow teeth.

There were sunflowers big as flowers
on Mars and thick cockscombs bleeding
the deep red fringe of theater curtains.
There were dizzy bees and bow-tied fruit
flies turning somersaults and humming in
the air. Sweet sweet peach trees. Thorn
roses and thistle and pears. Weeds like
so many squinty-eyed stars and brush
that made your ankles itch and itch until

you washed with soap and water. There were big green apples hard as knees. And everywhere the sleepy smell of rotting wood, damp earth and dusty hollyhocks thick and perfumy like the blue-blond hair of the dead.

Yellow spiders ran when we turned rocks over and pale worms blind and afraid of light rolled over in their sleep. Poke a stick in the sandy soil and a few blue-skinned beetles would appear, an avenue of ants, so many crusty ladybugs. This was a garden, a wonderful thing to look at in the spring. But bit by bit, after the monkey left, the garden began to take over itself. Flowers stopped obeying the little bricks that kept them from growing beyond their paths. Weeds mixed in. Dead cars appeared over-night like mushrooms. First one and then another and then a pale blue pickup with the front windshield missing. Before you knew it, the monkey garden became filled with sleepy cars.

Things had a way of disappearing in the garden, as if the garden itself ate them or as if with its old-man memory it put them away and forgot them. Nenny found a dollar and a dead mouse between two rocks in the stone wall where the morning-glories climbed, and once when we were playing hide-and-seek, Eddie Vargas laid his head beneath a hibiscus tree and fell asleep there like a Rip Van Winkle until somebody remembered he was in the game and went back to look for him.

This, I suppose, was the reason why we went there. Far away from where our mothers could find us. We and a few old dogs who lived inside the empty cars.

Think & Respond

Discuss the "pictures" or details you liked best in Cisneros's description. What words and phrases did Cisneros use to make these details stand out for you? To which of your senses do these words and phrases appeal? Do you have a similar place—a park, a backyard, a vacant lot—where you play? Describe your place to your classmates in a way that they will remember.

One Student's Writing

Japan
Alisa Monnier

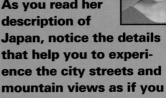

Japan is a group of wonderful islands off the coast of Asia. I look forward to going there every year. When I go to Japan with my mother and sister, we stay with relatives: my aunt Tomoko, my uncle Hideyuki and his wife, my cousin Hidenori, and my grandma Hideko. I enjoy exploring the cities of Kitakyushu and Beppu. I also love the large green mountains right behind the house where my relatives live.

Kitakyushu, my mother's hometown, is a big city. It has a population of over 1 million. It is filled with modern skyscrapers and department stores. Each summer Kitakyushu has a large day-long festival called Gion Matsuri [gē ́ ôn mät soo ́de]. This festival is an exciting combination of sights and sounds. People wear Japanese kimonos and other brightly colored outfits, and special entertainers dance down the street to the rhythm of music and the beat of a drum. Many vendors set up little tents along the streets where they sell cotton candy, barbecued meat, toys, and even pet turtles and goldfish. The party continues all day and lasts late into the night, filling the air with the delicious smell of barbecue and the wonderful sounds of music and laughter. I cherish living in such an exciting city as Kitakyushu during the summer.

Beppu, another city in Japan, is known for having the largest hot springs in the world! I, my mom, my sister Heidi, my aunt Tomoko, and my grandma Hideko all travel by train to Beppu. There we stay at the busy Suginoi [sōō gi noi] Hotel. This hotel contains gift shops, restaurants, pools, theaters, and hot springs. From the front gate of the Suginoi, which is located partway up a mountain, guests can see the nearby hot springs bubbling up from the ground. Farther up the mountain, there is an amusement park as well as a waterfall and lovely green gardens that delight the eyes.

Even though I enjoy the big cities and exciting hotels, I think what I love about Japan the most are the large, bright green mountains. There are not many things that could be compared to them. Japan is very humid, so there is often fog. The fog gives the mountains a soft, misty look. Each morning when I wake up, I see these gorgeous mountains with the sun rising behind them. I always look forward to seeing the mountains when I go to Japan. They are another beautiful part of our world.

Japan is a great place to visit. I love the summer festival in Kitakyushu, the hotel and hot springs in Beppu, and the beauty of the mountains. Japan is exciting, relaxing, and beautiful.

Two girls in traditional dress display their fans at the Gion Matsuri festival.

Think & Respond

Respond as a Reader

▶ What part of Alisa's description do you picture most clearly and vividly?

▶ What did you learn from her first paragraph?

Respond as a Writer

▶ What are some of the details that help bring Kitakyushu, Beppu, and the mountains to life?

▶ How does Alisa's use of paragraphs help her make clear the details she provides about Kitakyushu, Beppu, and the mountains?

INVITATION
TO
Write

Sandra Cisneros and Alisa Monnier both described places that were special to them. Through their descriptions, you explored an overgrown garden and visited Japan.

Choose a person or place that matters to you or interests you. Then write a vivid description that brings your subject to life.

PREWRITE AND EXPLORE

1. Find an interesting subject.   Have you been someplace you wish your friends could have seen? Do you know someone you'd like your parents to meet? If so, you may already have a subject you'd like to describe. If not, try one or more of the following activities.

Exploring Topics

- **Be on the lookout.**   Your subject might be someone or someplace you see every day. For example, Sandra Cisneros wrote about an abandoned garden that she used to play in.

- **Take a photo safari.**   Hunt through old snapshots to find people and places you might want to capture in a description. **List** the possible subjects you find.

- **Dig up the past.**   Reread old letters, postcards, or journal entries to recall some of the people and places that have been part of your life. Note the subjects you find especially interesting or still care about. Then explore them further by **freewriting.**

This float is one of many in a *Gion Matsuri* parade. This Japanese festival dates back to the year 869 and commemorates the end of a terrible epidemic that had struck Kyoto.

2. Choose a subject. Pick the subject that interests you most. If you can't make up your mind, freewriting about some of your favorites may help.

3. Gather details. To paint word pictures, you need details. These activities can help you gather details:

- **Go right to the source.** Look at photographs, post-cards, souvenirs, and other items that might trigger memories of your subject. If your subject is a person, ask questions of him or her. If your subject is a place you can revisit, do so to gather details.

- **Close your eyes and open your mind.** Imagine your subject. Ask yourself what you see, hear, smell, taste, and feel. Then draw a **sketch** or complete an **observation chart** or an **idea tree.**

- **Listen to yourself.** Describe your subject to a friend, letting your friend ask you questions. Then jot down the incidents, examples, sensory details, and comparisons you used as you answered your friend's questions.

You will have more fun writing if you choose a subject that you care about.

PROBLEM
S O L V I N G

"Where can I find out more about graphic devices?"

For more information on graphic devices, see

- Handbook 1, "Thinking with Pictures," pages 192–196

One Student's Process

Here's an idea tree that Alisa Monnier created to gather details about Kitakyushu, Japan.

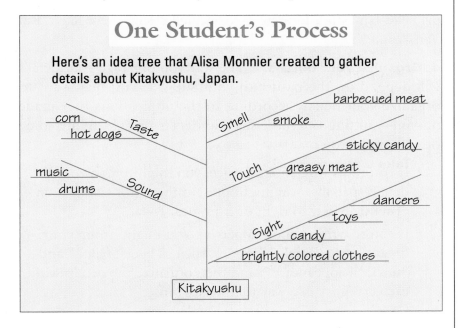

1. Start writing. Now begin drafting your description. You might start by describing the feature you like best or the one that is clearest in your mind. Then move on to descriptions of other details of your subject.

2. Create a main impression. As you write, decide what is most important to you about your subject. Then choose details that help show this feature or quality of your subject. For example, Cisneros focuses on the wildness of the garden, including many details that show what a free and untamed place the garden was.

3. Show, don't tell. For instance, you might describe specific incidents that show what a person or place is like. Cisneros provides two incidents to show that "things had a way of disappearing in the garden, as if the garden itself ate them or as if with its old-man memory it put them away and forgot them." She writes, "Nenny found a dollar and a dead mouse between two rocks in the stone wall . . . and once . . . Eddie Vargas laid his head beneath a hibiscus tree and fell asleep there like a Rip Van Winkle. . . ."

4. Organize your details. The way you organize your details will depend on the nature of your subject. You may want to organize your details according to the impressions they made on you—putting the most striking details first. Here are some other options you may want to try:

• If you're writing about a place, you might organize your details spatially. You might present them, for example, in order from left to right or from near to far.

• If you're writing about a person, you might group your details into general categories, such as "personality" and "physical appearance," and then organize the details within each category in a way that makes sense.

5. Think about your draft. How is your draft shaping up? Are you ready to share your writing with a peer reader? Here are some questions to ask yourself and your peer readers about your writing.

REVIEW YOUR WRITING

Questions for Yourself
- What is the main impression I want to create? Have I supported this impression with details?
- What matters to me most about my subject? Have I gotten this across?
- Do I want to show my thoughts and feelings or just hint at them?
- Where do I need to add more information or details?

Questions for Your Peer Readers
- What do you remember best about my description?
- What does my description make you think and feel?
- What details came across most clearly? least clearly?
- What else would you like to know about my subject?

One Student's Process

Here is part of Alisa Monnier's first draft, along with the comments her peer readers made. What comments would you make about Alisa's draft?

Kitakyushu is my mother's hometown. It is a big city. Each summer Kitakyushu has a large festival called Gion Matsuri. People wear Japanese clothes and special entertainers dance down the street to the music. Many vendors sell food and toys. The party lasts late into the night. Kitakyushu is an exciting place to be in the summer.

Peer Reader Comments

Just how big is Kitakyushu? I want to know more about it!

What kinds of food and toys can you get?

Your description makes me wish that I could go there.

1. Review your responses. Look over your peer readers' comments as well as your own notes. Then make any changes you think will improve your description.

2. Use sensory details, similes, and metaphors. Vivid sensory details, similes, and metaphors can help readers feel as if they are experiencing your subject firsthand. In the following passages, such details and devices bring readers ankle-deep into the monkey garden.

> "There were sunflowers big as flowers on Mars and thick cockscombs bleeding the deep red fringe of theater curtains."

> ". . . brush that made your ankles itch and itch until you washed with soap and water."

> "There were big green apples hard as knees. And everywhere the sleepy smell of rotting wood, damp earth and dusty hollyhocks thick and perfumy. . . ."

 Writer's Choice Descriptions can create different feelings, or moods. A description might create a feeling of suspense, mystery, or peace. Choose the mood you want to get across. Then select words, metaphors, and similes that will help create this feeling—for example, "The wind moaned like a sad old ghost."

3. Review your organization. Is the word picture you have painted clear? If not, you might be able to improve your draft by organizing your details differently. Also, check to make sure that you start a new paragraph each time you begin a new part of your description.

4. Check your beginning and ending. Think about how you want to begin and end your description. What details might you use at the beginning to get your readers' attention?

PROBLEM
S O L V I N G

"How do I create similes and metaphors?"

To learn more about similes and metaphors, see

• Handbook 19, "Appealing to the Senses," pages 266–273

PROBLEM
S O L V I N G

"What are some other ways to organize my details?"

To learn more about organizing details, see

• Handbook 7, "Organizing Details," pages 217–221

What might you say at the end of your description to give your readers a sense of closure—a sense that they've reached the end? Do you want to leave your readers with a powerful word picture or with some final thoughts about your subject?

 Paragraphs at Work Alisa Monnier describes each of her favorite places in Japan in a separate paragraph. The way you paragraph your description will depend on your subject and your organization.

- Start a new paragraph whenever you begin describing a new area within a place, such as a city within a country or a room within a building.
- Begin a new paragraph whenever you introduce a new aspect of a person, such as appearance or personality.
- Develop the main idea of each paragraph with vivid details that are organized in a way that makes sense.

Writing TIP

If your organization is sensible but your details are hard to follow, you may just need to connect your details with transitions. For more information on using transitions, see Handbook 11, "Transitions," pages 234–238.

One Student's Process

These are the changes Alisa made to her draft after she and her friends reviewed it. She would make even more changes as she revised her work.

Kitakyushu is my mother's hometown. It is a tall buildings and department stores. It has a population of over one million. It is filled with big city. Each summer Kitakyushu has a large

festival called Gion Matsuri. People wear Japanese clothes and special entertainers kimonos

dance down the street to the music. Many vendors sell food and toys. The party lasts into cotton candy, barbecued meat, the night. Kitakyushu is an exciting place to be in filling the air with great smells and sounds.

the summer. and pet turtles and goldfish.

1. Proofread your work. Check your spelling, grammar, usage, and punctuation.

L I N K I N G

MECHANICS AND WRITING

Using Commas in a Series

When you write descriptions, you will often use series of details. Remember to use commas to separate the items in a series—including a comma just before the conjunction *and* or *or.*

Original

> I love the summer festival in Kitakyushu the hotel and hot springs in Beppu and the beauty of the mountains.

Revised

> I love the summer festival in Kitakyushu, the hotel and hot springs in Beppu, and the beauty of the mountains.

For more information on using commas properly, see Handbook 43, "Punctuation," pages 566–599.

---

2. Make a clean copy of your description. Review your writing one last time, using the Standards for Evaluation in the margin. Then make a final copy.

- **Share your writing with someone who likes to draw.**
  Ask an interested classmate to create a drawing or painting based on your description.

Standards for Evaluation

DESCRIPTIVE
W R I T I N G

A description

- creates a main impression and supports that impression with details
- paints a clear and vivid picture of the subject
- shows readers what matters most about the subject to the writer
- reveals the writer's thoughts and feelings about the subject
- is well-organized
- possesses an attention-getting beginning and a satisfying ending

- **Illustrate your description.** Re-create your subject in a sketch, painting, or sculpture. Then, on a bulletin board or in a special area of your classroom, display your artwork beside your written description.

- **Submit your description to a local newspaper.** Neighborhood newspapers often publish articles about special local people and places. So if you have described a person or a place in your community, consider submitting your description to the local paper.

Mt. Fuji, with an elevation of 12,388 feet, is the highest mountain in Japan.

R EFLECT ON YOUR WRITING

W R I T E R T O W R I T E R

If you can first get away from worrying about spelling and following grammar rules, you'll find that your imagination is free to write.

Paul Zindel, novelist

1. Add your writing to your portfolio. In a note to yourself, jot down what you've learned in writing your description. Then attach your note to the final copy of your description. Thinking about the following questions may help you focus your thoughts:

- What did I notice or realize about my subject that I had never noticed or realized before?

- Did my attitude toward my subject change? If so, how?

- What would I have liked to get across more vividly?

- What helped me the most in doing this assignment? What got in my way?

2. Explore additional ideas. See the suggestions for writing a description of a cultural custom on pages 64–66 and Springboards on page 67.

FOR YOUR
PORTFOLIO

Culture and Customs

YOMARHI PURNIMA

by Elizabeth Murphy-Melas

What are some of the customs of your family or group? When you lose a tooth, do you sleep with it under your pillow? Do you take part in special religious ceremonies? Is there a day each year when you dress up in special clothing?

In this excerpt, Elizabeth Murphy-Melas describes a festival in Nepal (nə pôl´) known as Yomarhi Purnima (yō mä´ dē pōō ñē´ mä). As you read her description, think about what the details reveal about the people of Nepal and the way they live.

Tiny Nepal is an enchanting land of deep, picturesque valleys surrounded by the rugged, snowcapped Himalayas. In the heart of the country lies the beautiful Katmandu Valley. There, the Nepalese till the rich soil as they have for generations. . . . And each December, the people of the Katmandu Valley celebrate a special festival called Yomarhi Purnima in thanksgiving for their bountiful harvest. . . .

Yomarhi Purnima begins on the day of the full moon in December. Yomarhi is a Nepali word formed from yo ("fig") and marhi ("cake"); purnima is a Sanskrit word meaning "full moon." The Yomarhi cake is a sweet cake the Nepalese eat during the harvest celebration, just as Americans eat fruitcake at Thanksgiving and Christmas.

On the eve of the full moon, also called the harvest moon, the women and girls of the household spend all day baking Yomarhi cakes in brick ovens. The small cakes, about the size of a child's fist, are molded by hand into the shapes of animals, people, and Hindu gods and goddesses. In the evening, the family says prayers and visits local temples and shrines, making

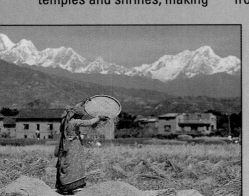

offerings of the cakes. The scent of incense from the shrines fills the streets.

The family then returns home for an evening of feasting and merrymaking. Children dress in their best festival clothes —the boys wearing trousers, high-necked tunics, and soft cotton topis; the girls, bright, colorful saris with bracelets and earrings. Because it's a special occasion, chicken or eggs are cooked. The Nepalese also eat rice mixed with dal, a thick sauce made from peas or lentils.

It's fun to sit upon woolen rugs on the floor, sip tea, and savor the meal!

That night, two special Yomarhi cakes—one shaped like Ganesh, the elephant-headed Hindu god of good luck, and one shaped like Laxmi, the goddess of wealth— are locked away in a cupboard. There they will remain for the four days of the harvest celebration. According to tradition, a miracle will occur,

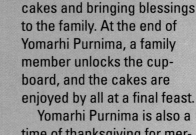

increasing the size of the cakes and bringing blessings to the family. At the end of Yomarhi Purnima, a family member unlocks the cup-board, and the cakes are enjoyed by all at a final feast.

Yomarhi Purnima is also a time of thanksgiving for mer-chants in the villages. They place Yomarhi cakes in their safe-deposit boxes, shops, and offices, hoping Laxmi will be pleased with their generosity and bring prosperity in the coming year. Students often wedge a few cakes in between their textbooks to bring them good luck in passing their school examinations!

Think & Respond

Which Yomarhi Purnima cus-toms do you like best? How are the customs described here similar to or different from your own holiday traditions? Point out some of the ways Elizabeth Murphy-Melas brings the Yomarhi Purnima festival to life by showing it rather than just telling about it.

In the process of describing Yomarhi Purnima, Elizabeth Murphy-Melas brings her readers into the homes and hearts of the people of Nepal.

Now write a description of an ethnic or religious custom that's familiar to you or one that you would like to learn more about.

The *Mani Rimdu* festival takes place each May in the Khumbu region of eastern Nepal. Monks dressed in colorful masks enact ancient legends that are based on the theme of good triumphing over evil.

E X P L O R I N G   C U S T O M S

1. Find a custom.   Can you think of a cultural or religious tradition you'd like to understand better or help someone else to understand? This tradition might come from your own culture or from any culture that interests you. Freewrite to come up with ideas, or try doing some of the following activities:

- **Holiday hop.**   Make a list of holidays that have special meaning to you and your family—one, for example, might be Rosh Hashana, Cinco de Mayo, Tet, or Easter. Create a **cluster** that explores the traditions associated with each holiday.

- **Interview.**   Talk with someone who has visited or lived in a culture different from yours. Ask questions and take notes on the customs of that culture.

- **Consider do's and taboos.**   What have you been taught about the traditions and customs of your culture? Do you always wear a head covering? Do you bow when you meet someone? Do you wear traditional clothing? Create a list of your customary practices and ways of behaving.

After exploring for a while, choose a custom that you would like to describe. Freewriting can help you discover which custom you want to describe and even what you want to say.

 Writer's Choice You may write about a custom of your own culture or one from another culture. Similarly, you may choose to describe a religious tradition that you know well or one you're interested in learning about.

2. Observe the custom and record details. If possible, become familiar with the traditional practice first hand by watching it or by doing it yourself. If that isn't possible, "observe from memory" by recalling the practice as vividly as possible. Then record the details of the custom in a **list** or a **cluster** or by creating an **observation chart** or a **sketch.** Be sure to include plenty of sensory details.

DESCRIBING A CUSTOM

1. Start your draft. Using your prewriting notes and your mind's eye, describe the sights, sounds, smells, tastes, and feelings you associate with the custom you've chosen. As much as possible, show rather than tell. Also, try to get yourself to write at top speed, without worrying about your word choices, grammar, or punctuation.

2. Consider your audience. Think about what your readers will need to know to understand the custom you are describing. Then make sure to include this information. For example, Murphy-Melas explains, "The Yomarhi cake is a sweet cake the Nepalese eat during the harvest celebration, just as Americans eat fruitcake at Thanksgiving and Christmas."

3. Think about your draft. Look for ways to improve your description. If you're comfortable sharing your draft, ask peer readers to comment on your description too.

PROBLEM
S O L V I N G

"How can I show rather than tell?"

For help in turning telling into showing, see

● Handbook 12, "Show, Don't Tell," pages 239–242

TIP

Comparisons of unfamiliar practices with familiar ones can help your readers better understand the unfamiliar practices. Similes (comparisons with *like* or *as*) can also help.

REVIEWING YOUR WRITING

1. Rework your description. Look at your own notes and your peers' comments. What needs improvement? Remember that adding sensory details, showing instead of telling, and replacing general words with more specific ones can all help bring a description to life.

2. Check your beginning and ending. In your introduction you should interest your readers in your subject and tell them what they will be reading about. To do this, you might begin by vividly describing an important feature of the custom. Another good way to begin is by pointing out a mistaken idea people have about the custom. You could also start by briefly telling about your first encounter with the tradition.

Your conclusion should leave your readers with a clear understanding of the custom you have described. Therefore, you may want to end by summarizing the important details you presented. You may also want to share what the custom means to you or what it taught you.

PROBLEM
SOLVING

"How do I write an effective introduction and conclusion?"

For information on introductions and conclusions, see

- Handbook 14, "Introductions," pages 247–249
- Handbook 15, "Conclusions," pages 250–252

PUBLISHING AND PRESENTING

- **Compile an anthology of cultural customs.** Include illustrations or photos. A brief biography of each writer also would be a nice touch.

- **Create a multicultural calendar.** Meet with classmates who wrote about holiday traditions. Then, for each month of the year, create an illustrated description of how one or more cultures celebrate holidays in that month. For some months, you may need to create a collage of illustrations.

- **Reenact customs.** Create short skits about the customs you and your classmates have described. Perform your skits in class or at a school assembly.

Spring boards

Social Studies

Choose an object from another time or place— a spinning wheel, a piñata, or a guillotine, for example. Then write about it in a way that describes its purpose or significance.

History

What historical events that are usually forgotten do you think people should celebrate or remember? Invent a holiday based on a historical event, and describe at least one custom you would observe on that day.

SCIENCE

Imagine you are an astronaut approaching a planet from space. This planet may be one you've heard of before or one that exists only in your imagination. What do you see from the cockpit of your spacecraft? What are your thoughts and feelings? Write a description of what you're seeing, thinking, and feeling.

Sentence

Unscrambling Sentences

Effective sentences often contain sentence parts, or chunks, that can be arranged in different ways. You can add variety to your writing by trying out different positions for your sentence chunks. Notice how you can unscramble sentence chunks and imitate sentences by professional writers.

Model	I was plain and tall, too tall for fourteen years, and without any shape. **Rosa Guy, _The Friends_**
Scrambled Chunks	and lacking any hair / very quiet for a newborn / the baby was small and quiet
Unscrambled Chunks	The baby was small and quiet, very quiet for a newborn, and lacking any hair.
Student Imitation	The diner is crowded and noisy, so noisy you can't always hear the waitress, and near the train station.

▶ **ON THE MARK** You generally place commas where you want readers to pause when they read your sentences.

A. Unscrambling and Imitating Sentences Unscramble each set of sentence chunks below to create a sentence that has the same order of chunks and punctuation as the model. Then write a sentence of your own that imitates the model.

1. Model   When I awoke, there were snowflakes on my eyes.
                                             Charles Portis, _True Grit_

in the sky / there was a rainbow / after the rain stopped

2. Model   Drawn by the scent of fish, the wild dogs sat on the hill, barking and growling at each other.
                                 Scott O'Dell, _Island of the Blue Dolphins_

yelling and screaming with delight / thrilled by the comeback of their team / the fans rushed onto the field

3. Model   Leaping out of the thickets like stags, the men of Soror were upon us before we could lift our weapons to our shoulders.

Pierre Boulle, *Planet of the Apes*

while the old dog watched / the young dog brought the Frisbee to the girl / with mild interest / running across the park like lightning

4. Model   She started quickly down the walk, waving to the boy who was making his way slowly up the street on a green motor scooter.

Betsy Byars, *The Summer of the Swans*

glancing toward the secretary / Wilbur walked nervously into the principal's office / with her finger on the trigger / who was holding the water gun securely

B. Unscrambling Sentences   Sometimes you can arrange sentence chunks in more than one acceptable order. Write two different sentences from each set of chunks below, adding punctuation as necessary. Then select the one you like best. Be prepared to explain why you prefer it.

1. staring out the window / I spent the entire day sulking / waiting for the rain to stop

Rosa Guy, *The Friends*

2. like sensible folk / and then / they waved until the boys were around the first bend in the road / they all went home to breakfast

Alexei Panshin, *Rite of Passage*

3. to meet him / each year / the faithful Sounder would come hobbling on three legs far down the road / after he had been gone for a whole winter and returned

William H. Armstrong, *Sounder*

4. in the very dead of night / then suddenly / clear, resonant, and unmistakable / there came a sound to my ears

Sir Arthur Conan Doyle, *The Hound of the Baskervilles*

Grammar Refresher   You can use commas between sentence parts to avoid confusion. For more information about using commas, see Handbook 43, "Punctuation," pages 566–599.

Sketch Book

Icarus, beating his wings in joy, felt the thrill of the cool wind on his face and the clear air above and below him. He flew higher and higher into the blue sky until he reached the clouds. His father called out in alarm. He tried to follow, but he was heavier and his wings would not carry him. Up and up Icarus soared, through the soft moist clouds and out again toward the glorious sun. He was bewitched by a sense of freedom; he beat his wings frantically so that they would carry him higher and higher to heaven itself.

"The Flight of Icarus,"
traditional Greek myth,
RETOLD BY SALLY BENSON

Detail of color engraving
The Fall of Icarus (1731),
Bernard Picart.

- Imagine that you could spread your wings and fly away. Tell the story of your flight.

- Tell a story about a memorable journey you have taken.

Show Don't Tell

Turn one of these *telling* sentences into a *showing* paragraph that has dialogue, action, description, or a combination of these techniques.

- Jason said the storm was frightening.

- We walked through the Monkey House at the zoo.

3

Narrative and Literary Writing

Guided Assignment
Personal Narrative

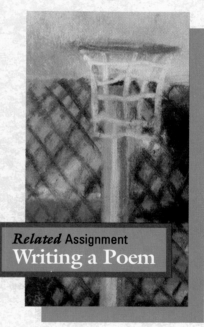

Related Assignment
Writing a Poem

You have special stories to share, and only you can tell them. No one else thinks what you think, knows the people you know, or has done what you have done. How can you help other people understand what it's like to be you? One way is to write about your personal experiences.

In this workshop, you will have the chance to explore your experiences in two ways. The guided assignment will help you write a personal narrative, or story. In the related assignment, you will write a poem to share your thoughts and feelings.

Personal Narrative

Sheyann Webb was eight years old in 1965 when she began participating in marches and rallies to help gain civil rights for African Americans. She was one of about seven hundred followers of Dr. Martin Luther King, Jr., who began a protest march from Selma to Montgomery, Alabama, that reached a violent climax on the Edmund Pettus bridge. As you read Sheyann's personal narrative, think about why she was able to conquer her fears that day.

from

A Child of the Movement

by Sheyann Webb

I remember being afraid on the first attempt of the Selma-to-Montgomery march (March 7, 1965). That was the first time that I was really afraid. The night before the march I slipped to the mass meeting. They began to talk about the strategies, like not fighting back. That right there told me that there was a possibility that there could be some fights. They were saying if you're

hit, or if something is said to you, just bow down. Out of all the times my parents had talked to me about what could happen, this is when it really came to me. But somehow I was still determined to go.

I got up the next morning, frightened to march. The people began to congregate and line up. I was looking for Mrs. Moore (a teacher who had befriended me) and I found her. I remember not wanting to get close to the front of the line because I was afraid. I remember Mrs. Moore telling me that I should go back home, and I was saying I was going to march. I got in the midway of the march. As usual, we knelt down to pray, and after we had prayed, we began to sing. A little of that fear began to leave me as we sang, because people were still joyful.

As we marched down the street to the downtown area, I began to see more spectators, blacks as well as whites, and this was different to me. Normally you didn't see a whole lot of spectators. And I began to see more police officers riding around on motorcycles. It was a little bit more exciting. We still clapped, and we sang all the way down. The closer we got to the bridge, the more I began to get frightened. At this time I could see

hundreds of policemen. The helmets, state troopers, dogs and horses, police cars. I got even more frightened then. I began to hold Mrs. Moore's hand tighter, and the person's hand on the other side of me. My heart was beginning to beat real, real fast. I looked up at Mrs. Moore, and I wanted to say, "I want to go home," but I didn't. She was looking straight ahead. Then the people began to kneel down and pray again.

We were still on the Edmund Pettus bridge. Going up, you can't see what's on the other side. But I had gotten up to the top, which is midway on the bridge, and you could see down. The big picture that I saw frightened me more. When we were asked to kneel down and pray, I knelt down with everybody. Shortly after we got up, a burst of tear gas began. I could see the troopers and policemen swinging their billy clubs. People began to run, and dogs and horses began to trample them. You could hear people screaming and hollering. And I began to run. I don't know what happened with Mrs. Moore. All I wanted to do was make my way back home. As I got almost down to the bottom of the bridge, Hosea Williams picked me up. I told him to put me down 'cause he wasn't running fast enough. I just continued to run.

Think & Respond

Discuss with your classmates how you would have felt if you had been marching alongside Sheyann Webb. What words and phrases signal the order of events in Sheyann's narrative?

One Student's Writing

What have you felt, seen, thought, or done that you will always remember? For one middle school student, Tim Stanley, the death of his grandfather was an experience he would never forget. He wrote this personal narrative about what happened and why it was important to him. As you read his narrative, think about how it makes you feel.

Grandpa

"Wake up, Tim," said Mom.

"What time is it?" I asked.

"About eleven-thirty," she answered.

"Eleven-thirty?" That's when I sensed that something was definitely wrong. I suddenly felt very scared, not for myself or my life, just scared that something bad was going to happen.

"Why did you wake me up?"

"Grandma just called."

"Which one?"

"Grandma Coberly."

My heart went into my throat. My Grandma and Grandpa Coberly were the older grandparents I had. They were also the more frail.

"What did she say?" I asked.

"Grandpa's in the hospital. He had a heart attack."

"Is he OK?" I asked.

"It doesn't look good," she replied.

I can remember thinking not about Grandpa, but why everyone always says, "It doesn't look good," instead of saying what they mean.

My grandpa died of kidney failure that night.

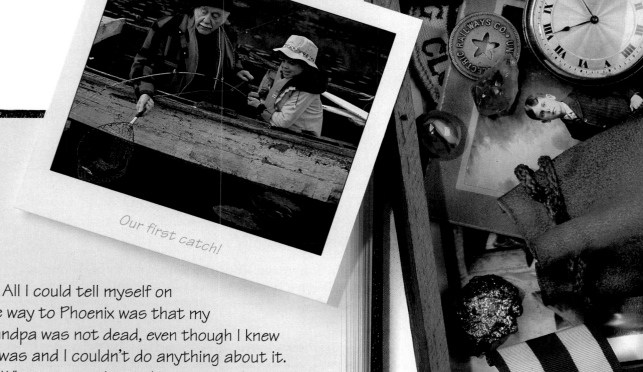

Our first catch!

All I could tell myself on the way to Phoenix was that my grandpa was not dead, even though I knew he was and I couldn't do anything about it.

When we got there, there was a planned viewing of the body. I didn't want to go to the viewing. My mom said I didn't have to, but somehow I ended up standing over my grandpa, crying.

Then there was the funeral. On television, funerals always happened on rainy days. I was mad because it was sunny the day of my grandpa's funeral.

We went to the service and then buried my grandpa.

I hadn't really cried much during those days, but on the way back to my grandma's house I cried continuously. Then we went home and went on with our lives, but there's still a hole where my grandpa was. It's the first time I faced death.

Think & Respond

Respond as a Reader

▶ How do you think writing about this experience helped Tim understand it better?

▶ What experiences of your own does Tim's experience remind you of?

Respond as a Writer

▶ How does the dialogue draw you into Tim's story?

▶ In what part of his story does Tim tell why it was so important to him? Why do you think he told about it there?

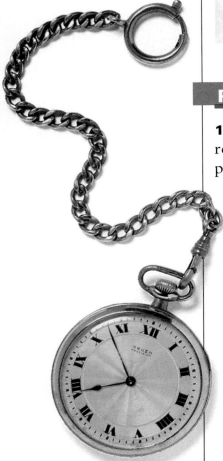

INVITATION ═ TO ═ *Write*

Sheyann Webb and Tim Stanley each wrote about an experience that made a difference in their lives. Personal narratives aren't always about major events like these, however. Sometimes writing about a small moment in your life can help you understand the moment's special meaning.

Write a narrative about a personal experience and tell why it was important to you.

P REWRITE AND EXPLORE

1. Search for ideas. Which incidents in your life do you remember best? Try some of the activities below to find personal experiences you might want to write about.

Exploring Topics

- **Unforgettable firsts** How did you meet your first friend? What was your first trip away from home like? List all the firsts you can think of. Then make some notes about ones that meant a lot to you.

- **Lifeline** What are the most memorable experiences in your life? **Graph** these experiences by marking off the years of your life on a horizontal line. Write each good experience above the year in which it occurred. Write each bad experience below the year in which it occurred.

- **Favorite things** Look through your scrapbooks or photo albums, or listen to some music. What memories do these images and songs spark? Freewrite about memories that have a special meaning to you.

2. Choose an idea for your narrative. Which of your ideas do you care most about? You might want to exchange story ideas with some of your classmates. Do other people's experiences give you any new ideas?

3. Think with your pencil. Freewrite about one or two of your favorite experiences. Just keep your pencil moving and see where your writing takes you.

 Writer's Choice Do you want to write about something that happened to you, or do you want to write about something that happened to someone else? The important thing is to choose a story that means a lot to you.

4. Explore your story. Begin gathering facts and feelings for your narrative. Try to relive the experience. Go there in your mind and write what you see, hear, smell, taste, and feel. You might want to freewrite for a few minutes about why this experience stands out in your memory. You could also explore your ideas in a cluster or make a time line listing the events of your story in the order in which they occurred.

PROBLEM
S O L V I N G

"How can I find an idea I care about?"

For help discovering the story you want to tell, see

- Sketchbook, page 70
- Springboards, page 89
- Handbook 2, "Finding a Starting Point," pages 197–202

One Student's Process

Tim Stanley wanted to write about his grandfather's death because his grandfather had meant so much to him. He made a cluster to help him explore his feelings.

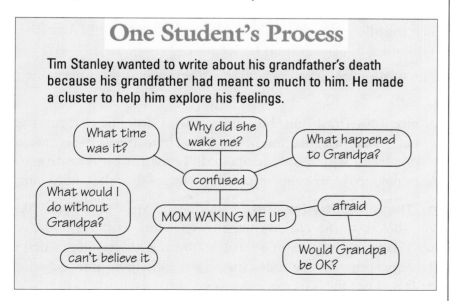

PROBLEM

S O L V I N G

"How can I make my narrative interesting to readers?"

For help finding lively details, see

- Handbook 12, "Show, Don't Tell," pages 239–242
- Handbook 19, "Appealing to the Senses," pages 266–273

DRAFT AND DISCOVER

1. Start writing.   A good way to begin is just to tell what happened. Feel free to explore new ideas as you put your thoughts down on paper. You also might begin thinking about what you want your readers to understand or to feel after they read your narrative.

2. Think about using dialogue.   Sometimes letting people speak for themselves can help readers experience events along with you. For example, notice how Tim Stanley records the conversation he had with his mother, telling most of the first part of his story in dialogue. In her narrative, Sheyann Webb uses a quotation to show how vulnerable she felt during the march. "I looked up at Mrs. Moore, and I wanted to say, 'I want to go home,' but I didn't."

3. Organize your draft.   Once you have put your ideas down on paper, you can start arranging them. Your narrative should have the following parts:

- **beginning**—sets the scene, or possibly tells why the experience was important to you
- **middle**—usually tells the story in chronological order (the order in which things happened)
- **end**—sums up the story or explains why it was important to you

Notice how Tim begins his narrative with dialogue that sets the scene: it's late at night, and he's in bed. He then tells the events in the order in which they happened. Tim ends his narrative by summing up the story and explaining why it was important to him.

4. Think about your draft.   Look over your draft. How do you feel about it? Do you want to continue working on it, or are you ready to get some feedback from your classmates now? The questions on the following page can help you review your draft and get the information you need to make it better.

Questions for Yourself
- How can I help readers share my experience?
- What part of my story do I like best? What makes it so interesting?
- Have I forgotten to mention any important details? How can I work them into my narrative?

Questions for Your Peer Readers
- What part of my narrative was most interesting to you? Tell me why.
- How did reading my story make you feel?
- Did you have any trouble following the events in my story? If so, where did you get lost?
- What would you like to know more about?

One Student's Process

Tim decided to ask some classmates to read and comment on the beginning of his draft. Read their comments. What would you say about Tim's draft?

"Wake up, Tim. What time is it?
About eleven-thirty."
"Eleven-thirty?" That's when I sensed something was definitly wrong.
"Why'd you wake me up?"
"Grandma just called."
"Which one?"
"Grandma Coberly."
She said that Grandpa was in the hospital.
"Is he OK."
"It doesn't look good." I remember thinking why does everyone always say it doesn't look good. Why don't they just say that someone's dying?

Peer Reader Comments

Your beginning makes me want to know what happens, but I'm not sure who's talking.

Can you say more about why you felt something was wrong?

Yeah, I agree! People should just say what they mean.

Personal Narrative   **79**

1. Think about the responses to your narrative. What good things did you or your peer readers notice about your narrative? Did your readers help you to see your draft in new ways? If you want to add more information or make parts of your draft more clear, check your prewriting notes. You may have jotted down details you can use as you revise.

2. Get personal. Since this is a personal narrative, help your readers get to know you. Does the writing sound like the way you speak now or spoke when the event took place? Have you showed how you felt about the experience?

For example, Sheyann Webb shows how she felt as an eight-year-old child during the march. "I began to hold Mrs. Moore's hand tighter, and the person's hand on the other side of me. My heart was beginning to beat real, real fast."

Paragraphs at Work In a personal narrative, paragraph breaks will help your readers follow your story. Divide your narrative into separate paragraphs to make the flow of events clear. As you revise, remember these tips:

- Begin a new paragraph whenever the scene or action changes.
- Begin a new paragraph when a different person begins speaking.
- Use transitional words and phrases such as *first, next, later, at the same time,* and *finally* to make the order of events clear.

3. Decide what changes you want to make in your draft. You may want to make only minor changes. Don't be afraid, however, to make major revisions or even to start over again. Do whatever is needed to turn your writing into something you care about and want to share with readers.

PROBLEM
S O L V I N G

"How can I make my writing sound like me?"

For help with finding your personal style, see

- Handbook 21, "Personal Voice," pages 276–277

COMPUTER
TIP

Try different ways of expressing an idea by moving your cursor down a line and typing in different wording. Keep the version you like best.

One Student's Process

After reviewing his draft and his peer readers' comments, Tim decided to make the following changes in his draft. He would change it even more before he was satisfied with his story.

"Wake up, Tim. ," said Mom. ¶"What time is it?," I asked.

,"About eleven-thirty. ," she answered.

"Eleven-thirty?" That's when I sensed something was definitly wrong.

"Why'd you wake me up?"

"Grandma just called."

"Which one?"

"Grandma Coberly."

She said that Grandpa was in the hospital. He had a heart attack.

"Is he OK? "

"It doesn't look good." I remember thinking why does everyone always say it doesn't look good. Why don't they just say what they mean? that someone's dying?

¶ My heart went into my throat. My Grandma and Grandpa Coberly were the older grandparents I had. They were also the more frail.

PROOFREAD

1. Proofread your work. When you proofread a personal narrative, make sure that you have spelled the names of people and places correctly. If you used dialogue, make sure you punctuated it properly. Then check for other errors in grammar, spelling, punctuation, and capitalization.

Writing Dialogue

When you write dialogue, be sure to indicate clearly who is speaking. Enclose the exact words of the speaker in quotation marks. Place commas, periods, and question marks inside the quotation marks as needed. Also, remember to begin a new paragraph each time the speaker changes.

Notice how Tim corrected his use of quotation marks when he revised his writing.

Original

"Wake up, Tim. What time is it?
About eleven-thirty."

Revised

"Wake up, Tim," said Mom.
"What time is it?" I asked.
"About eleven-thirty," she answered.

For more information about using quotation marks, see Handbook 43, "Punctuation," pages 586–588.

Standards for Evaluation

PERSONAL
WRITING

A personal narrative

- tells a story that is important to the writer
- has an introduction that draws readers in
- presents events in an order that makes sense
- makes it clear why the story is meaningful
- has a satisfying conclusion

2. Make a clean copy of your narrative. Take a last look at your narrative, using the Standards for Evaluation shown in the margin as a guide. Then make a final copy of your work.

PUBLISH AND PRESENT

- **Make a class booklet.** Collect stories in a booklet that can be displayed in class or in the school library.
- **Read your narrative aloud.** If possible, add music, photographs, or other props.

- **Submit your narrative to the school magazine.** If the school does not have a magazine, your class could start one.
- **Turn your story into a dramatic skit.** Act out your story with the help of your classmates.

REFLECT ON YOUR WRITING

> ## WRITER TO WRITER
>
> *The story's about you.*
>
> **Horace, Roman poet**

1. Add your writing to your portfolio. You have now read two personal narratives and written one of your own. Think about what you have learned from this experience. Then write your thoughts in a paragraph and attach it to your narrative.

Think about questions like these:

- How did writing about my experience help me to understand the event? What new thoughts or memories came to me while writing?

- What was easiest about writing my narrative? What was hardest?

- How did sharing my writing with my peers help me? How could I have gotten more help?

- What would I do differently if I wrote about the same experience again?

2. Explore additional writing ideas. See the suggestions for writing a poem on pages 86–88 and Springboards on page 89.

FOR YOUR
PORTFOLIO

Writing a Poem

A poem can capture a thought, a feeling, a scene, or any other experience. Writing poetry gives you a chance to play with language. You can think about how words sound and look, as well as about what they mean. You can be silly or serious, simple or sophisticated. As you read these poems, notice the different ways the poets use language.

Rain

Rain hits over and over
on hot tin,
on trucks,
on wires and roses.
Rain hits apples, birds, people,
coming in strokes of white,
gray, sometimes purple.
Rain cracks against my eyelids,
runs blue on my fingers,
and my shadow floats on the sidewalk
through trees and houses.

Adrien Stoutenburg

Scrapyard

Old, old cars, rusting away,
Some cars whole—in these we play.
Now I am swerving round a corner,
Streaking round a bend,
Zooming past the finishing line
To the checkered flag—
Finishing a perfect first,
Ready for the autograph hunters.

Michael Benson

Reggie

It's summertime
And Reggie doesn't live here anymore
He lives across the street
Spends his time with the round ball
Jump, turn, shoot
Through the hoop
Spends his time with arguments
    and sweaty friends
And not with us
He's moved away
Comes here just to eat and sleep
    and sometimes pat my head
Then goes back home
To run and dribble and jump and stretch
And stretch
And shoot
Thinks he's Kareem
And not my brother

Eloise Greenfield

Think & Respond

What feeling do you get from reading each of these poems? Which poem do you like best? Why? What words strike you the most? What ideas do these poems give you for your own writing?

Writing a Poem

INVITATION
TO
Write

A poem can be about a subject as common as rain or as personal as your brother. The only limit to what you say—and how you say it—is your own imagination.

Write a poem about something you've seen, felt, thought, or dreamed.

EXPLORING YOUR WORLD

1. Look inside your head.   Close your eyes and try to focus your thoughts inward. What images or ideas come to mind? Also check your journal for subjects you've been thinking about lately.

2. Explore ideas.   You might try freewriting about your observations and feelings. Write down or sketch words and images that occur to you, no matter how odd they seem. Look for these kinds of details:

- **Sensory images**   What do you see, hear, smell, taste, and feel when you think about your subject?

- **Words and phrases**   What words, phrases, or sounds remind you of your subject?

- **Comparisons**   Is your subject like anything else? Look for unexpected or unusual comparisons.

For example, notice the strong sensory images Stoutenburg uses to help readers see and feel the rain—"hot tin," "strokes of white, /gray, sometimes purple," "cracks against my eyelids," and "my shadow floats on the sidewalk."

PROBLEM
S O L V I N G

"How can I turn my ideas into a poem?"

To help bring your ideas to life, see

- Handbook 19, "Appealing to the Senses," pages 266–273

DRAFTING YOUR POEM

1. Write and rewrite. You actually started writing your poem when you began exploring your world. Now begin experimenting with images, ideas, words, and meanings. Keep the ones you like best and try out new ones. Many poets write their poems over and over before they really discover what they want to say.

2. Play with language. As you write, read your drafts aloud. Listen to the sound of the words. Try using words that use sound in an interesting way.

Words and Sounds

Words can

- begin with the same sound (slippery snow)
- end in the same sound (dark ink)
- have the same vowel sound (gray lake)
- sound like what they mean (buzz, crackle)

Writer's Choice Some poems rhyme and some don't. Experiment with your poem to see if rhyming the last words of lines makes your poem seem more rhythmic, more musical.

3. Think about the rhythm and shape of your poem. Notice the rise and fall of your voice as you read your poem. Also notice the way the poem looks on paper. Experiment with different words and ways of arranging them. Try short lines and long lines and different stanzas, or groupings of lines.

Notice how both Stoutenburg and Greenfield repeat certain words to give their poems rhythm. Stoutenburg repeats the word *on:* "on hot tin, / on trucks, / on wires and roses." Greenfield repeats the word *and:* "To run and dribble and jump and stretch / And stretch / And shoot."

REVIEWING YOUR POEM

1. Play it by ear. Put your poem aside for a few hours or a day. Then read it again, aloud. Listen for places where you stumble or don't like the way it sounds. Can you think of better words to use? Do you need to find more vivid images?

2. Share your poem with your peers. Read your poem aloud to your classmates. Then have them read it silently or aloud. Ask your classmates why they think you wrote this poem. What words and phrases do they especially like or dislike? What images create the most vivid pictures?

3. Cut it down. Poetry is a way of saying a lot with a few well-chosen words. Look for ways you can trim unnecessary words or thoughts. You might want to focus on only one part of an experience, a scene, or a feeling.

For example, in his poem, Benson tells readers that pretending to be a race-car driver in an old, junky car makes the speaker feel important and powerful. One line of the poem—"Ready for the autograph hunters"—says it all.

4. Make sure that your poem expresses who you are. As you rework your poem, consider the comments of your peers. Remember, though, that the poem represents your vision, and you get to decide what you say and how you say it.

PUBLISHING AND PRESENTING

- **Have a poetry reading.** Read poems aloud with your classmates. Invite another class to listen.
- **Make a poetry collection.** Gather your class's poems into a booklet.
- **Create a bulletin-board display.** Post your poems in the classroom. Add artwork to illustrate the poems.

Grammar
—TIP—

In poetry, the first word of every line is sometimes capitalized. However, you can use capitalization and punctuation in any way that helps you express your ideas clearly and strongly.

Springboards

History What historical event do you wish you could have experienced? The first walk on the moon? The eruption of Mount Vesuvius? Write a journal entry describing your imaginary experience.

Music Make up a rap in which you retell a personal experience. Use the rhythm and sound of your words to express your true feelings.

Literature Pretend that you are a character in one of your favorite stories. What if you could get up off the page and do anything you wanted? Write a narrative about an experience you would have.

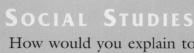

SOCIAL STUDIES How would you explain to someone in another country what a day in your life is like? Write your thoughts in a letter to a pen pal.

Sentence

Combining Sentences

Good writers often express more than one idea in a sentence. By combining information from two sentences, the writer quoted below made a sentence that was smoother and more interesting.

Model   Dead fruit trees rose like ghostly hands.
Dead fruit trees were all around us.

Combined   All around us, dead fruit trees rose like ghostly hands.
Laurence Yep, *Dragon of the Lost Sea*

▶ **ON THE MARK**   When you add information to a sentence, you often need to set off the new information with a comma.

A. Combining Sentences   Make a new sentence by putting the underlined part of the second sentence into the first sentence at the caret (∧).

1. Inside the cabin the boy's mother sat by the stove ∧ . She was <u>picking kernels of walnuts with a bent hairpin</u>. (*Put a comma before the added information.*)

William H. Armstrong, *Sounder*

2.   ∧ The kind of friends I had were what you'd expect. This was true <u>up until I turned twelve years old</u>. (*Put a comma after the added information.*)

Joseph Krumgold, *Onion John*

3. The three women had their fence half built ∧ . It was <u>a high fence enclosing an area behind the house</u>. (*Put a comma before the added information.*)

William E. Barrett, *The Lilies of the Field*

4. The children ∧ came charging back into their homeroom. The children were <u>shouting and screaming</u>. (*Put commas before and after the added information.*)

Rosa Guy, *The Friends*

B. Combining and Imitating Sentences Combine each group of sentences below by adding the underlined chunks to the first sentence. Make a sentence that has the same order of chunks as the model. Then write a sentence of your own that imitates the model.

1. *Model:* A shaft of sunlight, warm and thin like a light patchwork quilt, lay across his body.

   Marjorie Kinnan Rawlings, _The Yearling_

   A creature from outer space stepped from the flying saucer. The creature was tall and glowing like a giant firefly.

2. *Model:* Closer and closer they came, bumping and jolting each other, clawing and snorting in their own eager fury.

   Norton Juster, _The Phantom Tollbooth_

   Faster and faster they ran. They were pumping and stretching their legs. They were straining and sweating toward the finish line.

3. *Model:* Behind it stretched a graveyard, with groves of trees planted among the tombstones.

   Cynthia Voigt, _Homecoming_

   Before us stood the teacher. He stood with a stack of report cards. The report cards were held in his hand.

4. *Model:* From every window blows an incense, the all-pervasive blue and secret smell of summer storms and lightning.

   Ray Bradbury, _Dandelion Wine_

   After every touchdown comes a celebration. It is a loud and joyous moment. The moment is one of spirited cheers and laughter.

   Peter S. Beagle, _The Last Unicorn_

Grammar Refresher When you combine sentences, the information you add is often a fragment. It does not express a complete thought by itself. To learn more about sentences and fragments, see Handbook 34, "Understanding Sentences," pages 338–373.

SketchBook

- Guess the purpose of the item in the picture. Explain how someone might use it.
- Imagine you're from another planet. Observe an Earth game such as baseball or soccer. Beam instructions for playing the game to your home planet.

Show, Don't Tell

When you give directions for making or doing something, you strive to *show* the steps of a process, using descriptive details to help readers follow your thinking. Try turning one of the *telling* sentences below into a *showing* paragraph using specific directions.

- A successful party takes planning.
- Becoming a good sport takes effort.

4

Informative Writing: Explaining *How*

Guided Assignment
Directions

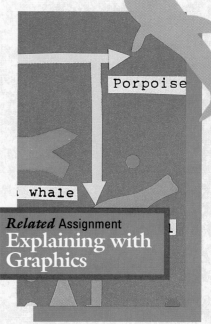

Porpoise

whale

Related Assignment
Explaining with Graphics

Wave one French fry in air for emphasis while you talk. Pretend to conduct an orchestra. Then place four fries in your mouth at once and chew. Turn to your sister, open your mouth, and stick out your tongue. . . . Close mouth and swallow. Smile.
Delia Ephron, *How to Eat Like a Child*

Directions can tell people how to perform all sorts of activities—even how to eat French fries. In this workshop you'll learn how to write clear directions. Then, in a related assignment, you'll learn visual ways of explaining how something works.

Guided ASSIGNMENT

Directions

Take TRACKS Home
by Ed Ricciuti

Starting from LITERATURE

Think about a time when you gave someone directions on how to get someplace or do something. Did you add any special tips or suggestions?

In this article from *Field and Stream* magazine, Ed Ricciuti explains how to make plaster casts of animal tracks, or footprints. As you read his directions, notice that he includes suggestions and descriptions so that you will understand exactly what materials to use and what to do.

One of the ways that many animals survive is by staying out of sight. They keep under cover and often move only at night. So even if they are around, you seldom see them, though you can tell they're in the area by what they leave behind—tracks.

Collecting tracks is a great way to keep a record of wildlife that lives in your area—or places you visit. You can even use tracks to make a natural history museum in your home.

How do you collect tracks? If you have artistic talent, you can sketch them. If you have a camera and know how to use it, you can photograph them. Another way is to make plaster casts of tracks.

All you need is plaster of Paris, water, stiff paper, and a paper clip or piece of tape.

The thin cardboard of a cereal box will work for the paper, and so will the covers of some

note pads, or manila folders. You'll want to identify the tracks you find. You can get field guides to track identification at a library or bookstore. Bring a book with you when you're out looking for tracks. . . .

Carry the plaster in a tightly sealed container.

A canteen will do for toting water. You can mix the water and plaster in an empty tin can, but make sure it's clean.

When you find a track, make a one- to two-inch-high circular collar around it with the paper. Secure it with a piece of tape or a paper clip. Then combine the plaster and the water in the can and stir. This is the tricky part: the

mix cannot be too thick or too thin. It should be slightly more fluid than pancake batter. You can follow the directions that come with the plaster, or figure on two parts plaster to one part water.

Mix quickly because plaster thickens and sets fast. When the mixture is ready, carefully pour it into the track. Make sure it fills the track entirely, and even overflows a little. Next, wait for the plaster to completely harden. It takes at least a half hour, so be patient. While you're waiting, you may want to make some notes. Describe the surroundings of the track—the vegetation, and whether the print was in mud, sand, or some other kind of soil. If there is a trail of tracks, make notes about its path.

When the cast is hard, dig around it with a pocket knife or garden trowel. Be careful not to cut into the

plaster. Then remove the cast from the ground. You can clean it later with water and a toothbrush. . . .

If you spend enough time scouting around for tracks,

you can build a nice collection, and at the same time, you'll learn about the habits of wildlife.

Think & Respond

Did Ricciuti's directions tempt you to try collecting tracks? Do you think you could follow Ricciuti's directions successfully? Why or why not? Can you think of activities you know how to do well enough to explain them to someone else?

One Student's Writing

Ed Ricciuti's purpose was to explain how to make plaster casts of animal tracks. Here, sixth-grader Doug Frieburg writes to explain how to clean your room. As you read Doug's piece, look for the similarities between his directions and those written by Ricciuti.

How to Clean Your Room in Ten Easy Minutes

by Doug Frieburg

Hey, Kids! Have you ever wondered how to clean your room without taking up your whole afternoon? I have that special answer for you in Doug's patented room-cleaning method.

BEGIN by dusting. Whirl away dresser dust with a blow-dryer set on high. Then terminate those nasty cobwebs by draping a not-so-well-liked T-shirt over the end of a baseball bat and running the bat around the ceiling infield.

NEXT, make your dirty clothes disappear in seconds by putting them in any of four major places. Stuff them into a laundry bag at the back of your closet. Mix your dirty clothes with the clean clothes in your dresser drawers. Simply shove them under your bed, or just pile them behind your door.

THEN have a little fun hanging up your clean clothes by turning this task into a game. Just tape a free-throw line on the floor a short distance from your closet. Then, one at a time, drape the items on hangers and toss them toward your

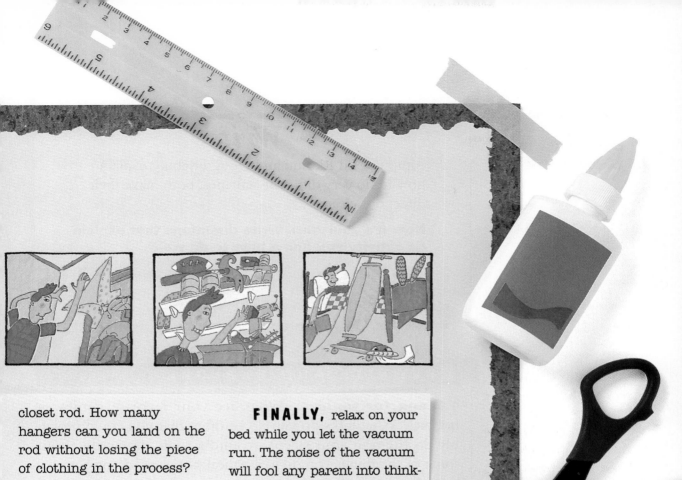

closet rod. How many hangers can you land on the rod without losing the piece of clothing in the process?

NEXT, maximize your shelf space. Do you have an accumulation of thing-a-ma-bobs you need to get rid of but can't bear to part with? Well, you can keep <u>everything</u> and still make your room look neat and organized just by putting these items into containers. Raid your mom's stash of old plastic containers and margarine tubs. Old coffee cans work well too.

FINALLY, relax on your bed while you let the vacuum run. The noise of the vacuum will fool any parent into thinking that you have actually vacuumed your room. After about five minutes, shut off the vacuum. Then go back to whatever you were doing before you started cleaning.

Many kids think cleaning their room is boring and a waste of time. However, if you follow my patented room-cleaning method, not only will you have fun cleaning your room, but you'll also be done in record time.

Think & Respond

Respond as a Reader
► Did you enjoy reading Doug's directions? Why or why not?
► What parts did you like best?

Respond as a Writer
► How does Doug get your attention in his opening paragraph?
► How are Doug's directions similar to Ricciuti's? How are they different?

INVITATION
TO
Write

Although Ed Ricciuti and Doug Frieburg explain how to do very different activities, both make their directions clear.

Now it's your turn. Write directions that explain an activity you know how to do well.

PREWRITE AND EXPLORE

1. Look for topics. What are your favorite games or hobbies? What tasks do you do so often that you could probably do them in your sleep? To find a topic, freewrite about some of the things you do in a typical day or try doing some of the following activities.

Exploring Topics

- **Taking stock** Are you the high scorer on a tricky video game? Do you bake cakes for special occasions? Are you a caretaker of fish, gerbils, or other pets? Take a moment to list your favorite activities, hobbies, and special skills.

- **Making a game of your search** Get together with a few classmates and pick a subject. Then spend a few minutes alone, listing everything about that subject you know how to do. For example, if you picked bicycles, you might list "riding with no hands," "patching inner tubes," and "changing flats." Then compare your list with those of your classmates. Who has the longest list? Did others think of any entries that you might add to your list?

- **Completing sentences**   Brainstorm alone or with friends or classmates to complete one or more of the following sentences. If you prefer, you can try completing a sentence of your own.

> "I know how to win at . . ."

> "You too can succeed at . . ."

> "Making a _____ requires some planning."

> "Being a good _____ takes know-how."

2. Pick a topic.   The activity you pick may be the one you know how to do best, one you think others should learn how to do, or one you think you'll have fun explaining. For help in making a selection, freewrite about your favorites to see which one interests you most.

3. Think about your activity.   If possible, carry out your chosen task or project. Then jot down the steps you follow. If performing your activity is not possible, simply imagine yourself doing the task. Also, note any materials and tools you need to perform your activity.

COMPUTER TIP

Listing your steps on a computer can make it easier to rearrange them or insert missed steps.

One Student's Process

Doug Frieburg thought about how he could add some fun to an unpleasant task as he imagined himself going through the motions of cleaning his room. Then he jotted down the following notes.

Steps	Tools and Materials
pick up dirty clothes	vacuum cleaner
put away clean clothes	blow-dryer
play closet "free throw"	laundry bag
dust	baseball bat
get rid of cobwebs	old T-shirt
vacuum	

Writer's Choice Do you want to treat your subject in a straightforward way, as Ed Ricciuti did? Would you rather take a humorous approach, as Doug Frieburg did?

DRAFT AND DISCOVER

1. Begin writing. If you took any notes or listed steps during prewriting, you might start by expanding on what you wrote. Otherwise, go through the activity in your mind and write about the steps as you picture them.

2. Think about your organization. As you write, make sure that you are presenting your information in a sensible order. For example, you would probably list any necessary tools and materials early on. Then present the steps in the order in which they should be followed—that is, in chronological order.

3. Keep your audience in mind. For example, what might you need to do to make your directions easy for a younger audience to follow? Make sure you explain what readers unfamiliar with your activity need to know. Sometimes making a comparison to something your readers are sure to be familiar with can help. Notice that Ed Ricciuti explains that the mixture of plaster and water "should be slightly more fluid than pancake batter."

4. Draw pictures. Sometimes it's easier to understand directions if you have a map or picture to follow. Would including a diagram, map, or picture help your readers?

Grammar
══TIP══

Imperative statements such as "Begin by dusting" can help you state your directions simply and clearly.

5. Evaluate your directions. Could someone unfamiliar with your activity follow your directions? To find out, you might have a peer reader try following your directions—if that's possible. The questions below can also help you evaluate your draft.

REVIEW YOUR WRITING

Questions for Yourself
- Have I missed any steps?
- What might I add or change to make the steps easier to follow?
- Where do I mention the tools and materials my readers will need? Is that the best place for them?
- Which terms might be unfamiliar to my readers?

Questions for Your Peer Readers
- Which steps come across most clearly? least clearly?
- Are my directions organized so that they're easy to follow? If not, where did you get lost or confused?
- What additional information, if any, would you need in order to follow these directions? Am I missing anything?

One Student's Process

Here is part of Doug's first draft. Read it and then review the peer comments.

Begin by dusting. Blow away dresser dust with a blow-dryer set on high. Then terminate those nasty cobwebs with a not-so-well-liked T-shirt and a baseball bat. Make your dirty clothes disappear in seconds by stuffing them into a laundry bag at the back of your closet, shoving them under your bed, or piling them behind your door.

Peer Reader Comments

I like your blow-dryer idea.

What do I do with the T-shirt and bat?

I stick my dirty clothes in with my clean ones.

Grammar
—TIP—

Adverbs can help make your directions more precise. In addition to telling how, when, or where to do something, as in "mix *quickly*," adverbs can tell readers to what extent, as in "mix *very* quickly."

PROBLEM
S O L V I N G

"Where can I learn more about using transitions?"

For more information about transitions, see

• Handbook 11, "Transitions," pages 234–238

1. Think about your responses. Read your peer responses as well as your own notes. Decide which parts of your directions are coming across clearly and which parts may need to be improved. Also, if a peer reader tried following your directions, pay attention to the outcome. Was he or she successful? Why or why not? Do you need to add information or make your wording more precise?

2. Add examples. Examples and suggestions can help your readers understand exactly what you mean. For instance, after telling his readers that they will need stiff paper, Ed Ricciuti adds, "The thin cardboard of a cereal box will work for the paper, and so will the covers of some note pads, or manila folders."

3. Be specific. Wherever possible, replace vague nouns and verbs with more precise ones. For example, don't say, "Write about the place" when saying "Describe the surroundings of the track" would be more precise.

4. Use transitions as needed. Transitions, or signal words, can make the order of your steps clear and guide your readers smoothly from one step to the next. Therefore, to introduce the steps in your directions, you may want to use transitions such as *first, second, third, then, next, before, after, meanwhile,* and *finally.*

5. Think about your beginning. Directions, like other forms of writing, have a beginning, a middle, and an end. Make sure that in your beginning you introduce your readers to the activity you're going to explain and get them interested in this activity. You may also want to give your readers a good reason for reading your directions. Ed Ricciuti, for example, promises his readers that they can learn about wildlife. Doug Frieburg promises to teach his readers how to clean their rooms quickly and easily.

6. Review your ending. You can simply end with your last step. You can also end by describing the result of following your directions. For example, Ricciuti ends his article by reminding readers of what they can gain by following his directions:

> If you spend enough time scouting around for tracks, you can build a nice collection, and at the same time, you'll learn about the habits of wildlife.

 Paragraphs at Work You can use paragraphs to make your directions easier to follow.
- Make sure to start a new paragraph whenever you introduce a new step or direction.
- Make sure that each paragraph contains two or more sentences that include all the details a reader will need.

One Student's Process

Read part of Doug's revised draft to see the kinds of changes he decided to make.

Begin by dusting. ~~Blow~~ Whirl away dresser dust (ceiling infield. Next,)

with a blow-dryer set on high. Then terminate

those nasty cobwebs ~~with~~ by draping a not-so-well-liked

T-shirt ~~and a baseball bat.~~ over the end of and running the bat around the Make your dirty

clothes disappear in seconds by ~~stuffing~~ putting them in any of four major places. them

into a laundry bag at the back of your closet,

~~shoving~~ shove them under your bed, just or ~~piling~~ pile them

behind your door.

Mix them in with the clean clothes in your dresser drawer.

1. Proofread your work. Correct any errors in grammar, usage, spelling, and mechanics.

2. Make a clean copy of your paper. Use the Standards for Evaluation in the margin to check your directions one last time. Then make a final copy.

LINKING
GRAMMAR AND WRITING

Using Prepositional Phrases

A prepositional phrase is a group of words that begins with a preposition and ends with its object—for example, "Just tape a free-throw line *on the floor.*" Because prepositional phrases often answer the questions *how, when,* and *where,* they are very useful in directions. When you use prepositional phrases, however, be sure to position them correctly. Improper positioning can result in confusing or even silly sentences.

Improperly Positioned

Finally, relax while you let the vacuum run on your bed.

Properly Positioned

Finally, relax on your bed while you let the vacuum run.

For more information on prepositional phrases, see Handbook 40, "Understanding Prepositions and Conjunctions," pages 502–525.

P UBLISH AND PRESENT

- **Give a demonstration.** Read your directions aloud for classmates, and demonstrate each step as you read.

- **Make a "how-to" booklet.** Form a class booklet of directions. Consider grouping directions under general headings, such as "Building Things," "Making Repairs," and "Cooking."

- **Mail your directions to a magazine.** Magazines for younger readers often publish articles about making craft items, conducting science experiments, caring for pets, and similar subjects. Your teacher or librarian may be able to help you contact one of these magazines.

R EFLECT ON YOUR WRITING

W R I T E R T O W R I T E R

I put down words fairly easily. It's being satisfied with what you write that's a problem.

Ralph Ellison, novelist

1. Add your directions to your portfolio. Now that you have written a set of directions and read two others, think about what you have learned. In a note, write down your thoughts and feelings. Attach this note to your final draft. The following questions may help you focus your thoughts:

- Is giving directions in writing harder or easier than giving directions orally?

- What advice would I give someone who was just starting this assignment?

- How was writing directions similar to other kinds of writing? How was it different?

- Were my peers' responses helpful? Why or why not?

2. Explore additional writing ideas. Try the suggestions for making a graphic on pages 108–109. You might also try the Springboards on page 110.

FOR YOUR
PORTFOLIO

Explaining with Graphics

Starting from A GRAPHIC

Ana Ortiz decided to create this chart of an ocean food chain to show who eats whom among the creatures in the sea. As you look at Ana's graphic, notice what other things you can learn about these creatures as well.

Phytoplankton
(tiny plants)

Zooplankton
(tiny animals)

Crinoids

Tripod fish

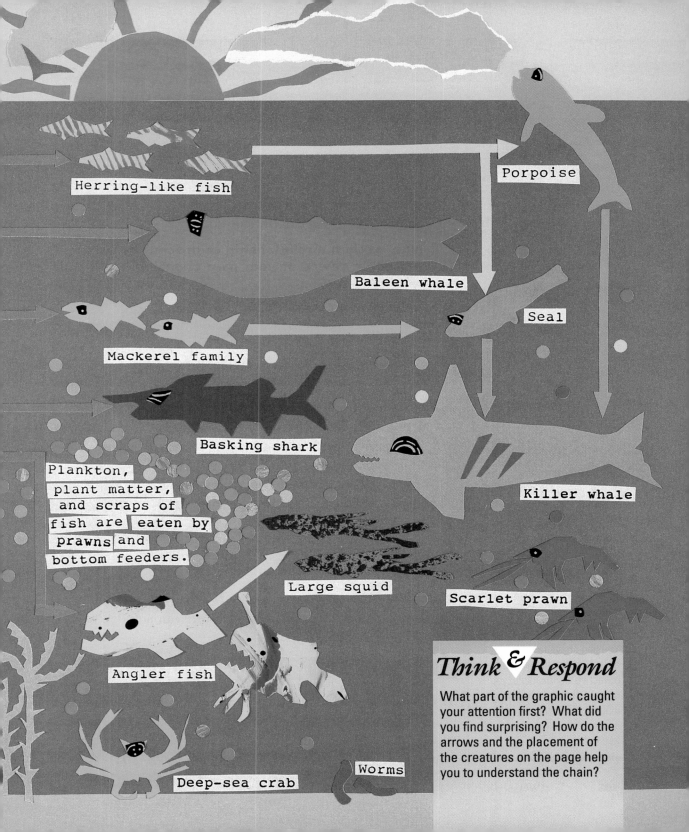

Herring-like fish

Porpoise

Baleen whale

Seal

Mackerel family

Basking shark

Killer whale

Plankton, plant matter, and scraps of fish are eaten by prawns and bottom feeders.

Large squid

Scarlet prawn

Angler fish

Deep-sea crab

Worms

Think & Respond

What part of the graphic caught your attention first? What did you find surprising? How do the arrows and the placement of the creatures on the page help you to understand the chain?

Ana Ortiz's chart helped you to understand feeding relationships among some of the creatures of the sea. Graphic devices such as this one often provide a simple way to explain difficult ideas.

Now explain a relationship or process by using a graphic device of your own choosing.

P LANNING YOUR GRAPHIC DEVICE

1. Find a subject. Are you writing a report for which you could use a graphic? If so, you may already have a subject. If not, brainstorm with classmates to come up with processes, cycles, or relationships you've learned about in science, social studies, or other classes. For example, you might consider showing how a tadpole becomes a frog.

2. Pick a subject. Choose something that you think you could explain more quickly and clearly in a graphic device than you could explain in words alone.

3. Jot down what you know. Try freewriting, sketching, or creating a cluster to gather details about your subject.

Writing
═══ **TIP** ═══

You don't have to be an artist to make your graphic attractive. For example, you can use photographs and magazine clippings to help illustrate the ideas you want to present.

C REATING YOUR GRAPHIC DEVICE

1. Choose a visual way to present your material. The graphic devices shown at the top of the next page are just two of the many forms your graphic can take. For other ideas, see Handbook 26, "Reading Skills," on pages 298–301.

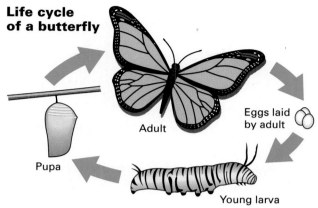

Life cycle of a butterfly

Adult

Eggs laid by adult

Pupa

Young larva

2. Use symbols. Make key relationships easy to spot by using symbols that your readers are sure to recognize. For example, you might use arrows, plus signs, or question marks in your visual.

3. Name and label your graphic. Title your graphic and label any important items or steps. The labels on the model, for example, identify the ocean creatures.

REVIEWING YOUR GRAPHIC DEVICE

1. Get feedback on your visual. Show your graphic to a friend or classmate. Your friend's questions and comments can give you ideas for improving your visual.

2. Revise your graphic. Adjust your graphic until you're sure that your relationship or process comes across clearly.

PUBLISHING AND PRESENTING

- **Be the teacher.** Use your graphic organizer to teach class-mates about the relationship or process you've chosen.

- **Display your graphic.** Would your visual make a great poster? Join with other students to create a display for your classroom or library. Add titles if necessary.

Human Heart Diagram

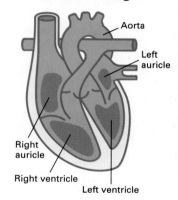

Aorta

Left auricle

Right auricle

Right ventricle

Left ventricle

Spring boards

HEALTH Create a poster for a younger audience. Show how to perform a simple task important to good health. You might show how to floss your teeth or how to stretch before exercising.

HOME ECONOMICS What household tasks can you do expertly? Make breakfast? Babysit? Dishes? Write a set of directions that explain to a friend how to do the job. Your directions can be humorous or serious.

Art Explain how to produce a particular kind of painting, sculpture, or craft.

Science Have you ever done a science experiment? If so, write directions explaining what to do. Be sure to explain especially well any parts of the experiment you found tricky or confusing.

Geography Write out a set of directions for getting from one city or town to another. If you wish, you might include a map that shows the exact route.

on the LIGHT side

For Your Eyes Only!

If you want to send a private message to a friend, write it in a secret code. Try these codes, then make up one of your own.

Tick-Tack-Toe Code

Did you know 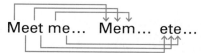 spells *theater?* The tick-tack-toe board below is your guide to this alphabet of symbols.

To write the letter T, for example, draw the outline of the part of the tick-tack-toe board that holds the letter: ⌞. Then place a dot in the middle part of the outline where the letter T is shown: ⌞̇.

```
A •  | J •  | S •
B •  | K •  | T •
C •  | L •  | U •
-----+------+-----
D •  | M •  | V •
E •  | N •  | W •
F •  | O •  | X •
-----+------+-----
G •  | P •  | Y •
H •  | Q •  | Z •
I •  | R •  | ? •
```

Can you read this message?

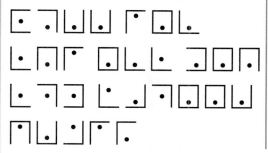

Will you try out for the school play?

Letter Scramble

If you want to send the message *Meet me after the show,* scramble the letters by rewriting the sentence as two words. Put the first letter, M, at the beginning of the first word and the second letter, e, at the beginning of the second word. Build each of the two words from every other letter of the message.

Meet me...   Mem... ete...

You end up with

Mematrhso etefetehw

If you wish, divide your two-word letter scramble into more words: Mem atrh so ete fetehw. To decode the message, divide the total number of letters in half. Write the second half directly below the first, and then read the letters from top to bottom.

What does this message say?

Ia et gfih hvsa ergt

Answers: I have stage fright.

Sentence

Sentence Openers

You can use single words or groups of words as sentence openers to add emphasis and to vary the rhythm of your writing.

Model A   <u>Outside</u>, he murmured to himself.

William H. Armstrong, *Sounder*

Model B   <u>Hobbling on one foot</u>, Wanda opened the closet door and turned on the light.

Betsy Byars, *The Summer of the Swans*

Model C   <u>Ever since I can remember</u>, I had wanted to know about the Land of the Golden Mountain, but my mother had never wanted to talk about it.

Laurence Yep, *Dragonwings*

▶ **ON THE MARK**   Put a comma after a sentence opener to separate it from the rest of the sentence.

A. Combining Sentences   Make a new sentence by adding the underlined part of the second sentence to the first sentence as a sentence opener. Write the complete sentence, putting a comma after the sentence opener.

1. He went to the door on the right and opened it. He opened it <u>without the slightest hesitation</u>.   **Frank R. Stockton, "The Lady, or the Tiger?"**

2. I set the cream puffs on the coffee table and stood back looking at them. This was <u>after Uncle Daniels had finished with his lamb-chop dinner</u>.

Rosa Guy, *Edith Jackson*

3. I looked at him with scorn and hatred, unable to imagine what I had ever seen in him. I was <u>still angry, still outraged by his attempt to betray me</u>.

James Gould Cozzens, "The Animals' Fair"

4. She dragged the boy inside, down a hall, and into a large kitchenette-furnished room at the rear of the house. She did this <u>when she got to her door</u>.

Langston Hughes, "Thank You, M'am"

B. Unscrambling and Imitating Sentences   Unscramble each set of sentence chunks below. Create a sentence that has a sentence opener, the same order of chunks, and the same punctuation as the model. Then write a sentence of your own that imitates each model.

1. Model   <u>With his remaining strength</u>, he dragged himself from the swirling waters.   **Richard Connell, "The Most Dangerous Game"**

onto their shoulders / the girls lifted their coach / after their stunning victory

2. Model   <u>Barely touching my waist and my fingers</u>, he began to dance with me.   **Alice Munro, "Red Dress—1946"**

to cross above us / the tightrope walker started / carefully keeping her balance and her concentration

3. Model   <u>When we arrived home</u>, we took a cold shower underneath a water hose.   **Francisco Jimenez, "The Circuit"**

the scouts told stories / as the stars twinkled above / around the campfire

C. Expanding Sentences   Use your imagination to add a sentence opener, followed by a comma, where the caret (∧) appears in each sentence below.

1. ∧ We could hear axes ringing in the woods, voices, and sometimes the fall of a tree.   **Alexei Panshin, *Rite of Passage***

2. ∧ Ralph laid the small end of the shell against his mouth and blew.
                              William Golding, *Lord of the Flies*

3. ∧ Mama Bellini picked him up by his antennae, tossed him into the cricket cage and locked the gate behind him.
                              George Selden, *The Cricket in Times Square*

Grammar Refresher   Some sentence openers are prepositional phrases. To learn more about prepositional phrases, see Handbook 40, "Understanding Prepositions and Conjunctions," pages 502–525.

"For today's youth, no issue ranks as high as the environment in shaping the world in which they are growing up," says the [Peter D. Hart Research Associates] report.

Connie Koenenn
LOS ANGELES TIMES

- What's your opinion about the environment? Jot down some of your thoughts.
- What issues do you care about? List some of them.

Show, Don't Tell

You can show your opinion on a subject by offering reasons and examples to support your point of view. Write a *showing* paragraph for one of the following *telling* sentences.

- I knew I was right.
- Television commercials are (are not) interesting.

5
Persuasion

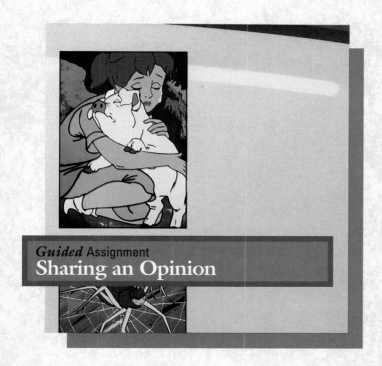

Guided Assignment
Sharing an Opinion

Related Assignment
Public Opinion Survey

Related Assignment
Writing for Assessment

Y ou express opinions every day. You're disappointed in a movie. You think a certain team is better than people realize. You think the rain forests should be protected. If some of your opinions seem stronger and more reasonable than others, it's probably because you have better reasons for them.

In this workshop you will learn to express your opinions effectively in writing. In the related assignments you'll conduct a public opinion survey and describe the opinions of others. You'll also practice writing a persuasive piece for assessment.

115

Sharing an Opinion

What do
you do when you get
steamed up about some-
thing—when you find
yourself holding a really
strong opinion? Do
you complain? Do you
try to persuade others?

Journalist Barbara
Brotman had a strong
opinion about a video
she saw. As you read
her column, notice how
she shows the reader
why she feels the way
she does. Also think
about whether you
agree with her.

Video "Web" Weaves an Inadequate Tale • by Barbara Brotman

There is a certain video you should
know about. You should know about it
because, despite what anyone else might
say, you should not watch it.

The tape is an outrage. It is video
refuse. It is a symbol of the decline of
American civilization.

It is *Charlotte's Web*.

You may think little permanent damage could be done by watching a cute
video featuring talking barnyard animals.

But you are wrong.

Before it was a video, *Charlotte's
Web* was a book—perhaps the finest
children's book ever written. It is a spectacular, magical journey into the lives
of a pig, a spider, and a little girl, written
in a matter-of-fact and yet luscious style

by E. B. White, a master of the English language.

It is a first taste of the miracle that is reading. Imagine: You can sit alone in a room, and hear Charlotte the spider cheerily say, "Salutations!" as clearly as you can hear yourself being called for dinner, and maybe more so.

You can smell the rotten goose egg that breaks and renders the barn "untenable," as Charlotte puts it (and if any children's book deserves to not be made into a video, it is one that uses the word *untenable*).

And if at the end of the book your heart does not break, you do not have one.

Charlotte's Web is a sweet video. But as I watch it, it seems terribly wrong.

In the book, Fern, who rescues Wilbur the pig from an untimely death, is a dreamy, mildly unkempt tomboy. In the video she is a generic animated girl. She could be Ariel in *The Little Mermaid*, or Belle in *Beauty and the Beast*; it doesn't seem to matter.

The book's Charlotte is a somewhat cerebral spider with a dry sense of humor and an aversion to sentimentality. She would never sing, "Up with your chinny-chin-chin!" in the voice of Debbie Reynolds. The video Charlotte would, and does.

Reading a book is a partnership. The author creates characters and action; you perceive them, through the wonders of imagination.

A video serves up the entire stew predigested. Imagination is neither required nor encouraged. You, the reader, deserve so much more.

This I wish for all of you:

That you may live in the big-sky prairie with Laura Ingalls Wilder; that you may watch the dancing light in Anna Karenina's eyes go tragically dark; that you may laugh and weep, sitting in rooms that are silent except for the eloquence of the written word; and that it may all start with a girl and a pig and a spider in Homer Zuckerman's barn.

Think & Respond

What parts of Brotman's column did you find most effective? What parts were not convincing? Can you think of times when watching a video of a book might be a good thing to do?

One Student's Writing

Barbara
Brotman felt that the
Charlotte's Web video
was an outrage, and she
said so. Her feelings
became the basis of a
strong opinion essay.

Dave Smith, a sixth-
grade student, has
strong feelings about
money and how much of
it some people are paid.
As you read his news-
paper opinion piece,
notice how he supports
his opinions with strong,
persuasive facts.

Kidviews

Those Sky-high Salaries
by DAVE SMITH

Many people in the United States today make somewhere between $5 and $10 an hour. That's not bad. But while they are making $5 to $10 an hour, there are some people making $12,000 an hour!

Who are these people? Who else? The professional athletes! The outrageous salaries of professional athletes just don't make sense.

First, no one is worth as much money as these athletes make. These people make millions of dollars a year, and they're not even doing that much work. Their qualifications are throwing a fastball ninety-plus miles an hour, hitting a twenty-foot jump shot sixty percent

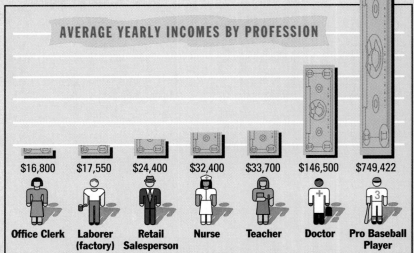

AVERAGE YEARLY INCOMES BY PROFESSION

Office Clerk	Laborer (factory)	Retail Salesperson	Nurse	Teacher	Doctor	Pro Baseball Player
$16,800	$17,550	$24,400	$32,400	$33,700	$146,500	$749,422

METRO EDITION

Sara

67th YEAR. No. 127 ★

of the time, or completing fifty-yard passes.

Bobby Bonilla and the New York Mets, for example, agreed to a five-year, $29 million contract. That averages to $5.8 million a year. Crazy, isn't it? I know this contract sounds outrageous, but it's becoming commonplace in professional sports today.

Second, there is no need for such a large salary. Average working Americans can live decently, yet they won't even come close to making in a lifetime what some pro athletes make in a year.

Let's use a factory worker to illustrate this point. We'll say this factory worker has worked for ten years and makes $30,000 a year. This hard-working factory worker would have to work two hundred years just to make as much as Bobby Bonilla will make in one year.

Finally, it doesn't make sense that people are mak-

ing so much money when so many Americans are homeless, when the world needs money to fund research on deadly diseases such as AIDS and cancer, and when our country has such a large national debt.

Why can't we put salary caps on the earnings of professional athletes and have some of the money go toward good causes like the ones just listed? I wish more athletes were like NFL quarterback Warren Moon, who donates a large portion of his salary to good causes.

If you only remember one thing from this essay, I hope it's this: No one is worth the kind of money pro athletes make today. But if anyone is going to receive that much money, it should be the men and women who get up early every morning, go to work, and work their hardest to support their families.

SUNDAY BLUE

INSIDE

Kidviews
Special pull-out section **1F**

'Romeo' opera restores missing music 1G

Think & Respond

Respond as a Reader

▶ What do you think of Dave's suggestion to limit salaries?

▶ How would professional athletes respond to Dave's opinion?

Respond as a Writer

▶ How does Dave use examples to make his point?

▶ How does he show when he is moving from one reason to the next?

INVITATION
TO
Write

Both Barbara Brotman and Dave Smith had strong opinions and expressed them in writing. Feeling strongly about an issue makes it easier to write about it. Writing about an issue also helps you sort out your thinking.

Write an essay stating your opinion on an issue that you feel strongly about.

PREWRITE AND EXPLORE

1. Search for opinions.   Do you believe in limiting violence in television programs? Should grading systems be changed? Should some kinds of music have warning labels? To discover issues you care about, try some of the following activities.

Exploring Topics

- **What bugs me is . . .**   Alone or with classmates, **brainstorm** about what makes you mad or about problems you feel should be corrected. Make a list of things that bother you. For example, do you disagree with Barbara Brotman about the video of *Charlotte's Web?*

- **Journal search**   Look through your journal for issues or problems that you have written about over and over again or with great emotion.

- **What's news?**   Listen to the local or national news on the radio or watch it on TV. You might also browse through newspapers or newsmagazines to see what's going on in the world. What controversial issues do you have an opinion about? Try making a **cluster** to explore your writing options.

One Student's Process

Dave Smith thought about the opinions he had on various subjects like recycling, rock song lyrics, and the homeless. Then he decided to try a cluster diagram based on one of his major interests. He started with "sports" and branched out in different directions. He realized he had a strong opinion about salaries in professional sports.

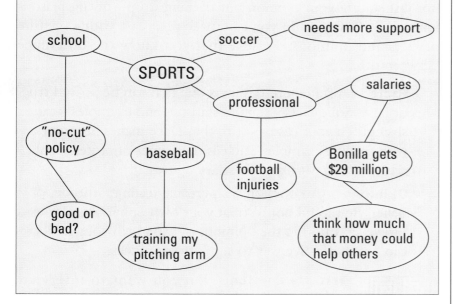

2. Pick an issue. Which issues do you care the most about? Try **freewriting** about some of them. Then choose the one you're most interested in writing about.

3. Explore ideas. In small groups, find out what your classmates think about your issue. You might get some new ideas. Then freewrite some more about the topic. Ask yourself, what is my opinion? Why do I feel this way?

4. Gather information. Do some research on your topic to find details you can use to support your opinion. Ask your librarian about books, newspapers, magazines, and other resources that might be helpful.

PROBLEM SOLVING

"What do I want my essay to do ?"

For help in pinpointing your purpose and personal goals, see

• Handbook 5, "Goals and Audience," pages 211–214

D RAFT AND DISCOVER

1. Start writing. If you're not really sure what you want to say, just begin putting down some ideas. You can change, organize, and add to them later. Try stating your opinion in one or two sentences. Then explain why you feel that way.

2. Support your opinion. Writing an opinion paper means not just stating your opinion but backing it up—giving reasons for it. Like Dave Smith, you can make your case with a mixture of facts and opinions. Be sure that you know the difference between the two.

- **Facts** A statement of fact is one that can be proved true or false. Solid facts—such as statistics and examples—can strengthen your case. Notice that Dave makes his point with specific examples, such as the names of professional athletes, and with specific salary figures.

- **Opinions** An opinion is a personal feeling, attitude, or belief. Be careful not to treat your own opinion as fact. However, quoting the opinions of experts in your subject can be an effective way to support your ideas.

 Writer's Choice Do you want to interview several people to get some quotes you can use for supporting evidence? Perhaps you can find an expert on your subject to interview.

3. Think about your readers. Aim your writing at your particular audience. Do they need more background information? If you think your readers disagree with you, how can you deal with their arguments against your ideas?

4. Organize your writing. Try to catch the reader's attention, as Barbara Brotman did, and state your opinion. Then give the background and present your reasons. It's often wise to save your best reason for last. For a conclusion, you might restate or summarize your opinion, as Dave Smith did.

PROBLEM

S O L V I N G

"How can I back up my opinion?"

For help in finding material to support your opinion, see

- Handbook 4, "Developing a Topic," pages 205–214

5. Think about your draft. Are you ready to share your writing now, or do you want to make some changes first? The following questions can help you review your draft and get good suggestions from your peer readers.

R E V I E W Y O U R W R I T I N G

Questions for Yourself
- Have I shown the importance of the issue I am writing about?
- Have I gathered enough evidence?
- Have I left out any reasons that support my opinion?
- Have I taken into account arguments on the other side?

Questions for Your Peer Readers
- Is my opinion on this issue clear? Tell it to me in a sentence or two.
- What part of this paper was most convincing to you?
- Did I support my opinion with enough facts and examples?
- What is your opinion on this issue?

One Student's Process

Here is the first draft of the beginning of Dave's paper. He asked some classmates for their responses. Would you add anything else?

The outrageous salaries of professional athletes just doesn't make sense. Ordinary working people don't make that kind of money. Many people in the United States today only make a few dollars an hour. But while they're making a few dollars an hour, there are some people making huge fortunes. It's insane. Who are these people? Who else? Professional athletes!

Peer Reader Comments

I like your point. I agree that the salaries are too high.

Some more facts would help me. What are the different salaries?

R EVISE YOUR WRITING

1. Think about your responses. If your readers thought your opinion was unclear, try stating it in just one sentence. Then build from there.

2. Check your reasons. You've probably heard young children support their opinions by simply saying "Because." Their friends say, "Because why?" Make sure you have supplied the "why."

3. Give the facts. Have you used facts or examples to support all of your reasons? Could you prove them if asked to do so? Dave Smith used real people and salary figures to back up his opinion.

 Paragraphs at Work When you state an opinion, you need to back it up with reasons. It's usually a good idea to put each of your reasons into a separate paragraph, along with the supporting facts, examples, and other details. Remember these tips.

- State your opinion in a separate paragraph at the beginning of your essay.
- Begin a new paragraph for each main reason you give to support your opinion.
- Make sure that all details in a paragraph are related.

4. Watch your language. Precise words make for clearer opinions. Some words cause emotional reactions. If you use words like *good* and *bad* or *right* and *wrong,* you should show readers what you mean. Barbara Brotman and Dave Smith used words like *outrageous,* but they based their opinions on reason as well as emotion.

5. Check your introduction and conclusion. Have you written an interesting introduction that makes your readers want to continue reading? Is your conclusion a strong one that your readers will remember?

PROBLEM

S O L V I N G

"How can I check my reasoning?"

To make sure your ideas make sense and you have used language effectively, see

- Handbook 30, "Thinking Skills," pages 320–322
- Handbook 20, "Levels of Language," pages 274–275

One Student's Process

After reviewing his draft with classmates, Dave Smith decided to change the beginning, add some facts, and change the organization. Here are the changes he made.

The outrageous salaries of professional ath-
letes just ~~doesn't~~ *don't* make sense. ~~Ordinary working~~
~~people don't make that kind of money.~~ Many peo-
ple in America today only make ~~a few dollars an~~ *somewhere between $5 and $10*
That's not bad. hour. But while they're making ~~a few dollars an~~ *$5 to $10*
hour, there are some people making huge ~~for-~~
~~tunes. It's insane.~~ *$12,000 an hour!* Who are these people? Who
else? Professional athletes!

PROOFREAD

1. Proofread your work. Look over your revised paper for errors in grammar, spelling, punctuation, and capitalization. Double-check numbers and statistics. In explaining your reasons for your opinion, you may have used transition words and phrases such as *for example, in addition, next,* and *finally.* Check with your teacher about the use of commas with these transition words.

GRAMMAR **AND** WRITING

Subject–Verb Agreement

Remember, a verb must always agree in number with its subject. The noun or pronoun closest to the verb is not always the subject of that verb. For example, if you refer to *one* of the factors in a problem or *one* of the reasons for your opinion, you should check for subject-verb agreement.

Dave corrected a problem in subject–verb agreement when he proofread and revised his writing. The plural word *reasons* is next to the verb in the following sentence, but the subject of the sentence is *one.* The singular verb *is* agrees with the subject.

Original

One of the reasons <u>are</u> that no one is worth that much money.

Revised

One of the reasons <u>is</u> that no one is worth that much money.

2. Make a clean copy of your paper.   Once you are satisfied with your paper, review it one last time, using the Standards for Evaluation listed in the margin. Then make your final copy.

Standards for Evaluation

PERSUASIVE
WRITING

An opinion paper
- has a strong introduction
- clearly states the writer's opinion
- provides support for ideas
- has a strong conclusion

PUBLISH AND PRESENT

- **Write a letter.**   Turn your opinion piece into a letter to the editor of a school or community newspaper. Perhaps you can pair it with another piece, expressing a different opinion on the same topic.

- **Turn your opinion into a poster.** Create headlines and illustrations to present your opinion.
- **Hold a class discussion.** Get together with your classmates and present your papers orally. Then share your reactions to each other's work.
- **Present your case.** Deliver your opinion personally to someone in a position of authority who might be able to help.

REFLECT ON YOUR WRITING

W R I T E R   T O   W R I T E R

One role of the writer today is to sound the alarm.

E. B. White, American writer

1. Add your writing to your portfolio. Include a note, to be attached to your paper, in which you reflect on your experience in writing your opinion paper. In this note you may want to write about the following questions:

FOR YOUR
PORTFOLIO

- How did I find a topic to write about?
- How did my opinion change as I thought and wrote about my topic?
- What happened when my classmates read my paper? How did their responses help me or get in my way?
- How would I change my essay now, if I were to revise it again?

2. Explore additional writing ideas. See the suggestions for writing a review on pages 130–132, and Springboards on page 137.

Public Opinion Survey

Reading a
PUBLIC OPINION SURVEY

Tina Smith, a sixth-grade student, was curious about the ideas and opinions of her classmates. So she satisfied her curiosity by taking an opinion survey. Then she wrote a report of her findings. Look at her survey form, shown here, and then read her report on the opposite page. Can you think of other questions you'd like to ask?

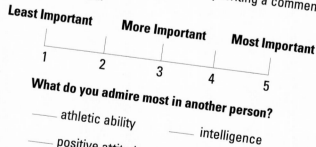

Personality Survey

Circle one: male female

Directions: This survey asks you to respond to a question by ranking five possible qualities from least important (1) to most important (5). First, read the question. Then write the number 1 next to the quality you think is least important, the number 2 next to the quality you think is next in importance, and so on until you reach number 5, the most important quality. If you wish, you can explain your responses by writing a comment in the space provided.

Least Important	More Important	Most Important
1	2 3	4 5

What do you admire most in another person?

—— athletic ability   —— intelligence

—— positive attitude   —— popularity

—— physical appearance

Comments:

Personality Survey

Question

I've often wondered why my friends like some people more than others. I started asking them what they admired most in a person. Some said intelligence was most important. Others mentioned good looks or personality. Sometimes, though, I wasn't sure they were being honest. So I decided to take an opinion survey. I wrote down five qualities that people mentioned the most. Then I made up a questionnaire.

Method

I conducted this survey at my school in March. I gave the survey form to 100 sixth-grade students, 50 girls and 50 boys. When I got the forms back, I added up all the numbers. If someone ranked a quality as number five, I gave that answer five points. The second choice got four points, and so on. Here are the choices the students made and the total points each quality got.

SURVEY RESULTS

Quality	Girls	Boys	Total
Positive Attitude	236	222	458
Intelligence	193	189	382
Athletic ability	117	132	249
Physical appearance	122	118	240
Popularity	81	89	170

Results

The most important quality of the five turned out to be a positive attitude. Out of the 100 students, 39 girls and 32 boys put it at the top of the list. The next most important trait was intelligence. It was rated number 2 by 35 girls and 26 boys. Almost one-fourth of the boys even gave it the highest rating. Third place was pretty close to a tie, but athletic ability came out a little ahead of physical appearance. Popularity came in last.

Conclusion

This survey tells me that boys and girls admire similar things. Both think a positive attitude and intelligence are most important. Girls seem to value physical appearance a little more than athletic ability, and with boys it's the other way around. Everyone put popularity last. I learned that most kids value more lasting things.

Think & Respond

What do you find to be the most interesting result of Tina's survey? Can you think of any reason why girls and boys disagreed about what to rank third? How do Tina's findings compare with your own experience?

INVITATION
═ TO ═
Write

Tina Smith used a survey to find out what her class-mates admired most in other people. Then she reported on her findings. You, too, can gather information about people's opinions by taking a survey.

Design a public opinion survey on a subject that interests you. Give the survey to a group of people, and then write a report about the results.

FINDING A FOCUS

1. Find a reason to take a survey. You can conduct a survey to get support for an idea—for example, that television violence is harmful to kids. You might use a survey to help you make a decision, such as which product to sell to raise money for your club. Perhaps you are simply curious about how other people think about an issue you care about, such as cafeteria menus or the length of the school day.

2. Consider your audience. Who will take your survey? That depends on what you want to learn. You may want to target certain groups, such as sports fans or skateboarders. On the other hand, you may simply want to survey students in general.

3. Choose the size of your survey. If, for example, you want to know how students feel about cafeteria menus, you would need to survey as many students as possible in order to get the most reliable information. If you want to know how the members of your club feel about meeting times, your survey would be limited to the club members.

CREATING YOUR SURVEY

1. Consider the form.   What form works best for the type of survey you are doing? Tina asked people to rank qualities from least to most important. The resulting data gave her numbers that she could compare. Multiple-choice questions are another useful form. They can be used for issues such as which radio stations are more popular or what kinds of books students like to read.

2. Write the questions.   Think about what you want to know. Brainstorm with some friends to come up with possible questions. Then try out different ways of wording the questions to make them as clear as possible.

3. Write directions.   Tell people what you want them to do. Your directions need to be very clear or else you may get answers that you do not understand or cannot count. Sometimes a sample question and answer helps clarify directions for the people who take your survey.

4. Test your form.   Try out your survey on a few of your classmates. Can they follow your directions? Do they understand your questions? If necessary, change the wording of questions or directions before giving your survey to a larger number of people.

COMPLETING THE SURVEY

1. Have people take the survey.   Find a convenient time and place for people to read and complete your survey. Collect the completed forms and keep them together until you are ready to count the answers.

2. Keep track of the responses.   Set up a chart or a list with which you can count responses and figure out the results of your survey.

3. Write a report. Think of an effective way of presenting the results of the survey. Your report will probably have the following sections:

- **Discuss the issue.** You can start your report by describing the purpose of your survey. Be sure to explain why you are interested in this information.

- **Describe the methods you used.** Explain who filled out the survey form. Describe how these people were chosen and when and where the survey was conducted.

- **Present the results.** Write a conclusion summing up the results. This might be a good place for a graphic presentation, perhaps a graph or a chart like the one Tina used. Then comment on the results of your survey. Tell why your results are interesting or important.

SHARING YOUR RESULTS

- **Display the findings.** Post the survey form and your report of the results on a school bulletin board. You might also give an oral report about the results of your survey.

- **Write an article.** Write an article for your school or community paper. Describe your survey and explain what you learned.

- **Share your report.** Give a copy of your survey report to those who might be particularly interested, such as student organizations or school administrators.

Writing for Assessment

Related ASSIGNMENT

More and more, writing is becoming an important part of the tests you take in school. You'll do better on a test if you know what to expect. One kind of test asks you to write a brief essay to show what you've learned about a school subject. In another type of test, a writing assessment, you write to show how well you can express your own thoughts and feelings.

Two of the questions on this page are essay-test questions and two are prompts for writing assessments. What does each question ask you to do?

- **SOCIAL STUDIES**   The ancient Egyptians believed in an afterlife. Define afterlife and tell the steps Egyptians took to prepare for the afterlife.

- **SCIENCE**   Dinosaurs lived on the earth millions of years ago. Discuss the theories about why they became extinct.

- **WRITING TEST**   You have received a letter from a sixth grader living in China who wants to know what life is like in the United States. Write a letter to this student. Describe what a typical school day is like for you.

- **WRITING TEST**   Imagine that your town is considering a law that would forbid people from skating on downtown sidewalks. Write a letter to the editor of your community newspaper. State your opinion on whether or not skating should be banned. Give reasons to back up your opinion.

INVITATION TO *Write*

Questions like those on page 133 test your knowledge, your thinking skills, and your writing ability. You can learn to examine test questions and find the clues that will help you write effective answers.

Follow the directions for the last question on page 133. Write a letter to the editor that tells your opinion and supports it.

PROBLEM
SOLVING

"What's the best way to study for a test?"

For more information on preparing for tests, see

• Handbook 33, "Taking Tests," pages 326–333

Writing
TIP

If a question doesn't specify the audience, it is often best to assume that your teacher is your audience.

READING THE QUESTION

1. Find out what you need to do. Key words in the directions can tell you what writing strategy to use. If you see words like *explain* or *compare* or *persuade,* for example, you know how your answer should be presented. Here are some key words to look for.

describe	discuss	persuade
explain	compare	contrast
define	tell how	give reasons

2. Know your audience. Some questions tell you to write for a specific person or group. Knowing the audience will tell you what kind of language to use or how much to explain. For example, the audience for the third question on page 133 is a sixth grader in China. You might use friendly, informal language for that reader.

3. Determine your format. Check to see what form your writing should take. You could be asked to write a letter, an editorial, or an essay, for example.

1. Plan your time. Before you start writing, take a few moments to decide how to use your time. For example, if you have thirty minutes to write an answer, you might budget ten minutes to plan your answer, fifteen minutes to write it, and five minutes to revise and proofread it.

2. Do some prewriting. You might want to make a list or a cluster or do some freewriting to find the ideas to include in your answer. Jot down ideas as they come to you. If possible, sketch out a quick outline of your answer.

One Student's Process

Leroy Collins jotted down a rough outline for an answer to the first test question.

Beliefs	Burial practices
Beliefs	Burial practices
— afterlife like real life	— mummies 5000 years old
— worshipped sun god	years old
— dead needed bodies	— food & weapons too
— dead should be comfortable	too
— mummies preserved	— pets and servants

WRITING YOUR ANSWER

1. Start with your main idea. Since time is limited, get right to the point. Try to state your main idea in a sentence or two. Then look at your prewriting notes to find details, facts, or reasons you can use to back up your main idea.

2. End with a strong conclusion. You might want to sum up the point you have made or restate your main idea.

Egyptian male mummy mask, painted wood, about 1400 B.C.

1. Reread the question. Make sure that you have fully answered the question. In the margins or between the lines, make any changes you want in your answer.

2. Proofread your work. Look for mistakes in grammar, spelling, capitalization, and punctuation.

One Student's Process

Here is how Leroy Collins's paper looked when he had finished it.

The Egyptians beleived that life continued

after death. They called this idea the Afterlife.

Defines afterlife

The Egyptians believed the afterlife would be

like real life. Therefore,

much the same. They wanted the dead to have

Explains why they had to prepare the dead

everything they would need to enjoy the afterlife.

the

Once an Egyptian died his body was perserved

Tells the steps Egyptians followed to prepare the dead for the afterlife

as a mummy. This was so the soul would be able

have a place when it returned.

to come back to it. Then the body was placed in a

tomb along with food and some of the persons

favorite things. Sometimes the bodies of ser-

Includes specific details

vants or cats and dogs were also included. The

insides of the tomb were often painted with

beautiful scenes from the persons life.

Spring boards

CONSUMER EDUCATION Write a consumer review of a product you have used. Tell your readers whether you recommend they use the product. Be sure to give specific reasons for your recommendation.

Keds (1961), Roy Lichtenstein

MEDIA Imagine that you work for an advertising agency. Choose a product and write an advertisement that will make people want to buy it. Illustrate your ad with your own drawings or with pictures you cut out of magazines.

Music

Who is your choice for best musical group, or best individual artist, performing today? Write a paper that presents—and supports—your opinion.

Science

How would you support the opinion that the earth is flat? How would you oppose it? Choose a scientific concept that we take for granted today. Then write a paper that either supports the concept or opposes it.

Speaking & Listening

Write a campaign speech for any candidate—living or dead—of your choice. Convince your listeners that they should vote for your candidate.

Sentence

Subject-Verb Splits

The underlined parts of the sentences below separate the subject (S) from the verb (V). Notice how these subject-verb splits add information about the subject of each sentence.

Model A Agatha's mother, <u>frantic now</u>, beat the door of the vault with her hands. **O. Henry, "A Retrieved Reformation"**

Model B The meat, <u>preserved for the feeding of the dogs</u>, hung in the smokehouse. **Marjorie Kinnan Rawlings, *The Yearling***

Model C Little Jon, <u>whose eyes were quicker than most</u>, should have seen the hole, but all his attention was on the stars.

Alexander Key, *The Forgotten Door*

▶ **ON THE MARK** Put commas before and after a subject-verb split to separate it from the rest of the sentence.

A. Combining Sentences Put the underlined part of the second sentence into the first sentence at the caret (∧) as a subject-verb split. Write the complete sentence, putting commas before and after the subject-verb split.

1. Boysie ∧ heard the door shut and came to the living room. Boysie was the one <u>who slept in the kitchen</u>. **Betsy Byars, *The Summer of the Swans***

2. The physical education teacher ∧ gave me an inquisitive look. The teacher was <u>dancing past energetically in the arms of a Grade Ten boy</u>.

Alice Munro, "Red Dress—1946"

3. The truck drivers ∧ were furious. This happened <u>when they heard that Maxie Hammerman had been released</u>. **Jean Merrill, *The Pushcart War***

4. The clerk ∧ tried to talk me into buying one big bottle. He was <u>a snappy-looking fellow, wearing a red bow tie, with a pink baby face but not a wisp of hair on his head</u>. **Robert Cormier, *Take Me Where the Good Times Are***

B. Unscrambling and Imitating Sentences   Unscramble each set of sentence chunks below. Create a sentence that has a subject-verb split and the same order of chunks and punctuation as the model. Then write a sentence of your own that imitates each model.

1. Model   Mr. McAlester, <u>who kept the store</u>, was a good Arkansas man.
Charles Portis, *True Grit*

who coaches our team / Andre's father / is a former professional football player

2. Model   His little legs, <u>bent sharply at the knees</u>, had never before seemed so fragile, so thin.   **James Hurst, "The Scarlet Ibis"**

surrounded completely by birch trees / had always seemed so comfortable, so cozy / their summer cottage

3. Model   My stomach, <u>a large distressing lump</u>, quaked and thrilled, making it hard for me to breathe the thin and tasteless air.
James Gould Cozzens, "The Animals' Fair"

a beautiful blue macaw / making it difficult for me / the parrot / to take a nap in peace / squawked and talked

C. Expanding Sentences   Use your imagination to add a phrase as a S-V split where the caret appears in each of the following sentences. Set off each phrase with commas.

1. The lion ∧ stared at the animals as hard as if he was going to burn them up with his mere stare.   **C. S. Lewis, *The Magician's Nephew***

2. My aunt ∧ pulled a chair up next to me, careful not to rake the legs across her shag carpet.   **Gary Soto, *A Summer Life***

3. Mr. Miyagi ∧ simply beamed.   **B. B. Hiller, *The Karate Kid***

Grammar Refresher   Adding words between the subject and the verb does not change subject-verb agreement. For more information, see Handbook 41, "Mastering Subject-Verb Agreement," pages 526–545.

- What do you think about this painting? Jot down your reactions.
- Tell a story about what you see in this painting.
- Is there a book, a poem, a painting, a song, or another work of art that has a special meaning for you? Explain why.

I and the Village (1911), Marc Chagall.

Show, Don't Tell

When you respond to a story or a poem, you try to connect your own experiences to something in the literature. Using examples from your life, you can explain how a piece of literature makes you feel. Select one of the *telling* sentences below and turn it into a *showing* paragraph by using examples from your own experience.

- The character did something that I would do.
- The story made me sad.

6

Responding to Literature

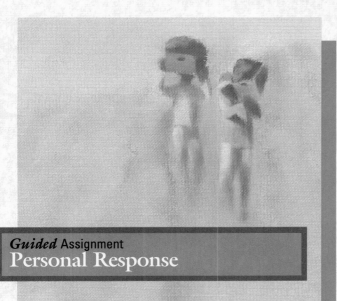

Guided Assignment
Personal Response

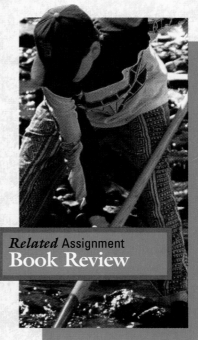

Related Assignment
Book Review

Y ou've just been watching a TV show with friends. You're complaining about the ending, but someone else liked the actors. Still another remembers the funny lines. You're all responding to the show. Sharing your reactions is not only natural and fun, it also helps you understand your own thoughts and feelings about a work.

In this workshop you'll get a chance to write what you think and feel about a short work of literature. In a related assignment, you'll share your responses to a book you've read.

Guided
ASSIGNMENT

Personal Response

Starting from
LITERATURE

Imagine how it might feel to move often and to change schools frequently. What if people at school did not speak your language? Panchito has to face such situations. He and his family are farm workers from Mexico who follow the crops in southern California. As you read "The Circuit," notice what you are thinking and feeling. Use your journal to write down your thoughts, feelings, and questions as you read.

The Circuit

from

by Francisco Jiménez

IT WAS THAT TIME OF YEAR AGAIN. Ito, the strawberry sharecropper, did not smile. It was natural. The peak of the strawberry season was over, and the last few days the workers, most of them *braceros,*[1] were not picking as many boxes as they had during the months of June and July. . . .

Yes, it was that time of year. When I opened the front door to the shack, I stopped. Everything we owned was neatly packed in cardboard boxes. Suddenly I felt even more the weight of hours, days, weeks, and months of work. I sat down on a box. The thought of having to move to Fresno and knowing what was in store for me there brought tears to my eyes.

That night I could not sleep. I lay in bed thinking about how much I hated this move. . . .

As we drove away, I felt a lump in my throat. I turned around and looked at our little shack for the last time.

At sunset we drove into a labor camp near Fresno. Since Papa did not speak English, Mama asked the camp foreman if he needed any more workers. "We don't need no more," said the foreman, scratching his head. "Check with Sullivan down the road. Can't miss him. He lives in a big white house with a fence around it."

When we got there, Mama walked up to the house. She went through a white gate, past a row of rose bushes, up the stairs to the front door. She rang the doorbell. The porch light went on and a tall, husky man came out. They exchanged a few words. After the man went in, Mama clasped her hands and hurried back to the car. "We have work! Mr. Sullivan said we can stay there the whole season," she said, gasping and pointing to an old garage near the stables. . . .

Early next morning Mr. Sullivan showed us where his crop was, and after breakfast, Papa, Roberto, and I headed for the vineyard to pick. . . .

After lunch we went back to work. The sun kept beating down. The buzzing insects, the wet sweat, and the hot dry dust made the afternoon seem to last forever. Finally the mountains around the valley reached out and swallowed the sun. Within an hour it was too dark to continue picking. The vines blanketed the grapes, making it difficult to see the bunches. *"Vamonos,"*[2] said Papa, signaling to us that it was time to quit work. Papa then took out a pencil and began to figure out how much we had earned our first day. He wrote down numbers, crossed some out, wrote down some more. *"Quince,"*[3] he murmured. . . .

The next morning I could hardly move. My body ached all over. I felt little control over my arms and legs. This feeling went on every morning for days until my muscles finally got used to the work.

It was Monday, the first week of November. The grape season was over, and I could now go to school. I woke up early that morning and lay in bed, looking at the stars and savoring the thought of not going to work and of starting sixth grade for the first time that year. Since I could not sleep, I decided to get up and join Papa and Roberto at breakfast. I sat at the table across from Roberto, but I kept my head down. I did not want to look up and face him. I knew he was sad. He was not going to school today. He was not going tomorrow, or next week, or next month.

He would not go until the cotton season was over, and that was sometime in February. I rubbed my hands together and watched the dry, acid-stained skin fall to the floor in little rolls.

When Papa and Roberto left for work, I felt relief. I walked to the top of a small grade next to the shack and watched the "Carcanchita"[4] disappear in the distance in a cloud of dust.

Two hours later, around eight o'clock, I stood by the side of the road waiting for school bus number twenty. When it arrived, I climbed in. No one noticed me. Everyone was busy either talking or yelling. I sat in an empty seat in the back.

When the bus stopped in front of the school, I felt very nervous. I looked out the bus window and saw boys and girls carrying books under their arms. I felt empty. I put my hands in my pants pockets and walked to the principal's office. When I entered, I heard a woman's voice say, "May I help you?" I was startled. I had not heard English for months. For a few seconds I remained speechless. I looked at the lady who waited for an answer. My first instinct was to answer her in Spanish, but I held back. Finally, after struggling for English words, I managed to tell her that I wanted to enroll in the sixth grade. After answering many questions, I was led to the classroom.

Mr. Lema, the sixth-grade teacher, greeted me and assigned me a desk. He then introduced me to the class. I was so nervous and scared at that moment when everyone's eyes were on me that I wished I were with Papa and Roberto picking cotton. After taking roll, Mr. Lema gave the class the assignment for the first hour. "The first thing we have to do this morning is finish reading the story we began yesterday," he said enthusiastically. He walked up to me, handed me an English book, and asked me to read. "We are on page 125," he said politely. When I heard this, I felt my blood rush to my head. I felt dizzy. "Would you like to read?" he asked hesitantly. I opened the book to page 125. My mouth was dry. My eyes began to water. I could not begin. "You can read later," Mr. Lema said understandingly.

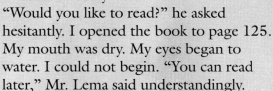

For the rest of the reading period I kept getting angrier and angrier with myself. I should have read, I thought to myself.

During recess I went into the restroom and opened my English book to page 125. I began to read in a low voice, pretending I was in class. There were many words I did not know. I closed the book and headed back to the classroom.

Mr. Lema was sitting at his desk correcting papers. When I entered he looked up at me and smiled. I felt better. I walked up to him and asked if he could help me with the new words. "Gladly," he said.

The rest of the month I spent my lunch hours working on English with Mr. Lema, my best friend at school.

One Friday during lunch hour, Mr. Lema asked me to take a walk with him to the music room. "Do you like music?" he asked me as we entered the building. "Yes, I like Mexican *corridos*,"[5] I answered. He then picked up a trumpet, blew on it, and handed it to me. The sound gave me goose bumps. I knew that sound. I had heard it in many Mexican *corridos*. "How would you like to learn how to play it?" he asked. He must have read my face because before I could answer, he added: "I'll teach you how to play it during our lunch hours."

That day I could hardly wait to get home to tell Papa and Mama the great news. As I got off the bus, my little brothers and sisters ran up to meet me. They were yelling and screaming. I thought they were happy to see me, but when I opened the door to our shack, I saw that everything we owned was neatly packed in cardboard boxes.

---

1. ***braceros*** (brä sä′ rōs): *Spanish:* hired hands; day laborers.
2. ***Vamonos*** (vä′ mô nôs): *Spanish:* Let's go.
3. ***quince*** (kēn′ sä): *Spanish:* fifteen.
4. **"Carcanchita"**: Papa's nickname for the old family car.
5. ***corridos*** (kô rē′ dôs): *Spanish:* ballads.

Think & Respond

How do you think Panchito feels about what happens at the end of the story? What are your thoughts and feelings about the story? **Freewrite** about your response to the whole story or to any part of it. Share your freewriting with your classmates.

145

One Student's Writing

Responding to "The Circuit"
by Vanessa Ramirez

When I read and reread "The Circuit" by Francisco Jiménez, I didn't understand why it made me feel sad, but then I realized at the end that it reminded me of when I was small, when I first started school.

In the story a boy named Panchito can't go to school because he has to work in the fields to help his family. When he finally goes to school in November, he forgets how to speak in English.

Panchito says that when he entered the school office, he heard a voice say, "May I help you?" Then he says, "I had not heard English for months. For a few seconds I remained speechless." I put myself in Panchito's place when I read this, because I

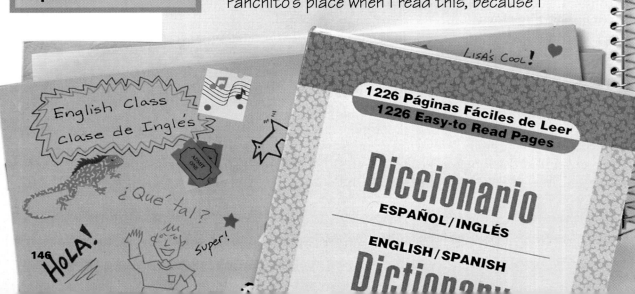

English Class
Clase de Inglés

¿Qué tal?

HOLA!

Super!

LISA's COOL!

1226 Páginas Fáciles de Leer
1226 Easy-to Read Pages

Diccionario
ESPAÑOL / INGLÉS

ENGLISH / SPANISH

Dictionary

had already experienced it before. When I first started school, I spoke only Spanish, but my parents spoke for me. So that was a great relief.

The reason I say it was a great relief is because in my situation my parents spoke for me in order to enroll me and in his situation Panchito had to speak for himself to enroll in school. This part of the story hit my heart.

When people are used to talking in one language, it is very hard when they realize they're being told something in another language. It must be sad because they don't understand, or maybe they do, but they are embarrassed because they don't know how to speak the other language well. That's how Panchito felt when he went to enroll in school and when the teacher asked him to read in class.

I liked writing about this story because as I was writing, I was imagining that I was there in the story and because it kind of has to do with what happened to me.

Think & Respond

Respond as a Reader

► How was Vanessa able to tie the story to her own experience?

► In what way was Vanessa's reaction to the story the same as or different from yours?

Respond as a Writer

► What parts of Vanessa's essay made the strongest impression on you? Can you say why?

► How does the end of Vanessa's paper tie in with the beginning?

Personal Response

INVITATION
TO
Write

Readers of "The Circuit" will respond to the story in many different ways. Vanessa Ramirez was touched by Panchito's struggle to speak English in school. Remembering her own experiences made it easier for Vanessa to connect to the story and to write about it.

Write a brief response essay, telling your own thoughts and feelings about a short work of literature.

PREWRITE AND EXPLORE

1. Find a story or a poem.   Choose a short literary work that you liked or disliked or were puzzled by. You will probably want to select a work that made a strong impression on you.

You could consider "The Circuit" by Francisco Jiménez or a short piece of writing suggested by your teacher. After making your choice, try some of the following activities.

Exploring Topics

- **Writing about it**   Notice your thoughts, feelings, and questions as you read. Try **freewriting** about your responses to the whole story or poem.

- **Sketching a response**   Try responding to the work with rough sketches or doodles, showing how you think or feel. Then freewrite briefly, explaining your drawing.

- **Talking about it**   Share your freewriting or your sketches with a small group of readers. Did others respond to the same work differently? Discuss the different responses. Feel free to change your mind as you listen to other ideas.

Writing
TIP

If you're having trouble deciding what to write about, find any short passage that you don't understand and write about why it is a problem for you.

2. Reread the piece. Read the story or poem again. This may give you some new ideas. Try some of these activities:

- **"Jump-in" reading** Try this with others who have read the same work. A volunteer begins reading it aloud, then pauses. Someone else jumps in and continues reading. If two jump in at once, they can read together. Afterwards, freewrite a new response.

- **Saying the lines** Readers call out lines they think are important, interesting, or difficult. It's fun and interesting to see what lines others find important.

- **Responding to a single line or sentence** Pick out a line that interests or amuses you or makes you think. Freewrite about why you chose it.

3. Think about your response. Review your notes, drawings, and freewriting to find a response you want to write about.

Writer's Choice Do you want to write about the work as a whole or focus on one part as Vanessa did? Follow your instincts. Write about what is most interesting to you.

One Student's Process

Vanessa wasn't sure how to write about her reactions to the story. So she did some freewriting, jotting down notes to help her sort out her feelings.

> This story make me feel sad—I don't know why. When the boy goes to the office somebody says, "May I help you?" and he is embarrassed. That made me feel bad. Also Mr. Lema the sixth grade teacher asks him to read and says "We are on page 125." I know how he might have felt.
> I'd like to write about the whole story, but the part about his trouble with English really hit my heart.

1. Start writing.   Trying to use any freewriting you've already done, write out a rough first draft. Connect your responses to specific things in the story or poem that triggered them. Use quotations from the work to show what you are responding to.

2. Think about the parts of your essay.   Some writers prefer not to start with a structure in mind. Still, it may help to think of these three parts of a response:

- **Introduction**   Mention the title and the author of the work, then tell what the work is about and why you're interested in it. Notice how Vanessa, in her first paragraph, identified the story, told how she felt about it, and briefly explained why.

- **Body**   Here you can give details of how you reacted to the work. If your response is based on your own personal experience, you can explain that. You can even tell a brief story. Vanessa described a key incident in the story and related it to something that had happened to her.

- **Conclusion**   You may not need a formal conclusion, but it's good to end with some final thought. You might explain what your response taught you about yourself or about the work. Vanessa ended her response by describing how she felt when writing it.

3. Think about your readers.   Who will be reading your response? What do they know about this story or poem? Note that Vanessa told just enough in her second paragraph to set up the incident she wanted to write about.

4. Think about your draft.   After you've finished your draft, let it sit awhile. Then read it again and make any changes you need to. Show it to classmates for their response. Here are some questions you might ask.

Questions for Yourself

- How honest is my response? Did I say what I really think or feel about this work?
- Have I told my readers enough about the work for them to know what I'm talking about?
- Have I explained why I responded to the work the way I did? Have I told how my own experiences may have caused me to respond this way?

Questions for Your Peer Readers

- What parts of my essay are most interesting to you?
- Did I tell you all you need to know about the work itself to understand my essay?
- Have I explained my thoughts and feelings clearly? Why do you think I reacted to the story the way I did?

One Student's Process

After looking over her prewriting notes, Vanessa wrote a first draft and asked some of her classmates to read it. Notice their comments. What would you have told her?

When I read "The Circuit" by Francisco Jiménez, it made me feel sad. In the story a boy named Panchito doesn't go to school until November, he works in the fields to help his family. He forgets how to speak in English.

Panchito says he heard a voice say "May I help you?" and he was startled. He had not heard English for months and he was embarassed and couldn't say anything right away. For a few seconds he remained speechless. I had already experienced this before. When I first started school, I only spoke Spanish, my parents spoke for me. So that was a great relief.

Peer Reader Comments

I wonder why it makes you feel sad.

That sounds interesting. Where did he hear this voice? In the fields?

PROBLEM

S O L V I N G

"How can I learn to write better paragraphs?"

For help in improving paragraphs, see

- Handbook 10, "Improving Paragraphs," pages 230–233
- Handbook 11, "Transitions," pages 234–238
- Handbook 17, "Revising," pages 257–259

1. Review your responses.   Think about how your readers responded to your essay. Do you want to follow up on any of their ideas or questions?

Paragraphs at Work   A good way to handle paragraphs in a response essay is to start a new paragraph whenever you move from one part of your response to the next part. The following guidelines may help you.

- Use at least one paragraph for your introduction.
- Start a new paragraph when you introduce and explain a new idea.
- Support each idea with specific details from the work itself.

2. Read your essay out loud.   Listen to your writing in your own voice. Can you hear sentences that don't quite work—words that don't quite say what you mean? Let your ear direct you to the parts that need to be rewritten. You might also try listening carefully as another student reads your essay to you.

3. Decide what changes you want to make.   You may think you're satisfied with your draft, but don't be afraid to go on revising it until it *effectively* says what you want it to.

One Student's Process

Vanessa's peer readers were confused about where certain scenes in the story took place and why Vanessa felt sad. So Vanessa made some changes in her draft to make her thoughts clearer.

> but then I realized at the end that it reminded me of when I was small, when I first started school.

> When he finally goes to school in November,

> I put myself in Panchito's place when I read this, because

When I read ~and reread~ "The Circuit" by Francisco Jiménez, ~I didn't understand why~ it made me feel sad. In the story a boy named Panchito doesn't ~can't~ go to school ~until November, he~ ~because~ ~has to~ works in the fields to help his family. He forgets how to speak in English.

Panchito says he heard a voice say ~that when he entered the school office,~ "May I help you?" ~and he was startled.~ ~Then he says, "I~ He had not heard English for months ~and he was embarassed and couldn't say anything right away.~ For a few seconds he remained speechless." I had already experienced this ~it~ before. When I first started school, I only spoke Spanish, ~but~ my parents spoke for me. So that was a great relief.

1. Proofread your writing.   Look for mistakes in grammar and spelling. Be careful when you include quotations from the story or poem. Make sure they appear exactly as they do in the original. Use quotation marks correctly, and spell proper nouns correctly.

LINKING

MECHANICS AND **WRITING**

Quoting from Literary Works

- When you quote from someone else's work, always enclose the quotation in quotation marks. Keep capitalization, punctuation, and spelling the way they are in the original.

- If you leave out part of a quotation, show the place where material is omitted by using ellipsis points (. . .).

Notice that when Vanessa quoted directly from the story, she put a comma after the explanatory words *he says* and before the quotation.

Original

Then he says he remained speechless.

Revised

Then he says, "I had not heard English for months. For a few seconds I remained speechless."

For more information about using quotation marks, see Handbook 43, "Punctuation," pages 566–598.

Standards for Evaluation

RESPONDING
TO LITERATURE

A personal response

- gives the author and the title of the work
- tells enough about the work for readers unfamiliar with it to understand the response
- clearly expresses a response
- gives the reasons for the response
- draws an overall conclusion

2. Make a clean copy of your response.   Read your paper over again, thinking about the Standards for Evaluation shown in the margin. Then make a final copy.

PUBLISH AND PRESENT

- **Have a round-table discussion.** Discuss responses with classmates who have read the same work.

- **Start a "Literature Response" file for the class.** Group together the responses to a particular work in a file, or bind them as a booklet. Other students can use this as a guide to reading.

- **Start a "Short Takes" review sheet.** For each work reviewed, list title, author, and source, along with a two- or three-line comment. Collect these reviews in a little magazine that can be shown to parents.

REFLECT ON YOUR WRITING

WRITER TO WRITER

'Tis the good reader that makes the good book.
Ralph Waldo Emerson, American poet and essayist

1. Add your writing to your portfolio. Write a brief introductory note for your paper, telling about how you wrote it and what you think of it now. As you write, think about questions like the following:

FOR YOUR
PORTFOLIO

- How did writing about the work help me learn about it?
- What did I learn about myself?
- How would readers with backgrounds different from mine respond to the work?
- What was hard about writing this essay? What was easy about it?

2. Explore additional writing ideas. See the suggestions for writing a book review on pages 158–159 and Springboards on page 160.

Reading a
STUDENT MODEL

Sometimes after you've read a good book, do you almost want to force your friends to read it too? Do you sometimes want to warn them to leave it alone? Writing a book review is a good way to share your reactions to what you read. Jeff Hayden, a student at Wilson School in St. Louis, Missouri, wrote a book review that was later published in the magazine *Creative Kids.* As you read, notice how he shows his enthusiasm for the book.

Jeff Hayden

A Review of <u>What Would We Do Without You?</u>

How can you help? Just read this book to find out how kids can help kids, how kids can help the environment, and how kids can help adults. In fact, this book shows different ways in which people of all ages can help. <u>What Would We Do Without You?</u> by Kathy Henderson is great for individuals from elementary school to college age. It suggests many different activities to meet the needs of people of all ages.

The chapter "Just Do It: Volunteering on Your Own" tells of activities you can do without special permission. There are guidelines for recycling, cleaning a park or neighborhood, or even about how to become a tutor.

The chapter "Protecting the Environment" gives suggestions as to how kids can save plant life and wildlife. For example, you could cut up soda-can holders before you throw them out. Or you could clean up a beach or a piece of land.

But the chapter "Kids Helping Kids: Peer Support Groups" is my favorite. It tells how kids can invent ways to help their peers who have problems. This chapter involves inventing solutions to everyday dilemmas or writing a story or rap to help kids with health or emotional problems. It tells kids how to organize a fund drive to get money to help save a life.

A really neat part of this book comes at the end of each chapter. It is called For More Information. If you find one chapter to be really interesting and want additional information, addresses are here to write to for more guidance and help.

I hope you read this book. You may find it interesting. And so will the people and animals you help!

Think & Respond

What kinds of information does Jeff Hayden give you about the book? On the basis of his review, would you want to read this book? Why or why not? What ideas does his review give you for books you might review?

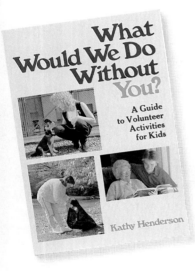

What
Would We Do
Without
You?

A Guide
to Volunteer
Activities
for Kids

Kathy Henderson

COMPUTER
TIP

If you have strong reactions as you read, enter these into your computer. Afterwards, create a split screen if your computer has one, and freewrite about why you had those strong reactions.

INVITATION
TO
Write

Jeff Hayden gave readers a clear picture of what one book was about and how he felt about the book. A good book review gives readers enough information to decide if they want to read the book themselves.

Write a review of a book that interests you. Give your readers a feeling for what the book is like and how you responded to it.

CHOOSING A BOOK

1. Find a book to read. Do you like mysteries? science fiction? comedy? history? Do you have a favorite author? Is there a subject you'd like to learn more about? Think about your interests. Look for a book that appeals to one of them.

2. Read and respond. Make notes of your reactions as you read. Copy passages you might want to refer to in your review. After reading, freewrite about what pleased or bothered you. Pretend that you are writing a letter to a friend. What would you want to tell him or her about your book? What might you want to ask the author, if you had a chance?

WRITING YOUR BOOK REVIEW

1. Begin writing. Check your prewriting notes for ideas. Remember, in a book review you need to tell what the book is about, describe your reactions to it, and say whether you think readers might enjoy it. Start anywhere; get some thoughts down on paper. Later you can decide how to arrange them.

2. Organize your draft.   Here's one good approach:

- **Introduce the book.**   Give the title, the author, and perhaps something about the author's background. You may also want to state the main point you intend to make.

- **Summarize the book.**   Give readers a general idea about the content of the book, as Jeff does in his review. If the book is fiction, you might discuss plot, setting, and characters. Normally, you shouldn't give away the ending.

- **Evaluate the book.**   Tell why you admire or dislike the book. You may want to discuss the author's purpose. Did the book make you laugh or perhaps get you to accept a new idea? Support your reactions with specific examples from the book.

- **Conclude the review.**   You can restate your view or perhaps give a recommendation, as Jeff Hayden did.

REVIEWING YOUR WRITING

1. Think about your audience.   Have you given your readers enough information for them to decide whether they might like the book? Did you explain unfamiliar terms?

2. Apply the final touches.   Does your introduction draw the reader in? Is your conclusion convincing? Did you support your reactions? Did you check your grammar and punctuation?

PUBLISHING AND PRESENTING

- **Publish your review**.   Submit it to a magazine, as Jeff did, or to a class or school publication.

- **Make an advertisement.**   Use words and artwork—as in a movie poster—to show your reactions to the book you reviewed.

- **Hold a book-review round table.**   Get together with classmates to discuss, compare, and recommend various books.

PROBLEM SOLVING

"How can I get a good start on my draft?"

For help in getting started, see

- Handbook 2, "Finding a Starting Point," pages 197–202
- Handbook 6, "Drafting," pages 215–216

Grammar **TIP**

Check to be sure you have capitalized and spelled all proper names correctly.

Spring boards

Speaking and Listening

In a book, story, or play, find a scene that you think is particularly moving. Then, with the help of some of your classmates, act it out or present an oral interpretation.

MEDIA   Imagine that you are the entertainment critic for your local TV station. Prepare a brief on-air presentation. It should give your personal response to a movie, play, television show, or literary work.

Music   Think about current events and personalities in the news. Make up a rap or a folk song that tells your personal response to some person or event.

Reading

Write a "lit letter" to a friend. Describe a book you are reading. Tell your friend why you loved or hated the book.

fine Arts   Make a

drawing, a collage, a painting, a sculpture, a mobile, or another piece of art that expresses your reaction to an event in your life or to a piece of literature. Write a paragraph to go with the art, telling what it means.

Reading Back and Forth

What do the words *eye, pop, dad, mom, noon,* and *civic* have in common?

They are all *palindromes*— words, phrases, or sentences that read the same way backward and forward. Try this one: *No lemon, no melon.*

An old joke says that Adam introduced himself to Eve with a palindrome: "Madam in Eden, I'm Adam."

Perhaps you've heard this famous one: "A man, a plan, a canal, Panama!"

Try reading these palindromes forward and backward.

- Rise to vote, sir.
- Never odd or even.

- Was it a rat I saw?
- Doc, note, I dissent. A fast never prevents a fatness. I diet on cod.
- Now, sir, a war is won.

What happens when you read the word *palindromes* backward? You get a *semordnilap,* a word that is another word in reverse. For example, *on* backward is *no, pots* backward is *stop,* and *star* backward is *rats.* Read *No evil repaid* backward, and you get *Diaper live on.*

Make your own list of palindromes or semordnilaps to share with friends. A dictionary can sometimes help. When you read back and forth, you never know what you might find.

What does *race car* spell backwards?

Sentence

Sentence Closers

At times, the last part of something is the best part—the finale of a fire-works display, dessert at the end of dinner, even the last part of a sentence. Like sentence openers, sentence closers are single words or groups of words that add important details to sentences.

Model A   The man was about fifty, <u>overweight but solid-looking</u>.

Frank Bonham, *Chief*

Model B   They were in the schoolroom again, <u>the five boys and Lina and the teacher</u>.

Meindert DeJong, *The Wheel on the School*

Model C   One of the pups came slowly toward me, <u>a round ball of fur that I could have held in my hand</u>.

Scott O'Dell, *Island of the Blue Dolphins*

▶ **ON THE MARK**   Put a comma before a sentence closer to separate it from the rest of the sentence.

A. Combining Sentences   Make a new sentence by adding the underlined part of the second sentence to the first sentence as a sentence closer. Write the complete sentence, putting a comma before the sentence closer.

1. My sister and I were working by our dock. We were <u>scraping and painting the little dinghy</u>.   **Shirley Ann Grau, "The Land and the Water"**

2. I jumped to my feet. I was <u>completely thunderstruck</u>.

Antoine de Saint-Exupery, *The Little Prince*

3. She stayed behind because she thought it would be worthwhile trying the door of the wardrobe. She thought this <u>even though she felt almost sure that it would be locked</u>.

C. S. Lewis, *The Lion, the Witch, and the Wardrobe*

4. The pounding came up the stairs. It was <u>crashing on each step</u>.

Shirley Jackson, *The Haunting of Hill House*

5. They were the same kind of thunderheads as on the day of the ball game. The thunderheads were <u>white and piled up over the hills like a sky full of fresh dried laundry</u>.

Joseph Krumgold, *Onion John*

B. Unscrambling and Imitating Sentences   Unscramble each set of sentence chunks below. Create a sentence that has a sentence closer and the same order of chunks and punctuation as the model. Then write a sentence of your own that imitates each model.

1. Model   Mr. Underhill came out from under his hill, <u>smiling and breathing hard</u>.

Ursula K. Le Guin, "The Rule of Names"

stood behind the cash register / the sales clerk / chatting and making change

2. Model   They were eating borsch, <u>the rich, red soup with sour cream so dear to Russian palates</u>.

Richard Connell, "The Most Dangerous Game"

too difficult for many figure skaters / a dangerous, demanding move / she was practicing a triple jump

3. Model   It was a good thing I had no homework that night, <u>for I could not possibly have concentrated</u>.

Jean Stafford, "Bad Characters"

because the storm would definitely have interfered / we took our hike this morning / it was a lucky break

Grammar Refresher   Some sentence closers are appositives. To learn more about punctuating appositives, see Handbook 43, "Punctuation," pages 566–599.

Sketch Book

- Invent a history for one of these objects (or an object of your choice). You might try to trace its history back to the materials it was made from, or you could make up a story about what its history *should* have been like.

- What would you like to know about one of these objects? Write as many questions as you can.

Show, Don't Tell

You can make a report interesting by giving facts and examples to *show* what you've learned about a topic. Expand one of the sentences below, adding information that *shows* instead of *tells*.

- Young people like many different kinds of music.
- Leisure activities have changed a great deal in the past fifteen years.

Informative Writing: Reports

Guided Assignment
Report of Information

Brooklyn Signs N
First in ...

...ed baseball was signed
tonight by the Brooklyn Dodgers for
their International League farm ...
Montreal Royals Th...

Jackie Robinson, one...
halfback ace and recer...
the Kansas City N...
put hi...

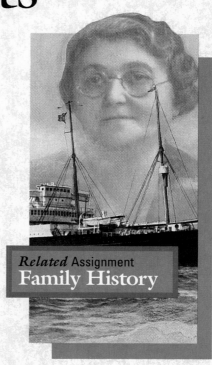

Related Assignment
Family History

H ave you ever learned a little bit about a fascinating subject—and then wished you knew more? In this workshop you'll have the chance to find answers to some of your questions about a topic you care about. Then, you can write a report of information about what you learn, sharing your knowledge with others. You'll also be able to put your report-writing skills to work in a related assignment, as you write your very own family history.

Guided ASSIGNMENT

Report of Information

Reading a
STUDENT MODEL

Jonathan Moskaitis, a sixth-grade student, needed to write a report for his social studies class. The final report would be displayed on a school bulletin board honoring Black History Month. As you read Jonathan's report, think about how he was able to put his love of baseball to good use in completing this assignment.

Baseball card
Dad's collect

Brooklyn Signs Negro Player, First in Organized Baseball

1945

MONTREAL, OCT. 23 (AP)– The first Negro player ever to be admitted to organized baseball was signed tonight by the Brooklyn Dodgers for their International League farm, the Montreal Royals. The Royals wanted

Jackie Robinson, one-time U.C.L. halfback ace and recent shortstop the Kansas City Negro Monarch put his signature on a contract ca ing not only for a regular playe salary but also for a guarantee

Dad's pin

Jackie Robinson's induction into the Baseball Hall of Fame, 1962.

Jonathan Moskaitis

Mrs. Flynn

Social Studies 6B

1 February 1993

A Baseball Pioneer

Jackie Robinson was the first black baseball player in the Major
Leagues, but getting there wasn't easy. Because of the color of his skin,
he was taunted, hated, and turned away. Jackie was a great athlete,
though, and he never gave up.

Jackie Robinson was born in Georgia on January 31, 1919, but his
family moved to California when he was a baby. The family was very
poor and didn't always have enough to eat. As he was growing up, Jackie
hung out with a gang of kids in the neighborhood, and he used to get in
trouble with the police all the time. A neighborhood mechanic who really
liked Jackie tried to get him to leave the gang and stay out of trouble.
With the help of the pastor in the family's church, it worked. They
convinced him that it was better to be different and not to follow the
crowd. Jackie spent time playing sports instead.

Throughout high school and junior college, Jackie was a star in
every sport. He was so good that universities were offering him sports
scholarships for his last two years of college. Jackie finally picked UCLA
to attend. Jackie was super in all the sports he played, and now
professional scouts were observing him!

However, Jackie never made a deal with these sports scouts.
Instead, he took a job at a children's camp. He wanted to send some of
the money he earned to his mother.

In 1942, Jackie Robinson was drafted into the army. He faced a lot

4/10/47
The Montreal
Royals

of discrimination there. He played on the military's football team, but he found out other teams wouldn't play against a team that included a black man.

At that time, major-league teams were all white. Minorities had to play in separate leagues. After Jackie left the army in 1944, he joined the Kansas City Monarchs, a baseball team in the Negro leagues. Life in the Negro leagues was tough. The Negro leagues' food, pay, schedules, and hotels weren't nearly as good as those the white leagues got. Players sometimes had to sleep and eat on the bus. Then came the event that changed Jackie's life and the history of baseball forever.

Branch Rickey, the general manager of the Brooklyn Dodgers, asked Jackie to join his team. Rickey knew many players and fans would be against Jackie because he was black. Rickey told Jackie he was looking for a player who would have the guts not to fight when others were cruel to him. Jackie said yes and swore that he'd prove himself by playing great baseball instead of by fighting. Jackie also felt that if he did well, other teams would draft black players too.

Before he could play in Brooklyn, Jackie had to play for the Dodgers' farm team, the Montreal Royals. At first Jackie was rejected by the Royals' fans and his teammates, but as time went on they accepted and liked him. Jackie became a hero in Montreal for his great playing. When he played in other cities, though, the crowd and other teams made fun of Jackie or wouldn't play when he played.

In 1947 Jackie signed a contract with the Dodgers. Again the fans booed him, the team didn't like him, and other teams refused to play with him. But Jackie did what his manager wanted. He ignored the bad things other people said and did to him and tried his hardest to play well. Jackie

began hitting and stealing more bases. The fans loved it. He was good at defense and hitting in pressure situations, so the team liked him too. At the end of his first year, Jackie's team won the pennant, and Jackie won the National League Rookie of the Year.

During his baseball career with the Dodgers, Jackie led his team to win five pennants. In 1955, the Dodgers even won the World Series! Jackie retired from baseball in 1957. He was inducted into baseball's Hall of Fame in 1962, and the Dodgers retired his number. By then Jackie's real job was done. He had opened the door for blacks, and now more black players were coming into the league.

On October 24, 1972, Jackie Robinson died. We will always remember his contributions to baseball. Of course, we will remember the pennants and World Series he helped win, but probably his most important contribution was his successful fight for blacks' rights on the field and off.

List of Sources

David, Lester. "Jackie Robinson: He Changed Baseball." Boys' Life Feb. 1991: 16.

Epstein, Sam, and Beryl Epstein. Jackie Robinson: Baseball's Gallant Fighter. Champaign: Garrard, 1974.

"Robinson, Jackie." Encyclopaedia Britannica. 1985 ed.

Rudeen, Kenneth. Jackie Robinson. New York: Crowell, 1971.

Scott, Richard. Jackie Robinson. New York: Chelsea House, 1987.

Think & Respond

Respond as a Reader

► What new things did you learn about Jackie Robinson?

► How does Jonathan get you interested in his topic?

Respond as a Writer

► What details does Jonathan include that show how Jackie Robinson struggled to make it in major-league baseball?

► What does Jonathan's conclusion say about why he chose to write about Jackie Robinson?

INVITATION
═ TO ═
Write

For Jonathan Moskaitis, completing a school assignment was a chance to learn more about a subject that had always interested him. When you write a report, you investigate a topic you care about, assemble your information, and share your knowledge with others.

Find a topic you're interested in and learn more about it. Then write a short report that shows what you have learned.

PREWRITE AND EXPLORE

1. Find a great topic.   First, think of subjects you already know something about—a special collection or hobby, for example. Then think of subjects you're curious about. Try some of the following activities to find the best report topic.

Exploring Topics

Jackie Robinson is caught off first base by the Boston Braves' Frank McCormack in 1948.

- **Looking inside**   Take some time to think about who you are and what you most like to do. Do you have a special talent or skill? Perhaps you're a whiz at computer games or you play a musical instrument well. Maybe you most enjoy reading animal stories or building model airplanes. Make a list of your special interests and **freewrite** about them in your journal.

- **Looking around**   What's happening in your world? Look through a newspaper or a magazine aimed at students your age to see what subjects are covered there. You may find stories on everything from space stations to archaeological digs. What catches your eye? Get together with classmates to share ideas and find the best angle on a topic.

- **Suiting yourself** Has your teacher assigned a general topic for your report? If so, try to find an angle you care about, a subtopic that will hold your interest. For example, if your teacher assigned a report on nutrition, you might focus on the benefits of a vegetarian diet.

One Student's Process

Jonathan Moskaitis needed to write a report honoring Black History Month. He explored his own interests and discovered ways to connect them to his assignment for school. Notice how Jonathan got stuck in the music and movies categories, but saw real possibilities in the sports category.

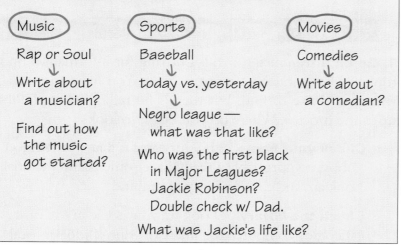

Music
Rap or Soul
↓
Write about a musician?

Find out how the music got started?

Sports
Baseball
↓
today vs. yesterday
↓
Negro league — what was that like?
Who was the first black in Major Leagues? Jackie Robinson? Double check w/ Dad.
What was Jackie's life like?

Movies
Comedies
↓
Write about a comedian?

2. Choose the topic that interests you most. Which of your possible topics do you know the most about? Which one do you want to explore further? Choose a topic now and spend some time freewriting about it to make sure it will hold your interest.

Writer's Choice Do you want to investigate a topic that is totally new to you? Would you rather explore something you know quite a bit about already? Which would be more fun for you? The choice is yours.

PROBLEM
S O L V I N G

"How can I find the right topic for my report?"

For help finding the topic that's right for you, see

- Handbook 1, "Thinking with Pictures," pages 192–196

- Handbook 2, "Finding a Starting Point," pages 197–202

- Handbook 3, "Finding a Focus," pages 203–204

- Springboards, page 185

3. Focus your topic.   If your topic is too broad, you may have trouble exploring it in a short report. For example, the broad topic *horses* can be narrowed by focusing in on one kind of horse (Clydesdales, for example). Doing some reading or talking with others about your topic can help you narrow it and find a more specific subject.

4. See what you know and what you want to find out. Review any freewriting you may have done on your topic to see what you already know, and put a star by those ideas you want to know more about. Then make a list of questions about your topic that you can find answers to later.

RESEARCH YOUR TOPIC

1. Go on a treasure hunt.   Looking for information on your topic is like going on a treasure hunt. You have an idea about what you'd like to find, but there's no telling what you'll turn up in the process. Where do you begin to look?

- **Check your home.**   If your topic is a favorite subject or hobby, you probably already have some useful materials. Look around to see what you can find.

- **Check the library.**   Look up your topic in the card catalog or computerized index of your school or local library. Also check the *Readers' Guide to Periodical Literature* for magazine articles on your topic.

- **Talk to people who can help.**   A reference librarian can steer you toward useful sources of information, including electronic resources. Interview friends, parents, or teachers who know something about your topic. Take careful notes!

2. Review your sources and prepare source cards.   Check your sources to make sure that they tell you what you most want to know about your topic. Write down the publication

PROBLEM

SOLVING

"How can I find the information I need?"

For help finding what you want to know, see

- Handbook 29, "Library Skills," pages 312–319
- Access Guide, "Using Electronic Resources," pages 627–632

information for each source on a separate index card. Assign a number to each source card for later reference when you take notes. You will also use this information when you create a List of Sources to attach to the end of your report. Always record the author's name (if given) and the title of the book or article. Also write down the following information:

- **Book**—city of publication, publisher's name, copyright date
- **Magazine article**—name of the magazine, issue date, page numbers
- **Encyclopedia**—article title, copyright date

3. Take notes from your sources.   You may want to take notes on index cards, using one card for each piece of information. Number each note card with the number of the source. That way you'll know where to look in case you have to go back and read some more. When you're ready to plan your organization, you can put the cards in any order you like.

4. Use your own words.   It's very important that you take notes using your own words instead of copying out of your sources. Rewriting information helps you understand what you read. Also, using someone else's words in your writing without saying where you got them is dishonest.

Jonathan took notes from one of his sources on this note card.

Writing TIP

If you are using electronic sources such as CD-ROMs or videos, you need to include other information on your source cards. For help, see page 632 of the Access Guide.

Topic

Source card number — ③

Early life

—very poor, hungry a lot, hung out with a gang of kids

—neighborhood mechanic and the pastor helped Jackie leave gang and learn to think and act for himself

—was encouraged to do well in sports   p. 21–23

Note written in Jonathan's own words   Page number from source

5. Think about your information. Now that you've done some research, what do you think are the main ideas you want readers to know about your subject? Try sorting your note cards into groups, with each group representing a main idea. Set aside any cards containing information that seems less important to you now.

6. Create a graphic to show the parts of your report. A cluster, a list, or an informal outline can help you see the parts of your report and how they fit together. A graphic can also help you find out where you need to do more research. Use your main ideas as headings, and chart the details beneath the headings.

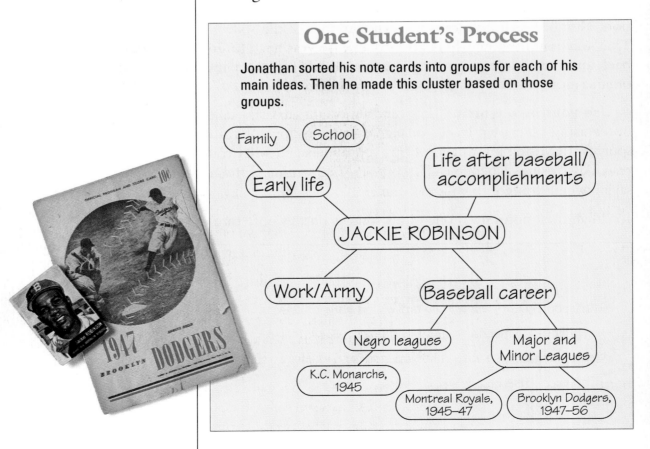

One Student's Process

Jonathan sorted his note cards into groups for each of his main ideas. Then he made this cluster based on those groups.

Family   School

Early life

Life after baseball/ accomplishments

JACKIE ROBINSON

Work/Army   Baseball career

Negro leagues   Major and Minor Leagues

K.C. Monarchs, 1945

Montreal Royals, 1945–47   Brooklyn Dodgers, 1947–56

1. Start writing any section you wish. You may want to begin drafting the part of your report you've learned the most about. However, if you have a clever idea for an introduction, then start at the very beginning and go from there.

2. Write one or more paragraphs for each main idea. Use your prewriting notes—your graphic and your note cards—as a guide to your writing.

3. Stay open to new ideas. As you write, you may find yourself heading off in unexpected directions. Go back to your sources for more information as you discover what you really want to say.

4. Assemble your draft. Put the pieces of your draft in an order that makes sense. Look again at Jonathan's final report on pages 167–169. You can see that he put his clusters of information in chronological, or time, order. Chronological order works well when you're describing events in history or when you're writing about someone's life. Other organizational patterns—such as order of importance or order of familiarity—may also work for the information you want to present.

5. Write an introduction and a conclusion. Your introduction should include a **thesis statement** that tells the main idea or purpose of your report. Your opening paragraph should also draw your readers into your writing and make them want to read on.

Your conclusion might summarize your main points, ask a question, or make a prediction. Notice how Jonathan's conclusion summarizes the importance of Jackie Robinson's contribution to baseball and to the fight for equality for all people.

6. Think about your draft. Do you want to share your draft with classmates now or work on it some more first? The following questions will help you and your readers review your report.

PROBLEM SOLVING

"What's the best way to organize my ideas? Would a more formal outline help?"

For help outlining your main ideas and ordering your details, see

• Appendix, page 608
• Handbook 7, "Organizing Details," pages 217–221

Questions for Yourself

- What is the focus of my report?
- Did I find answers to the questions I had about my topic? What do I still need to research?
- Does my report read smoothly from beginning to end? Is anything missing? What parts should I rearrange?

Questions for Your Peer Readers

- What do you think is the main point of my report?
- Which parts interest you the most?
- Which parts need more explanation?

One Student's Process

Jonathan shared his draft with a friend whose comments appear in the margin.

> Before he could play in Brooklyn, Jackie had to play for the Montreal Royals. At first he was rejected by the Royals' fans and his teammates, but as time went on they accepted and liked him. Jackie became a hero in Montreal. Soon Jackie signed up with the Dodgers. Again the fans booed him, the team didn't like him, and other teams refused to play with him. But he began hitting and stealing more bases. The fans loved it! He was good at defence and hitting in pressure situations too, so the team liked him too!

Peer Reader Comments

I've never heard of the Royals. Were they in the Major Leagues back then?

It must have been awfully hard for him! What did Jackie do when he was treated so badly?

REVISE YOUR WRITING

1. Review your responses. Think about how you and your readers responded to your draft. What changes do you want to make? Will you add information and details? Will you take out information that's not related to your main focus?

One Student's Process

Jonathan thought about his friend's comments and added specific details and examples to support his ideas.

for his great playing. When he played in other cities, though, the crowd and other teams made fun of Jackie or wouldn't play when he played.

Before he could play in Brooklyn, Jackie had to play for the Montreal Royals. *the Dodgers' farm team,* At first *Jackie* he was rejected by the Royals' fans and his teammates, but as time went on they accepted and liked him. Jackie became a hero in Montreal. ¶ *In 1947* Soon Jackie signed *a contract* up with the Dodgers. Again the fans booed him, the team didn't like him, and other teams refused to play with him. But he began hitting and stealing more bases. The fans loved it! He was good at defen*s*ce and hitting in pressure situations too, so the team liked him too.

Jackie did what his manager wanted. He ignored the bad things other people said and did to him and tried his hardest to play well. Jackie

Paragraphs at Work Your outline, list, or cluster headings can help you see where your paragraph breaks should go. Remember these tips.

- Focus on one idea in each paragraph.
- Use a topic sentence to state the main idea.
- Include in each paragraph only those details and examples that support the main idea.

Report of Information

GRAMMAR AND WRITING

Using Transitions

You can show how your ideas are connected by using **transitions** between sentences and paragraphs. Words such as *however, also, therefore,* and *instead* are transitions that connect ideas. You can also repeat key words to link ideas. Transitions used at the beginning of a sentence are often followed by a comma. The transitions Jonathan uses to connect two paragraphs are underlined below.

Jackie was super in all the sports he played, and now professional scouts were observing him!
    However, Jackie never made a deal with these sports scouts. Instead, he took a job at a children's camp.

For more information about using transitions to connect ideas, see Handbook 11, "Using Transitions," pages 234–238.

2. Make an alphabetical List of Sources. Only list those books or articles you actually took notes from and used in writing your report. Also list any people you interviewed. Notice on page 169 how Jonathan prepared his List of Sources.

PROOFREAD

1. Proofread your report. Slowly and carefully reread your report. Correct any mistakes you might have made in grammar, spelling, capitalization, and punctuation.

2. Make a final copy. Read the Standards for Evaluation in the margin and decide if you were successful in completing the assignment. Make any additional changes you feel are necessary. Then write or print out a clean, final copy.

Standards for Evaluation

INFORMATIVE WRITING

A report

- has an interesting introduction that clearly states the subject
- focuses on a single topic
- includes facts and details to support main ideas
- uses information from more than one source and includes a List of Sources
- ends with a strong conclusion

PUBLISH AND PRESENT

- **Present your report to another class.**   Add visuals, such as models or graphs, to make your presentation more interesting.

- **Have a panel discussion.**   If any classmates researched related topics, present these reports orally. You and the other presenters can then answer questions from the rest of the class.

- **Illustrate your report with drawings or photographs.** Then display your work on a class or school bulletin board.

Jackie Robinson smashed a three-run home run against the Jersey City Giants during his minor league baseball debut, April 18, 1946. Here a teammate congratulates Robinson.

REFLECT ON YOUR WRITING

WRITER TO WRITER

I do a lot of research in books, and I read a lot of old diaries. There's an enormous amount of material available if one will take the time to get it.

Louis L'Amour, writer

1. Add your report to your portfolio.   First, take some time to reflect on your writing process. Attach your answers to these questions to your final draft.

- How did I find my topic?
- What part of this project was most fun for me?
- What are the special strengths of my final draft?
- How have other types of writing I've done helped me to write this report?

2. Explore additional writing ideas.   See the suggestions for researching and writing a family history on pages 182–184 and Springboards on page 185.

FOR YOUR **PORTFOLIO**

Family History

Starting from LITERATURE

Parents, grandparents, aunts, uncles, cousins. These are the people you call *family*. But what do you know about them? What were their lives like before you were born?

Researching and writing your family history, your family's story, connects you to the past. Writer Merrill Wilk researched her family's history and traced one side of her family back to Poland at the turn of the century. As you read, think about why she might have chosen to focus her family history on the immigration of her grandfather to the United States.

Finding Home

by
Merrill
Wilk

My grandfather Louis Zaremski (known now as Poppa Lou) was born in 1904 in a small, rural town in Poland. He was the first of six children born to Jacob and Molly Zaremski. Two other children, Frances and Morris, would be born in Poland before my family's dream of a better life in the United States finally came true.

Jacob was the first to arrive, settling in Chicago, Illinois, in 1910. He was a shoemaker by trade, as was his father before him. He set up shop and, by 1913, he had earned enough to send for his wife and children. Poppa Lou, then nine years old, still remembers the long journey to the United States.

Since they could only take with them what they could carry, Molly, Poppa Lou, Frances, and Morris packed their most precious belongings into a few small bags. Ironically, however, the day before my family was to leave Poland forever, their home burned to the ground. My family escaped with their lives, the clothes on their backs, and the money and passage papers Jacob had sent them. And on they went. . .

Over two thousand immigrants spent more than two weeks in steerage, below the decks of the steamship New Amsterdam. Canvas hammocks for sleeping lined the walls. Benches and long tables filled the room. Each night, heaping platters of boiled herring were served family style, two or three to a table. One night a very large woman sat across from Poppa Lou, quickly eating as much as she could. When she thought no one was looking, she took a whole plate of herring and put it between her feet, hiding it under the skirts of her floor-length dress! My clever grandfather had watched her from the corner of his eye. When he thought she wasn't looking, he slid beneath the table, found the plate of herring, and put it back on the table for everyone to share.

After my family reached New York, they took a train into Chicago's La Salle Street Station. They arrived a day early, however, so Jacob wasn't there to meet them. A traveler's aide who spoke Yiddish and English helped Molly give directions to a driver who then took my family to Jacob's address. Unfortunately, Jacob wasn't home. The driver didn't know what to do, so he asked a police officer for help.

Unwilling to leave them on the street, the officer took my family to jail. Molly, Poppa Lou, Frances, and Morris spent their first night in Chicago on two cots in a jail cell on the second floor of the 48th Street Station. But when the officer brought my family breakfast the next morning before taking them to Jacob's shop, they knew a better life had already begun.

Think & Respond

What details does Merrill Wilk include to bring the characters—and the situations—to life for her readers? What sources might she have used to find this information about her family?

INVITATION
=== TO ===
Write

Writing a family history, like the one Merrill Wilk wrote, makes connections between today and yesterday, between who you are and who your ancestors were. When you write a family history, you research your family's past and write about it in a report.

Gather information about one aspect of your family's past. Then write a family history based on your research.

P LANNING YOUR FAMILY HISTORY

1. Discover what you know.   What interesting or funny stories about family members have you heard? What do you know about the lives of your grandparents or great grandparents? Your immediate family members may have much of the information you need. Ask them to go through family photograph albums or scrapbooks with you and to share stories about people and events.

2. Choose a focus.   It would be nearly impossible to tell all there is to know about your family in one short report. You could probably fill several books with stories about their past! Instead, think about what part of your family's history you'd most like to write about.

Writer's Choice   Would you like to focus on one person's story, as Merrill Wilk did? Would you rather write about the way your relatives' lives were changed by an event in history, such as a natural disaster? Perhaps you'd prefer to trace one side of your family back in time. The choice is yours!

RESEARCHING YOUR HISTORY

1. Begin your research. First, make a list of research questions. You may want to know, for example, when and where your ancestors lived and died, when they came to this country, and what kinds of work they did.

2. Talk to members of your extended family. Ask your parents for the names and phone numbers or addresses of other people you might contact. You could even send a questionnaire to family members who live far away. Be sure to include a letter explaining your purpose.

3. Gather documents written by your family members. Journals, diaries, and letters are wonderful sources of information about your family's past. As you review them, take notes on what's most interesting to you and what suits your focus.

Writing
═ TIP ═

You may wish to tape-record your interviews with family members. That way, you can replay the conversation later and write down the information you want to include in your report.

WRITING YOUR FAMILY HISTORY

1. Tell your family's story. You don't want to only list the facts—the "who married whom and when" kind of information. These facts may be part of your report, but be sure to include some of the personal stories your family members shared. Don't just *tell about* what happened to someone; include the kinds of details that *show* what people actually experienced.

2. Share your draft with others. Before you write your next draft, you may wish to share your work with a friend or a family member. A friend might help you find ways to check your organization or make your writing more interesting. A family member might help you fix any mistakes you might have made or fill in any gaps in your story.

Ships such as the one shown in this poster ad carried hundreds of thousands of immigrants from Europe to the United States in the early 1900s.

R EVIEWING YOUR HISTORY

1. Think about your limits. Check to see if you've tried to do too much in a short report. Are there too many names and dates? Does your history sound like a boring list of facts rather than an interesting story about interesting people? If so, think about how you can narrow your focus in your next draft. For example, you might zoom in on a smaller span of time, describing in detail what happened to two or three family members.

2. Does your story flow smoothly from beginning to end? Family histories are most often told in chronological order. Making a time line of the facts and events you've included can help you check your organization. Rereading your draft aloud is another way to see if the order of events is clear. Is any information out of place? Include any transitions, details, or stories that would make your history easier to follow.

TECHNOLOGY
— TIP —
You could turn your written family history into a multimedia presentation. For help, see pages 636-638 of the Access Guide.

European immigrants at Ellis Island, New York

P UBLISHING AND PRESENTING

• **Make copies of your family history.** Share your final piece with any family members who helped you with your research. You may also wish to send copies of your history to family members living far away.

• **Display your family history on a class bulletin board.** Include a drawing of your family tree and photographs of the people you've written about. Be sure to write a caption for each photo so your readers will be able to connect people's names with their faces.

Spring boards

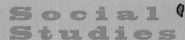

Current Events Pick a topic from the news that interests you, and gather more information on it from several sources. Then stage a radio or television news program—recording it on videotape or audiotape—and present it to other classes.

Social Studies Working in small groups, choose a country that you'd like to learn more about. Each person should select one aspect of that country to research—geography, culture and customs, industry, natural resources, or government, for example. Assemble the reports to make a class encyclopedia.

A Village Scene in the Punjab (about 1820), Gulam Ali Khan.

Art Visit an art museum or look through art books at the library to find an artist whose work you especially like. Then find out what you can about the artist or about the artist's style (expressionism or pop art, for example).

LITERATURE Do some research on a place or time period described in a favorite story or novel. Then write up your findings in a report or make an oral presentation to your class. You may wish to read aloud passages from the work that bring the time and place to life.

Sentence

Reviewing Sentence Composing Skills

In the preceding sentence-composing exercises, you saw different ways professional writers add variety and interest to their sentences.

Sentence Opener	Outside, he murmured to himself. **William H. Armstrong, *Sounder***
Subject-Verb Split	Agatha's mother, frantic now, beat the door of the vault with her hands. **O. Henry, "A Retrieved Reformation"**
Sentence Closer	The man was about fifty, overweight but solid-looking. **Frank Bonham, *Chief***

A. Identifying and Imitating Sentences   The sentences below illustrate the sentence-composing skills you have studied. For each sentence, write whether the underlined part is a sentence opener, subject-verb split, or sentence closer. Then write a sentence of your own that imitates each sentence.

1. Templeton, asleep in the straw, heard the commotion and awoke.
E. B. White, *Charlotte's Web*

2. John dusted off his best chair, a rocker with its runners off.
Joseph Krumgold, *Onion John*

3. Mr. Simpson, director of the Order, looked up from the work on his desk and was surprised to see Maggie.
Olive W. Burt, "Banker Maggie Walker"

4. Tall, beautiful, fair, the youth's appearance was greeted with a low hum of admiration and anxiety.   **Frank R. Stockton, "The Lady, or the Tiger?"**

5. Then, wildly, like animals escaped from their caves, the children ran and ran in shouting circles.   **Ray Bradbury, "All Summer in a Day"**

B. Unscrambling and Imitating Sentences Unscramble each set of sentence chunks below. Create a sentence that has the same order of chunks as the model. Then write a sentence of your own that imitates each model.

1. Model One of them, a tan Jersey named Blind Tillie, was Cold Sassy's champion milk producer.

Olive Ann Burns, *Cold Sassy Tree*

a Vulcan called Spock / an officer on the *Enterprise* / was George's favorite *Star Trek* character

2. Model Instead of answering, the minister let out a startled yelp and sprang to his feet.

Farley Mowat, "Owls in the Family"

the runner reached out his hand / and grabbed for the water bottle / rather than stopping

3. Model I saw Lottie for the first time one afternoon in our own kitchen, stealing chocolate cake.

Jean Stafford, "Bad Characters"

setting the home run record / in the memorable game that year in Atlanta / my grandfather saw Henry Aaron

4. Model When flour was scarce, the boy's mother would wrap the leftover biscuits in a clean flour sack and put them away for the next meal.

William H. Armstrong, *Sounder*

and wash them down with soft drinks / after the game was over / at their favorite stand / would buy hot dogs / the little league team

5. Model The hawk, ruffled in misery, brooding in ferocity, came forth in hunger and hate.

D'Arcy Niland, "The Parachutist"

received their medals with honor and pride / exhausted from competition, glowing from victory / the Olympic team

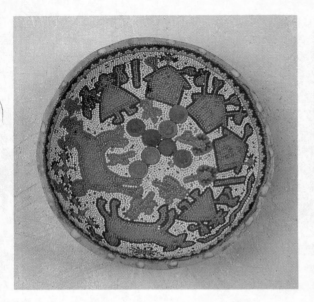
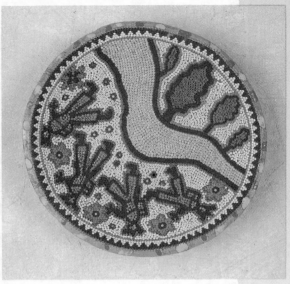
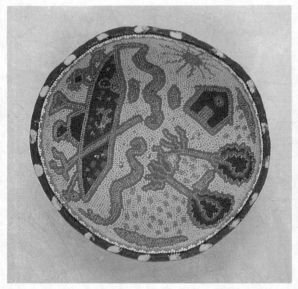
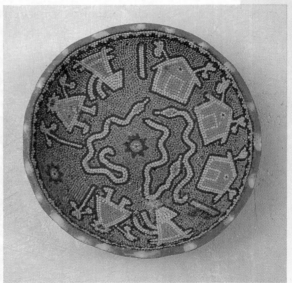

These ceremonial bowls are made by the Huichol people of central Mexico. Each bowl is made from half of a gourd. An artist coats the gourd with wax and then, using a needle, carefully presses glass beads and other objects into the wax. The illustrations on the bowls tell stories from Huichol mythology.

Writing Handbook

MINI-LESSONS

Sketch Book

- What would you like to design? Try drawing some of your ideas.
- Where did you get your ideas for your design? Jot down some of your thoughts.
- What is important to you? Write about some of the things you care about.

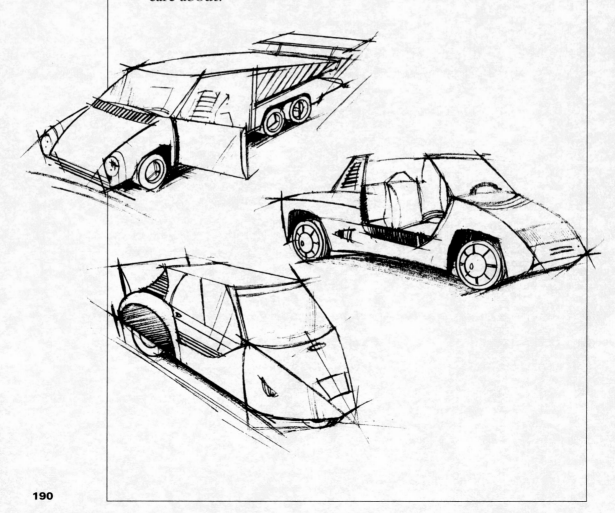

Writing Process

A lot can happen between the time a designer starts scribbling and the time a project is finished. There may be many false starts and many trips back to the drawing board. Then, at last, the final design takes shape.

The process of writing can be like that too. As you start exploring your thoughts, you may come up with new ideas, or even change your mind about what you want to say. Finally, though, your ideas take shape. The handbooks that follow can help you make the most of your own writing process.

How Do I Get Started?

Thinking with Pictures

"I need an idea!" How many times have you said this? You might need an idea for a Halloween costume or for a theme party. Maybe you're trying to think of that perfect gift for a friend. Perhaps you want to think up a story for a skit at school. You might just need an idea for something to do in your spare time or for a way to solve a misunderstanding with a friend.

GRAPHICS YOU CAN USE

Thinking doesn't always have to involve words. Sometimes sketching a picture or making a chart can help you find an idea you didn't know you had. These graphics can also help you organize ideas you've already collected.

In the following sections, you will learn about graphic devices you can use to help you work out your ideas. Pictures and clusters help you discover new ideas. Observation charts, compare-and-contrast charts, and story maps help you organize and expand ideas you presently have. These devices are useful in everyday situations and also in writing.

Pictures

Drawing a diagram, a picture, or a map can help you try out your ideas. For example, maybe you want to rearrange the furniture in your room. Before you start moving the furniture, you might draw a diagram of the new arrangement to see if you like it. Your diagram might even lead you to discover arrangements you like better.

In the following example, Jody drew a diagram of how she wanted to rearrange the furniture in her room. Notice how the first diagram led to new ideas and a better arrangement of the furniture in the second diagram.

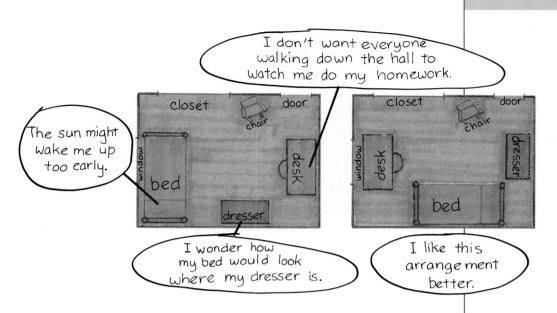

Clusters

A good way to find new ideas and details is to make a **cluster,** a graphic that connects ideas. For example, imagine you are trying to think of a costume to wear for Halloween. To make a cluster, write down your starting point in the middle of a sheet of paper and circle it. Write related ideas around this circle as you think of them. Circle each one and draw a line connecting it to the main idea or to one of the other ideas you added. Continue adding ideas to the cluster until you find one you'd like to use.

Look at the cluster one sixth grader made to find an idea for a costume. Notice that once he decided on a costume, he made a second cluster, listing items needed for the costume.

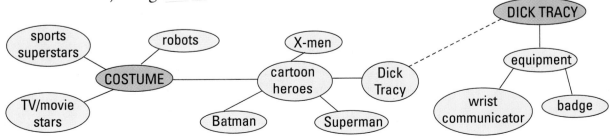

Observation Charts

Sometimes you need to think of details about a person, a place, a thing, or an experience. Your friends in the neighborhood might be having a homemade-cookie contest with you as a judge. You might be doing a science experiment to find out how the color of food affects taste. You might be making a collage about a day at the beach. An **observation chart** can help you.

To make an observation chart, first choose a subject. Then make five columns, one for each of the senses. Think about details related to the subject—things you see, hear, feel, taste, and smell. Write them in the proper columns.

The observation chart below shows the details one sixth grader thought of for a collage of pictures about a day at the beach.

Observation Chart

A Day at the Beach				
Sight	**Sound**	**Touch**	**Taste**	**Smell**
sand	crashing of	hot sand	salty ocean	salt air
waves	waves	cool water	water	seaweed
sunbathers	kids laugh-	greasy	soft drinks	sunscreen
lifeguards	ing	sunscreen	snacks	lotion
sand	lifeguard's	lotion		
castles	whistle			
boats	blowing			
seashells	music from			
flies	radio			
	bells on ice			
	cream			
	cart			

Compare-and-Contrast Charts

A **compare-and-contrast chart** can help you chart similarities and differences between items. Perhaps you are doing a science experiment, for example. You want to prove that green plants cannot grow without sunlight. Making a compare-and-contrast chart can help you find the details you need to report your results.

Compare-and-Contrast Chart

Characteristics	Subjects Compared—Changes After Two Weeks	
	Green plant in dark closet	**Green plant in sunlight**
Height	No change	Grew 2.5 cm
Thickness of stem	No change	Increased by 2 mm
Number of leaves	No change	2 new leaves
Appearance	Clear yellow color, wilted, almost dead	Green color, strong and still growing

Story Maps

A **story map** helps you to sort out the plot of a story and to see areas that need more work. For instance, imagine that you and your friends want to put on a skit at a neighborhood party. You could use a story map to plan and organize your skit. Start by listing the characters. Then describe the setting, or where the story takes place. Finally, outline the plot, or the events that make up the action of your story. Be sure to organize the events in the order they will take place.

The story map on the next page shows a skit planned by a group of friends for younger children in their neighborhood. The story map also shows a hole in the plot.

Characters	Goldilocks, Papa Bear, Momma Bear, Baby Bear
Setting	The Bears' apartment

Plot

Background	Momma Bear makes three pizzas. The bears hop on their dirt bikes and go out to buy pop.
Event 1	Goldilocks is on her way to Peggy's apartment for dinner. She gets confused and goes into the Bears' apartment by mistake.
Event 2	She samples each pizza. One is too spicy. One tastes fishy. She eats the whole cheese pizza.
Event 3	She's tired. One bed has a broken spring. She's allergic to the feathers in the second bed. She falls asleep on the water bed.
Event 4	The Bear family returns from the store.
Event 5	(WHAT TWIST SHOULD WE USE NEXT?)
Ending	Goldilocks makes friends with the Bears. They phone Peggy and invite her over for pizza.

Practice Your Skills

A. Choose one of the topics listed below and make a drawing, a diagram, or a map to develop ideas for the invention.

a homework robot   a iand-sea-air bike

B. Choose one of the topics listed below and make a cluster to develop ideas for a club for people interested in the subject.

food   computers   travel   fan club

C. Choose one of these topics and make an observation chart, a compare-and-contrast chart, or a story map about it.

a camping trip   meeting friends at the mall   a parade

Finding a Starting Point

Ideas for writing can come to you in many ways. Sometimes you can see an idea in a photo, for example. What writing ideas can you get from this photo? Probably the best source of ideas, however, is *you*. Both your personal world and the larger world around you can provide an endless supply of ideas. All you need to do is learn how to tap into them.

WRITER TO WRITER

The first place I go to find ideas is in my head.

Jaime Carr, student
York, Pennsylvania

FINDING IDEAS

"I can't think of anything to write about." If you've said this to yourself, the problem may be that you don't know where to look for writing ideas. Here are some places you can begin your search.

Your Personal World

The first place to look for writing ideas is in your personal world. Your daily life and all your memories, hobbies, and interests can be sources for writing ideas.

Your Daily Life   Your everyday experiences with family, friends, people you meet, things you read, and events you observe may be sources of writing ideas. Your experiences may make you surprised, excited, angry, or disappointed. Behind each of these experiences, there's a story waiting to be told.

Memories   How can you jar loose memories of experiences in your life? You might begin by reading your journal or by looking at photos. Talk with family members and friends about memories you share with them. What experiences and feelings come to mind?

Hobbies and Interests   You may not realize it, but you are an expert in something. Think about your skills, hobbies, and interests. What might your readers want to know more about?

The Larger World

What are people talking about? What's going on in your town and around the world? Look for things around you, in the news, or on TV that interest you, puzzle you, or concern you. The special section of the newspaper shown here has articles about the Olympics, Columbus, and kids in Russia. Are there writing ideas here for you?

When you see interesting newspaper articles, ads, and photos, clip them out or copy them. Then save the clippings in a notebook, a folder, or a section of your journal. A clip file can be a gold mine of writing ideas.

WAYS TO TAP IDEAS

Now that you know where to look for writing ideas, you need to know how to dig into these idea sources. Here are some ways you can start getting ideas down on paper.

Freewriting

Just as the name says, **freewriting** means writing freely. You write down anything that comes to mind. Don't worry about spelling, grammar, punctuation, or even making sense. The goal is to discover what you are thinking about. A good way to start is to choose one idea and write for a set period of time—say three minutes. Try to keep your pencil moving, even if you can't think of anything. If you keep at it, something will come to mind.

Look at the example below. This student came up with a wide range of ideas. Notice how he kept finding ideas even after he thought he had run out.

OK. I like science fiction. Books, movies—Terminator II, Star Trek, Android, Aliens—even comics—Flash Gordon, ray guns. Its funny to see the old movies with their bogus (special effects.) I saw one where the spaceship looked like a tin can on a string. Now what? My mind is blank. Empty, empty, empty. Outer space is empty. How big is outer space? (Are people living on other planets?) I can't think of anything else. Nothing. I could list my favorite (space movies.) I could rate all the movies I've seen. Time's up!

Student
MODEL

How special effects have changed over the years could be a good topic.

I might want to do some more freewriting on this idea.

I could write a review of some space movies.

Finding a
Starting Point   **199**

When you have finished freewriting, look over your paper and circle the ideas that catch your interest. Then freewrite on one of those ideas. This second freewriting is a good way to discover details about a subject. It also lets you decide whether you really like the topic enough to continue writing about it.

Talking with Others

A good way to examine a writing idea, and possibly to find a better idea, is to talk with other people. Try bouncing ideas off your classmates, friends, and family members. Give everyone a chance to talk. Build on one another's suggestions. If you listen carefully and ask questions, you may find new ways to look at your topic.

This is my idea . . .

What if we look at it this way?

What do you mean?

Listing

Another way to tap into writing ideas is to create a list. When you make a list, you start with a broad subject or idea. You then write examples or details related to the broad topic. Here is Lisa's list of things she and her friends collect.

COLLECTIONS

stamps
shells
comic books
bugs
rocks
baseball cards
compact discs
board games

After looking over her list, Lisa decided to explore one of the ideas. She made another list. Then she realized that she had enough ideas to begin drafting.

SHELLS

colors   jewelry
labels   conch shells
displays   cowrie shells
shapes   decorations

Drawing

You can also draw pictures, diagrams, and charts about people, places, and events that you might want to write about. Your drawings can help you "see" a subject and think about what you want to say. See Handbook 1, "Thinking with Pictures," pages 192–196, for more ideas on using graphic devices to explore ideas.

MAKING AN IDEA YOUR OWN

Writing becomes better when you care—when you have a reason for writing. Look for a personal connection to a topic. Don't just pick "my dog." Find an angle you care about. Was your dog your best friend at a time when you especially needed a friend?

For example, Luis was assigned to write a report on the history of a sport. He knew he wanted to write about baseball, but he wasn't sure where to go from there. To find an idea he truly wanted to write about, he thought about these questions.

- What is my personal experience with this topic?
- What special knowledge do I already have about this topic?
- What do I wish I knew more about?

Here is the way Luis answered the questions.

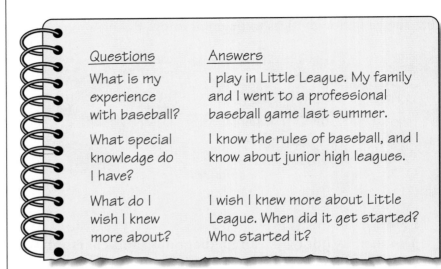

Questions	Answers
What is my experience with baseball?	I play in Little League. My family and I went to a professional baseball game last summer.
What special knowledge do I have?	I know the rules of baseball, and I know about junior high leagues.
What do I wish I knew more about?	I wish I knew more about Little League. When did it get started? Who started it?

For additional suggestions about how to make a topic your own, see Handbook 3, "Finding a Focus," pages 203–204.

Practice Your Skills

A. Look through a room in your house to trigger a memory of a person, a place, a conversation, or an experience. Then write about that memory.

B. Use listing, freewriting, or drawing to find writing ideas about a person, a place, an object, an event, or a conversation.

C. Use listing, freewriting, or drawing to find a list of writing ideas related to one of the following subjects.

    heroes   school   summer   TV   clothes

D. Choose one of the following subjects. Use one or more of the methods you learned in this lesson to make the subject meaningful to you personally.

    jobs   achievement   hobbies   travel   school

Finding a Focus

The shoes you wear, the soft drink you buy, and the TV you watch all come in sizes. You buy the size you need or want. In writing too, the size of your topic must fit your needs. To find the right size, think about what your purpose for writing is and what details you want to cover.

WRITING
HANDBOOK
3

NARROWING THE TOPIC

Asking questions and making graphic devices will help you divide a subject into parts. You may decide that you especially want to write about just one of the parts. On the other hand, you may see how several parts fit together to create a topic that you can manage.

Writing
TIP

You can use the subheads in an encyclopedia article or the table of contents in a book to find the parts of a topic.

Asking Questions

One student narrowed her topic on pets after asking these *who, what, when, where, why,* and *how* questions.

Why do people have pets?

I'd have fun interviewing my friends.

When should you get a pet?

What animals make good pets?

I wonder what animals make good pets in other countries.

How should you take care of a pet?

I'll write about this one. I could tell how Digger's first dog house was so small that he got stuck when he tried to turn around in it.

Where should a pet live?

Who are famous people with pets?

Using Graphic Devices

You can also use graphic devices, such as clusters, diagrams, observation charts, lists, and drawings, to see the parts of a topic. Another student started the following cluster about storms. What would you add to the cluster? What do you think would be a good topic about storms for a two-page paper?

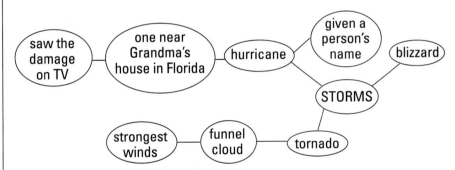

For more information on using graphic devices, see Handbook 1, "Thinking with Pictures," pages 192–196.

Practice Your Skills

A. Choose one of the topics below or one of your own. Then ask questions to focus the topic.

    rock music   cars   art   holidays   comedy

B. Choose one of the topics below or one of your own. Then use a cluster, an observation chart, a list, or another graphic device to divide the topic into parts.

    animals   snow   cities   sports   friends

Developing a Topic

> **The Wonderful Wizard of Oz:** A tornado carries a girl and her dog from their home to another land.

Would you want to read *The Wonderful Wizard of Oz* on the basis of the summary above? If the summary included vivid details, however, you might want to read the book. Details about the tornado, the girl, her dog, their home, and the characters she meets would make the writing come alive. You too can learn ways to make your writing lively. Simply add details that explain, show, or illustrate your message.

KINDS OF SUPPORTING DETAILS

How would you describe the taste of a pizza? What is the nutritional value of pizza? Who invented pizza? To answer each of these questions, you would need to use different kinds of details. The details you choose will vary, depending upon what you want to accomplish. Here are some types of details that can help you in different writing situations.

Sensory Details

You can make descriptions easy to remember by using your senses. Think of ways to tell your readers how things look, sound, feel, smell, and taste. Look at the description of a picnic on the next page. The author could simply state that a delicious selection of food was gathered. But she does much more. (Be careful; her description could make you hungry.)

Writing
TIP

You can explore your senses by making an observation chart. See Handbook 1, "Thinking with Pictures," pages 192–196.

Sense of sound ⎯
Sense of sight ⎯
Sense of taste ⎯

Sense of touch ⎯

> On the barbecue pit, chickens and spareribs sputtered in their own fat. . . . Orange sponge cakes and dark brown mounds dripping chocolate stood layer to layer with ice-white coconuts and light brown caramels. Pound cakes sagged with their buttery weight, and small children could no more resist licking the icings than their mothers could avoid slapping the sticky fingers.
>
> **Maya Angelou, *I Know Why the Caged Bird Sings***

Facts

You can support your main idea with facts from experts or from reference books, such as encyclopedias and almanacs. A **fact** is any piece of information that can be proved true. The location of Edison's laboratories in New Jersey is a fact. What other facts does the paragraph below tell you about early movies?

Professional
MODEL

> On February 1, 1893, Edison opened the world's first motion picture studio at his laboratories in West Orange, New Jersey. After producing numerous filmstrips to be viewed through the Kinetoscope [a box-like device for one viewer at a time], Edison opened the first movie theater on April 14, 1894, at 1155 Broadway, New York City. For a nickel, a customer could watch a brief filmstrip of the great bodybuilder Eugene Sandow lifting weights and performing gymnastics, or of Buffalo Bill mounting a horse and shooting his pistols. The new "theater" was a great success.
>
> **Charles Panati, *The Browser's Book of Beginnings***

Reasons

Don't leave your readers asking why. Give them reasons to support an opinion or tell why something happened. **Reasons** are explanations or logical arguments. The paragraph on the next page tells why scientists want to know when Merapi, a volcano in Indonesia, will erupt.

> Why is it important to know when Merapi might blow? If many of the people living around the volcano's base don't leave in time, they could be killed. Hurricanes of 1,400-degree-Fahrenheit volcanic ash would burn the villagers and farmers. Or flows of mud caused by heavy rain mixed with the ash would bury them alive.
> **Brianna Politzer, "Magma P.I."**

Professional
MODEL

— Main reason
— Supporting reasons

The celebrated aviator Amelia Earhart sits in the cockpit of her aircraft after setting a new altitude record, April 1931.

Examples

Sometimes the best way to help your readers understand a point is to give them an **example,** or instance of something. You can introduce an example with words such as *for instance,* or *to illustrate.* Look for examples in the paragraph below. Which ones support the main idea that the famous airplane pilot Amelia Earhart and her sister were athletic?

Professional
MODEL

> From an early age, Amelia and her sister were athletic. They turned a lawn swing into a jungle gym and hung by their knees on the top bar. They played baseball and football with equipment their father bought them. In the barn, they climbed on an old carriage where they took imaginary journeys behind teams of galloping horses while fighting off nonexistent attackers.
> **Ginger Wadsworth, "The Adventure Begins"**

Stories or Events

Another way to add details is to tell a story or describe an event that will help your readers understand your idea. A **story** or **event** can come from your experiences or from talking to others. It can also come from reading or from your imagination.

The following paragraph tells a story about a real event that happened to Valerie Taylor, an Australian diver and underwater photographer. The details support the main idea that divers sometimes meet sharks unexpectedly.

> Valerie remembers one such occasion many years ago. She was diving with two friends along the Great Barrier Reef near her home in Australia one sunny day. "Suddenly I sensed something swimming very close to me," she recalls. "Thinking it was one of the other divers, I looked around—straight into a large black eye. It belonged to a huge tiger shark, nearly fifteen feet long. I knew instinctively it was not going to hurt me. If it had wanted to bite, it would have done so before I ever saw it."
>
> **Judith E. Rinard, "Sharks Are Our Business"**

WAYS TO EXPLORE A
TOPIC FURTHER

During prewriting you explore your ideas and collect some details. To find out if you have enough details to support your ideas, ask yourself these questions:

- Can I accomplish my purpose with the details I have?
- Will the details I have get my ideas across clearly?
- Will my readers need more information to understand my ideas?

WRITER TO WRITER

The thing I like most about writing is the way it allows me to express myself.

**Ben Everett, student
Charleston, Illinois**

Perhaps you need more details for a paper on the knights of the Round Table. Try these strategies.

Common Ways to Find More Details

Recalling   Remember a movie you've seen about King Arthur and his knights. Have you read a book about Merlin the magician or about King Arthur's magic sword?

Observing   Study an illustrated book to learn about life during the time of King Arthur. Pay close attention to the way the people dressed and the places they lived.

Imagining   Ask yourself questions such as "What if I were a knight of the Round Table?" or "What if I were Guinevere's best friend?"

Interviewing   Plan to talk to your reading teacher or a librarian who knows about your subject. Write out the questions you want to ask. Then interview the person. Listen carefully and ask more questions if you don't understand.

Researching   Visit the library. Look for details in encyclopedias, in books such as *King Arthur and the Knights of the Round Table, The Tale of Sir Gawain,* and *The Legend of King Arthur.* Enjoy movies such as *Knights of the Round Table, Camelot,* and *The Sword in the Stone.*

Try to use several or all of these strategies. The more information you gather, the more familiar you will become with your topic. Then it will be easier for you to include interesting facts, stories, and specific details.

What can you do if you are writing a story about an imaginary character? You will probably rely on imagining. You might, however, blend in details from your memories, observations, and everyday experiences.

PROBLEM

S O L V I N G

"How do I know which facts, stories, and details to include?"

For more information on narrowing your topic and organizing details, see

- Handbook 1, "Thinking with Pictures," pages 192–196

- Handbook 3, "Finding a Focus," pages 203–204

- Handbook 7, "Organizing Details," pages 217–221

Practice Your Skills

A. Choose one of the following main ideas. Write a paragraph about it, using the suggestion in parentheses. For this assignment you don't need to do any outside research. You can just make up the kinds of details you need.

1. In the summer heat, the ice cream cone began to melt. (Use sensory details to show what happened.)
2. Living creatures were discovered on Mars in 2094. (Make up the facts about this discovery.)
3. Girls should (or should not) play on the same Little League teams as boys. (Give reasons to support your position.)
4. I like listening to several types of music. (Give examples of the music you like.)
5. You can learn a lot from your mistakes. (Tell a story about what you learned from a mistake you made.)

B. Imagine that you need to add details to support each of the following main ideas. For each idea, name one or more types of details that would make the piece of writing lively and informative. Choose from these types: sensory details, facts, reasons, examples, and stories or events.

1. the ways computers influence our lives today
2. watching a fireworks display
3. the origins of modern basketball
4. why video games are worthwhile
5. your scariest experience

C. Choose one of the topics below or a topic of your own. Write your topic on a piece of paper. Then list two or three concrete details you might use to develop the topic. Use one of the strategies for finding details covered in this handbook.

mummies   roller coasters   fire alarms   sunken ships

Why Am I Writing and Who Am I Writing for?

Goals and Audience

A gymnast leaps onto the balance beam and begins her routine. All her energy, talent, and training are focused on one audience—the gymnastics judges—and one goal—a medal-winning performance.

You may not expect to win a medal for your writing. Like the gymnast, however, you do need to think about your goals and your audience. Your writing will be more effective if you first consider why you're writing. At the same time keep thinking about your audience.

GOALS

When you write, you usually have some **goal,** or reason for writing, in mind. Think about what makes the subject important to you. Why is it worth writing about? For example, you may want to tell a friend about an exciting baseball game you attended. You may want to express your opinion about a movie you've seen.

You may have more than one goal in mind for a particular piece of writing. For example, you may want to write about a baseball game both to tell what happened that day and to help your friend understand why the game was so special to you. You may want to express your opinion about a movie both to convince your classmates to see it and to share your impression of the star.

Identifying your goals can help you focus your writing. You might begin by asking yourself the following questions:

- Why am I writing?
- What do I want my writing to do?
- How do I want my readers to react?

Sometimes you will have clear goals in mind before you begin writing. At other times you will discover your goals as you write. You may even change your goals as you draft and revise. Thinking about your goals can help you identify your personal connection to your topic. Clear goals will also help you write clearly and strongly.

AUDIENCE

Just as important as why you are writing is whom you are writing for—your **audience.** These are the people with whom you will share your writing.

Often in your school assignments, your audience will be chosen for you. For example, if your social studies teacher assigns a report on ancient Egypt, your audience will be your teacher and possibly your classmates. In other cases, you will choose your audience. For instance, you might decide to write a letter to a friend or a grandparent, or you might jot down your thoughts and feelings in your journal—for you alone to read.

Thinking about your audience can help you figure out what you want to say. You might ask yourself questions like the following:

- Who is my audience?
- What do they already know about my subject?
- What do I want them to know?
- What details might they find most interesting?

As you consider your audience, also think about the kind of language you will use to present your ideas. For example, if you were writing for younger readers, you would use simpler language and shorter sentences than you would use if you were writing for adults.

Use a graphic organizer like the one shown on the next page to help you think about your goals and audience.

Writing
TIP

To help you figure out what kind of language to use in a piece of writing, imagine you are having a conversation with your audience.

Topic: <u>Dolphin language</u>

Goals	Audience
Why am I writing? to explain what scientists have learned about how dolphins communicate with one another	**Who is my audience?** my classmates
	What do they already know about my subject? They may have seen a program about dolphins on TV; our class has already learned that dolphins are mammals.
What do I want my writing to do? to make my readers better informed about dolphin communication	**What do I want them to know?** how dolphins make noises, what kinds of noises they make, what the noises might mean, and how scientists study dolphin language
How do I want my readers to react? with interest and amazement	**What details might they find most interesting?** specific examples of how dolphins communicate

Practice Your Skills

A. For each of these topics, suggest one or more possible goals for writing.

1. a funny incident
2. a book you enjoyed reading
3. performing onstage
4. one dark, dreary night
5. tidal waves
6. medieval armor

B. Select two of the topics listed below. For each topic, choose a possible audience and tell the reasons for your choice.

1. why cities need to plant more trees
2. how to get along with a younger brother or sister
3. earthquakes
4. safety tips for in-line skaters
5. the best music videos
6. the best sneakers to buy

on the LIGHT side

Way Out West

Over a period of seventy years, "Frosty" Potter collected a list of sayings he heard cowboys use. Can you come up with other expressions for the adjectives listed here?

Afraid He bolted like a jack rabbit in tall grass.

Brave He'll fight a rattler an' give him first bite.

Crazy He was plumb weak north of his ears.

Hard to do Like tryin' to scratch yore ear with yore elbow.

Hot We had to feed the chickens cracked ice to keep 'em from layin' hard-boiled eggs.

Lazy He was always settin' on the south side of his pants.

Mad Mad 'nough to kick his own dog.

Quiet So quiet yuh could hear daylight coming.

Short Would have to borrow a ladder to kick a grasshopper on the ankle.

Smart As full of information as a mail-order catalog.

Tall So tall he couldn't tell when his feet were cold.

Thin Had to stand twice in the same place to cast a shadow.

Unhappy As unhappy as a woodpecker in a petrified forest.

Worthless His family tree wasn't no more better than a shrub.

Cold Shakin' like a Chihuahua pup with a chill.

How Do I Create a First Draft?

Drafting to Explore

Imagine that you have an idea for a painting. How would you begin? You might first draw a sketch of your idea and then follow the sketch as you paint. Perhaps you would rather paint your idea right on the canvas and then make changes or start over as new ideas come to mind.

You can draft your writing ideas using similar methods. **Drafting** is the process of trying out ideas on paper. As you draft, your writing begins to take shape.

HOW DO I START?

As with any creative process, there is no "right" way to draft. Some writers follow a plan they have constructed. Others try out their ideas as they work. Try both techniques.

Follow a Plan

Plan your draft by making an outline or listing your ideas and details in the order you want to write about them.

Follow your plan as you draft.

Submarines

I. How a submarine dives
A. Flood storage tanks
1. Water replaces air
2. Added weight sinks ship
B. Tilt diving planes down
II. How a submarine surfaces
A. Drain storage tanks
1. Air replaces water
2. Lighter ship begins rising
B. Tilt diving planes up

Submarines

You can't sink a toy boat in the bathtub, so how does a submarine sink? A submarine has special storage tanks. When the captain issues the order to dive, the crew floods the tanks with water. The water pushes air out of the tanks. Because water is heavier than air, the submarine sinks. When the diving planes, or fins, on the

Follow the Flow of Your Ideas

Write down the ideas that are clear in your mind.

Arrange the ideas in the order you want them. Delete unrelated ideas.

Add new ideas as they come to mind.

> Being Left-handed
>
> I think our school should have a club for left-handed people. We lefties could use the support, because being left-handed isn't easy. Many school supplies, like ~c~ sissors, are made only for right-handers. Even some school desks are made only for rightees. people who write with their right hands. Once during arts and crafts class, my teacher tried to teach me to knit. It was hopeless! It's harder for a lefty to learn how to do some things from a right-handed teacher.

Start over again if you're not happy with the results.

Writing TIP

Once you have completed a draft, it's a good idea to set it aside for an hour or two—or even a day. You may be surprised by the new ideas that occur to you when you look at your draft again.

HOW DO I KNOW WHEN I'M DONE?

You may think you're done after you complete your first draft. That's not the case. After you finish a draft, read your work and decide what you like and what you want to improve. Then start a draft with those changes. Like most writers, you may write several drafts until you are satisfied with your writing.

Practice Your Skills

Look in your journal and choose an entry you would like to turn into a finished piece of writing. Decide whether you want to start by making a plan or by letting your ideas flow as you write. Then write a draft of your piece.

What Is the Best Order for My Writing?

Organizing Details

You have chosen a topic, and you have developed that topic with sensory details, facts, reasons, examples, and stories or events. Now you must organize all of these ideas and related details in paragraphs. Where do you begin?

There are different methods of organization you can use, depending on the type of writing you are doing. In some types of writing, such as a story that includes description, you may even use more than one method.

On the following pages you will learn ways in which you can organize details in paragraph form. The chart below is a summary of these methods.

Methods for Organizing Details

Method	Type of Writing	How to Organize Details
main idea with supporting details	reports, opinion	Write the main idea, perhaps as a topic sentence. Support it with facts, reasons, anecdotes, events, or examples.
chronological order	stories, process, directions	Write events or steps as they occur.
spatial order	descriptions	Describe details in a scene by moving up, down, to the left or right, or from near to far or far to near.
order of importance	persuasive, informative	Organize details from most important to least important or from least important to most important.

MAIN IDEA WITH
SUPPORTING DETAILS

Some of the details you have gathered may be reasons, facts, examples, brief stories, or events. You can organize these details by starting with a sentence that expresses the main idea of the paragraph. Then write the reasons, facts, examples, stories, or events that develop and support the main idea.

Notice the development in the paragraph below, about the work of zoologist Dr. Jane Goodall. The first sentence tells the main idea—Goodall found that chimpanzees act like humans in many ways. All of the other sentences provide details that explain how chimpanzees act like humans.

Professional
MODEL

Details that support the main idea

> Dr. Goodall noticed many ways in which chimpanzee behavior resembles that of humans. Chimpanzee mothers form close ties with their young and care for them for many years. The young learn from their mothers how to raise their own young. Chimpanzees communicate by sounds and gestures. They hold hands and kiss. They pat each other on the back. After being separated for a while, two chimps may hug.
>
> **Sharon L. Barry, "Asking Questions, Finding Answers"**

PROBLEM
SOLVING

"How can I organize the events in my story?"

For information about using story maps, see

- Handbook 1, "Thinking with Pictures," pages 192–196

CHRONOLOGICAL ORDER

The details you have gathered may be events that happened in a certain order in time. Other details may be the steps in which something happens. You can organize these details in **chronological order,** or the order in which events or steps occur, as in the paragraph on the next page.

SPATIAL ORDER

Spatial order is the order in which details are arranged in space. This order helps your readers picture scenes, people, or objects.

To organize details in spatial order, start at a specific place and then move on. For example, you might describe a skyscraper by starting at the bottom and moving up to the top story. You might describe a person from head to toe. You could describe a beach scene from left to right or near to far.

Notice how in the model below, Virginia Hamilton helps her readers picture the inside of a barn. She starts at the entrance and then directs her readers' attention first to the crossbeam above and then to the walls at the sides.

ORDER OF IMPORTANCE

Another way to arrange details is to rank them in **order of importance.** Your most important detail may be the one that impressed you the most or the one that you think your readers might not know. Your least important detail may be the one that impressed you the least or the one your readers know already. Arranging details in order of importance is useful when you present arguments and opinions or write reports.

Look at this student's paragraph presenting an opinion on the destruction of Florida's coral reefs. Notice how she catches her readers' attention at the beginning with a detail that made a great impression on her.

Student
MODEL

Most important detail
Less important details

> Whenever a careless diver or boater stands on or even bumps into our coral reef, their actions damage a living structure that took nature about six thousand years to create. Also, water pollution and litter from boats contribute to the destruction and death of coral. For these reasons, fishing and diving near the coral reefs should be limited.

You can also put the less important details first, leaving your readers with the most important idea at the end. In the passage below, Robert C. Gray begins with some interesting details about two East Coast islands. Notice how he tells about Assateague's most famous animals at the end of the paragraph.

Professional
MODEL

General details about the islands
Wildlife listed in order from common to endangered
Most famous island wildlife mentioned last

> A few miles off the eastern shore of Virginia and Maryland lie two small islands: Assateague and its smaller companion, Chincoteague. Assateague is home to great blue herons, sika deer, and even the endangered peregrine falcon. But the island's most famous inhabitants are the wild ponies, called Chincoteague ponies even though they live on Assateague.
> **Robert C. Gray, "The Wild Ponies of Chincoteague"**

Practice Your Skills

A. Imagine you are viewing the scene shown in this painting by Thomas Hart Benton. Write a description of everything that is happening around you. Use spatial organization to present your descriptive details so that your readers can picture the scene just as you see it.

Fire in the Barnyard (1944), Thomas Hart Benton.

B. Reorder each set of details below, using one of the organizational strategies shown in this handbook. Use the strategy that presents the details in the most logical order.

1. Soon the boy surfaced on the other side of the pool.
   Pedro stood poised on the high diving board and studied the water beneath him.
   He spouted water from his mouth as he let the air out of his lungs.
   The hometown crowd exploded into applause and wild cheers.
   He bounced once, lifted off the board, shot downward, and sliced through the water.
2. For one thing, skateboarding is fun, and just about anyone can do it.
   I think our town should reserve space in the park for a special skateboarding area.
   The most important reason, however, is that there are very few public places where kids are allowed to ride their skateboards.
   Also, it is very popular among junior-high students.
   Instead, dedicated skateboarders must skate in unsupervised, possibly dangerous places.

What Is a Paragraph?

Examining Paragraphs

A paragraph is as easy to spot as a zebra with purple polka dots. All you have to do is look for a group of sentences with the first line indented. However, a well-developed paragraph is more than just a series of sentences.

GOOD PARAGRAPHS

A **paragraph** is a group of sentences that all work together to express and develop the same main idea. In a well-written paragraph, the sentences are also arranged in an order that makes sense. Notice how all the sentences in the following model work together to describe a dog's bark.

Literary
MODEL

> There was no price that could be put on Sounder's voice. It came out of the great chest cavity and broad jaws as though it had bounced off the walls of a cave. It mellowed into half-echo before it touched the air. It was louder and clearer than any purebred's voice. Each bark bounced from slope to slope in the foothills like a rubber ball. It was not an ordinary bark. It filled up the night and made music.
>
> **William Armstrong, *Sounder***

Developing a Main Idea

When you first draft a paragraph, just try to get down everything that comes to mind. Then, to improve your draft, you can do the following:

- Think about your main idea or purpose. What important idea do you want to get across?
- Take out any details that are not related directly to the main idea.
- Add details that help to develop the main idea further and make your paragraph more interesting.

Identify the main idea of the following paragraph. Then check to see whether or not all the details develop this idea.

> During the winter of 1838-39, U.S. troops forced fifteen thousand Cherokee men, women, and children to march from Georgia to Oklahoma through snow and bitter cold. Most were barefoot. All were hungry. Over a fourth of them died on the journey, which became known as the Trail of Tears. Many of the survivors started farms in Oklahoma. Farming was difficult, though, because cattle ranchers often drove their herds of cattle right across the Cherokees' fields.

The details about farming are interesting, but they have nothing to do with the Cherokees' forced march, which is the topic of the paragraph. When the sentences about farming are removed, the main idea comes across much more clearly as in this revised student model.

Student MODEL

> During the winter of 1838-39, U.S. troops forced fifteen thousand Cherokee men, women, and children to march from Georgia to Oklahoma through snow and bitter cold. Most were barefoot. All were hungry. Over a fourth of them died on the journey, which became known as the Trail of Tears.

Arranging Sentences Sensibly

Once you have settled on the details you want to include in a paragraph, you need to arrange them in a way that makes sense. If you don't do this, you're likely to confuse your readers. For example, read the following paragraph.

> Snack-sized pizzas are easy to make. You just broil them for three to five minutes or until the cheese is melted. First, you have to toast and butter both halves of an English muffin. Then you can add extras such as cooked hamburger, onions, olives, and mushrooms. Don't forget to spread a thin layer of spaghetti sauce or pizza sauce on each half. Put mozzarella cheese on top.

Could you follow these directions? Do you know whether to put the sauce on before or after you add the extras? When do you put on the cheese? When do you broil the pizzas? Now see how much easier it is to follow the directions when the steps are presented in a sensible order.

Student
MODEL

The steps are arranged in chronological order.

Transitions help make the order of the steps clearer.

> Snack-sized pizzas are easy to make. **First,** toast and butter both halves of an English muffin. **Next,** spread a thin layer of spaghetti sauce or pizza sauce on each half. **On this layer of sauce,** add extras such as cooked hamburger, onions, olives, and mushrooms. **Then** put mozzarella cheese on top. **Finally,** broil them for three to five minutes or until the cheese is melted.

You can help your readers understand the arrangement of your sentences by using transitional words and phrases. Some of these words and phrases signal time: *soon, after a while.* Others signal place: *to the left, on top.* To learn more about transitions, see Handbook 11, "Transitions," on pages 234–238.

For help in finding the best ways to organize different types of details, you might want to review Handbook 7, "Organizing Details," on pages 217–221.

Practice Your Skills

A. Decide which of these two examples is a weak paragraph. Then improve the weak paragraph by getting rid of the sentences that stray from its main idea.

1.   People all over the world love baseball. Canadians love it enough to have two teams competing in the Major Leagues. People in many Latin American countries and in Japan love the game enough to have formed their own baseball leagues. What's more, in Japan a single baseball game often attracts more than fifty thousand fans.

2.   Wolves communicate by using different types of howls. One kind of howl signals that a wolf wants to "talk." Another type of howl warns that danger is near. Many people think that wolves are vicious beasts, but they aren't. Wolves rarely attack people. In addition, they show mercy to one another. When wolves gather to hunt, they howl to greet one another. Then, to begin the hunt, they let out a wilder sort of howl. If you want to read a good book about wolves, read *Julie of the Wolves*.

B. Use what you've learned about good paragraphs to improve the following paragraph.

Some hot-air balloons hold only two passengers, but others hold more. Just how does a balloonist fly a hot-air balloon? Here are the basics. To take off, the balloonist lights a propane burner under the balloon. To land, the balloonist turns down the burner or opens the vent at the top of the balloon. To make the balloon go higher, the balloonist turns up the propane burner. A group of colorful balloons is quite a sight.

A propane burner heats the air inside a hot-air balloon, causing the air to expand. The balloon rises when the escape of some of the air decreases the overall weight of the balloon.

How Do I Write a Paragraph?

Creating Paragraphs

Look over some of the paragraphs you've written. Which ones seem to work best? What makes them successful?

As you draft other paragraphs, keep in mind what has worked for you in the past. Also, consider using topic sentences and supporting details to express and develop your main ideas.

DRAFTING TOPIC SENTENCES

A **topic sentence** states the main idea or purpose of a paragraph. Here, for example, is the topic sentence from a paragraph about a computer game:

> If you've ever wanted to explore the universe with a crew of creatures from different planets, StarVoyager is the ideal game for you.

You don't have to put a topic sentence in every paragraph you write. However, including a topic sentence is a simple and direct way to make the main idea of a paragraph clear to readers. Furthermore, writing a topic sentence can help you stay focused on your main idea as you draft.

A good topic sentence can also get readers interested in your subject. To create attention-getting topic sentences, use the tips on the following page.

DEVELOPING PARAGRAPHS

A paragraph is more than just a topic sentence. As you learned in Handbook 8, "Examining Paragraphs," a paragraph is a group of sentences that develops one main idea. In a well-developed paragraph, these sentences contain the details needed to explain the main idea fully. They also support the main idea effectively.

As you develop your paragraphs, remember to do the following:

- Supply your readers with all the important information they need.

- Stay focused on your main idea.

- Explain and support your main idea with details such as facts, statistics, sensory details, incidents, examples, reasons, and quotations.

For more help in developing your ideas with supporting details, review Handbook 4, "Developing a Topic," pages 205–210, and Handbook 12, "Show, Don't Tell," pages 239–242.

Writing
TIP

Avoid using wordy phrases such as "This paragraph is about . . . ," "I am going to write about . . . ," or "My topic is. . . ." Instead, just start with what you want to say.

Now read the following paragraph. Is it well developed?

> My new guitar is great. It looks really neat. I like it a lot.

Why is the new guitar great? What are some of its neat looking features? Why do you like it so much? Since the paragraph fails to support its main idea with details, it is not well developed. A version that's more fully developed with reasons and sensory details gets across the main idea much more effectively.

> My new guitar is great. Its wood is as golden yellow as maple leaves in autumn. There's a really fancy design around the sound hole. Its nylon strings are easy for my fingers to press down. Best of all, it sounds gorgeous.

Now decide whether or not the following paragraph is well developed.

> Watch out! The advertisers are after you! They're trying to get you to buy all sorts of things.

The second sentence states the paragraph's main idea—but not very precisely. Who, exactly, is "you"? What, specifically, are these advertisers trying to get you to purchase? Notice how much stronger and more complete the paragraph is once it answers these questions.

Writing — **TIP** —

If your paragraph raises more questions than it answers, it is probably missing important information.

> Watch out! If you're between the ages of nine and sixteen, the advertisers are after you! They're trying to get you to buy expensive athletic shoes, computers, and other costly items. Many advertisers are even trying to sell you family products because they know that you can influence how your parents spend their money.

Practice Your Skills

A. Write a topic sentence for the paragraph below. Remember, this sentence should both tell what the paragraph is about and interest readers.

_____. Tacos and tortilla chips appear on many American restaurant menus and most grocery store shelves. We use Spanish phrases such as "Hasta la vista." Also, the fashion industry has made Mexican symbols, color combinations, and patterns quite popular.

B. Read the topic sentences below. If a topic sentence is weak, revise it to make it clearer and more interesting. If the sentence is fine as is, write _No revision needed_.

1. Frightened and injured, the only survivor made his way through the thick jungle.
2. I am going to tell you why you should recycle paper.
3. The Olympic Games are exciting to watch.
4. Have you ever wondered what your doodles mean?
5. This is a story about a bad day I had.

Intricate cross-stitch needlework decorates a Chatino Indian blouse from Oaxaca, Mexico.

C. Create a well-developed paragraph about either a topic of your choice or one from the following list. The choice of whether or not to include a topic sentence in this paragraph is up to you.

- why your classmates should vote for you (or someone else) for class president
- how to do something you enjoy doing
- an exciting event

How Do I Create Better Paragraphs?

Improving Paragraphs

When you compare an artist's sketch with a finished painting, you notice many differences. The sketch is usually pretty simple—just pencil lines on paper. The finished painting, however, is much richer. It has color, details, and feelings that aren't present in the sketch.

Think of your drafts as simple sketches. As you revise your writing, try to add color, details, and feelings to your work.

Sailor at Lunch (1914), Diego Rivera. *Sailor's Head,* second version (1914), Diego Rivera. The artist did this pencil sketch as a study for the painting *Sailor at Lunch.*

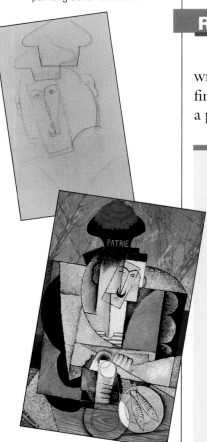

REVISING PARAGRAPHS

Once you've completed a draft, you can improve your writing by referring to the following guidelines. You may also find it helpful to refer to these guidelines when you're acting as a peer reader.

Guidelines for Revising a Paragraph

- **Make your first sentence a real attention getter.** You may want to start with a question, a startling fact, or vivid details or by addressing the readers.

- **Identify the main idea.** Does your main idea come across clearly? If not, adding a topic sentence can help.

- **Make sure all of your details develop the main idea.** Take out any unrelated details.

- **Check that you've included enough details.** If your paragraph raises more questions than it answers, you probably need to add more information.

- **Be sure the order of your sentences makes sense.** Rearrange sentences and add transitions as necessary.

Now look at one student's first draft of a paragraph about his father's weekend hobby. Imagine that you are the writer's peer reader. Can you see ways to improve this paragraph? You may want to refer to the guidelines for help.

> My father goes to his office every Saturday. It's about five miles from our house. Sometimes I come with him. He goes there to play computer games. He's one of the millions of adults who is hooked on computer games. I can see why. On the computer he flies airplanes, drives tanks, and even battles with aliens.

The student writer found a couple of ways to improve his paragraph. He revised his first sentence to make it more of an attention getter. He decided to take out some details that, on second thought, didn't really seem to relate to his main idea. He also added a sentence. Look for these changes as you read his revision.

> On the weekends, my father flies airplanes, drives tanks, and even battles with aliens. No, he's not a comic-book superhero. He's just one of the millions of adults who is hooked on computer games.

Student
MODEL

Here is the first draft of another student's paper. This paragraph expresses an opinion about censorship and school newspapers. Think about the ways you might improve this student's paragraph.

> I don't think school officials should tell us what to publish in our student newspaper. Every time the principal tells us to take out an article he doesn't like I get angry. What right does he have to tell us what to print? It's not fair!

Now read the revised paragraph. Can you see what the writer did to improve her paragraph?

> I don't think school officials should tell us what to publish in our student newspaper. First of all, the newspaper is written for students. So why should the articles in it have to please the principal? Second and more importantly, don't sixth-graders have the right to free speech just like every other citizen in this country?

Writing notes to yourself can help you remember what you want to do to improve your draft. When you review your work, you may want to note in the margin the changes you'd like to make. Notice how one writer used his notes to improve his writing.

Student
MODEL

I need to rewrite my topic sentence so that it grabs people's attention.

It would make more sense to begin at the beginning of the process, putting the blastoff at the end.

This sentence doesn't really belong.

~~Here is~~ Have you ever wondered how a rocket blasts off *actually* ? Basically, a rocket ~~launches~~ *moves* in one direction by pushing in the opposite direction. As *the* gases force their way out the back of *the* a rocket, they send *the* a rocket skyward. ~~A rocket launch must be an amazing sight.~~ The whole process starts with the burning of fuel inside *the* a rocket. The burning fuel produces hot gases. These gases build up inside the rocket until they fill all the space in the compartment where they're being created. At that point, they start escaping through an opening in the back of the rocket,

Practice Your Skills

Read each of the following drafts of student paragraphs. Then read the student comments that accompany each paragraph. Use the student comments in the margin to revise each paragraph. If you have your own ideas about how to make each paragraph better, add those to your revision also.

1. Whales' behavior suggests that a great deal of what they sing about must have to do with relationships. For example, the relationship between a female whale and her child is an extremely strong one. Female whales will risk their lives to protect their young. Whale offspring, called calves, can double in size during their first year of life. Adult whales may grow to weigh as much as 150 tons. What's more, even a fully grown adult may return to its mother during times of trouble. I can understand that. No matter how old I get, when I'm sick or hurt I always want my mom to take care of me. Adult whales will also come to the aid of a sick or injured companion. Furthermore, if a very sick whale decides to beach itself rather than die by drowning, the rest of the whales in its herd may beach themselves too rather than abandon their companion. Clearly, the attachments whales form in life are very strong and important to them.

Peer Reader Comments

Get rid of details that don't develop the main idea.

2. During summer, my brother likes going to the neighborhood pool. I like spending my time at the Hill of Three Oaks. There are lots of great reasons to hang out at the hill. First, the hill is a perfect launching place for my glider. Since no one else is ever there, it's a great place to practice the harmonica. When I try to practice at home, either my mom asks me to stop or my brother makes fun of me. Best of all, though, the hill is a good place to read and think. The book I've been reading lately is *Rumble Fish* by S. E. Hinton.

Write an attention-getting topic sentence.

Get rid of the details that don't develop the main idea.

Add a transition to link the second reason to the others.

How Can I Connect My Ideas?

Transitions

Not all relationships are as easy to identify as the one between these twins—especially when the relationships are between ideas or details in a piece of writing. To make such relationships clear, writers sometimes use transitions. **Transitions** are words and phrases that tell readers how details are related to one another. For example, "We have similar tastes in many things. *However,* I like chocolate frozen yogurt, and my sister prefers vanilla."

KINDS OF TRANSITIONS

Writing
TIP

Transitions can link paragraphs, sentences, and details within sentences.

You can use transitions to tell how details are related in time, space, or importance. You can also use transitions to signal whether details are similar or different.

Time Order   When you want to show how details are related in time, you can use the words *first, second,* and *third.* Other words that signal a link to the past, present, or future are shown on the following chart.

Time Order Transitions		
Past	**Present**	**Future**
before	now	later
yesterday	today	finally
earlier	next	tomorrow
	during	afterwards
	meanwhile	then

Now notice how J.R.R. Tolkien uses transitions in the following passage to help readers follow Bilbo and his friends on a journey.

At first they had passed through hobbit-lands, a wild respectable country inhabited by decent folk, with good roads, an inn or two, and now and then a dwarf or a farmer ambling by on business. **Then** they came to lands where people spoke strangely, and sang songs Bilbo had never heard before. **Now** they had gone on far into the Lone-lands, where there were no people left, no inns, and the roads grew steadily worse.

J.R.R. Tolkien, *The Hobbit*

Spatial Order   To show the position or location of something, try using the following transitions.

Writing
TIP

You can create clear word pictures and give precise directions with spatial order transitions.

Spatial Order Transitions

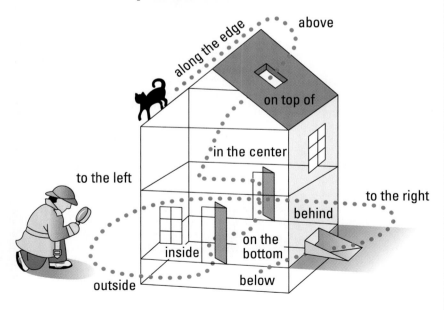

Look for the transitions in the model on the next page. Could you picture the scene as clearly without these transitions?

> The hills had flattened and given way to low fields of sedge [grasslike plants]. A scent of brine and brackish water reached Taran's nostrils. **Ahead,** the river widened, flowing into a bay, and **beyond that** to an even greater expanse of water. **To his right, on the far side** of towering rocks, Taran heard the rush of surf.
>
> **Lloyd Alexander, *The Castle of Llyr***

Order of Importance   When you want to draw attention to how important each detail is, organize your details from least to most important or from most to least important. Then, introduce your details with transitions that show the details' order of importance.

Transitions That Show Order of Importance

First
Second
Third

Good
Better
Best

Least important
More important
Most important

Best
Better
Good

Some transitions can be used to show more than one relationship. For example, *first, second,* and *last* can signal both time order and order of importance. Look at the model on the next page. Notice how transitions show the order of importance of these tips for beginning runners.

If you're interested in running, it's **important** to start by getting some information on the subject. Do some reading or talk to a coach. Even **more important,** invest in a good pair of shoes. Your feet need support. **Most important,** take it easy at first. Gradually, you will be able to increase your speed and distance.

Comparison and Contrast   The following transitions can help you make clear which details are similar to one another and which are different. Remember, comparisons show similarities, while contrasts show differences.

Comparison Transitions	
Comparison	
as	both
similarly	like
than	also
likewise	by comparison
Contrast	
yet	instead
but	by contrast
however	on the contrary
unlike	on the other hand

RABBIT TRANSIT

1939   1940   1942   1948

Now read the following model to see how transitions help the narrator point out the similarities and differences between two girls she hasn't seen all summer and a third girl who is new to her.

Grace and Carol are browner, less pasty; their features are farther apart, their hair lighter. The third girl is the tallest. **Unlike** Grace and Carol, who are in summer skirts, she wears corduroys and a pullover. **Both** Carol and Grace are stubby-shaped, **but** this girl is thin without being fragile.

Margaret Atwood, *Cat's Eye*

Practice Your Skills

A. Choose a time order transition to fill in each blank.

You can make a model volcano erupt in your own kitchen. (1) _____ , you'll need to get some newspapers, a six-ounce paper cup, some modeling clay, four tablespoons of baking soda, and one-fourth cup of vinegar. (2) _____ , cover the table with four layers of newspaper. Put the empty cup, right side up, on the table. (3) _____ , press and shape the clay around the sides of the cup so it looks like a mountain. (4) _____ , put the baking soda into the cup. (5) _____ , add the vinegar and watch your volcano erupt.

B. Each of the following groups of sentences is related. The relationship is stated in parentheses. Rewrite the italicized sentence in each group so that it begins with a transition showing how it is related to the others. The first item has already been done for you.

1. Second, it tastes good. *It's good for you.* (importance)
   Most important, it's good for you.
2. First, Jamie slid into third base. *She stole home.* Now she's up to bat again. (time order)
3. Both Deloris and Marcia prefer salty snacks. They love munching on peanuts and pretzels. *Mae has a terrible sweet tooth.* (contrast)
4. Rico peered into the canyon. *A bright yellow raft floated along a muddy river.* (spatial order)
5. Raji can play any tune after hearing it only once. *His sister has an ear for music.* (comparison)
6. First, I don't know anyone on the team. *I've only played first base, never catcher.* (importance)
7. Frogs have moist, smooth skin. *Toads have dry, warty skin.* (contrast)
8. We warmed ourselves in front of the fireplace. *The wind howled and the snow continued to pile up.* (spatial order)

What's the Best Way to Present My Information?

Show, Don't Tell

Two friends are discussing a race one of them ran:

JAMIE: The other runner was gaining on me. She was getting closer and closer. I was afraid she would win.

MARIA: How could you tell she was getting closer? What did you do?

JAMIE: As I rounded the last bend, the crunching of footsteps on the cinder track got louder and louder. Then I felt the brush of her sleeve against mine as she tried to pass me. I pumped my arms and pushed my legs harder, thinking, You've got to do it! You've got to win!

Jamie's first description *tells* what happened in a general way, providing no details. Her second description *shows* what actually happened while she was running. By sharing the thoughts and feelings she experienced during the race, Jamie makes it possible for Maria to experience what happened too.

In writing, as in conversation, the details are what people care about. Whether you're writing a letter or a report for school, you can develop and expand your ideas by including interesting, lively details that capture and hold your readers' attention.

How to *Show* Rather Than *Tell*

Showing an Experience When you write about a personal experience, show what happened by using specific sensory details to bring the people and places to life. Look at the passage from "Baseball in April" on the next page. Notice how Gary Soto uses vivid description to show what he remembers about a visit to Disneyland.

What does Disneyland look like? What's special about it? What fun things did you do?

Literary
MODEL

Telling

Disneyland's a great place. Our trip there was fun.

Showing

Disneyland stood tall with castles and bright flags. The Matterhorn had wild dips and curves that took your breath away if you closed your eyes and screamed. The Pirates of the Caribbean didn't scare anyone but was fun anyway, and so were the teacups and It's a Small World. . . . Maria's younger sister, Irma, bought a Pinocchio coloring book and a candy bracelet. Her brothers, Rudy and John, spent their money on candy that made their teeth blue.

Gary Soto, "Baseball in April"

Showing a Process When you explain the steps in a process or give a set of directions, you need to be especially clear and complete. Notice how the telling sentence below leaves many questions unanswered. The showing paragraph includes all the important details.

How do you get him to sit the first time? What do you repeat?

Professional
MODEL

Telling

To train your dog to sit, make him sit down, then repeat the command over and over.

Showing

Stand him on your left side, holding the leash fairly short, and command him to sit. As you give the verbal command, pull up slightly with the leash and push his hindquarters down. Do not let him lie down or stand up. Keep him in a sitting position for a moment, then release the pressure on the leash and praise him. Constantly repeat the command as you hold him in a sitting position, thus fitting the word to the action in his mind.

William D. Wescott, *How to Raise and Train a Keeshond*

Showing an Opinion   Your opinions and beliefs are based on your experiences and on what you have learned from others. To show rather than tell your opinions, support them with facts, examples, or reasons. This student writer revised her telling sentence. She showed why she believes that solar energy is part of a solution to the world's environmental problems.

Telling

    We should rely more on solar energy because it's better for the environment.

Why is solar energy better for the environment? Better than what? How does it compare with other forms of energy?

Student
MODEL

Showing

    To save the environment, we need to rely more on solar energy. Solar energy—energy from the sun—is a cleaner form of energy than the energy that comes from burning fossil fuels, such as coal and oil. That means there will be less pollution and the air will be cleaner. The rate of global warming will slow down, and less wildlife will be displaced or killed by people searching the wilderness for new oil supplies.

A woman uses a solar box cooker to prepare food.

Showing Information   Showing information in a report or essay means supporting each of your main points with plenty of facts, examples, and details.

Telling

    Animals play when they're young. That's how they learn survival skills.

Which animals? What survival skills do they learn?

Showing

Do animals really "play"? The next time you're at a zoo, watch how the lion cubs frolic. One will crouch low against the ground, stalk slowly toward its littermate, and then pounce on the surprised "victim." Such roughhouse sessions occur frequently among most carnivores such as wolves, tigers, cheetahs, raccoons, and coyotes. As they play, these young develop the abilities they need to become efficient predators.

Eugene J. Walter, Jr., "Why Do They Do What They Do?"

Practice Your Skills

A. Rewrite the following telling sentences, turning them into showing paragraphs. Use the writing strategies suggested in parentheses.

1. The movie was disappointing. (Show your opinion by supporting it with reasons and other evidence.)
2. There's a greeting card for every occasion. (Show why this is true by giving several examples.)
3. You need to know how to make a good first impression. (Show the steps in this process.)
4. The party was great. (Show the experience by using vivid sensory details to describe what happened.)
5. She stood out from the crowd. (Show this character by describing physical details and actions.)

B. Write a showing paragraph based on each of the following sentences.

1. It was a moment no one would forget.
2. I love making my favorite food. You can do it too.
3. Our lunch period should be fifteen minutes longer.
4. Junk food is being replaced by more healthful food choices for both snacks and meals.
5. I felt out of place.

How Do I Put Everything Together?

Creating Longer Pieces of Writing

Exploring an idea can be like tugging on a magician's scarf: you start with one idea and it leads you to another, which leads to another, and so on. What then? If you want to write about all these ideas, you really can't do so in just one paragraph. After all, a good paragraph develops only one main idea. To explore a number of ideas, you write a composition.

WHAT IS A COMPOSITION?

A **composition** is a group of paragraphs that work together to develop a single topic. If this definition reminds you of the definition of a paragraph, that's because the two forms are very much alike. Just look at some of the similarities between a paragraph and a composition.

Paragraph		Composition
Topic Sentence	• states the main idea • gets the reader's attention	Introductory Paragraph
Supporting Sentence		Body Paragraph
Supporting Sentence	• develops the main idea	Body Paragraph
Supporting Sentence		Body Paragraph
Clincher	• reinforces the main idea • paragraph clincher is optional	Concluding Paragraph

The strategies you use to write good paragraphs will also help you create strong compositions. So keep those techniques and guidelines in mind as you draft.

Drafting a Composition

When you start drafting, you may want just to explore and develop your ideas without giving any thought to how many paragraphs there will be. You can group and organize ideas later. On the other hand, you may know what your main ideas are, and you may want to develop each one as a paragraph. Refer to the guidelines for drafting paragraphs that appear in Handbook 10, "Improving Paragraphs," on pages 230–233.

Revising a Composition

Once you've gotten your ideas down on paper, you can improve your composition by following these guidelines.

Guidelines for Revising a Composition

- **Check to see that your first paragraph identifies your topic and gets your reader's attention.**

- **Make sure that each supporting paragraph develops only one main idea.** Break paragraphs overloaded with ideas into smaller paragraphs, each focusing on one main idea.

- **Check to see that the order of your paragraphs makes sense.** Rearrange paragraphs and add transitions as necessary.

- **Make sure that your last paragraph ties your ideas together effectively and does not introduce new thoughts that need to be developed or explained.**

Writing
TIP

You might want to make a rough outline of your composition. Then use each main point in your outline as the main idea of a paragraph.

PROBLEM
SOLVING

"I need to know more about developing the different kinds of paragraphs in a composition."

For more information about developing paragraphs in a composition, see

- Handbook 4, "Developing a Topic," pages 205–210

- Handbook 14, "Introductions," pages 247–249

- Handbook 15, "Conclusions," pages 250–252

Now look at how one student used these revision guidelines to improve his composition.

Are video games worthwhile or not? There are strong arguments to support both answers to this question. ¶ Some people argue that video games are

For instance,

just a waste of time and money. ∧ My dad says, "You should have more to show for the time and money you spend than what you get from those games." He

time

thinks that playing video games just takes ∧ away

players

from doing homework and chores and gives ~~you~~ ∧ nothing in return.

However, other people point out that

∧ Video games provide entertainment and help build important skills. Kids get a lot of fun out of playing

At the same time,

video games. ∧ Because many games involve quickly pushing buttons or moving a joystick, players also develop faster reflexes and better coordination. ~~When you get one of the top scores you get to put your name on the screen. I've done that in one game already. Your name stays there until someone else gets a better score.~~ Also, with practice, the games

players

make ∧ you able to concentrate better and solve

players

puzzles faster. ¶ Clearly, video games give ∧ you quite a

their *Therefore,*

lot in return for ∧ your time and money. ∧ In my opinion video-game playing is a worthwhile hobby.

Keep opener—question should get my readers' attention.

Begin a new paragraph when a new idea is introduced.

Add a transition to help readers see that this is my next main idea.

Getting off the point here???

Oops—players, not readers

Separate out conclusion and connect the last sentence with a transition word.

Creating Longer
Pieces of Writing   **245**

Practice Your Skills

Revise the draft below by making the following changes:

- Break the writing into four paragraphs, each focusing on one main idea.
- Delete the two sentences that don't support any of the main ideas.
- Add any transitions that are needed to make the connections between details clear.
- Fix the run-on sentence.

When Gail Devers flashed across the finish line at the 1992 Summer Olympics, her run was an amazing achievement. Not only did she win a gold medal in the 100-meter dash, she did so even though she suffered from a serious illness. In 1988, Devers came down with Graves' disease, a gland problem that often causes weight loss and extreme tiredness. George and Barbara Bush also have this disease. Doctors found it difficult to treat her illness. The treatments they gave Devers ruined her health. After a while, she couldn't even walk. In 1991, doctors finally figured out how to get rid of the side effects. They changed her treatment within a month she was able to walk around a track. Two months later she won a race. One year later she won an Olympic gold medal. Her coach at the Olympics was Bob Kersee. To win an Olympic gold medal at all is a triumph. To win one as Devers did is a truly amazing accomplishment. *Sports Illustrated* called her achievement "the greatest comeback in modern track history."

Introductions

Worms, flies, a bit of a cheese sandwich—to catch a fish, you've got to use the right bait. To catch a reader's attention, a writer also relies on bait. However, a writer's "bait" is a well-written introduction—not a day-old sandwich.

WAYS TO BEGIN

A good introduction both interests readers and lets them know what they will be reading about. Here are some good ways to get started.

Ask a Question

If you start with a question, curiosity will probably cause your readers to read on to find the answer. Would you continue reading to discover the answer to the question that begins the following introduction?

> Is the Leaning Tower in Pisa, Italy, falling down? Some Italians think so—even though the 817-year-old monument has survived earthquakes, World War II and nearly one million visitors a year.
>
> **"Pisa in Pieces,"** *3-2-1 Contact*

Professional
MODEL

Facts First

Jump right in with a surprising fact or statistic that will catch your reader's attention. Here, for example, a writer begins with several startling bits of information.

> United States manufacturers sold some 388 million pairs of athletic shoes last year. The beauty of that dizzying number varies greatly from beholder to beholder. Runners see lots of miles run. Retailers see $12.1 billion. And environmentalists see 776 million shoes heading straight for landfills (and those are just last year's shoes).
>
> **David Arneke, "Sole Searching"**

Talk to Your Reader

Have you ever noticed that it's hard to ignore someone who speaks straight at you? Readers tend to find it equally difficult to ignore writing that talks directly to them. Notice, for instance, how you respond to the following introduction.

> Are you feeling sad and "blue"? Or are you happy and "in the pink"? Believe it or not, whether you are sad or happy may have a lot to do with color: the color you're wearing, or, more likely, the color you're looking at.
>
> **Deborah Heligman, "There's a Lot More to Color Than Meets the Eye"**

Writing
TIP

Remember not to use the pronoun *you* unless you really mean "the reader."

Tell a Story

Interest your readers by telling an unusual or a funny story. After all, who can resist a good story? Remember, however, that it's just the introduction to your main subject. So keep the tale short. For example, read the brief tale told in the introduction on the next page.

> It was a chilly October night. A family was driving along a lonely mountain road in northern Oregon. Suddenly, they saw a nine-foot-tall, hairy figure moving swiftly along the roadside. It was caught in the head-lights of their car as they passed. But they were too scared to turn around and investigate.
>
> **Russell Ginns and Michael Rozek, "Tracking Bigfoot"**

Professional
MODEL

This story makes readers want to find out what happened next. What did the family see?

W R I T E R   T O   W R I T E R

When I can't think of how to begin a story, I start with dialogue.

Alyce Arnick, student
Aurora, Colorado

Practice Your Skills

A. Look through the models in the Writer's Workshops. Find three introductions that made you want to read more. Tell why each introduction is effective.

B. The following are four weak introductions. Choose two of them. Use what you learned in this handbook to rewrite the two introductions, making them more interesting.

1. Computers can do amazing things. Things that seem fantastic now may be common in the future.
2. Mercury is an interesting planet. It travels around the sun at about 106,000 miles per hour. It is faster than the other planets in the solar system.
3. Bicycle helmets are a great way to protect yourself when you're riding. Everybody should wear one.
4. The weather affects many people's moods. On cold, gray winter days, the lack of sunshine makes some people feel like hibernating.

How Do I End My Writing?

Conclusions

Ending a piece of writing without a conclusion is like hanging up in the middle of a phone conversation. You leave your reader wondering, "Is this really the end?"

WAYS TO END WRITING

A good conclusion tells readers, "This is the end," and also leaves them with something to think about. Here, for example, are some good ways to conclude your writing.

Say It Again

When you want your readers to remember the main points that you've made, restate them in a new way in your conclusion. For example, this writer reminds his readers that collecting baseball cards is and will continue to be a popular hobby.

> Baseball cards have been sold with everything from the first bubble gum, in the 1930s, to dog food. And baseball fans will keep on buying them, trading them, and treasuring them for as long as players continue to play ball.
>
> **"Hot Hobby: Collecting Baseball Cards,"**
> ***National Geographic World***

Writing
——**TIP**——

Be careful not to introduce any new supporting details or unrelated ideas in your conclusion.

Professional
MODEL

Summarizes the details that support the main idea.

Tell Readers What to Think or Do

Sometimes your purpose for writing is to get your readers to change their mind or take an action. Then you may want to end by telling your readers exactly what you feel they should think or do. What actions does this writer suggest?

> The Bronx Zoo isn't the only place where you'll find bits of wilderness created for zoo animals. Other zoos have been building similar exhibits. Take the time to get to know some of the animals who live there. Remember, they're ambassadors from a disappearing world. And once you've made some new friends, find out how to keep their wilderness homes from disappearing.
>
> **Richard Chevat, "Monkey Business: A Zoo Exhibit Makes Baboons Feel at Home"**

Professional
MODEL

Suggests an action

Suggests something to consider

Suggests an action

End with a Picture

If you want to leave your readers with a powerful word picture, sensory details can help. Here, one writer ends a story about a trip to Mount Rainier with a portrait of the mountain.

> I step outside the lodge door and into the **softly glowing** night. The earth is **silent,** the land **pure white,** here at the top of the world. Blinking away snowflakes on my eyelashes, I stare at the white slopes, trying to imagine them as meadows in bloom, the way they will look in a few short weeks. It seems impossible. But this is, after all, the magic mountain.
>
> **K. M. Kostyal, "Mount Rainier National Park"**

Professional
MODEL

These sensory details help to make the mountain seem like a magical place.

Words such as *blinking, stare, impossible,* and *magic* help to communicate a feeling of wonder.

Save the Last Event for Last

If you're writing a story, you may just want to end it by telling the last thing that happened. For example, notice the model on the next page that shows how one writer ended a story about a clerk who loses his job in a flower shop.

Literary
M O D E L

The final sentence leaves no doubt that these are the last things that happen.

> Teruo took the bills and rang up the cash register. "All right, I'll go now. I feel fine. I'm happy. Thanks to you." He waved his hand to Mr. Sasaki. "No hard feelings." . . .
>
> He walked out of the shop with his shoulders straight, head high, and whistling. He did not come back to see us again.
>
> **Toshio Mori, "Say It with Flowers"**

Practice Your Skills

A. Below are five weak conclusions. Select three of them. Then rewrite each one to make it stronger.

1. It was the end of the race. I didn't think I would have the strength to reach the finish line. Then I heard my teammates cheering me on, and I won the race.
2. World hunger is a big problem, and people should do something about it. I really wish we could end hunger throughout the world.
3. I'll never forget what our house looked like after the tornado. Everything was completely wrecked—except for the living room.
4. Science fiction stories make really great reading. So the next time you're looking for a really great book, why not try the sci-fi section?
5. It was worth all of the planning and the work to see Lorenzo's reaction. He was completely surprised by the party.

B. The following two ideas are the main points expressed in a composition. Now, write a conclusion to the composition in which you restate these two ideas in a new way.

- Dogs that roam the streets can get hurt in any number of ways.
- People who care about their dogs keep them close to home.

What Help Can Others Give Me?

Peer Response

W R I T E R T O W R I T E R

What helps [when I get stuck] is to read it to a friend and ask for ideas. Maybe read it to two friends.

Melissa Starr, student
Houston, Texas

Have you ever asked a friend to give you advice or to help you solve a problem? If so, you may have gotten a welcome pat on the back along with the advice. Maybe your friend even saw some new ways to solve the problem.

Friends can help you with your writing in the same way. The classmates who read and comment on your work are called **peer readers.** The comments and suggestions they give are **peer responses.** Asking peers to respond to your work may be one of the most important things you can do as a writer.

GETTING PEER RESPONSES

You can get help from peer readers at any time during the writing process. During prewriting, you can bounce your ideas off friends and see how they react. During drafting and revising, you can find out if you've gotten your ideas across clearly. Peer response is helpful at whatever point you choose to use it.

Helping Your Reader

At first your peer readers may not know what kinds of comments you want. They may also be afraid of hurting your feelings. You can help your peer readers by using the guidelines and questions on the next page.

GIVING PEER RESPONSES

When you are the peer reader, try putting yourself in the writer's shoes. You are a writer yourself, so all you need to do is to remember how you feel when someone reads your writing. Think about the kinds of comments *you* would like to receive. Then give the writer your honest advice and support. The chart on the next page gives some tips that peer readers should keep in mind.

Responding as a Peer Reader

- **Read carefully.** You may want to read the draft twice so that you are sure you understand it.

- **Be considerate.** Think about the writer's feelings. Remember that you are reading a work in progress.

- **Give useful feedback.** If you are asked specific questions, answer them helpfully and honestly.

- **Be supportive.** A writer needs to know what is good about a piece of writing, too.

- **Be specific.** Don't just say "This was good." Tell what was good and why.

- **Use "I" statements.** You are giving your opinion, not telling a writer what is "right" or "wrong." Don't tell a writer "This sentence isn't clear." Instead, say "I don't understand this."

Ways of Responding

You may find that three kinds of responses—*pointing, summarizing,* and *identifying problems*—are especially helpful when you are a reader. The paragraph below is from a student's first draft. The questions and the responses that follow it show how these kinds of responses work.

My sister and I learned an important lesson when we went hiking. A sign at the beginning of the trail read "TAKE A FLASHLIGHT." We didn't have one, and it was a sunny day, so we ignored the sign.

After a while we came to a tunnel and walked into total darkness. Walking slowly and cautiously, we crept along. Suddenly, a twig snapped behind us. Then, we heard breathing. Nervously, we stumbled forward. Suddenly the end of the tunnel and daylight were ahead. We squinted in the bright sun and breathed a sigh of relief.

Student
MODEL

Pointing   "What words or phrases do you especially like?"

> "I like how you quoted the words on the sign. I like the words *crept* and *stumbled.*"

Summarizing   "What do you think is my main idea?"

> "Ignoring instructions can lead to trouble. Is that your main idea?"

Identifying Problems   "Was there anything you did not understand or that you wanted to know more about?"

> "Why did you go into the tunnel? Were you scared? Also, did you find out who or what was behind you?"

Practice Your Skills

A. Read the first draft below. Then respond to the writer's questions that follow.

> Making pennies doesn't make sense. In the first place, pennies are practically worthless. Abraham Lincoln's image is on pennies. Pennies are also a nuisance. Each year nine billion pennies are minted, and each year six billion disappear from circulation. Why? No one wants a pocket or purse full of pennies, so the coins get tossed into a drawer or a jar. If you want my two cents worth, we should pitch the penny.

1. What comes across as my main point?
2. Which words or phrases do you especially like?
3. Was there anything you wanted to know more about?
4. Was anything confusing?
5. What are your ideas on this topic?

B. Choose something you have written recently. Read it again and write questions about it to ask a peer reader. Then ask a classmate to respond to your writing by answering the questions you have written.

How Can I Make My Writing Better?

Revising

You too can improve your writing by revising. Revising can be much more than taking out one unnecessary word, however. It is your chance to look back at your work and see what you like about it and what you want to change. You might want to reword a description or add to an explanation. You may even decide to start over again.

Keep in mind that writing is a very personal activity. Some writers like to revise as they go along. Others wait until they have completed a draft. Use whatever method is right for you.

STRATEGIES FOR REVISING

When you have completed a draft put it aside for a while. When you look at it again, you will be able to see it with fresh eyes. You may be surprised at the things you notice.

One good approach is to read your draft aloud. Hearing the sound of the words can help you decide how well you like your writing. Also, you may find places where you stumble as you read. Think about revising those passages.

Your peers can give you valuable advice for revising your writing. See Handbook 16, "Peer Response," on pages 253–256 for ways to get the best advice from others.

In addition, questions and suggestions like the ones shown on the next page might help you as you revise.

A cut-and-paste function can be very helpful for moving or deleting sentences as you revise.

Guidelines for Revising

Ask Yourself
- Is my main idea obvious?

- Have I included enough information to support my points?

- Should anything be taken out?

- Is my writing easy to follow?

- Is my writing interesting?

Try This
- Rewrite your introduction or opening sentences.

- Add supporting details as needed to make your points clear.

- Leave out details that don't develop your main idea.

- Check the order in which you present information. Start a new paragraph for each main idea. Add transitions where needed.

- Spice up your writing with vivid nouns, verbs, and modifiers.

One student made these revisions to a draft.

Student
M O D E L

Made introduction more interesting
Unimportant details deleted
New paragraph for a new main idea

Details added

Sentence moved

Transition added

Have you ever
~~I've always~~ wondered what was inside a baseball.
                                                                    ?
Yesterday I took ^one^ apart ~~an old~~ baseball ^to find out^ ~~I found in a~~
~~vacant lot.~~ ¶ The first layer I took off was pieces of
leather. They were held ^stitched^ together with ^thick^ red thread.
                      yards and yards
Then I unwrapped layers ^of^ wool yarn wound very
tightly. (At the center I discovered a small ball of
                    Under the yarn I found
cork.) ~~That was covered by~~ ^two^ layers of rubber. | Now
you won't have to destroy your own baseball to see
what's inside.

Practice Your Skills

A. The passages below need to be revised. Use the Guidelines for Revising on page 258 and make any changes you think are needed.

1.　　　Frank Drake, the President of the SETI Institute, said he thinks their new project will succeed. SETI stands for Search for Extraterrestrial Intelligence. SETI and NASA scientists are looking for intelligent life on other planets. They have started a 10-year, $100 million search for radio signals from space.

2.　　　What makes popcorn pop? The Native Americans were the first people to make popcorn. One way they made popcorn was to put an ear of corn on a stick and roast it over a fire. They gathered up the kernels that popped off the ear. The corn kernels that are used for popcorn contain a lot of water. When they are heated, the water expands and turns into steam. This causes the kernel to explode into a mass. The Native Americans scraped kernels from the cob and threw them directly into a fire. They ate the pieces that came out of the fire. One method was more complicated. They heated coarse sand in a shallow clay pan. When the sand was hot, they put corn kernels into it. The cooked kernels popped to the surface of the sand. There is nothing more tasty than fresh-popped popcorn. Eating popcorn became very popular with the explorers and settlers who came to America. Today people in the United States eat almost two pounds of popcorn per person a year.

B. Choose a piece of writing you completed recently, or something from your writer's portfolio. Revise it, using the ideas presented in this handbook. Then write a note to attach to the revised paper. Discuss the changes you made and the reasons you made them.

How Do I Know My Writing Is Correct?

Proofreading

What would you think if you saw this sign? If you're like most people, you would think that whoever created the sign needs a spelling lesson!

When you write, little errors like the one on the sign can take a reader's attention away from your message. By proofreading your work, you can find and correct errors in spelling, punctuation, capitalization, and grammar. You can help your readers concentrate on your writing, not on accidental mistakes.

PROOFREADING STRATEGIES

To catch the little mistakes in your writing that might slip by, you need to look carefully at your work. Here are some strategies you can try.

Proofread more than once. It's a good idea to read over your work several times. You can look for different kinds of mistakes each time. Put your paper aside between proofreadings. With fresh eyes, you may see errors you missed the first time.

Read aloud for end punctuation.   As you read your work aloud, pause where you think each sentence ends. Find the subject and verb. Be sure that you have used the correct end punctuation—a period, a question mark, or an exclamation point—for that type of sentence.

Read aloud for commas within sentences.   Notice where you pause naturally. Such a pause may mean that a comma is needed. If you stumble over the words, you may be able to delete a comma that is not needed.

Proofread for initial capitals.   Find the end punctuation mark of each sentence. Check to see that the next word begins with a capital letter.

Read your work backwards.   Read backwards one word at a time to check your spelling. Circle any spellings you are unsure of. After you finish reading, check the spellings of the circled words in a dictionary.

Proofreading Checklist

Step 1: Look at your sentences.
Do all sentences express complete thoughts?
Are there any run-on sentences?
Do subjects and verbs agree?

Step 2: Look at your words.
Are words spelled correctly?
Have you used the correct forms of verbs to show tense?
Have you used the correct forms of pronouns?
Have you used adjectives and adverbs correctly?

Step 3: Look at your capitalization and punctuation.
Have you capitalized the first words of sentences?
Have you capitalized proper nouns and adjectives?
Have you used commas correctly?
Have you used end marks correctly?
Have you used other punctuation marks correctly?

Proofreading Symbols

∧	Add letters or words.	/	Make a capital letter lowercase.
⊙	Add a period.	¶	Begin a new paragraph.
≡	Capitalize a letter.	∾	Switch the positions of
⌣	Close up a space.		letters or words.
⌄	Add a comma.	— or ℮	Take out letters or words.

Notice how the symbols were used in this passage.

> Roller Skates ^was^ (were) invented by Joseph Merlin in 1759. (the 1760s) he biult the skate's so that he could make a stunning entrance at a costume party. Unfortunately he didn't know how to stop, he crashed through a miror.

Practice Your Skills

Proofread the paragraph below for mistakes in grammar, capitalization, punctuation, and spelling. Rewrite the paragraph correctly.

In the age of hand-held Computer Games, its strange to think that the first computer game was played on a machine that took up a whole room. In january of 1962 students began expeirmenting with a giant computer at Harvard University. They find a way to make a dot skip across the computer screen, and soon they changed the dot to a spaceship, and by febuary, they had two space-ships flying across the screen. Each spaceship was controlled by a box with a lever and a button on top. Pushing the button made the spaceship shoot at it's opponent. There new game, called Spacewar, set the stage for a new use of computers.

on the LIGHT side

In the News

Under the pressure of a deadline, you work fast, even furiously, to get things done. You probably make mistakes in the process. Even professional journalists goof sometimes, as you can see here.

An eighth of everyone in this country lives in California.

Montreal Gazette

A story in *The Gazette* yesterday incorrectly identified a Cree as James Boffish. In fact, his name is James Babbish. In addition, he was described as an elder. In fact, he is too young, but was an acting elder for this occasion. *The Gazette* regrets the errors.

All river buses are now monitored by an electronic advanced Datatrak system that which enables means that at any time the airport to can be informed of the progress of the boats on their way down-river service.

Pennysaver

Three Ambulances Take Blast Victim to Hospital

KETCHUP CORRECTION
Top-quality ketchup would take at least 75 years to flow across Canada. An incorrect figure was given yesterday, owing to an error in the thinking process.

Ability to Swim May Save Children from Drowning

Storm Delayed by Bad Weather

Helicopter Powered by Human Flies

TODAY IN HISTORY
1775 Paul Revere began his famous ride from Charlestown, S.C., to Lexington, Mass., warning the American colonists that the British were coming.

San Francisco Chronicle

*Skimming
an asphalt sea
I swerve, I curve, I
sway; I speed to whirring
sound an inch above the
ground; I'm the sailor
and the sail, I'm the
driver and the wheel
I'm the one and only
single engine
human auto
mobile.*

Lillian Morrison,
"THE SIDEWALK RACER"

©K.Haring

Untitled painting (1986), Keith Haring.

- Describe your special skateboarding style or dancing style, or . . .
- Imagine you are an object. Tell what you are like.
- If you could design your own skateboard, what would it look like?

Style

The way you ride a skateboard, dance, or pitch a ball is special. Your personal style shows in the individual way you move. Even the activity you choose is a reflection of who you are.

The way you write has just as much personal style as the way you move. The handbooks that follow will show you how to make your special style come through in your writing.

How Can I Bring My Writing to Life?

Appealing to the Senses

Good writers are good observers. They write about the look and feel, the smell and taste, and the sounds of things.

> ## W R I T E R   T O   W R I T E R
>
> *What worries me is that each day something out of the ordinary will happen and I won't take notice.*
>
> **Anna Quiroz, student**
> **Kenosha, Wisconsin**

SIGHT

All writers notice details and then search for precise words to describe them. Practice making notes on the sizes, shapes, colors, and conditions of the things around you. In the following description, the writer uses precise words to help readers "see" the scene: *blackest, biggest horse; white, frilly nightcap; arms folded.*

Literary
MODEL

> Out of the trees on the right side of the house came walking the blackest, biggest horse Thomas could remember seeing.... Riding on it was a tiny girl, sitting straight and tall. She had a white, frilly nightcap on her head and she wore red flannel pajamas with lace at the neck and sleeves. She had no shoes on her feet and she sat well forward, her toes clasped in the horse's mane. With her arms folded across her chest, she stared into the distance. She was serene and happy and seemed not to notice Thomas.
>
> **Virginia Hamilton, *The House of Dies Drear***

Sound

Do you ever tune out sounds? To be a good observer, you need to listen carefully. Think of words that describe sounds: *buzz, whir, squeak.* Each word conveys a precise sound. Notice how the writer of the following passage uses precise words to describe sounds. Also note that when you say some of the words aloud, you almost make the sounds yourself.

> Every whale everywhere moves in a sea of total sound. From the moment of its birth until its final hour, day and night, it hears the endless orchestra of life around its massive frame. Silence is an unknown thing. The snapping and crackling of tiny shrimps and crablike organisms, the grunting and grating, puffing and booming, of a hundred fishes, the eerie whining and squealing of dolphins, the sad voices of sea birds overhead, the chatter of its own companions, the undertone of moving water and the drone of wind, all these notes and many more come flooding through its senses all the time. It *feels* the music, too, for water presses firmly on its frame—a smooth continuous sounding board.
>
> **Victor B. Scheffer,**
> ***The Year of the Whale***

Writing
TIP

Many factual articles begin with descriptions. Use sensory details to catch your readers' interest.

Literary
MODEL

Appealing to the Senses

TOUCH, TASTE, AND SMELL

Good writers combine senses to make their descriptions vivid. We often take the senses of touch, taste, and smell for granted. However, they are important tools for all writers.

Touch Read the following description, and notice how the writer uses precise touch words such as *downy, smooth, soft,* and *cotton* to describe a small donkey. He helps you imagine what it might feel like to run your hand over Platero's coat.

Literary
MODEL

> Platero is small, downy, smooth—so soft to the touch that one would think he were all cotton, that he had no bones. Only the jet mirrors of his eyes are hard as two beetles of dark crystal.
>
> **Juan Ramón Jiménez,** *Platero and I*

Taste and Smell Notice how taste and smell are part of one woman's memories of food she loved in China. The writer uses taste words such as *crunchy, sweet, creamy-soft.* She also describes smells: *good, stinky smell for waking up your nose.*

Literary
MODEL

> The lettuce heart, for example, it was thick like a turnip, crunchy but sweet, easy to cook. And the bean curd, we could buy that from a man who rolled his cart by our house every morning, calling, *"Cho tofu! Cho tofu!"* It was fried on the outside, and when you broke it open, inside you'd find a creamy-soft middle with such a good, stinky smell for waking up your nose.
>
> **Amy Tan,** *The Kitchen God's Wife*

USING SIMILES AND METAPHORS

Sometimes the best way to describe something you sense is to compare it to something else. Writers often use comparisons to make their descriptions vivid. One kind of comparison, called a **simile,** uses the word *like* or *as.* Read these comparisons:

The icicles were **like** frozen waterfalls.

The sunlight feels **as** sharp **as** a thousand needles.

When you use similes to describe something, be sure to make vivid, interesting comparisons. Finish the following phrases, once with the first words that come to mind, and then with vivid words:

as cold as . . .

as hard as . . .

as slippery as . . .

The first words you thought of may have been *ice, a rock,* and *an eel* because you have heard those comparisons many times before. Words and phrases that have lost their power to interest people are called **clichés.** Good writers avoid clichés by making refreshing new comparisons.

Another kind of comparison is called a **metaphor.** A metaphor compares two things without the word *like* or *as.* The following are examples of metaphors:

The treetops were a soft sea of green.

The seaweed was a slippery golden snake.

In the first metaphor, treetops are compared to the sea. In the second metaphor, seaweed is compared to a snake.

Whether you write similes or metaphors, always search for new comparisons to make your writing lively and appealing.

Sight Words

Fast Movements
hurry
scamper
dart
spring
streak
trot

gallop
dash
rush
zoom
zip
hurl
flick
whisk
rip
swerve
dive
swoop
plunge
fly
twirl

Slow Movements
creep
crawl
plod
slouch
tiptoe
amble
saunter
loiter
slink
stalk
edge
sneak
waddle
drag
drift

Shapes
flat
round
domed
curved
wavy
lean
ruffled
flared
oval
skinny
square
chubby
portly
swollen
lumpy
padded
tufted

jutting
angular
tapering
thin
spindly
wiry

Appearance
freckled
spotted
blotched
wrinkled
mottled
striped
bright
shiny
glowing
glossy
shimmering
flowery
flashy
glazed
sheer
transparent
turquoise
green

muddy
grimy
drab
dingy
dull
dark
dismal
worn
untidy
gold
maroon
shabby
ramshackle
arid
awkward
crooked
loose
rigid
cluttered
crowded
jammed
bruised
erect
supple
lively
muscular
pale
small
miniature
massive
dazzling
fiery
sturdy
hardy
healthy

Sound Words

Loud Sounds

crash
thud
explode
roar
screech
whistle
whine
squawk
blare
rumble
grate
slam
stomp
jangle
rasp
clash
racket
thunderous
hubbub
deafening
raucous
piercing
bang

Soft Sounds

sigh
murmur
whisper
whir
rustle
twitter
patter
hum
hiss
bleat
peep
buzz
gurgle
swish
chime
tinkle
clink
mute

Speech Sounds

stutter
stammer
giggle
guffaw

Appealing to
the Senses

laugh
sing
yell

scream
snort
bellow
growl
chatter
coo
whimper

Touch Words

cool
slimy
icy
lukewarm
dusty
hot
steamy
sticky
damp

slippery
spongy
mushy
oily
waxy
rubbery
leathery
silky
satiny
velvety
smooth
soft
woolly
rough
sharp
furry
feathery
fuzzy
prickly
gritty
sandy

Taste and Smell Words

buttery
salty

bitter
smoky
sweet
sugary
sour
vinegary
fruity
tangy

medicinal
fishy
spicy
peppery
burnt
rotten
perfumed
earthy
piney
briny
acrid
reeking
rancid
musty
nutty

Practice Your Skills

A. Recall the start of a race, a game, a concert, or some other event that you have participated in or observed. Try to relive the moment in your mind. Write down vivid sensory details that describe what you experienced. List the details under the four categories (1) sight, (2) sound, (3) touch, and (4) taste and smell. Use the details to write a description of your experience.

B. Practice describing different things. Choose three of the items below and describe each one in terms of two or three senses. For one item, try your hand at writing a simile or a metaphor to describe it.

1. a campfire   **4.** a pickle   **7.** a rose
2. a police siren **5.** a fish   **8.** a bus
3. a caterpillar   **6.** a skyscraper   **9.** a baseball glove

C. Sensory details make any writing better—whether it is fiction or nonfiction. Write a story about a true or imaginary incident. Use details to make your writing lively and inter-esting. The following examples may give you some ideas.

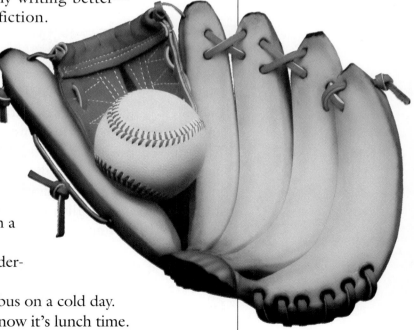

1. A bee tries to land on your sandwich.
2. You are walking home in a rainstorm.
3. A tiny puppy tries to under-stand your commands.
4. You wait for the school bus on a cold day.
5. Your stomach lets you know it's lunch time.

How Do I Make My Language Fit My Audience?

Levels of Language

> Propel, propel, propel your craft
> Smoothly down the liquid solution . . .
> **From *A Prairie Home Companion Folk Song Book***

Perhaps you would prefer to row, row, row your boat gently down the stream. In fact, the version of a well-known song quoted above would be much easier to understand if you replaced its formal vocabulary with more familiar words.

As you write and speak, you make choices about what words you will use. By thinking about your audience (a best friend, classmates, PTA members) and the kind of writing or situation (friendly letter or speech), you can learn to adjust your language to match any occasion.

CHOOSING THE RIGHT WORDS

Careful writers and speakers use **standard English,** language that follows the rules of grammar and usage. **Nonstandard English** is language that does not conform to rules of grammar and usage. Most of the time, you will be using standard English. When you use standard English, however, you will still need to make some decisions. Standard English can vary greatly in style, from formal to informal. **Slang,** for example, is a very informal kind of English used by a particular group. Choose language that is appropriate for your audience and type of writing.

Look at the chart on the next page. It shows some of the characteristics that distinguish formal language from informal language.

Levels of Language

Characteristics	Formal	Informal
	Advanced vocabulary, long sentences, no contractions	Simple vocabulary, shorter sentences, contractions
Type of writing	Report, business letter, speech, job application, letter to the editor	Friendly letter, journal entry, note to your best friend
Tone	Serious, reserved	Conversational, casual

Here are some examples of the differences between formal and informal language.

Formal Students who wish to attend the concert should assemble in front of the gymnasium in the morning.

Informal Students who want to go to the concert should meet in front of the gym in the morning.

Formal If you cannot attend, please advise your teacher by 3:00 P.M. today.

Informal If you can't make it, please tell your teacher by 3:00 P.M. today.

Practice Your Skills

Rewrite the passage below in a form appropriate for sending to the mayor of your town.

The kids on our block need your help. The streets are pretty busy here. There isn't a safe place to hang out. The old lot on Elm St. would be a great place for a playground. Right now, it's got heaps of trash. Suppose we kids clean up the lot. Could you OK the change for a playground and give us some equipment?

How Can I Make My Writing Sound Like Me?

Personal Voice

When you call your friends on the phone, do you have to tell them who's calling? Of course not—they recognize your voice. How? Well, there is something unique about the way you sound and the way you put words together.

The same is true of your writing. You have a special way of choosing words and putting them together that is yours and yours alone. It's called your **writing voice.**

YOUR OWN VOICE

Have you ever tried to impress someone by using vocabulary or a formal way of talking that just isn't you? If you did, you most likely sounded unnatural—maybe even completely phony. The same thing can happen with your writing.

Young writers sometimes think they need to use big, important-sounding words and long, complicated sentences to make their writing sound grown-up and sophisticated. Often, though, their writing ends up sounding strained and unnatural. Here, for example, is how Lindsay wrote when she began keeping a journal for her writing class.

> **September 15**
> Today we have been assigned the task of keeping a writing journal. Through the coming months, we are to record our personal impressions and thoughts and use them as ideas for future writing projects. I shall attempt to observe the people and nature surrounding me and write about them in meaningful new ways.

At first, Lindsay's journal entries sounded unnatural, as if she were writing to impress some unknown reader. After several weeks, though, she began to find her own voice.

Compare this later journal entry with the first one. Which one sounds more natural to you?

> **November 9**
> It seems like we spent all weekend raking leaves and cleaning up the yard for winter. Will and I piled up a HUGE mound of leaves, then we decided to jump in it like we did when we were little. The leaves went flying. They looked like a flock of red and yellow birds settling on the grass.

LEARN BY DOING

An effective way to discover and develop your writing voice is to write as often as you can. Try these strategies.

- **Write in your journal regularly.** When Lindsay finally relaxed and wrote just for herself in her journal, she discovered her own writing voice.
- **Freewrite at the start of every writing assignment.** You'll be expressing your ideas in your own words.
- **Read your writing aloud.** When you hear your writing spoken, you can more easily tell what sounds natural.
- **Write letters to friends.** Write in the same words you would use if you were speaking to your friends.
- **Use peer readers.** Have friends read your writing. After they finish, ask them, "Is it me? Do you know this writer?"

Practice Your Skills

Read this paragraph. How would *you* express the ideas in this paragraph? Rewrite the paragraph using your own voice.

> I urge all my fellow students to take part in the process of electing officials to govern our class. When one exercises the right to vote, one is taking part in one of our nation's most cherished traditions.

WRITING
HANDBOOK
22

How Do I Make My Characters Sound Real?

Using Dialogue

Dialogue is conversation—people talking to each other. You can use dialogue in your writing to clearly *show* readers what happens and what people are like. Read the following paragraph. It doesn't use dialogue. It just tells about a conversation between two characters.

> Grandpa wanted to know how long I'd been saving the money. I told him it was two years. He was really surprised.

Now listen to the characters talking to each other.

Literary
MODEL

> "How long have you been saving this?" he asked.
> "A long time, Grandpa," I said.
> "How long?" he asked.
> I told him, "Two years."
> His mouth flew open and in a loud voice he said, "Two years!"
>
> **Wilson Rawls, *Where the Red Fern Grows***

Dialogue makes the characters seem like real people. You "hear" how surprised Grandpa is. You can picture the scene between him and his grandson as if you were there.

H OW TO USE DIALOGUE

You can use dialogue in any kind of writing, from stories to newspaper articles. By presenting people's actual words, you can both provide information and show how the people think and feel.

Providing Information Dialogue can provide information about action, characters, and setting. What can you learn about these parts of a story from the following dialogue?

> "Here I am trying to get home to cook me a bite to eat, and you snatch my pocketbook! Maybe you ain't been to your supper either, late as it be. Have you?"
>
> "There's nobody home at my house," said the boy.
>
> "Then we'll eat," said the woman. "I believe you're hungry—or been hungry—to try to snatch my pocketbook!"
>
> "I want a pair of blue suede shoes," said the boy.
>
> "Well, you didn't have to snatch my pocketbook to get some suede shoes," said Mrs. Luella Bates Washington Jones. "You could of asked me."
>
> **Langston Hughes, "Thank You, M'am"**

Showing Personalities Dialogue can also bring out the personalities of the characters and set the tone of your writing. For example, the tone could be humorous, angry, or sad. In the following example, the way the character speaks shows that he is used to ordering people around and that he is a little ridiculous. The dialogue gives the story its humorous tone.

> "I want you to get the moon," said the King. "The Princess Lenore wants the moon. If she can have the moon, she will get well again."
>
> "The moon?" exclaimed the Lord High Chamberlain, his eyes widening. This made him look four times as wise as he really was.
>
> "Yes, the moon," said the King. "M-o-o-n, moon. Get it tonight, tomorrow at the latest."
>
> **James Thurber, "Many Moons"**

Guidelines for Writing Dialogue

- Dialogue should sound like real people talking. It can include slang and sentence fragments, for example.

"Ken, did you hear me? Don't swim too far out," his mother warned.

"Yeah, yeah," he muttered. "Parents!"

- Use speaker's tags—such as "I said" and "she asked quietly" — to show who is speaking and how the words sound.

"Everybody out of the water," the lifeguard shouted.

"What's going on?" Ken asked anxiously.

- Begin a new paragraph each time the speaker changes.

"Ken," I yelled, "get out of the water! They've seen a shark."

"Wow! Let's get movin'."

- Notice that the first words of quotations are capitalized. The first words of new sentences within a quotation are also capitalized as in the first example above.

- End marks are usually placed inside quotation marks.

PROBLEM
S O L V I N G

"I'm not sure how to use periods and commas with quotation marks."

For information on punctuating dialogue, see

- Handbook 43, "Punctuation," pages 566–599

Practice Your Skills

Rewrite the story described below, using dialogue.

Carla brings her new pet frog to school. Its croaking disrupts Mr. Lugonez's social studies class. Carla tries to cover up the croaking by giving a long and complicated answer to Mr. Lugonez's social studies question, but she eventually runs out of things to say. Mr. Lugonez then asks her if she stopped talking because of a frog in her throat.

How Can I Write Better Sentences?

Correcting Sentence Errors

Sometimes you start a sentence and you keep thinking of things to add and your sentence goes on and on and you don't know when to stop. Other times a different problem. Not enough information.

Sentences like these are confusing and hard to follow. To communicate clearly, you need to revise sentences that go on and on, as well as groups of words that do not express complete thoughts. Here are some strategies you can use to write better sentences.

REVISING FRAGMENTS

A sentence expresses a complete thought. A group of words that doesn't express a complete thought is a **fragment.** A subject, a verb, or both are missing from a fragment. The groups of words below are fragments.

Missing a subject	Anxiously waited for the results
Missing a verb	The star of the show
Missing a subject and a verb	From the roof of the building

You can correct fragments by adding the missing parts.

> *The contestants* anxiously waited for the results.
> The star of the show *signed autographs for her fans.*
> *The stuntman jumped* from the roof of the building.

Yves Klein's *Saut dans le vide,* 1960, as photographed by Harry Shunk. In English, the French phrase could be translated "leap into the void."

Sometimes you can correct a fragment by adding it to a complete sentence.

Sentence	The ship was thrown off course.
Fragment	By the violent storm and strong ocean currents
Revised	The ship was thrown off course by the violent storm and strong ocean currents.

For more help with writing sentences that express complete thoughts, see Handbook 34, "Understanding Sentences," pages 338–345. For more suggestions on ways to combine sentences and sentence parts, see Handbook 24, "Sentence Combining," pages 286–291.

Revising Run-on Sentences

A **run-on sentence** expresses more than one complete thought. Sometimes there is no end mark at the end of the first thought. At other times a comma incorrectly joins two thoughts. You can correct run-ons by breaking them into separate sentences.

Run-on	Julianne plays the flute, her little sister plays the clarinet.
Revised	Julianne plays the flute. Her little sister plays the clarinet.

If the thoughts are closely related, you can use a comma and a conjunction to link them.

Run-on	The quarterback threw the football the receiver caught it.
Revised	The quarterback threw the football, and the receiver caught it.
Run-on	The music critic disliked the concert the fans loved it.
Revised	The music critic disliked the concert, but the fans loved it.

You can use the conjunctions *and, but,* and *or* to join sentences. Each word draws attention to a different type of relationship between thoughts.

REVISING STRINGY SENTENCES

In a **stringy sentence,** many thoughts are strung together with the word *and.* This type of sentence is dull to read and is often hard to follow. You can break up stringy sentences into separate sentences.

Stringy	Blue smoke curled from the stone chimney and light glowed from the windows and we caught the delicious smells of supper cooking.
Separate Ideas	Blue smoke curled from the stone chimney. Light glowed from the windows. We caught the delicious smells of supper cooking.

Sometimes writers want to string thoughts together because the ideas are related. However, it is generally better to separate the thoughts by writing them as separate sentences. Then you can use transition words and phrases to show how the thoughts are related.

Stringy	We read about the planets and we watched a movie about Venus and Mars and we went to the planetarium.
Separate Thoughts	We read about the planets. We watched a movie about Venus and Mars. We went to the planetarium.
Revised	We read about the planets. *The next day* we watched a movie about Venus and Mars. *Then* we went to the planetarium.

Correcting
Sentence Errors **283**

For more help with using transitions to link thoughts, see Handbook 11, "Transitions," on pages 234–238.

Practice Your Skills

A. Revise each sentence fragment below. Add a subject, a verb, or a subject and a verb to make a complete sentence.

1. The day before the big game
2. The lead singer of the band
3. Leaped over the fence
4. Through the secret passageway
5. Reminded me of my first piano concert

B. Correct each of the following run-on sentences.

1. We climbed all the way to the top of the hill we weren't even tired.
2. Arlyn's head ached she had the flu.
3. Jake thought the animal was an alpaca, it was a llama.
4. The theater was packed there was a line around the block.
5. The doorbell rang, the mail carrier was at the door.

C. Rewrite these stringy sentences to make the relationships between thoughts clear.

1. Brent started to walk to Kathy's house and he stopped to talk to Charlie and he stayed to play video games.
2. The wind howled outside and an owl hooted in the distance and the boards in the old house creaked.
3. I had a dream about *Alice in Wonderland* and I thought I was Alice and I chased the White Rabbit.
4. First we raked the leaves and we discovered an old baseball and we quit raking.
5. Emma knows how to use a computer and she has a program for drawing pictures and she can print the pictures in color.

Tongue Twisters

You probably know that Peter Piper picked a peck of pickled peppers. But did you know that Bonnie Bliss blows big beautiful blue bubbles? Or that old, oily Ollie oils oily autos?

Tongue twisters like these have been around for centuries. Test your tongue on these troublesome twisters [from *A Twister of Twists, a Tangler of Tongues,* a torturous collection by Alvin Schwartz].

A noisy noise annoys an oyster.

Sheep shouldn't sleep in a shack.
Sheep should sleep in a shed.

Which is the witch that wished the wicked wish?

Which wristwatches are Swiss wristwatches?

A tooter who tooted a flute
  Tried to tutor two tutors to
  toot.
Said the two to the tutor,
  "Is it harder to toot or
To tutor two tutors to toot?"

Betty Botter
  bought some butter,
But, she said,
  the butter's bitter.
If I put it
  in my batter,
It will make
  my batter bitter.
But a bit
  of better butter—
That would make
  my batter better.

Does this shop stock short socks with spots?

How Do I Fix Choppy Sentences?

Sentence Combining

A pair of jeans, a T-shirt, a vest—by themselves, these clothes might seem fairly dull. Put them together in an interesting way, though, and you've got style.

You can add style to your writing in a similar way. By combining sentences with related ideas and details, you can make your writing livelier and more interesting.

COMBINING SENTENCES
AND SENTENCE PARTS

As you review your writing, look for short, choppy sentences that give information about the same topic. Often, you can combine these sentences into one sentence that includes all the information. You can join related sentences or sentence parts with conjunctions such as *and, but,* and *or.*

Combining Complete Sentences

Sometimes two sentences contain ideas that are alike. You can join the sentences with a comma and the word *and.*

Separate   The baseball stadium is filled with fans.
               The game is about to begin.
Combined   The baseball stadium is filled with fans**, and** the
               game is about to begin.

You can use a comma and the word *but* to join two sentences that state contrasting ideas on the same topic.

Separate   The two teams are ready to play. The umpire is
               nowhere to be found.
Combined   The two teams are ready to play**, but** the umpire
               is nowhere to be found.

If two sentences offer a choice between ideas, use a comma and the word *or* to join the sentences.

Separate	Is the umpire on his way? Did he forget about the game?
Combined	Is the umpire on his way**, or** did he forget about the game?

Combining Sentence Parts

Sometimes two sentences are so closely related that some of the same words or ideas appear in both sentences. You can join those sentences by using *and, but,* or *or* and leaving out the repeated words or ideas.

Separate	Seals are speedy swimmers. *They are* skillful divers.
Combined	Seals are speedy swimmers **and** skillful divers.
Separate	Seals need to breathe air. *They* can stay underwater for more than thirty minutes at a time.
Combined	Seals need to breathe air **but** can stay underwater for more than thirty minutes at a time.
Separate	Are seals fish? *Are they* mammals?
Combined	Are seals fish **or** mammals?

Grammar
═ TIP ═

Use a comma before a conjunction that joins two complete sentences. Don't use a comma before a conjunction that joins two sentence parts.

Practice Your Skills

A. Combine each pair of sentences, using a comma and the conjunction shown in parentheses.

1. Yellowstone National Park was crowded. Most of the campgrounds were full. (*and*)
2. Did you see Old Faithful? Were you too late? (*or*)
3. A family of bears approached our car. The mother bear led her cubs away. (*but*)
4. We took our new video camera with us. My sister taped some of our adventures in the park. (*and*)

B. Combine the ideas in each pair of sentences. Leave out the words shown in italics.

1. I walked along the sandy beach. *I* looked for shells *in the sand.*
2. Pelicans dove into the water to catch fish. *The birds* often came up with their beaks empty.
3. I saw a dark shape speeding through the water. *I watched it* leaping over the waves.
4. Was that a dolphin? *Could it have been* a killer whale?

ADDING WORDS TO SENTENCES

Using *and, but,* or *or* to connect related ideas is just one way to make your writing livelier. You can also take important words from two or more related sentences and put them together to make a new sentence.

Adding Single Words

You can join sentences by taking an important word from one sentence and adding it to another. Leave out the rest of the words.

Separate	The jet rolled quickly down the runway. *The jet was* gleaming.
Combined	The **gleaming** jet rolled quickly down the runway.
Separate	The jet waited to leave the airport. *The plane was* huge. *The airport was* busy.
Combined	The **huge** jet waited to leave the **busy** airport.

When you add more than one word to the main sentence, you may need to use a comma or the word *and.*

Separate	Bats poured out of the cave. *The cave was* cool. *It also was* dark.
Combined	Bats poured out of the **cool, dark** cave.

Separate	A flock of bats flew over the sleeping city. *The bats flew* swiftly. *They moved* silently.
Combined	A flock of bats flew **swiftly and silently** over the sleeping city.

Sometimes the group of words can be put in more than one place in the new sentence.

Combined	**Swiftly and silently,** a flock of bats flew over the sleeping city.

Adding Words That Change Form

In some cases you must change the form of a word before you add it to another sentence. For example, you may have to add *-y* to the end of the word.

Separate	I threw my jeans into the washer. *They were covered with* dirt.
Combined	I threw my **dirty** jeans into the washer.

You may need to use the *-ed* or *-ing* form of the word.

Separate	Then I mended the hem. *It had begun to* rip.
Combined	Then I mended the **ripped** hem.

Separate	I love these jeans. *They are starting to* fade.
Combined	I love these **fading** jeans.

You might have to add *-ly* to the word before you use it in the new sentence.

Separate	I changed into my jeans. *I was* quick.
Combined	I **quickly** changed into my jeans.

Sometimes a word ending in *-ly* fits in more than one place in the new sentence. Pick the place that best suits your meaning.

Combined	**Quickly,** I changed into my jeans. I changed into my jeans **quickly.**

Practice Your Skills

A. Combine each group of sentences, following any instructions in parentheses. Omit the words in italics.

1. My friend Ali competed in a race. *It was a* bicycle *race. The race was* yesterday.
2. The weather was hard on the racers. *The day was* hot. *The air felt* humid. (Use *and.*)
3. The race followed a trail up a mountain. *The mountain looked* huge. *The trail was* steep.
4. Ali rode his new mountain bike along the trail in the race. *The path was* rough.
5. He steered around the big rocks in the road. *He tried to be* careful. (Use *-ly.*)
6. On our map we traced Ali's route up the mountain. *The road seemed to* wind *back and forth.* (Use *-ing.*)
7. We met the cyclists at the end of the race. *They were all* exhausted. *The race had been* difficult.
8. After the race everyone drank lemonade. *The lemonade tasted* cool. *It made a* refreshing *drink.* (Use a comma.)

B. Combine the sentences in each of the following groups, leaving out any unnecessary words. You may need to change the forms of some words.

1. Thousands of people streamed into the stadium for the skating competition. The crowd made a lot of noise.
2. When the stadium lights dimmed, a hush fell over the audience. The audience was excited.
3. In the spotlight we saw a skater in a green costume. Her costume sparkled. It was a dress with many ruffles.
4. As the music began, she skated across the ice. Her movements were slow. She skated gracefully.
5. The skater completed many jumps. The jumps were complicated. She performed them perfectly.
6. The crowd cheered when this skater won a medal. She won a silver medal. Everyone was delighted.

ADDING GROUPS OF WORDS
TO SENTENCES

Sometimes a group of words in one sentence can add important information to another sentence. You can move the word group from one sentence to the other. If the words you move tell something about a person, a thing, or an action in the other sentence, put them near the name of the person, thing, or action.

Separate	Mom asked me to wash the dog. *She asked me twice today.*
Combined	Mom asked me **twice today** to wash the dog.

However, the group of words might make sense in more than one place in the new sentence.

Twice today, Mom asked me to wash the dog.

Practice Your Skills

A. Combine each pair of sentences by moving a word group from one sentence to the other. Omit the words in italics.

1. The woman is my grandmother. *She is* wearing a ring.
2. Grandma moved here in 1940. *She came here* from Norway.
3. The most important thing she brought with her was a ring. *It is a* beautiful ruby *ring.*
4. Grandma lost her ring. *She lost it* the year I was born.

B. Combine each pair of sentences by adding important words from one sentence to the other sentence.

1. The postcard is from Grandfather. It is on the table.
2. He is visiting Mexico. He is there for the winter.
3. The card shows the ruins of an ancient city. The city is called Chichén Itzá.
4. Chichén Itzá was built by the Maya. They built the city hundreds of years ago.

Writing
TIP

After you join two sentences, read the new sentence carefully. Words added in the wrong place can make a sentence confusing, wrong, or even funny—for example, "Mom asked me to wash the dog *twice today.*"

Sketch Book

- What kind of book would you like to write? Jot down some thoughts about what your book would be like.
- What fascinates you? Make a list of things you would like to find out more about.
- What is the most interesting thing you have learned in school this year? Tell why it is important to you.

Academic Skills

Whether you write them or read them, books can take you to new worlds. To get the most out of these worlds, you need to be able to read, study, think, and research effectively.

The handbooks that follow can teach you skills that will help you explore new worlds, in school and on your own.

How Can I Become a Better Student?

Study and Research Skills

Do you ever wish that it were possible just to open up your head and pour in knowledge? Unfortunately, learning doesn't work that way. To get the most out of your studies, you need to actively participate in the learning process. There are skills you can learn that will make your study time more efficient and enjoyable.

THE KWL APPROACH

Whether you are reading a textbook, doing a research report, or working on a project, using the KWL approach is a good way to focus your thinking. The letters stand for three questions you should ask yourself about your subject:

"What do I already know about my subject?" Before you start studying, make a list of everything you already know about the subject. The list will get you thinking about the subject and about what you don't yet know.

"What do I want to know?" Make a list of the things you would like to know about the subject. As you study, see if you find the answers to your questions.

"What did I learn?" After you have studied the subject, look back and list the things you have learned. Are there still things you want to know? Have your thoughts about the subject changed?

LEARNING LOGS

Writing about a subject helps you understand it better and often prompts you to think about things you hadn't noticed before. One of the best ways to take charge of your learning is to keep a learning log. A **learning log** is a journal you keep for one subject. Like your writing journal, your learning log is a place to record ideas, thoughts, and questions. You might want to keep separate learning logs for each of your subjects.

All sorts of things can go into a learning log. It is a perfect place to record your answers to the KWL questions and to note key facts about the subject. You can write about your reactions to the things you are learning and ask yourself questions about things you don't understand. You can also draw pictures or graphic aids to help you understand the subject.

<u>Science Journal</u>

4/13 Alligators and Crocodiles
   <u>K</u>: reptiles, look like floating logs, dangerous huge teeth, short legs, alligators live in swamps in Florida
   <u>W</u>: How are alligators and crocodiles different? How can you tell them apart? Do they both attack people?

4/14 Field trip to the zoo
   <u>L</u>: I touched an alligator! Alligators aren't as ferocious as crocodiles. The zookeeper could hold the alligator's snout shut with one hand because the muscles to open the jaws are pretty weak. Alligators usually avoid people, but crocodiles will attack. One way to tell them apart is by the shape of the snout.

alligator snout:

crocodile snout:

It would be fun to actually see alligators in the wild! Where besides Florida could I find them?

Try these ideas to make the most of your study time.

- **Keep track of assignments.** Use a special assignment notebook to record exactly what is expected, what materials you will need, and when the assignment is due.
- **Plan ahead.** Schedule your activities on a weekly calendar to make sure you have time for everything.
- **Keep a separate notebook or folder for each subject.**
- **Take notes as you study.** Include only the main ideas.
- **Review your notes as soon as you can.** Revise or add to them as needed, and highlight important points.

Writing **TIP**

Your notes are for your eyes only. Don't worry about grammar, punctuation, and spelling. Feel free to use abbreviations and to make up symbols.

Memorizing

Do you think some people are born with good and bad memories, just as some people are tall and others short? Actually, there are skills anyone can learn to improve memory.

- **Write it, recite it.** The action of writing and the sound of your voice will help you remember information.
- **Find connections between items.** For example, remember items in the order they happened or recall items alphabetically.
- **Create a crazy picture.** Arrange the facts you want to remember in a vivid picture in your mind. Then, when you want to recall those facts, visualize the same picture.
- **Make up catchy sayings.** Develop a sentence or phrase using the initials of the words you want to memorize. For example, HOMES could help you remember the names of the Great Lakes: *H*uron, *O*ntario, *M*ichigan, *E*rie, and *S*uperior.

A crazy picture can help you remember that *core* is the innermost part of the earth.

Practice Your Skills

A. Use the KWL approach to write a learning log entry about one of the topics below. First make a list that tells what you already know about the subject. Then list what you want to know about the subject.

pyramids	Olympic Games	sharks
lasers	earthquakes	Australia

B. Obtain a list of the nine planets of the solar system. Use a memorizing strategy to learn the planets. Explain your strategy.

C. Memorize the basic four food groups important for good nutrition: dairy products, meat, fruits and vegetables, and grains. Make up a saying in which each word begins with the first letter of one of the groups.

D. Read the selection below, taking notes as you read. Then share your notes with a small group of classmates. Discuss the main idea of the selection and develop a list of things the group would like to know about the subject.

> It's like being inside a video game. You are in an artificial world where you can interact with the computer-generated objects around you. You might see a ticking clock and decide to pick it up. You watch as your hand reaches down and grabs the clock. You bring it closer and the ticking gets louder. It is not reality. But it isn't just computer graphics either. It's virtual reality.
>
> Virtual reality is a very advanced form of computer simulation. Already, it is being used for everything from letting architects walk through houses before they are built to helping scientists study the surface of Mars. And one day it may be as much a part of your schoolwork as a notebook and pen.
>
> **Nancy Day, "Get Real!"** *Odyssey,* **June 1992**

How Can I Become a Better Reader?

Reading Skills

Sprinters dash toward the finish line as fast as possible. In contrast, marathon runners carefully pace themselves so that they have enough energy to finish the race. No single method or plan will work for every runner or every race. Similarly, good readers learn to vary the way they read depending on their purpose for reading.

TYPES OF READING

You read for a variety of purposes—to learn about a subject, to find enjoyment, or to locate some specific fact or piece of information. Depending on the kind of material you are reading and your purpose, you may read very quickly or quite slowly and carefully.

Skimming and Scanning

Skimming is a kind of fast reading that helps you get a general idea of what a book or passage is about. To skim, read the most important parts and skip everything else. Look for titles, headings, italicized words, and any pictures, charts, or graphs.

This method of reading is also a useful technique for study and review. Skim headings and topic sentences and then recall specific details.

Scanning is a speedy way to find a specific piece of information. Think of searching for an object with a flashlight. The beam of light focuses on a very small area. Similarly, when you scan, you glance quickly over the page until you spot key words or phrases that show you are near the information you need. Use this skill for tasks such as locating a name and number in the phone book or a certain date in an encyclopedia article.

In-depth Reading

The goal of **in-depth reading** is to get everything you can from a piece of writing. Here are some techniques for in-depth reading.

1. Preview   Read the first paragraph of a selection to get a general idea of the topic. Also read titles and headings and look over any charts and graphs. Skim the first sentence of paragraphs within the body of a selection and then read the last paragraph. Writers often summarize or draw conclusions in this last paragraph.

2. Read   After you preview, go back and read carefully. Look at topic sentences for key terms and main ideas. Focus on details. Notice how ideas fit together and reread passages until the meaning really sinks in.

3. React and record   Respond to the author's ideas. Do you agree or disagree? Take notes as you read and list any questions you may have.

Writing
TIP

As you read, use your journal, reading log, or notebook to record your questions, reactions, and opinions. Also jot down key information.

USING THE PARTS OF A BOOK

Knowing how to use three parts of nonfiction books can help you locate information efficiently.

Three Parts of a Nonfiction Book

	Table of Contents	Glossary	Index
Where:	Front of the book	Usually back of book	Back of the book
What:	Chapter titles and chapter page numbers	Defines special words used in the book	Lists important topics with page numbers
Use:	Gives an overview of the book. Tells you if the book meets your needs and interests	Quick and easy source for definitions	Helps you find specific details quickly and easily

Graphic aids arrange information in a visual way. For example, one type of graphic aid is a table. What does the table below tell you about different types of graphic aids?

Types of Graphic Aids

	Purpose	Reading Tips
Photograph	Puts ideas into picture form	Read the title or caption.
Diagram	Identifies parts of an object	Read all the labels.
Map	Shows land areas and bodies of water	Read the title and study the symbols in the map key.
Tables and Charts	Presents groups of facts—often in column form	Read the title and column headings.
Graph	Shows how facts or sets of numbers are related	Read the title, symbol key, and all printed text.

UNDERSTANDING GRAPHS

Two common types of graphs are the bar graph and the circle graph. The **circle graph,** or pie chart, is drawn like a pie. Each wedge or slice shows how parts relate to the whole. Compare the size of each slice in the pie chart on the next page. Which "slice" is the largest? What does this tell you?

A **bar graph** uses the lengths of bars to show relationships. Often numbers run along the bottom of the graph, and words run along the left side. What is the subject of the bar graph on the next page?

Most Popular Restaurant Desserts

Ice Cream 30%
Mousse 16%
Pie 16%
Chocolate Cake 20%
Cheesecake 18%

Source: Survey of 400 adults for advertising campaign.

What People Fear Most

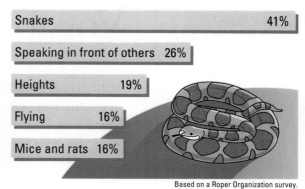

Snakes	41%
Speaking in front of others	26%
Heights	19%
Flying	16%
Mice and rats	16%

Based on a Roper Organization survey.

Practice Your Skills

A. Answer the questions below about "Take Tracks Home" on pages 94–95 by using the reading strategies shown in parentheses.

1. (Skim) What is the main idea of the passage?
2. (Scan) How long does it take for the plaster cast to harden?
3. (Read in depth) How can you make your own set of plaster casts of tracks?

B. Tell whether you would use the table of contents, glossary, or index in this book to answer the following questions. Then answer the questions.

1. Which pages tell you how to use question marks in quotations?
2. What is the definition of "brainstorming"?
3. What topics are found in Handbook 30, "Thinking Skills"?

C. Answer these questions by referring to the graphs in this lesson.

1. What two categories of things are people least afraid of? How do the numbers in these two categories compare?
2. Which is ordered more often, pie or cheesecake?

How Can I Increase My Vocabulary?

Vocabulary Skills

Like Lucy, have you ever struggled to find just the right word to say what you mean? When you have a strong vocabulary, you won't need to invent strange new words to express your ideas. Instead, you'll be able to communicate clearly right from the start. Here are some simple techniques you can use to increase your vocabulary.

Strategies for Building Vocabulary

Read	One of the easiest ways to build your vocabulary is to do a lot of reading. As you read about many subjects, you will learn a variety of new words.
Ask about meanings of unfamiliar words	When you come across a word you don't understand, ask what the word means. Such questioning is a good way to help you learn about new words.
Keep vocabulary lists	Keep your own list of new words. Write down the new words you read or hear each day in your journal or another notebook. Use a dictionary to look up the words you've listed. Next to each word write its definition.
Write sentences	Create sentences using the new words you have listed and defined. Whenever you use a new word in your writing, you are more likely to remember it.

There are other skills you can develop to help you figure out the meanings of words. Like a detective, you can look for clues. So get out your magnifying glass and become a word sleuth as you learn new ways to unlock word meanings.

USING CONTEXT CLUES

You may find important clues to a word's meaning in its **context,** or the words and pictures around it. These context clues often take the form of definitions, restatements, or examples.

Definitions and Restatements

Sometimes a writer tells you what an unfamiliar word means. The writer may define the word directly or restate its meaning in other words. Here's one example:

> The researcher checked the readings on a *seismograph,* which is a device used to measure earthquakes.

In this sentence, the writer provides a definition of the word *seismograph.* The sentence tells you that *seismograph* means "a device used to measure earthquakes."

Now look at these examples:

> He was a *vagabond,* a wanderer, who traveled the world on his bicycle.

> In 1774, the British placed an *embargo* on Boston Harbor. In other words, they prevented ships from entering or leaving the harbor.

In these sentences, the writer restates the meaning of the words *vagabond* and *embargo.* Whenever you read, look for the following key-word clues. They often signal a definition or restatement.

Key Words That Signal a Definition or Restatement

that is	or	this means
in other words	which is	also called

Examples

Sometimes a writer will give you an example that helps you understand the meaning of an unfamiliar word.

> Most *amphibians,* such as frogs and toads, feed on insects.

The sentence above tells you that frogs and toads are two examples of amphibians. These examples give you an idea about the meaning of the word *amphibians.*

Sometimes the example itself is an unfamiliar word. In such a case, you may be able to use the general term to help you understand the meaning of the new word.

> Weather instruments, such as the thermometer and the *barometer,* can help meteorologists forecast the weather days or even weeks in advance.

Although you may be unfamiliar with the term *barometer,* the context clues tell you that a barometer is a type of weather instrument.

In the sample sentences above, the writers use the words *such as* to introduce the examples. Here are other words that writers often use to introduce examples.

Key Words That Signal an Example

and other	for example	like
especially	for instance	these

USING WORD PARTS

An unfamiliar word is like a secret code. Sometimes you can crack the code by breaking the word into its parts. Each word part has its own meaning. Once you know what each part means, you can put the parts together to figure out the meaning of the whole word.

Base Words

The main word to which other word parts are added is called the **base word.** When you add a word part to a base word, you form a new word. For example, you can add the word part *mis-* to the base word *direct* to form *misdirect,* a word that means "to direct wrongly." In the same way, you can add the word part *-or* to the base word *direct* to form *director* a word that means "a person who directs."

direct   mis**direct**   **direct**or

Prefixes

A **prefix** is a word part that is added to the beginning of a base word. A prefix changes a base word to a new word with a new meaning. When you know the meanings of common prefixes, you can often figure out the meanings of unfamiliar words that contain those prefixes.

For example, look at the word *illegible.* The prefix *il-* means "not." The base word *legible* means "able to be read." So *illegible* means "not able to be read."

Here are some common prefixes and their meanings.

Prefixes	Meanings	Examples
il-, im-, in-, ir-	not	illegal, impossible, insane, irregular
mis-	wrong	mislead, misplace
non-	not, without	nonfat, nonsense
pre-	before	preheat, prehistory, preschool
re-	again	reappear, rebuild, recharge, reconsider
un-	not	unexpected, uncommon

Keep in mind that not all word parts that look like prefixes are prefixes. For example, the *mis-* in *missile* is not a prefix because *-sile* is not a base word. When you analyze word parts, watch out for prefix look-alikes.

Suffixes

A **suffix** is a word part that is added to the end of a base word. Like a prefix, a suffix changes a base word to a new word with a new meaning. For example, the suffix *-ous* means "full of" or "having." When *-ous* is added to the base word *danger,* the new word *dangerous* means "full of danger." When *-ous* is added to *courage,* the new word *courageous* means "having courage."

Here are some common suffixes and their meanings.

Suffixes	Meanings	Examples
-able, -ible	capable of being	washable, collapsible
-en	to make	lengthen, frighten
-er, -or	a person who does	teacher, governor
-ily	in what manner	speedily, happily
-ful, -ous	full of	successful, joyous
-hood, -ness	state of	falsehood, statehood, kindness, goodness
-less	without	heartless, restless
-like	relating to	childlike, lifelike

Practice Your Skills

A. Use the context clues in each sentence to write a definition of the word in italics. Check your definition in a dictionary.

1. Our new neighbor is a *polyglot*—that is, she can speak several languages.
2. They put the pottery in a *kiln,* or oven.
3. Some *condiments,* especially mustard, can really make food appealing.

TIP

Sometimes the spelling of the base word changes when you add a suffix to it. If you're not sure about the spelling, check a dictionary.

4. The cages held *quetzals* and other tropical birds.
5. Sue is *ambidextrous*—that is, she can use both hands with equal ease.
6. Some *predators,* such as wolves and hyenas, hunt in packs.
7. The concert tickets were *complimentary;* in other words, she got them for free.
8. Some mythological creatures, like the *griffin,* combine the features of several different animals.
9. We heard a *quintet,* a group of five musicians, play folk songs.
10. *Carcinogens,* like cigarette smoke, are the focus of studies on the causes of cancer.

B. Look up the following words in a dictionary. Then use each word in a sentence that contains context clues to the meaning of the word.

1. veranda   2. opulence   3. marsupial   4. artifact

C. Use what you learned about word parts in this handbook to answer the following questions.

1. If *zeal* means "strong feelings" or "intense support for a cause," what does *zealous* mean?
2. If *daunt* means "to discourage," what is a *dauntless* person?
3. If *belligerent* means "ready to fight," what does *nonbelligerent* mean?
4. If *classify* means "to place in a class or category," what does *reclassify* mean?
5. If *attain* means "to gain through effort," what does *attainable* mean?
6. If *natal* means "dating from birth," what does *prenatal* mean?
7. If *toxic* means "poisonous," what does *nontoxic* mean?
8. If *spite* means "feeling of anger or annoyance toward someone," what does *spiteful* mean?

Where Can I Find Information About Words?

Using the Dictionary and the Thesaurus

Mark Twain wrote, "The difference between the *almost right* word and the *right* word is . . . the difference between the lightning bug and the lightning." How can you capture lightning in your writing? A dictionary and a thesaurus can help you find just the right words.

USING A DICTIONARY

You know that a dictionary contains the spellings and definitions of words. There is, however, much more information packed into this helpful book. To use a dictionary effectively you first must know how it is organized.

Alphabetical Order

The words that appear in a dictionary are called **entry words.** Like the names in a phone book, the entry words in a dictionary are listed in alphabetical order—the order of the letters in the alphabet.

Words that begin with the same first letter, such as *elephant* and *envelope,* are alphabetized by the second letter. Words that have the same first and second letters, such as *festival* and *fertile,* are alphabetized by the third letter, and so on.

Guide Words

The two words in boldface type at the top of each page of a dictionary are called **guide words.** Guide words can help you find words in a dictionary quickly and easily.

The guide word on the left tells you the first entry word on that page. The guide word on the right tells you the last entry word on that page. As you flip through a dictionary searching for a word, the guide words can help you quickly find the right page. When the word you're looking for falls alphabetically between two guide words, you're on the right page.

drill / drone   **417**

thread⟧ a coarse linen or cotton cloth with a diagonal weave, used for work clothes, uniforms, etc.
drill⁴(dril) *n.* ⟦< ? native term⟧ a short-tailed, bright-cheeked monkey *(Mandrillus leucophaeus)* native to W Africa, resembling the mandrill but smaller

Dictionary Entries

The information a dictionary gives about an entry word is called a **dictionary entry.** Each entry has several parts, as you can see in the example at the top of the next page.

Entry Word   The first part of a dictionary entry is the entry word. In most dictionaries, spaces or centered dots divide the entry word into syllables. Knowing how a word is divided into syllables enables you to hyphenate words correctly.

Pronunciation   The next part of a dictionary entry is the **pronunciation guide,** often shown in parentheses. The pronunciation guide is a respelling of the word using symbols that stand for sounds. These symbols are explained in a **pronunciation key,** which often is found at the bottom of a dictionary's right-hand pages or at the front of the dictionary.

In the pronunciation guide, words of more than one syllable are shown with accent marks (´). These marks tell you which syllables to emphasize when you pronounce the word.

Part of Speech   Most dictionaries tell you the part of speech of each entry word. Some words can be used as more than one part of speech. In those cases, the dictionary defines each part of speech separately. Notice in the dictionary entry on page 310 that *surprise* is defined first as a verb **(vt.).**

Word Origin   Next the dictionary entry shows the origin of the word—how the word developed from words in other languages. In the entry for *surprise,* **ME** stands for Middle English, and **OFr** stands for Old French. The abbreviations used are explained in the front of the dictionary.

Entry word ——

Pronunciation guide   Part of speech   Word origin

sur·prise (sər prīz´, sə prīz´) **vt. -prised´, -pris´ing** ⟦ME *surprysen* <
OFr *surpris,* pp. of *sorprendre,* to surprise, take napping < *sur-* (see
SUR-¹) + *prendre,* to take (see PRIZE²)⟧ **1** to come upon suddenly or
Definition ———— unexpectedly; take unawares **2** to attack or capture suddenly and
without warning **3** *a)* to cause to feel wonder or astonishment by

Synonyms——— ***SYN.* —surprise,** in this connection, implies an affecting with wonder
because of being unexpected, unusual, etc. *[*I'm *surprised* at your
concern*];* **astonish** implies a surprising with something that seems
unbelievable *[*to *astonish* with sleight of hand*];* **amaze** suggests an
astonishing that causes bewilderment or confusion *[amazed* at the

Definition   The definition tells you what the entry word
means. Many words have more than one definition, and the
different definitions are numbered. Usually the oldest definition
is given first and the newest definition is given last.

Synonyms   Following the definition, a dictionary may
provide **synonyms,** or words with similar meanings.

Using a thesaurus

A thesaurus contains synonyms and antonyms for commonly used words. Synonyms are words that have similar
meanings. **Antonyms** are words that have opposite meanings.
A thesaurus can help you find the word that best expresses the
meaning you have in mind.

Some thesauruses are organized alphabetically. Others have
an index at the end. The index tells you where to find the
synonyms for a specific word.

Suppose you have used the word *ran. Ran* is a general verb
that means "to move quickly." Perhaps a more specific verb
would make what you have written more interesting or exciting.
Look at the thesaurus entry for *run* at the top of the next page.

> **run,** *v.* [To go swiftly by physical effort] —*Syn.* rush, hurry, spring, bound, scurry, skitter, scramble, scoot, travel, run off *or* away, dash ahead *or* at *or* on, put on a burst of speed, go on the double, have effect, go on the double-quick, hasten (off), light out, have a free play, make tracks, dart (ahead), gallop, canter, lope, spring, trot, single-foot, amble, pace, flee, speed, spurt, swoop, bolt, race, shoot, tear, whisk, scamper, scuttle.

Words like *bound, scramble, dart,* and *scamper* are all more specific than the word *run. Bound,* for example, means "to move by leaping" and might be a better verb to describe the way a dog runs after a squirrel.

Practice Your Skills

A. Use a dictionary to to find the answer to each of the following questions.

1. From what language did the word *plumage* come? What did it mean originally?
2. What parts of speech can *record* be?
3. How would you pronounce *echidna?* What syllable would you emphasize?
4. What does *gregarious* mean?
5. What is a synonym for *ridiculous?*

B. For each of the following sentences, look up each word in italics in a thesaurus. Then rewrite each sentence using a more precise word.

1. The car *went* slowly up the mountain road.
2. The hungry children *ate* the pizza.
3. The detective *looked* at the footprints in the snow.
4. The exhausted marathon runner *walked* across the finish line.
5. She *carried* the overloaded suitcase through the airport.

WRITING
HANDBOOK

29

Library Skills

Imagine that there was one place where you could do all of these things: listen to a compact disc, use a computer, find a movie, see an art display, read a book. There is such a place—the library. You can find these resources and more in most libraries today. A world of information, ideas, and activities is available to you at the library.

THE SECTIONS OF THE LIBRARY

You may be surprised at what you can find in the library, if you just know where to look. Most libraries are arranged into the following sections.

Library Floor Plan

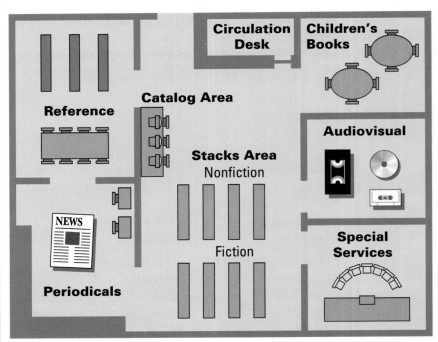

The Way Books Are Arranged

Librarians divide books into two main types, fiction and nonfiction.

Fiction   Made-up stories, such as novels and short stories, are fiction. Fiction books are grouped together in one part of the stacks and arranged alphabetically according to the author's last name. For example, a book by Lewis Carroll will be shelved under *C.* If the library has more than one book by the same author, the books by that author will be arranged alphabetically by the first word of the title. Words like *a, an,* and *the* are skipped when alphabetizing. Some libraries keep collections of short stories in a special section of the stacks.

Nonfiction   Books that provide factual information about people, events, and other subjects are nonfiction. They are arranged according to their subject. Libraries use special numbering systems to group nonfiction books into broad subject categories. Most school libraries use the Dewey Decimal System to classify books.

Dewey Decimal System

000-099	General Works	Encyclopedias, directories
100-199	Philosophy	Self-help, psychology
200-299	Religion	The Bible, mythology, theology
300-399	Social Science	Politics, education, folklore
400-499	Language	Languages, dictionaries
500-599	Science	Mathematics, astronomy, geology
600-699	Useful Arts	Computers, cooking, business, cars
700-799	Fine Arts	Music, painting, acting, sports
800-899	Literature	Poetry, plays, essays
900-999	History	Biography, travel, geography

Many libraries have a special area in the nonfiction stacks for biographies and autobiographies. These books are shelved alphabetically according to the last name of the person the book is about. Reference books are also nonfiction books, but they usually are kept in a separate section of the library.

Using Call Numbers

Every nonfiction book in a library has a **call number.** The call number is like a street address. It tells you the location of the book in the stacks. In libraries that use the Dewey Decimal System, the call number is based on the book's Dewey number. Libraries that use other classification systems have different call-number codes.

A call number may show other information, such as the author's initials or **section letters.** Section letters tell you in which section of the library you can find the book. Here are some commonly used section letters:

R, REF = Reference	B, BIO = Biography
C, CHILD = Children's	X, J, JUV = Juvenile
X, Y, YA = Young Adult	F, FIC = Fiction
A V = Audiovisual	P, PER = Periodicals
SF = Science Fiction	MYS = Mystery

Call numbers are usually printed on the book's spine. Look at one library's call number for the book *The Mysterious World of Caves* by Ernst Bauer.

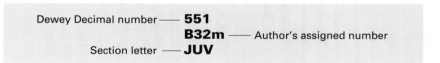

Dewey Decimal number —— **551**
B32m —— Author's assigned number
Section letter —— **JUV**

This book would be found in the children's section of the library. It would be shelved between books that have the Dewey Decimal numbers 550 and 552.

LIBRARY CATALOGS

When you want to know if the library has a book you are looking for, you can use a library catalog, which lists every book the library has. Entries in the library catalog give you a great deal of information about a book, including what the book is about and where you can find it.

Some libraries use card catalogs—file cabinets filled with cards that list information for every item you can check out. Other libraries have computer catalogs. You type in key words, such as the subject or the title of the book. Then complete publication information appears on a computer screen for all the titles that match your request. For more about computer catalogs, see page 627 of the Access Guide.

Catalog Entries

There are three ways to look for a book in a library catalog. You can look up the subject, the author, or the title of the book. Each of these three types of entries shows the same basic information about a book, but the specific details may appear in a different order for each type.

Subject Entries   Do you want to learn more about caves for a class report? A good way to start would be to look under *Caves* in the subject entries of the library catalog. You would probably find several books listed. This subject entry for *The Mysterious World of Caves* is an example from a card catalog. Notice all the information it provides.

Subject Card

Call number	CAVES — Subject
	Bauer, Ernst — Author
x551	The mysterious world of caves — Title
B32m	[by] Ernst Bauer.
	New York: F. Watts, 1971 — Copyright date
Publisher	129 p. : illus.
Length	
Illustrated	

Author Entries   Suppose you especially enjoyed reading *Where the Red Fern Grows* by Wilson Rawls, and you would like to find another of his books. This time you would start by looking up the author's last name in the author entries section of the library catalog. You will find entries for all the library's books by Wilson Rawls. Here is a sample of a single computer catalog entry you might find after doing a search of all the listings for Wilson Rawls. Notice that this computer entry gives the same kinds of information that the card-catalog entry does.

Computer Catalog Author Entry

```
     AUTHOR:   Rawls, Wilson
      TITLE:   Summer of the Monkeys
  PUBLISHER:   Doubleday [1976]
DESCRIPTION:   239 p.


## ----Call number ------Material          Location
1      Y                  Young Adult Book  Jr. Hi Room
```

Title Entries   Suppose you needed a book called *The Wright Brothers* for a report about airplanes. How would you find out if this book was in your library? You could look up the title in the library catalog. In a card catalog, title entries are listed alphabetically by the first word in the title. Remember, though, that *A, An,* and *The* do not count as first words for alphabetizing. For example, *The Wright Brothers* is listed under *W,* not *T.* Notice that in a title entry, the first line shows the title of the book, not the author's name as in an author entry.

Title Card

```
          WRIGHT BROTHERS, THE
     Y       (by) Freedman, Russell
     629.13   The Wright Brothers
          New York: Holiday House, 1991
          129 p.: illus.
```

R EFERENCE WORKS

What's the capital of India? How does photosynthesis happen? Who won the Super Bowl in 1992? You can find the answers to these questions and just about any others you might have by looking in the reference section of the library. Your librarian can help you find the works that have the information you are looking for. Here are some of the most common types of reference works. Many of these are available on-line.

Library Reference Materials

Reference Source	Contents	Examples
Encyclopedias	articles on a wide range of topics	*The World Book Encyclopedia*
Almanacs and Yearbooks	up-to-date facts, statistics, and unusual information	*Guinness Book of World Records, Information Please Almanac*
Atlases	maps and geographical information	*Hammond World Atlas*
Periodicals	newspaper and magazine articles	*USA Today, National Geographical World*

COMPUTER
TIP

Many libraries have computer indexes for finding periodical articles.For more about accessing on-line reference sources, see pages 628–631 of the Access Guide.

Calvin and Hobbes
by Bill Watterson

Using the Encyclopedia

The reference work you will probably turn to most often for your school work is the encyclopedia. You can use an encyclopedia to find information on a wide variety of subjects. This information will be helpful to you when you write research papers or other pieces of informative writing. You can also browse through the volumes to get ideas for topics you could write about or just to learn some interesting facts.

You will find encyclopedia articles arranged alphabetically by subject, or you can look up your topic in the index. This sample page from *The World Book Encyclopedia* shows many features that can help you learn about a subject.

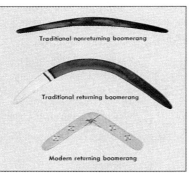

Benjamin Ruhe Collection (WORLD BOOK photo by Vince Finnigan & Assoc.)

Many boomerangs are made of wood, such as the Australian ones shown above. Nonreturning boomerangs are used as tools and weapons. Returning types are thrown mainly for sport.

Boomerang is a curved, flat implement that is thrown as a weapon or for sport. Most boomerangs are made of wood or plastic. Boomerangs measure from 1 to $6\frac{1}{2}$ feet (0.3 to 2 meters) long and $\frac{1}{2}$ to 5 inches (1.3 to 13 centimeters) wide. They weigh from 1 to 80 ounces (30 to 2,300 grams). Boomerangs spin when thrown correctly, and some boomerangs are shaped so they return to the thrower.

Boomerangs are commonly associated with the Aborigines, the original people of Australia, who use them for hunting and many other specialized tasks. However, scientists believe boomerangs were developed independently by a number of prehistoric hunting peoples. Ancient boomerangs have been found in many parts of the world, including Africa, Asia, Europe, and North America.

Kinds of boomerangs. There are two kinds of boomerangs, *returning* and *nonreturning.* Returning

Some Aborigines decorate boomerangs with carved or painted designs that are related to their legends and traditions. They treat these decorated boomerangs with respect and use them in religious ceremonies. The Aborigines also clap boomerangs together to provide rhythm for songs and chants.

How a boomerang flies. A boomerang's flight depends on its shape and size and how it is thrown. Winds also influence its flight. Most boomerangs have a bend near the middle that forms two wings shaped like airplane wings. Each wing is flat on the bottom and curved on top. One edge is thicker than the other. As a boomerang spins wing over wing in flight, its shape causes lower air pressure above each wing than below it. This difference in pressure helps keep the boomerang airborne. Some boomerangs have a shallow, hollowed-out area on the underside of one wing to provide added lift. See **Aerodynamics** (Principles of aerodynamics).

Forces acting on the boomerang, combined with its spin, make it follow a curved path in the air. A skillful thrower can make a returning boomerang travel about 150 feet (45 meters) before it begins its return. Nonreturning boomerangs can be thrown about 300 feet (90 meters). Hanns Peter

Parts of a returning boomerang

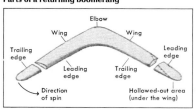

Each wing has a flat bottom and a curved top. When thrown, the boomerang spins forward so the leading edges cut through the air. The hollowed-out area helps the boomerang gain height.

Practice Your Skills

A. Arrange these fiction books in the order in which you would find them in the fiction stacks.

> Blume, Judy. *Deenie*
> Peck, Richard. *Ghosts I Have Been*
> Bonham, Frank. *Chief*
> Blume, Judy. *It's Not the End of the World*
> Rodgers, Mary. *Freaky Friday*

B. Refer to the Dewey Decimal System chart on page 313. Write the number category for books on each of these topics:

1. the history of Greece
2. ice hockey
3. automobile repair
4. Japanese poetry
5. adding and subtracting fractions

C. Which type of catalog entry—subject entry, author entry, or title entry—would you use for each situation below?

1. You want to read a book by Ursula LeGuin.
2. You want to find the book *Dragondrums*.
3. You want to find a book on beekeeping.

D. Look up one of the topics below in an encyclopedia. On your paper, write down the name of the encyclopedia, the volume number, the title of the article, the guide word at the top of the page where the article begins, any special features the article includes (such as maps, charts, or pictures), and any cross-references.

> cliff dwellers   laser
> Mohandas Gandhi   volcano

Gandhi beside his spinning wheel, 1946, as photographed by Margaret Bourke-White.

How Can I Present My Ideas Convincingly?

Thinking Skills

"Mom, I want to go to Cheryl's party because it's really important to me. Everyone will be there, and either I show up or I'll be labeled for life!"

Have you ever made a plea like this one? If you have, you probably weren't too successful. To present your ideas clearly and convincingly, you need to think critically. You must be able to judge whether an argument is logical, truthful, and based on facts rather than just on feelings. Then you can judge both your own ideas and those presented to you by others.

COMMON ERRORS IN REASONING

How can you decide whether the ideas in your writing make sense? Study the following common errors in reasoning. Watch for errors like these in your own writing.

Overgeneralization   An overgeneralization is a statement that is too broad or general to be true in every case.

> Everyone wants to be rich and famous someday.

This may seem to be true, but think about it. Although everyone may wish to be successful, success may not mean wealth and fame to everyone. Be careful about using such words as *everyone, no one, always,* and *never* in your writing. Would words such as *most, few, usually,* and *seldom* be more accurate?

Circular Reasoning   This error occurs when someone tries to support a statement by simply restating it in different words.

> Michele is the most qualified candidate for class president because she is the best person for the job.

What have you learned about Michele's qualifications? Nothing, really. The last part of this statement just repeats what the first part already said.

Always support statements with logical, truthful details: "Michele is the most qualified candidate for class president because she was vice-president last year, she has helped with a number of school projects, and she works well with people."

Either/Or Argument   An either/or argument suggests that there are only two sides to an issue.

> Either we raise the price of tickets to this year's class dance, or we will lose money.

Are there really only two ways to deal with the situation? Would cutting costs or having fund-raising activities help?

APPEALS TO EMOTION

When people try to convince others of something, they sometimes appeal to emotion rather than to reason. Watch out for these common appeals to emotion.

Bandwagon Appeal   This appeal tries to convince you to do something just because everyone else is.

> You have to learn this new dance! Everyone else has.

Has *everyone* really learned the dance? It's not likely, but does that matter? Just because other people are doing something doesn't mean it's right for you. Always look for sensible reasons *why* you should do something.

Loaded Language   Language that stirs up either positive or negative feelings in people is called loaded language. Notice the difference in the two statements on the next page.

> John comes up with unusual and creative ideas.
> John comes up with weird and far-fetched ideas.

Both statements suggest the same thing—that John's ideas are new and different. Yet the second statement gives a very negative impression of John's suggestions. When you write, avoid using such loaded language to persuade your readers.

Name-calling Making statements that attack or criticize a person so that the person's ideas will not be taken seriously is known as name-calling.

> Why would anyone want a loser like Ian on this committee? He's so unpopular.

Ian may not be the best-known kid in school, but that doesn't mean he's not intelligent or capable of offering useful ideas. When you hear statements like the one above, ask yourself what the *real* issue is. The real issue here is whether Ian can handle certain responsibilities, not whether he can win a popularity contest.

Practice Your Skills

Identify the error in reasoning or the appeal to emotion in each statement below. Then rewrite the statement to correct the error. You can make up any facts you need to correct the statements.

1. Lisa shouldn't choose the music for the party because she's a real featherbrain and she can't even carry a tune.
2. Luciano Pavarotti is famous because he is an internationally known opera star.
3. You should buy Rockin Roller in-line skates because everyone is buying them.
4. In this age of computers, no one uses typewriters anymore.
5. Either I sign up for lessons now, or I'll never learn to play the guitar.

Writing
TIP

You can use facts, statistics, and quotations from experts to back up the statements you make.

How Can I Become a Better Listener?

Interviewing Skills

An interview can help you get firsthand information to use in your writing. Unlike Calvin, as you ask follow-up questions and listen carefully, you will gather useful information that will make your writing lively and detailed. This handbook will help you prepare and conduct an effective interview.

WRITING
H A N D B O O K
31

GUIDELINES FOR INTERVIEWING

Planning an Interview

1. **Contact the person.** Set a time and place to meet.

2. **Explore your subject.** Read about the subject and try to learn more about the expert and his or her field.

3. **Prepare questions.** Write a list of questions that require more than a yes or no answer. For example, instead of asking, "Do you enjoy your work?" you could ask a musician you are interviewing, "What kind of music do you most enjoy playing?"

4. **Organize your supplies.** Gather paper, pencils, and perhaps a cassette recorder.

Conducting an Interview

1. **Listen closely.** Take notes as you listen. If you need more time to write, ask the person to repeat his or her answer.

2. **Ask questions.** Use follow-up questions to clear up anything you don't understand.

3. **Review your notes.** Immediately after the interview, go over your notes.

Calvin and Hobbes
by Bill Watterson

How Can I Make Better Oral Presentations?

Oral Reports

W R I T E R   T O   W R I T E R

Write as if [you] were speaking to an audience.

Jason Edwards, student
Clovis, California

Writing is not the only way to communicate with an audience. Sometimes, speaking directly to a group is the best way to share your ideas. Yet, like many people, you may not know how to make an effective oral presentation. With preparation and practice, you will feel more confident when addressing a group.

PREPARING AN ORAL REPORT

Use what you already know about the writing process as you prepare your oral report. Follow these steps:

- Pick a topic and consider your audience and goals.
- Gather information and explore your ideas through freewriting or drafting.
- Organize and write down the main ideas and key supporting points on note cards.
- Use visual aids such as charts, maps, or pictures to support your ideas. Make sure your visual aids are large enough to be seen by everyone in your audience.

PRACTICING AND PRESENTING

The more you practice your talk, the more confident you'll feel when you present it. Here are some guidelines to help you.

Writing
═══ **TIP** ═══

Highlight key words on your note cards to jog your memory as you present your talk. This will help you unglue your eyes from your notes and look directly at your audience.

Guidelines for Oral Reports

Practicing

1. **Review your notes.** Read through your notes several times.

2. **Rehearse.** Tape-record your report and listen to see if you are speaking clearly and neither too quickly nor too slowly.

3. **Present your report before family members or friends.** Ask for honest feedback and helpful suggestions.

Presenting

1. **Stand up straight and look natural.** Take a deep breath before you begin. This will help you relax.

2. **Establish eye contact with your audience.** Look directly at your audience as much as possible.

3. **Use natural gestures and facial expressions.** Don't smile if you are talking about a sad subject. Keep any gestures simple and natural.

4. **Use your voice effectively.** Speak clearly and loudly enough to be understood by all your listeners. Pause briefly after you make an important point.

The Fourth of July Oration

Practice Your Skills

Prepare an oral report on a subject listed below or on one of your own choosing. Write down key ideas on your note cards before you rehearse your talk. Finally, present your report in front of your classmates.

how to care for a pet   a movie you have seen recently
robots   hurricanes

How Can I Score Better on Tests?

Taking Tests

No matter what Peppermint Patty says, taking tests doesn't have to be hard. You can improve your test scores by learning how to prepare for a test and how to answer different types of test questions.

PREPARING FOR A TEST

The secret to successful test-taking is careful preparation. The following strategies will help you take charge of any testing situation.

- **Know what to study.** Ask your teacher exactly what the test will cover. That way you can use your study time to focus on the most important information.

- **Make a study plan.** It helps to study a little bit every day. The night before the test, review what you have learned.

- **Review your materials.** Look over the notes you took in class, skim chapters you have read, and review any other materials you may have studied. Think of questions that you would ask if you were making up the test, and try to answer them.

- **Memorize important facts.** Look for and memorize important names, dates, events, vocabulary words, and other important information. For suggestions about how to memorize information, see Handbook 25, "Study and Research Skills," pages 294–297.

- **Rest and relax.** You will perform best when you are alert and well rested. Get a good night's sleep before test day. Then be confident as the test begins. If you studied well, you should do just fine.

TYPES OF TEST QUESTIONS

Studying the information that will be covered on a test is important. Just as important is knowing how to answer different types of test questions.

Some test questions ask you to choose one answer from among three or four. Other questions ask you to write a phrase or a sentence. Still others require an entire essay. You might be asked to decide whether a statement is true or false. The following guidelines will help you to recognize and answer different types of test questions. In the process, you will become a better test taker.

True-False Questions

To answer this type of test question, you must read a statement and decide whether it is true or false. The following strategies can help you decide.

- If *any* part of the statement is false, the answer is "false."
- Statements that include such words as *all, never, always, and none* are often, though not always, false.
- Statements that include such words as *generally, some, most, many,* and *usually* are often, though not always, true.

1. T (F) All reptiles are coldblooded and walk on four legs.

Although all reptiles are coldblooded, reptiles such as snakes do not have legs. Because the second part of the statement is false, the answer is "false."

Matching Questions

Matching questions ask you to match items in one column with related items in a second column.

- First read all the items in both columns. Then match the ones you know for sure.
- Cross out the items as you match them. This way you won't be distracted by items you've already matched.

1. Write the letter of the definition next to its term.

_B_	**1.** index	**A.** a list of chapter titles and subheadings
_C_	**2.** glossary	**B.** an alphabetical list of topics
_A_	**3.** table of contents	**C.** an alphabetical list of terms and their definitions

Be sure to choose the most *exact* match for each item. For example, both an index and a glossary are alphabetical lists, but only a glossary includes definitions of terms.

Multiple-Choice Questions

A multiple-choice question asks you to choose the best answer from three or more possible answers.

- Read each choice carefully.
- Cross out any answers that are clearly wrong.
- Choose the answer that is most complete or correct.

1. Which of the following best describes a river?
   A. a large stream of saltwater
   B. a large stream of water that empties into an ocean, a lake, or another body of water
   C. a large body of water separating two continents
   D. a body of water completely surrounded by land

Answers *C* and *D* are clearly incorrect. Answer *A* is only partly correct. Therefore, *B* is the correct answer.

Fill-in-the-Blank Questions

Fill-in-the-blank questions ask you to complete a sentence by adding an appropriate word or phrase.

- First fill in the answers that you know for sure.
- Then go back and try to answer the questions you left blank. An "educated guess" is better than no answer at all.
- Check each fill-in for correct capitalization and spelling. Also, be sure your answer fits grammatically with the rest of the sentence.

Sumerian clay tablet, about 1980 B.C.

> **1.** The first writing system was developed by the
> _Sumerians_ .

This question requires an answer that tells *who* developed the first writing system. Telling *where, when,* or *how* writing was invented would be incorrect.

Short-Answer Questions

Short-answer questions ask you to write a brief answer, usually just a sentence or two.

- First read the directions to find out if each answer must be a complete sentence.
- If you must write a complete sentence, begin by restating the question. Then give the answer.
- Reread the answer to be sure you used correct grammar, spelling, punctuation, and capitalization.

> **1.** Name the three social classes in ancient Rome.
> _The three social classes in ancient Rome were the_
> _elite, the "more humble," and the slaves._

Notice how this answer first restates the question and then provides the answer.

Essay Questions

When you answer an essay question, you must write your answer as one or more paragraphs.

- First identify the topic you are to write about.
- Look for key words that tell how to answer the question, such as *compare, explain, describe, identify,* and *discuss.*
- Note the form you are supposed to use, such as a letter, an explanatory paragraph, or an essay.
- Note also whether your audience is your teacher, other students, or adults.
- Before you start writing, jot down some notes about the key points you want to make.
- Proofread your writing.

Writing
TIP

If you want to add additional information after you've finished writing, place it in the margin. Draw an arrow to indicate where the information should go in the paragraph.

STANDARDIZED TESTS

In addition to the tests prepared by your teacher, you will also take standardized tests. These tests, sometimes called achievement tests, are used to measure your understanding of many subjects, including mathematics, reading comprehension, vocabulary, science, and social studies.

Standardized tests often include some of the same types of questions you have already studied. In addition, there are two other types of questions you may come across.

Reading Comprehension Questions

These questions test how well you understand something you have just read. You are given a passage to read, followed by one or more questions about the passage. For example, you might be asked to state the main idea of the passage, recall a detail, or draw a conclusion.

- Read the questions first, if you're allowed to. Then you will know what information to look for as you read.

- Read the passage carefully but quickly.
- Read each question carefully. Then select or write the best, most complete answer.
- If allowed, look back over the test to check answers you're unsure of.

Read the following passage carefully. Then answer the question that follows it.

> Jack London was an American adventurer and writer. Before he was twenty, he sailed the world. He achieved fame and fortune in his lifetime. His travels to Alaska spawned his most well-known adventure tales, *The Call of the Wild* and *White Fang.* London was a self-educated man who wrote about his concerns for the poor and the powerless. His novels and stories emphasize the cruel side of nature.
>
> **1.** In his writing, what was Jack London concerned about?
> **A.** fame and fortune   **C.** education
> **B.** the poor and the powerless   **D.** sailing

Although all of the answers are mentioned in the passage, only *B* answers the question.

Vocabulary Questions   These questions test how well you know the meanings of words. **Synonym questions,** for example, ask you to find words that have the same, or almost the same, meanings as other words.

> Choose the phrase that is closest in meaning to the underlined phrase.
> **1.** <u>a costly</u> computer
> **A.** a cheap   **C.** a thrifty
> **B.** an expensive   **D.** an efficient

Answer *A* is a word that means the opposite of *costly*. Answers *C* and *D* have different meanings than *costly*. Answer *B* is the word that is closest in meaning.

Antonym questions ask you to find words that have opposite meanings.

> Choose the word that is opposite in meaning to the underlined word.
> **1.** a <u>fascinating</u> story
>   **A.** interesting   **C.** boring
>   **B.** challenging   **D.** attractive

Answers *A* and *D* both have meanings that are similar to *fascinating*. Answer *B* has a different meaning, but not an opposite meaning. Only *C* means the opposite of *fascinating*.

TAKING A TEST

When it's time to sit down and take a test, these tips can help you do well.

- **Look over the whole test.** See how long it is and what types of questions it includes.

- **Budget your time.** Read all the directions first. This will let you know whether you will need more time for one type of question, such as an essay.

- **Read the directions carefully.** Ask questions if you don't understand the directions. Follow the directions exactly.

- **Answer easy questions first.** Mark the questions you can't answer right away. Then go back to these questions later.

- **Mark answer sheets carefully.** If the test you're taking includes a computer-scored answer sheet, mark each answer in the correct space, filling in the answer circles or boxes neatly.

- **Review your answers.** Check that you have not left out any answers and that your answers make sense. Make any necessary changes.

Practice Your Skills

A. Answer the following questions.

1. T   F   Standardized tests always include reading-comprehension questions.
2. T   F   Before you begin a test you should look over the entire test, if this is allowed.
3. Questions that ask you to choose the best answer from three or more choices are _____ questions.
4. A word that means the opposite of a given word is an _____ .

B. Read the following passage. Then answer the questions.

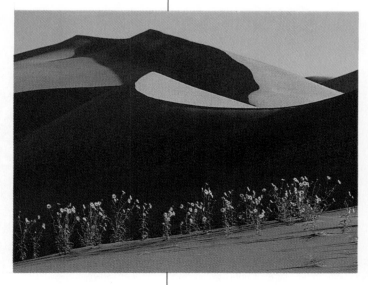

A desert is a hot, barren region that receives little rainfall. However, scientists do not agree on a specific definition. Some scientists define deserts by the amount of rainfall and evaporation. Some define them by the type of soil or plant life present. Others use a combination of all of these factors. The largest desert in the world is the Sahara in Africa. The Sahara covers an area about the same size as the United States.

1. What factors do some scientists use to define deserts?
   A. rainfall and evaporation   **C.** plant life
   B. type of soil   **D.** all of the above
2. Which word is closest in meaning to the word *barren?*
   A. empty   **C.** tame
   B. fertile   **D.** rich

Detail of a pieced, appliquéd, and embroidered quilt, about 1870. The artist depicts over one hundred colorful log cabins, as well as scenes of community members engaged in a variety of daily tasks. Perhaps the quilt was made to show what life was like for African Americans after the abolition of slavery.

Grammar and Usage Handbook

MINI-LESSONS

ASSESSMENT   PRETEST   **Grammar Handbooks**

Directions   One or more of the underlined sections in the following sentences may contain an error in grammar, punctuation, spelling, or capitalization. Write the letter of each incorrect section. Then rewrite the section correctly. If there is no error in an item, write *D.*

> **Example**   The first navigator to sail <u>completely</u> around the world
>   **A**
> was Juan Sebastián del Cano in <u>1522. Magellan</u> did not
>   **B**
> <u>live. To complete</u> the expedition. <u>No error</u>
>   **C**   **D**
>
> **Answer**   C—live to

1. We will visit my <u>Grandpa</u> in Mexico for the *posada* celebration before
                   A
<u>Christmas. He</u> will make piñatas for all of <u>us.</u> <u>No error</u>
   B   **C**   **D**

2. The <u>butterflys</u> name may have come from <u>folklore.there</u> are stories about
      A   **B**
<u>witches</u> taking the form of a butterfly to steal butter and milk. <u>No error</u>
  C   **D**

3. A drop of water is <u>smaller</u> than you might think. There <u>is</u> 120 <u>drops</u>
                A   **B**   **C**
in a teaspoon. <u>No error</u>
         D

4. The parachute was <u>invented</u> to help <u>people</u> jump out of burning buildings
              A   **B**
<u>safe</u>. <u>No error</u>
 C   **D**

5. <u>First, the</u> veterinarian showed <u>Ian and I</u> how to clip the <u>cats</u> claws. <u>No error</u>
   A   **B**   **C**   **D**

6. Look at <u>them</u> two crystals. The <u>largest</u> one grew <u>more slowly</u> than the
        A   **B**   **C**
other. <u>No error</u>
     D

7. Either of the <u>witnesses</u> will tell <u>their</u> story to the <u>Judge</u>. <u>No error</u>
　　　　　　A　　　　　　　**B**　　　　　　　　**C**　　　**D**

8. The people of North <u>Africa</u> make food, medicine, cooking oil, bowls,
　　　　　　　　　　　A
baskets, sandals, <u>rope, and</u> <u>fuel, From</u> parts of the date palm tree. <u>No error</u>
　　　　　　　　　B　　　　　**C**　　　　　　　　　　　　　　　　**D**

9. Everyone should be careful about <u>their</u> diet. ~~Setting~~ *Sitting* down regularly to
　　　　　　　　　　　　　　　　A　　　　　**B**
meals high in sugar and fat can lead to certain <u>diseases</u>. <u>No error</u>
　　　　　　　　　　　　　　　　　　C　　　　　**D**

10. Only fourteen out of every one hundred <u>wives</u> in the United States <u>are</u>
　　　　　　　　　　　　　　　　　　　　A　　　　　　　　　　　**B**
older than <u>their</u> husbands. ⟨<u>No error</u>⟩
　　　　　C　　　　　　**D**

11. In ancient England, the <u>fierce</u> Celtic warrior Boadicea <u>rided</u> *rode* into London
　　　　　　　　　　　A　　　　　　　　　　**B**
with her soldiers and <u>burned</u> the city to the ground. <u>No error</u>
　　　　　　　　C　　　　　　　　　　　　**D**

12. At the <u>Pentagon</u> building in <u>Arlington, Virginia</u> there are almost seventy
　　　　A　　　　　　　　　**B**
thousand miles of telephone <u>lines!</u> <u>No error</u>
　　　　　　　　　　C　　　**D**

13. On Christmas Eve, the organ in Joseph Mohr's church <u>broke</u> down.
　　　　　　　　　　　　　　　　　　　　　　　A
Within three hours, <u>him</u> and the church organist <u>had wrote</u> "Silent
　　　　　B　　　　　　　　　　　**C**
Night" so the church members would have music. <u>No error</u>
　　　　　　　　　　　　　　　　　　D

14. Thousands <u>searched</u> for gold in the Klondike at the <u>hieght</u> *height* of the gold rush.
　　　　　　A　　　　　　　　　　　　　**B**
<u>now</u>, almost one hundred years later, people are still digging there. <u>No error</u>
C　　　　　　　　　　　　　　　　　　　　　　　**D**

15. <u>Balloons</u> were stuck to the <u>ceiling, they</u> <u>fell</u> down later. <u>No error</u>
A　　　　　　　　　**B**　　　**C**　　　　　**D**

Sketch Book

- Imagine you could interview any famous person—living or dead. Write down some questions you would ask and the answers you think the person would give.

- You are telling a reporter about your greatest achievement. Write what you would say.

Understanding Sentences

After a press conference, reporters must make sense of the information they received. When they tell their readers what was said, they may restate the questions and even quote some of the answers. Reporters will use various kinds of sentences in their articles. The headline may even be a question or an exclamation.

This handbook explains the parts of sentences and shows you the types of sentences you can use in your writing. It can help you write sentences that express your ideas clearly and confidently.

Understanding
Sentences   **339**

WHAT IS A SENTENCE?

A **sentence** is a group of words that expresses a complete thought.

Look at this group of words:

Visitors to Yellowstone National Park

This group of words is about visitors to Yellowstone National Park. The words do not, however, say what happens to the visitors or what the visitors do. They do not express a complete idea.

Now consider this group of words:

Hike through rugged wilderness

This group of words tells you *what happens.* However, it does not tell *who* or *what* hikes through the wilderness. These words also present only part of an idea.

A **sentence** expresses a complete thought. Every sentence must tell whom or what the sentence is about. It must also tell what happens. Read the following group of words. Since it expresses a complete thought, it is a sentence.

Visitors to Yellowstone National Park hike through rugged wilderness.

Practice Your Skills

A. CONCEPT CHECK

Sentences and Incomplete Sentences   Label each group of words *Sentence* or *Not a Sentence.*

1. The Yellowstone area was part of the Louisiana Purchase.
2. Belonged to the United States government after 1803.
3. Home of Native Americans.
4. Hunted in the Yellowstone region for thousands of years.

Writing
——TIP——

Do not leave your readers with only part of an idea. Make sure every sentence you write tells a complete thought.

Writing Theme
Yellowstone National Park

5. President Jefferson sent Lewis and Clark on an expedition.
6. The two explorers never saw the Yellowstone region.
7. Heard stories about it from Native Americans.
8. Around 1807, the trapper John Colter.
9. Discovered geysers and hot springs.
10. Other trappers explored the region in the 1830s and 1840s.
11. Spread stories about the Yellowstone area's natural wonders.
12. Few people believed these incredible tales.
13. Finally, in 1870, a United States government expedition.
14. By 1872, Yellowstone National Park.
15. The oldest national park in the world.

B. REVISION SKILL

Correcting Incomplete Sentences   Label each group of words *Sentence* or *Not a Sentence*. Add words to change the incomplete sentences to complete sentences.

16. Tourists marvel at the scenery in Yellowstone National Park.
17. More than two hundred geysers and thousands of hot springs.
18. Old Faithful is the most famous geyser.
19. Shoots water and steam 160 feet into the air.
20. During the summer, meadows with beautiful wildflowers.
21. Gazes at their bright colors.
22. Forests of pine trees cover most of the park.
23. Roam freely in the dense forest.
24. Builds a nest in a tree.
25. Large animals, such as grizzly bears.

C. APPLICATION IN WRITING

Paragraph   These notes from a journal tell about a vacation in Yellowstone National Park. Use the list and make up details to write a brief paragraph about the trip. Add words to make each note a complete sentence.

long trip in the car
the warm glow of the fire
a huge, brown grizzly bear!

pitched our tent
hiked through the forest
paddled a canoe

FOR MORE PRACTICE
See page 366.

The **subject** of a sentence tells *whom* or *what* the sentence is about. The **predicate** tells what the subject *does* or *is*.

Every sentence has two parts. The **subject** tells whom or what the sentence is about. The **predicate** tells what the subject does or did or what the subject is or was.

Look at the subjects and predicates in these sentences.

Subject (whom or what)	Predicate (what the subject does, did, is, or was)
Babe Ruth	was a superstar in professional baseball.
His great skills	drew huge crowds in the 1920s.
Baseball	is still a popular sport today.
Fans everywhere	flock to ballparks during the summer.

Notice that every sentence can be divided into two parts. All the words in a sentence are part of either the subject or the predicate.

Sentence Diagraming For information on diagraming subjects and predicates, see page 617.

Practice Your Skills

A. CONCEPT CHECK

Subjects and Predicates Write each of the following sentences. Draw one line under the subject and two lines under the predicate.

> EXAMPLE   The history of baseball dates back hundreds of years.

1. People in England played rounders in the 1600s.
2. This English game was similar to baseball.

3. Players hit a ball with a bat.
   4. American colonists in the 1700s enjoyed rounders too.
   5. Americans changed the game into baseball.
   6. Alexander Cartwright was probably the father of baseball.
   7. He organized the first baseball club in 1845.
   8. The name of his team was "Knickerbocker Base Ball Club."
   9. The Knickerbocker Club lost its first game.
   10. Cartwright developed many of the rules of baseball.
   11. He decided the size of the baseball diamond, for example.
   12. Today's rules are similar to Cartwright's rules.

B. APPLICATION IN LITERATURE

Subjects and Predicates   Label each italicized word or word group *Subject* or *Predicate*.

   13 *Our team* started to argue with one another. **14** *Our play* was sloppy, nothing like the cool routines back at Hobo Park. **15** Flyballs that lifted to the outfield *dropped at the feet of open-mouthed players.* **16** Grounders *rolled slowly between awkward feet.* **17** The pitching *was sad.* . . .

   18 *My teammates* were grumbling because they thought I was going to strike out, pop-up, roll it back to the pitcher, anything but hit the ball. . . .

   19 *I* came up scared of the fast ball and even more scared of failing. **20** Mary *looked on from the bleachers with a sandwich in her hand.* **21** The coach *clung to the screen* . . .

   Gary Soto, "Baseball in April"

FOR MORE PRACTICE
See page 366.

Detail of *Baseball* (1990), Paul Giovanopoulos.

Understanding
Sentences   **343**

SENTENCE FRAGMENTS AND RUN-ON SENTENCES

A **sentence fragment** is a group of words that does not express a complete thought. A **run-on sentence** is two or more sentences written as one sentence.

Readers find both sentence fragments and run-on sentences difficult to understand. A sentence fragment is confusing because something is left out. A run-on sentence incorrectly joins ideas that should be separated.

Sentence Fragments

A group of words that is not a sentence is called a **sentence fragment.** Some fragments do not tell what happened. Other fragments do not tell whom or what the sentence is about. You can correct a fragment by adding a missing subject or a missing predicate. Look at these examples:

Fragment	Some kinds of insects. *(What happens?)*
Sentence	Some kinds of insects fool their enemies.
Fragment	Looks like a brown twig. *(What is this about?)*
Sentence	The stick caterpillar looks like a brown twig.

Run-on Sentences

A **run-on sentence** is two or more sentences written as if they were one sentence. Sometimes there is no end mark at the end of the first complete thought. Sometimes a comma is used incorrectly to separate two complete thoughts. To correct a run-on, add the proper end mark at the end of the first sentence. Then capitalize the first letter of the next sentence.

Incorrect	This fox changes color it is white in the winter.
Incorrect	This fox changes color, it is white in the winter.
Correct	This fox changes color. It is white in the winter.

Practice Your Skills

A. CONCEPT CHECK

Fragments and Run-ons   Label each group of words *Sentence, Sentence Fragment,* or *Run-on Sentence.*

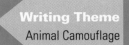
Writing Theme
Animal Camouflage

1. A nest of baby rabbits with gray and brown fur.
2. Matches the leaves and grass of their surroundings.
3. A fox approaches, the baby rabbits lie very still.
4. Finally, the danger passes.
5. The baby rabbits are safe they blend in with the background.
6. Fawns also fool their enemies.
7. Sometimes they stand as stiff as trees.
8. Their color protects them, their fur has specks of white.
9. Almost disappear in the sunlight and trees.
10. Clever tricksters in the animal world.

When nestled in foliage, the flap-neck chameleon of Africa is nearly invisible to predators.

B. REVISION SKILL

Correcting Fragments and Run-ons   Add words to make the fragments complete sentences. Rewrite the run-on sentences as separate sentences.

11. Insects have very short lives they have many enemies.
12. Their chances of survival.
13. Some insects copy the faces of dangerous animals, the appearance of these insects scares their enemies.
14. Some swallowtail caterpillars have fake eyes on their backs they look like a snake's eyes.
15. Probably frighten away hungry birds.
16. Many other kinds of disguises.
17. The lantern fly lives in Brazil the shape of its head is unusual.
18. Looks like a big hollow peanut.
19. The lantern fly's head has weird markings they are not just for decoration.
20. Markings like the teeth of an alligator, for example.

FOR MORE PRACTICE
See page 367.

Understanding Sentences   **345**

Read the following letter about a trip to Washington, D.C. Label each numbered group of words *Sentence, Fragment,* or *Run-on Sentence.* Then rewrite the letter. Change each fragment into a complete sentence by adding a subject or a predicate. Correct the run-on sentences.

Dear Adam,

1Our trip to Washington, D.C., is really fun, we left on Monday morning. **2**This city is a terrific place. **3**Many visitors from across the United States. **4**Huge government buildings. **5**The White House was our first stop. **6**Showed us some of the famous rooms. **7**I liked the Red Room the best, it has beautiful furniture and paintings. **8**Next, we visited the National Air and Space Museum. **9**Contains all sorts of old airplanes and rockets. **10**Famous spacecraft of U.S. astronauts. **11**Rocks from the first trip to the moon. **12**The Smithsonian Institution building is nearby. **13**Looks just like a castle in a fairy tale.

14Then we walked to the Lincoln Memorial this white marble building reminds me of a great temple. **15**Honors Abraham Lincoln. **16**A gigantic statue of the president. **17**We also went to the Washington Monument. **18**The tallest building in Washington, D.C. **19**An elevator inside the monument carried us to the top. **20**Had a great view of the city.

Your friend,
Daryl

A view of Washington, D.C., with the Potomac River in the foreground and the Lincoln Memorial, the Washington Monument, and the Capitol in the distance.

THE SIMPLE PREDICATE, OR VERB

A **verb** is a word that tells about action or that tells what someone or something is. A verb is the most important word in a complete predicate.

You know that a sentence can be divided into two main parts. We call the subject part the **complete subject.** The complete subject includes all of the words that tell whom or what the sentence is about.

The predicate part of the sentence is called the **complete predicate.** The complete predicate includes all of the words that tell what the subject is, what the subject does or did, or what happened to the subject.

Read the following examples of complete subjects and complete predicates.

Complete Subject	Complete Predicate
A large silvery spacecraft	landed.
A large silvery spacecraft	landed in a field.
A large silvery spacecraft	landed in a field near school.
Hairy green aliens	invaded.
Hairy green aliens	invaded the planet..
Hairy green aliens	invaded the planet at midnight.

Look at each complete predicate above. What is the key word in each one? The most important word in the first three complete predicates is *landed*. The most important word in the last three complete predicates is *invaded*.

The most important part of every complete predicate is the **verb.** It is sometimes called the **simple predicate.** In this book, however, we will call the simple predicate the **verb.**

Types of Verbs

There are two types of verbs. Some verbs tell about an action. These are **action verbs.**

Mario *gazed* at the strange creature outside his window.
The alien *leaped* toward the house.
It *banged* on the door with its steel fist.

Other types of verbs may tell that something is, or they may link the subject with words that describe it. These are called **state-of-being verbs.** They are also called **linking verbs.**

The space creature *is* small and chubby.
Sara *seemed* surprised at the alien's sudden appearance.

Common Linking Verbs

am	was	has been	seem	become
are	were	have been	look	feel
is	will be	had been	appear	taste

You will learn more about verbs in Grammar Handbook 36, "Using Verbs," pages 394–430.

Practice Your Skills

A. CONCEPT CHECK

Verbs   Write each sentence on your paper. Underline the complete predicate once. Draw a double line under the verb.

1. *The War of the Worlds* is a story about space monsters.
2. In the story creatures from Mars invade the earth.
3. These invaders are huge and ugly.
4. Their skin looks like wet leather.
5. The Martians carry powerful weapons.
6. They terrify people on the East Coast.
7. The monsters catch a common earth disease.
8. Deadly germs destroy the cruel Martians.
9. Not all aliens in science fiction are mean.

10. The alien in the movie *E.T.* is lovable and cute.
11. Children learn about friendship from this creature.
12. Many friendly, helpful aliens appeared on *Star Trek.*
13. For example, Mr. Spock worked closely with earth people.
14. He gave Captain Kirk good advice.
15. Like humans, aliens have been both good and evil.

B. REVISION SKILL

Using Vivid Verbs   Write the following sentences. Replace each italicized word or phrase with a vivid verb from the list.

> EXAMPLE   Weird monsters in science fiction *scare* people.
> Weird monsters in science fiction *terrify* people.

craved	grew	starred	grabbed	caused
trudged	gobbled	oozed	invaded	stormed

16. Giant creatures without brains *moved* through the jungles on the planet Venus.
17. They *took* everything along the way.
18. In a story by Robert A. Heinlein, a speedy, eight-legged monster *went* across the earth.
19. This hungry alien *ate* metal.
20. It really *wanted* old cars for dinner.
21. The Blob *was* in a popular movie.
22. This famous monster *went into* a small town.
23. It *made* all kinds of trouble.
24. The slimy alien *came* slowly through the town.
25. With each human meal, the Blob *got* bigger and bigger.

C. APPLICATION IN WRITING

Science Fiction Story   Write a story about a space creature that lands in your neighborhood. Be sure to describe the creature and its actions. In your story, use five of the vivid verbs in the following list.

rescue	struggle	search	invade
stare	scream	quarrel	command
topple	chuckle	explode	flee

FOR MORE PRACTICE
See page 367.

The **simple subject** is the most important part of the complete subject.

In a complete sentence, every verb has a subject.

Complete Subject	Verb
The princess	danced.
The lovely princess	danced.
The lovely princess in the red gown	danced.
The prince	bowed.
The handsome prince	bowed.
The handsome prince from England	bowed.

Look at each complete subject above. What is the key word in each one? In the first group, the most important word is *princess;* in the second group, it is *prince.*

The most important word in a complete subject is called the **simple subject** of the sentence. Another name for the simple subject is the **subject of the verb.**

To find the subject of a verb, first find the verb. Then ask *who* or *what* before the verb. The answer indicates the simple subject of the sentence. Look at these examples:

> The red dragon in the cave thundered mightily.
> Verb: *thundered*
> Who or what thundered?   dragon
> *Dragon* is the subject of *thundered.*

> The young girl spun gold from straw.
> Verb: *spun*
> Who or what spun? girl
> *Girl* is the subject of *spun.*

Elves are magical beings in fairy tales.
>Verb: *are*
>Who or what are?   elves
>*Elves* is the subject of *are*.

Practice Your Skills

A. CONCEPT CHECK

Simple Subjects   Write the verb and the simple subject of each of the following sentences.

Writing Theme
Fairy Tales

1. Very few children's books existed before 1700.
2. Children learned lessons about good behavior from these first books.
3. Later stories entertained young readers.
4. Many early books were collections of fairy tales.
5. These tales are among the oldest kinds of literature.
6. People handed fairy tales down from generation to generation.
7. Two brothers collected German fairy tales during the early 1800s.
8. Their names were Jakob and Wilhelm Grimm.
9. German farmers told tales to the brothers.
10. The Grimms wrote down the farmers' exact words.
11. Then they published these ancient tales.
12. Their collection of fairy tales became very popular.
13. Authors in other countries published fairy tales too.
14. In Denmark, Hans Christian Andersen wrote 168 fairy tales.
15. Young readers around the world enjoy Andersen's magical tales.

Arthur Szyk illustrates Hans Christian Andersen's tale "The Nightingale" by showing the little bird singing to cheer an unhappy emperor.

B. DRAFTING SKILL

Using Subjects and Verbs Creatively   Find the simple subject and the verb in each sentence. Then rewrite the sentence. Keep the same simple subject and verb, but replace the other words to create a new fairy tale.

> EXAMPLE   The Pied Piper was a magical musician.
> The Pied Piper was a rock-and-roll star.

16. The Pied Piper played a magical fife.
17. His music charmed people and animals.
18. One day, rats overran the town of Hamelin, Germany.
19. The number of rats grew quickly.
20. The people of Hamelin promised the Pied Piper a rich reward for his help.
21. Soon every street echoed with the Pied Piper's magical fife music.
22. The sound of the music drew rats from every house in Hamelin.
23. A great parade of rats wound its way to the river.
24. Bunches of rats floated down the river.
25. Then the selfish people threw the piper out of town without a cent.
26. Angrily, the musician promised revenge.
27. The Pied Piper raced from the city.
28. Years later, the magical fife music again played in the town.
29. This time the Pied Piper led all the children away.
30. The townspeople cried over the loss of their children.

C. APPLICATION IN WRITING

Fairy Tale   Write a short fairy tale. Use at least five of the simple subjects below.

king	dragon	frog
forest	knight	princess
sword	horse	giant
apple	castle	cave
cottage	townspeople	countryside
crown	moon	raven

FOR MORE PRACTICE
See pages 367–368.

CHECK ✔ POINT
MIXED REVIEW · PAGES 347–352

A. Create a chart with two columns. Label one column *Simple Subject* and the other *Verb*. Write the simple subject and the verb of each sentence in the correct columns.

1. In July 1940, the Tacoma Narrows Bridge opened in the state of Washington.
2. This bridge was 2,800 feet long.
3. On a windy day, the deck of the bridge bounced up and down.
4. Newspapers named the wild bridge Galloping Gertie.
5. On Sunday afternoons, traffic was very heavy.
6. Many people drove across the bridge just for fun.
7. The trip was like a ride on a roller coaster.
8. However, the fun stopped in November 1940.
9. The wind blew at forty-two miles an hour.
10. Suddenly, the bridge crashed into the water below.

The Leaning Tower of Pisa, a bell tower, was begun in 1173 and completed between 1360 and 1370 in Pisa, Italy. Built on unstable soil, it tilts an additional twentieth of an inch each year.

B. Write each of the following sentences. Draw one line under the simple subject and two lines under the verb.

11. Over eight hundred years ago, architects in Pisa, Italy, designed a beautiful marble tower.
12. However, builders soon discovered a big mistake.
13. The foundation under the tower was only ten feet thick.
14. It was not strong enough for the huge tower.
15. As a result, the foundation sank into the ground.
16. The whole tower tilted to one side.
17. Over the centuries, the base of the tower settled even more.
18. Today this unusual building still tips sideways.
19. Tourists flock to the Leaning Tower of Pisa.
20. Many people consider it one of the wonders of the world.

Understanding
Sentences   **353**

> The subject does not always come at the beginning of a sentence.

The subject is usually near the beginning of a sentence and before the verb. Writers, however, can change the order of sentences to add variety to their writing.

> Animal paintings appear on the cave walls.
> On the cave walls, animal paintings appear.
> *(The subject is near the end of the sentence but before the verb.)*

> On the cave walls appear animal paintings.
> *(The order of the subject and the verb is reversed.)*

To find the subject of a sentence in which the order is unusual, first find the verb. Then ask *who* or *what* before the verb.

> Who or what *appear? Paintings* appear.
> *Paintings* is the subject of the sentence.

Sentences Beginning with *Here* and *There*

In a sentence beginning with the word *here* or *there,* the subject usually follows the verb.

> There is the paintbrush.
>> Verb: *is*
>> Who or what is? paintbrush
>> *Paintbrush* is the subject of *is.*

> Here are the drawings.
>> Verb: *are*
>> Who or what are? drawings
>> *Drawings* is the subject of *are.*

Practice Your Skills

A. CONCEPT CHECK

Subjects in Different Positions   Write each of the following sentences. Draw one line under the subject of the verb and two lines under the verb.

1. There is a wonderful cave in southern France.
2. Here are the world's oldest paintings.
3. Scientists from all over the world study the paintings in the Grotte de Lascaux.
4. On the walls and ceilings are pictures of animals.
5. Everywhere are creations from the distant past.
6. Inside the dark cave, a scientist imagines a scene from twenty thousand years ago.
7. In the middle of the cave sits an ancient artist.
8. Beside the artist are hollow bones.
9. These bones are the artist's paintbrushes.
10. Near him is a torch.
11. By firelight the artist begins his work.
12. Patiently, the artist draws a buffalo.
13. For early people, rock paintings had a magic purpose.
14. For example, they meant good luck to hunters.
15. Even today, there is mysterious power in these pictures.

B. REVISION SKILL

Varying the Positions of Subjects   Rewrite each sentence so that the subject comes after the verb.

16. Many examples of rock art are in southern Africa.
17. Many drawings are there from thousands of years ago.
18. Examples of rock art appear on the walls of cliffs in Rhodesia.
19. An animal scene is over here.
20. A deer comes from the forest.
21. A band of hunters gathers around the deer.
22. Bows and arrows are on the hunters' backs.
23. A huge rhinoceros is nearby.
24. Clouds of smoke are in the distance.
25. Other scenes of events in daily life are next to this drawing.

FOR MORE PRACTICE
See page 368.

Understanding
Sentences   **355**

Writing TIP

Use different types of sentences to make your writing more interesting.

There are four types of sentences: **declarative, interrogative, imperative,** and **exclamatory.**

People use four types of sentences to express different kinds of thoughts and emotions. Sentences can state facts, ask questions, make requests, and show strong feelings.

Type of Sentence	Definition	Punctuation	Example
Declarative	tells or states something	.	The ghost town looks like a western movie set.
Interrogative	asks a question	?	Did you see those crumbling buildings?
Imperative	makes a request or gives an order	.	Imagine life in a ghost town.
Exclamatory	expresses strong feeling	!	This ghost town is amazing!

Practice Your Skills

A. CONCEPT CHECK

Identifying Kinds of Sentences   Write each of the sentences in the following dialogue, adding the correct punctuation. Then label each sentence *Declarative, Interrogative, Imperative,* or *Exclamatory.*

1. JORGE: What is the name of this ghost town
2.   LIN: Its name is Hamilton
3.   What a fantastic place this is
4. JORGE: How long has the town been deserted
5.   LIN: Hamilton has been empty since about 1870
6. JORGE: Why did everyone leave
7.   LIN: The silver in the mines ran out

Writing Theme
Towns in the Old West

8. JORGE: Where were the mines located
9.   LIN: Two of the biggest mines were in that mountain
10. JORGE: That certainly is a steep climb in this desert heat
11.   Just imagine the hard life of the miners
12.   LIN: Watch your step
13.   The board on the sidewalk is loose
14. JORGE: Let's leave now
15.   This place is just too spooky

B. PROOFREADING SKILL

Correcting Errors in Sentences   Write the following paragraph, correcting errors in grammar, capitalization, punctuation, and spelling. Pay special attention to the punctuation of different kinds of sentences. (10 errors)

Read this newspaper headline from the 1870s! "Miners find gold!" Discoverys of gold and silver in the western states. Created new towns overnight. Why did many of these new towns later turn into ghost towns. After a while, the mines became empty? Than the settlers moved too other towns. However, Last Chance Gulch still exists today, this town is now Helena, montana. Find this city on a map of the united states.

C. APPLICATION IN WRITING

A Travel Brochure   Pretend you live in a town next to a gold mine. Write a travel brochure describing your town. Use all four types of sentences in your brochure. Punctuate correctly.

FOR MORE PRACTICE
See pages 368-369.

A ghost town of the Old West

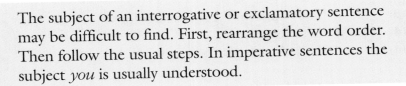

The subject of an interrogative or exclamatory sentence may be difficult to find. First, rearrange the word order. Then follow the usual steps. In imperative sentences the subject *you* is usually understood.

Interrogative, exclamatory, and imperative sentences often have unusual word order. To find the subject of an interrogative sentence, change it to a declarative sentence. Then find the verb and ask *who* or *what* before it.

Interrogative Sentence	Is Bill afraid of roller coasters?
Declarative Sentence	Bill is afraid of roller coasters.
	Who is? Bill
	Bill is the subject of the verb *is*.

Find the subject of an exclamatory sentence in the same way. First, change it to a declarative sentence. Then find the verb and ask *who* or *what* before it.

Exclamatory Sentence	Was that ride fantastic!
Declarative Sentence	That ride was fantastic.
	What was? ride
	Ride is the subject of the verb *was*.

Most imperative sentences appear to have no subject.

Buy your ticket.   Have fun.

In these sentences, *you* is understood to be the subject.

(you) Buy your ticket. (you) Have fun.

Sentence Diagraming   For information about diagraming interrogative, exclamatory, and imperative sentences, see page 617.

Practice Your Skills

A. CONCEPT CHECK

Subjects in Different Positions   Write each of the following sentences. Draw a line under the subject of the verb. If the subject you is understood, write (*you*).

1. Listen to my news about this wild roller coaster.
2. Have you ever heard of Greezed Lightnin'?
3. This exciting ride is at Astroworld in Houston, Texas.
4. It zooms at sixty miles an hour!
5. Are you ready for the thrill of your life?
6. Take an imaginary ride on Greezed Lightnin'.
7. Here comes an eighty-foot loop!
8. Next, climb 138 feet in the air.
9. Your face is as white as a ghost's!
10. Can you stop the screams?

B. REVISION SKILL

Varying the Types of Sentences   Change each sentence to the kind described in parentheses. You will need to add or drop words in some of the sentences. Punctuate correctly.

11. Is "The Beast" the name of a roller coaster? (declarative)
12. It is in Kings Island, Ohio. (interrogative)
13. The Beast is terrifying. (exclamatory)
14. Passengers think about the eight scary turns. (imperative)
15. Imagine dropping 135 feet into a tunnel! (interrogative)

C. PROOFREADING SKILL

Correcting Errors in Punctuation   Write the following paragraph from a letter, correcting all errors in grammar, capitalization, punctuation, and spelling. Pay special attention to the punctuation of different kinds of sentences. (8 errors)

What a great day we had? Do you remember my freind annie. She and me rode our bikes to the amusement park. The best ride was the roller coaster, it was really scary! The roller coaster was over five storys high. Was it ever fast.

Writing Theme
Roller Coasters

FOR MORE PRACTICE
See pages 368–369.

Understanding
Sentences   **359**

A. Write each sentence and label it *Declarative, Interrogative, Imperative,* or *Exclamatory.* Underline the subject of each sentence. If the subject *you* is understood write (*you*).

1. Are you interested in twins?
2. Do you like festivals?
3. Find out about a really fun event.
4. First, look at a map of Ohio.
5. Can you find the town of Twinsburg?
6. This little town is near Cleveland, Ohio.
7. Why is this town so special?
8. Since 1976, identical twins have come to Twinsburg each summer for a festival.
9. In 1989, a total of 2,356 sets of twins came here!
10. Picture that many twins in one place.
11. How unusual is this festival?
12. The twins take part in parades and magic acts.
13. There are also more than a hundred contests for twins at the festival.
14. One of the contests is for twins with the widest smiles.
15. Imagine the happy winners.

B. Write the subject and the verb of each of the following sentences.

16. Here is the story of the "Jim twins."
17. Different parents raised them.
18. After thirty-nine years, they finally met each other.
19. Besides their appearance, these twins had many other things in common.
20. Here are some examples.
21. In each of their driveways was the same kind of blue car.
22. Among the favorite hobbies of each twin was woodworking.
23. In the late afternoon, both men got headaches.
24. There were also other similarities.
25. They both named their dog Toy.

COMPOUND SUBJECTS

A **compound subject** has two or more parts.

Notice that the subject of each sentence below has two parts.

Subject	Predicate
Nick and *Elena*	learned about animals.
Birds and *snakes*	are their favorites.

When a subject has two or more parts, it is called a **compound subject.** *Compound* means "having more than one part."

The word *and* is often used to join the parts of a compound subject, but the word *or* can also be used. The words *and* and *or* are conjunctions. A **conjunction** is a word used to join sentence parts.

Sometimes a subject has three or more parts. Then use commas to separate the parts. Place a conjunction before the last part. Look at this example:

> *Owls, raccoons,* and *squirrels* sometimes live in hollow logs.

Compound subjects can make your writing and speaking flow smoothly. Use them to combine sentences that repeat similar ideas.

Awkward	Moose use their antlers as weapons.
	Deer use their antlers as weapons.
Better	Deer and moose use their antlers as weapons.
Awkward	Clams and oysters have hard shells.
	Mussels also have hard shells.
Better	Clams, oysters, and mussels have hard shells.

Grammar TIP

When a compound subject has three or more parts, use a comma before the conjunction. See page 574 in Handbook 43, "Punctuation," for more about punctuating compound subjects.

Practice Your Skills

A. CONCEPT CHECK

Compound Subjects   Write each of the following sentences. Draw two lines under each verb and one line under each part of the compound subject.

1. Carpenters and architects exist in the animal world.
2. Many birds and other animals are excellent builders.
3. Grass, twigs, and leaves are the materials for birds' nests.
4. Birds' beaks and feet make handy tools.
5. Rats and mice build nests in different places.
6. Cracks and corners often become their homes.
7. Feathers, leaves, and bits of fur line their nests.
8. Their jaws, teeth, and claws are their tools.
9. Chipmunks and prairie dogs build underground tunnels.
10. Their paws and noses act like shovels.

B. DRAFTING SKILL

Sentence Combining   Find the sentences with compound subjects, and write the parts of the subject and the verb of each. Combine the sentences in items 12, 13, 14, 17, 18, and 20 to form single sentences with compound subjects. You may need to change or drop some words as you combine the sentences.

11. Insects and birds thrive in the rain forest.
12. Bees are everywhere. Beautiful butterflies are everywhere.
13. Spiders grow to a giant size. Ants also grow huge.
14. Hummingbirds sip nectar from flowers. Sunbirds also get their nectar this way.
15. Large birds and snakes prey on smaller animals.
16. Snakes, lizards, and frogs live among the branches.
17. Anteaters hang by their tails. Opossums also hang by their tails.
18. Monkeys leap from tree to tree. Squirrels also leap among the tree branches.
19. Deer and antelope roam the forest floor.
20. Leopards prowl through the jungle at night. Tigers prowl through the jungle at night.

COMPOUND PREDICATES

> A **compound predicate** has two or more parts.

Notice that the predicate of the sentence below has two parts.

Subject	Predicate
King Arthur	*grabbed the sword* and *pulled it from the stone.*

When a predicate has two or more parts, it is called a **compound predicate.** When a predicate has three or more parts, use commas to separate the parts. Place the conjunction before the last part, as in this sentence:

> King Arthur *stood before the Round Table, looked at his knights,* and *talked about his plans.*

Compound predicates help make your writing and speaking flow smoothly. Use them to combine sentences with similar ideas.

Awkward	King Arthur rode toward Sir Lancelot. King Arthur welcomed him home.
Better	King Arthur rode toward Sir Lancelot and welcomed him home.

Sentence Diagraming For information about diagraming compound subjects and compound predicates, see page 618.

Practice Your Skills

A. CONCEPT CHECK

Compound Predicates Write the following sentences. Draw one line under the subject or subjects of each sentence. Then draw two lines under each verb of the compound predicate.

1. King Uther lived in a castle and ruled all of Britain.
2. He and his wife had a baby son and named him Arthur.

Writing Theme
The Legend of King Arthur

3. King Uther worried about Arthur and asked Merlin the Magician for advice.
4. Merlin thought for a moment and then advised his king.
5. "You send Arthur away and tell no one about him."
6. Merlin took the baby and placed him in Sir Ector's home.
7. Sir Ector cared for Arthur and taught him about knighthood.
8. After King Uther's death, Sir Ector and Arthur left their home and went to a tournament of knights.
9. At the tournament Arthur saw a sword in a stone and pulled it out.
10. Before Arthur, many brave knights also wanted the sword and pulled at it with all their might.
11. Sir Ector saw the sword in Arthur's hand and told him about King Uther.
12. Arthur finally learned the secret of his birth and became the new king.

B. DRAFTING SKILL

Sentence Combining   Combine each of the following sentence pairs into one sentence. Use a conjunction to form a compound subject or a compound predicate.

EXAMPLE   King Lot wanted Arthur's lands. Lot's sons also wanted Arthur's lands.
King Lot and his sons wanted Arthur's lands.

13. King Lot gathered an army. King Lot attacked Arthur.
14. During the battle Merlin appeared before Arthur. Merlin told him about the powers of the magic sword and then vanished.
15. Arthur drew his magic sword. Arthur leaped toward his enemies.
16. Light flashed from the sword. The light blinded King Lot and his troops.
17. King Lot fled from the battlefield. His army fled from the battlefield.
18. Arthur celebrated the victory. His loyal followers celebrated the victory.

FOR MORE PRACTICE
See page 369.

CHECK ✔ POINT
MIXED REVIEW • PAGES 361–364

Make two columns on your paper. Label them *Subjects* and *Verbs*. Write the subjects of the following sentences in the first column. Write the verbs in the second column.

1. Sequoyah's mother, his uncles, and other people in his village taught him the Cherokee way of life.
2. Traditions and laws were important to the Cherokees.
3. As a young man, Sequoyah fought in battles and was a brave warrior.
4. Friends and relatives admired his courage.
5. Sequoyah also painted pictures and made silver objects.
6. He trapped and hunted animals too.
7. One day Sequoyah and his friends were in the forest.
8. They met and talked with white hunters.
9. One white hunter had a book and read from it.
10. The book and its strange symbols amazed Sequoyah and made him curious.
11. The Cherokees and other Native Americans had no written language.
12. Sequoyah studied the language and created a new alphabet, with a symbol for each syllable in the Cherokee language.
13. English, Greek, and Hebrew were the sources of his symbols.
14. Sequoyah worked on the alphabet for twelve years and finished it in 1821.
15. Both children and older people learned the new Cherokee alphabet easily.
16. Cherokee leaders translated treaties and read them to the people.
17. In 1828, the Cherokees started their own newspaper and called it the *Cherokee Phoenix.*
18. Sequoyah's hard work and creativity earned him respect.
19. The Cherokees honored Sequoyah and named him their president.
20. During the rest of his life, Sequoyah traveled to different countries and studied different languages.

Understanding
Sentences   **365**

Writing Theme
The Western Frontier

A. Recognizing Complete Sentences   Label each group of words *Sentence* or *Not a Sentence*. Add words to make the incomplete sentences complete.

1. In the 1870s, circuses were very popular on the Western frontier.
2. Unlike today's circuses, traveled in wagons from town to town.
3. Pioneer families loved the circus.
4. A parade of circus animals and colorful wagons.
5. Watched the brass bands and the elephants.
6. Wild animals in their cages.
7. Followed the parade to the edge of town.
8. Then workers put up the big tent for the circus acts.
9. Some children earned free tickets to the circus.
10. Did chores for the circus performers.
11. Watered the elephants, for example.
12. The townspeople applauded the performers.
13. A tightrope walker in a beautiful costume.
14. Silly clowns in enormous shoes.
15. A lion tamer with a whip.

B. Finding Complete Subjects and Predicates   Write each of the following sentences. Draw one line under the complete subject and two lines under the complete predicate.

16. A wagon train headed west of the Mississippi River on May 19, 1841.
17. Seventy brave pioneers went on a dangerous journey to California.
18. They traveled along the Oregon Trail.
19. Herds of cattle followed closely behind the wagons.
20. The captain of the wagon train gave a signal at sunset.
21. The wagons left the trail one by one.
22. They formed a large circle.
23. Families started campfires for the evening meal inside the circle.
24. Some boys played tag after dinner.
25. Other children read books by the glow of the campfires.

C. Correcting Fragments and Run-ons   Add words to each fragment to make a complete sentence. Rewrite each run-on as separate sentences. Write *Correct* if the sentence is correct.

26. Some advertisements twisted the truth about the West.
27. Newspaper editors also spread fabulous stories they made the West seem like a place in a dream.
28. Promised people in the East a better life.
29. The valleys were greener the skies were bluer.
30. Beets grew three feet thick, turnips measured five feet around.
31. Golden wheat with stems as thick as canes.
32. Mines with gold and silver.
33. Headed west in search of riches and adventure.
34. They believed the advertisements and newspaper stories.
35. However, few people became wealthy, many settlers on the Western frontier were poor.

D. Finding the Verb   Write the verb in each sentence.

36. Many African Americans were pioneers during the 1800s.
37. For example, Biddy Mason blazed new trails for others.
38. She found adventure and freedom on the Western frontier.
39. Because of her courage, she escaped slavery in the South.
40. Her journey began in Mississippi during the early 1850s.
41. She walked all the way to California behind a wagon train.
42. Slavery was against the law in California.
43. In this free state, Biddy Mason finally won her freedom.
44. Later, she became a rich and powerful woman.
45. She owned businesses and land in Los Angeles.

E. Finding the Verb and Its Subject   Write each of the following sentences. Draw two lines under the verb and one line under the subject of the verb.

46. Pioneers in a Kansas town celebrated on July 4, 1871.
47. Harriet wrote about the day's events in her diary.
48. At sunrise a soldier fired a cannon in the center of town.
49. Families in the area decorated their wagons and buggies.
50. Even horses wore tiny American flags.

51. The settlers rode into town for a day of fun.
52. By the courthouse the sheriff gave a patriotic speech.
53. Then the choir sang "The Star-Spangled Banner."
54. Many people brought food for a big picnic.
55. After lunch the boys played games.
56. Some men competed in wagon races and horse races.
57. At night, fireworks burst in the sky.

F. Finding Subjects in Different Positions Write the subject of each of the following sentences. Then tell whether it comes *before* or *after* the verb.

58. Here are some facts about education on the frontier.
59. At first there were no schools in the wilderness.
60. A pioneer woman usually taught boys and girls at home in her cabin.
61. Around her gathered a circle of children.
62. With a stick she scratched out numbers on the dirt floor.
63. Her students learned arithmetic and other subjects.
64. Later, pioneers built one-room schoolhouses.
65. There were many one-room schoolhouses in the Wild West.
66. Outside the schoolhouse door hung an iron bell.
67. Each morning the teacher rang the bell loudly.
68. Then the students rushed to their seats.
69. Along one side were rows of hard wooden benches.
70. In the front of the room was a blackboard.
71. Near the center of the room was a big potbellied stove.
72. There were students of all ages in the same classroom.

G. Identifying Kinds of Sentences Label each of the following sentences *Declarative, Imperative, Interrogative,* or *Exclamatory.* Then write the correct punctuation mark for the end of each sentence.

73. What was life like in Granite, Oklahoma
74. Are you ready for an adventure in history
75. Then take an imaginary journey in a time machine
76. Pretend you are a visitor to this frontier town
77. Pioneer families stop at the shops along Main Street

78. How busy the general store is
79. Horses gallop through the middle of town
80. So much action happens here

H. Finding Subjects and Verbs in Sentences Write each of the following sentences. Draw two lines under the verb and one line under the subject of the verb. If the subject *you* is understood, write it in parentheses.

81. Imagine a square dance in the 1800s.
82. Where is your partner?
83. Find one in a hurry!
84. What a fun time awaits you!
85. Listen to the caller.
86. "Are you all ready?"
87. "Swing your partner round and round."
88. "Form a star and then a chain."
89. "Now stampede!"
90. How loudly the dancers stamp their feet!

I. Finding Compound Subjects and Verbs Write each of the following sentences. Draw two lines under the verb(s) and one line under the subject(s).

91. Pioneer boys and girls had many chores.
92. On an ordinary day, most parents and their children woke up at four o'clock in the morning.
93. Younger children fed the chickens, gathered twigs, and picked berries.
94. Older children plowed the fields, planted the crops, and carried buckets of water.
95. Usually boys and their fathers worked in the fields.
96. In contrast, girls helped their mothers and worked at home.
97. They baked bread, washed clothes, and stitched embroidery.
98. Margaret Mitchell and her family were pioneers in Kansas during the 1870s.
99. As a young girl, she and her sisters trapped wild turkeys and hunted wolves.
100. Margaret, her parents, and her sisters built a log cabin.

Writing Theme
Exploring Places

A. Subjects and Predicates   Write the italicized words in the following sentences. Label these words *Subject* or *Predicate*.

1. Your plane *circles above a snowy field.*
2. You *see a land of lakes and streams from your window.*
3. *Not a single road* is visible anywhere.
4. *This huge, lonely, and wild land* is the tundra.
5. The tundra *stretches north to the ice fields of the Arctic.*
6. Your plane *lands near an icy patch of land.*
7. With several other people, *you* explore this unusual place.
8. Very few trees *grow here because of the cold weather.*
9. However, *wild animals* roam everywhere.
10. *Some animals, such as arctic hares and polar bears,* blend in with the snowy background.
11. Reindeer *graze on the short grasses.*
12. *A gray wolf* howls in the distance.
13. Gulls *build their nests on the arctic cliffs.*
14. Along the coast, *walruses* float on blocks of ice.
15. *They* use their long white tusks as giant hooks.

B. Fragments and Run-ons   Label each numbered group of words *Sentence, Fragment,* or *Run-on.* Then correct the fragments and run-ons.

¹⁶Two deep-sea divers explored a cave off the eastern coast of Mexico. ¹⁷One diver was a photographer, the other diver was a scientist. ¹⁸Suddenly, a shark. ¹⁹Held a movie camera in front of the shark. ²⁰The shark almost bumped the photographer's face mask. ²¹The camera surprised the shark it remained very still. ²²Stared peacefully at the divers. ²³The shark's two dozen sharp teeth in the front of its lower jaw. ²⁴Sharks sometimes attack people. ²⁵However, the sharks in these caves are gentle their behavior here is very odd.

²⁶Carlos Garcia discovered these caves and their unusually calm visitors, at first, the sharks seemed dead. ²⁷Looked like a graveyard for sharks. ²⁸Actually, these caves are shark "hotels" under the sea. ²⁹Sharks visit these caves when they become sleepy. ³⁰Provide a restful place for sharks.

C. Simple Subjects and Verbs   Write the simple subject and verb of each sentence.

31. You follow a sandy path to the top of a hill.
32. At the top, great waves of sand seem endless.
33. These hills of sand are dunes on the Oregon coast.
34. The ocean piles the sand into huge dunes along the coast.
35. Their form changes often.
36. Violent winter winds reshape the dunes almost overnight.
37. Many dunes even "sing."
38. Sometimes the sand shifts in the wind.
39. Then the grains of sand brush across one another.
40. The movement sounds squeaky.

D. Types of Sentences   Label each complete sentence *Declarative, Interrogative, Imperative,* or *Exclamatory.* Correct the sentence fragments.

41. Explore the seas with Jacques-Yves Cousteau.
42. Discovered families of octopuses in a bay south of France.
43. Cousteau named this area Octopus City.
44. Dive beneath the ocean's surface.
45. What a strange world this is!
46. Where are the octopuses' homes?
47. Holes under those piles of rocks.
48. Is the octopus a terrible monster?
49. Frightens many people because of its scary appearance.
50. However, the octopus is really a very shy creature.

E. Subjects in Different Positions   Write each of the following sentences. Draw one line under the simple subject and two lines under the verb. Write understood subjects of imperative sentences in parentheses.

51. How adventurous are you?
52. Are you ready for a trip to the Southwest?
53. Explore the desert in Arizona.
54. Here is some important advice.
55. Bring canteens of water.

56. Wear long pants, high boots, and a hat with a brim.
57. Before your eyes stretches a beautiful desert.
58. How weird it looks!
59. The desert reminds me of a strange planet.
60. There are almost no trees.
61. Only ten inches of rain fall here every year.
62. How strong the sun is!
63. Are you too hot?
64. Under those rocks is a shady place.
65. Be careful!
66. Nearby is a rattlesnake.
67. The sharp fangs on that snake are really scary!
68. Where are the other animals in the desert?
69. See all the different holes in the ground.
70. Creatures in the desert stay cool underground.

F. Compound Subjects and Compound Predicates

Combine each group of sentences into one sentence by making a compound subject or a compound predicate.

71. You walk out on this glacier. You inspect it.
72. The beauty is unmistakable. The power is unmistakable.
73. The blue and green colors are lovely. The shapes are lovely.
74. Great cracks develop in the ice. Towers develop in the ice.
75. Glaciers covered much of North America during the Ice Age. Glaciers shaped the land.
76. Glaciers cut valleys. Glaciers dug lakes. Glaciers carved mountains.
77. Alaska still has glaciers. Canada still has glaciers. Some Rocky Mountain states still have glaciers.
78. Mountains are the homes of today's glaciers. Polar regions are the homes of today's glaciers.
79. Glaciers begin as mounds of snow. Glaciers grow slowly.
80. Snow falls. It builds up each year.
81. The snow gets thicker. It packs into ice.
82. The ice slides downhill. The ice forms a glacier.
83. You go to the glacier's edge. You see a mound of gravel.
84. The glacier scraped up rock. The glacier crushed it.
85. Only heat stops glaciers. Only the sea stops glaciers.

Revise the following draft about a personal experience by using the directions at the bottom of the page. Then proofread your revision for errors in grammar, capitalization, punctuation, and spelling. Pay special attention to sentence fragments and run-ons.

¹Lewis and I were always alike. ²We were the same age. ³Had the same interests. ⁴We were even the same size. ⁵We loved to play basketball against each other for hours at a time the games were always close. ⁶My favorite player is Michael Jordan. ⁷However, last year Lewis began to grow. ⁸He was beating me all the time. ⁹At first it made me mad. ¹⁰I accused him of cheating on the score. ¹¹I said he was fouling me, even when he wasn't. ¹²I couldn't beleive that he played basketball better than I did. ¹³My attitude changed last labor day, when our familys got together for a picnic. ¹⁴I looked at Lewis's parents and brothers, I noticed something for the first time. ¹⁵Everyone in his family is about a head taller than everyone in mine. ¹⁶The problem isn't that Lewis is better than I am. ¹⁷He's bigger. ¹⁸His height and wieght are things I cant change.

1. Combine sentences 2 and 3 to correct the sentence fragment.

2. Add the transition word "Soon" to the beginning of sentence 8 to make the order of events clearer.

3. Add the phrase "than I am by six inches and twenty-five pounds" to sentence 17.

4. Delete the sentence that doesn't belong.

5. Divide the passage into two paragraphs.

Personal and Expressive Writing

Writing in your journal gives you a chance to explore your thoughts and to record your experiences. (See Workshop 1.) When you revise journal entries for others to read, you need to polish your rough ideas. Make sure that every sentence expresses a complete thought. Correct sentence fragments and run-ons, which may confuse your readers.

Understanding
Sentences

Sketch Book

You'll like
MAYBE, MICHIGAN
...maybe.

Welcome to
Bread Loaf Mountain, Vermont

Now Entering
SMILE
Kentucky
No frowners in this town!

Friends Xing

You've got a friend in
FRIENDSHIP, AR

- Invent your own town. Give it a name and then explain the meaning of the name.
- Make up the setting for a science fiction story. Write about the weird and wonderful objects in your setting.
- Imagine you have discovered the royal tomb of an Inca ruler. Tell about the fascinating artifacts you have found within it.

Understanding Nouns

- **What Are Nouns?**

- **Common and Proper Nouns**

- **Singular and Plural Nouns**

- **Nouns That Show Possession**

A town can have an unusual name (Muleshoe, Texas) or a plain name (The Plains, Ohio). The names of persons and things can be just as simple or fancy. Dinosaur, Colorado, is a place. A dinosaur is (or was) a thing. Both names are nouns. You need nouns to name the people, places, things, and ideas you write about.

In this handbook you will study the different types of nouns. You will learn how you can use them to make your writing precise and interesting.

A **noun** names a person, a place, a thing, or an idea.

Many names tell who you are. You may be an artist, a student, and a leader. These different names for you are nouns. Nouns are used to name persons, places, things, or ideas.

Many nouns name things that can be seen. Some examples are *spaceship, airport,* and *mountain.* Some nouns name things that can be neither seen nor touched. These include nouns such as *justice, courage, fear,* and *happiness.*

Here are some other examples of nouns.

Persons	Places	Things	Ideas
captain	desert	robot	loyalty
engineer	solar system	meteor	curiosity
Kirk	Asia	Eiffel Tower	knowledge
Uhura	Lima	*Enterprise*	love

A noun can name something in general, or it can be a precise name. Compare these sentences:

The travelers explored the area.
The astronauts explored the crater.

Did you notice how much more the second sentence tells in the same number of words? The word *astronauts* is more specific than *travelers,* helping a reader guess where these travelers might be. *Crater* gives a picture of the place, while the general term *area* does not. In your writing, always try to use specific nouns. They will make your ideas and descriptions clearer.

Writing
── **TIP** ──

Notice how specific nouns in "Finding Home" on pages 180–181 record the persons, places, things, and ideas that were important to Merrill Wilk's family.

Data and Captain Picard from the television series *Star Trek: The Next Generation,* with Captain Kirk and Mr. Spock from the original *Star Trek.*

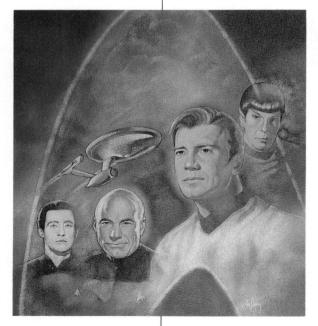

Practice Your Skills

A. APPLICATION IN LITERATURE

Nouns   Write each of the italicized nouns and tell whether each refers to a *Person*, a *Place*, a *Thing*, or an *Idea*.

Writing Theme
Fantastic Fiction

¹In a far corner of the *universe,* on one of the forest *moons* of the planet *Endor,* there lived a *tribe* of small furry *folk* called *Ewoks.* ²In a *village* perched high in the *branches* of the ancient *trees* they lived happy *lives,* with *love* and *goodwill* for their fellow Ewoks. . . .

³One of these young Ewoks was named *Teebo.* . . . ⁴He could daydream and watch the *rivers* of color that flowed across the *sky.* ⁵The sky *colors* seemed to sing a bright *song.* . . . ⁶In these *songs* Teebo could hear different *voices.* ⁷He could sense the *happiness* when the voices rejoiced at the planting of a new *birth-tree,* and the *sorrow* when the voices mourned the *end* of a tree's *lifetime.*

Joe Johnston, *The Adventures of Teebo*

B. DRAFTING SKILL

Using Precise Nouns   Finish the following sentences. Using your imagination, complete each sentence with precise nouns.

8. Keisha rode her _____ to the _____.
9. When she reached the _____, she spoke to the _____.
10. Keisha didn't know that the _____ was from another _____ in the universe.
11. The _____ from his head made the _____ blink on and off.
12. Suddenly, a feeling of _____ came over Keisha as she ran to call the _____.

C. APPLICATION IN WRITING

Fantasy   Imagine you are writing about a strange event that occurs in another universe. Before you begin writing, make a list of nouns you might use in your story. Go over your list to make each noun as specific as possible.

Writing
━TIP━

Choose the noun that names exactly what you mean. Do not say *tool* if you mean *hammer.* Do not write *boat* if you mean *canoe.*

FOR MORE PRACTICE
See page 388.

Understanding
Nouns   **377**

A **common noun** is a general name for a person, a place, a thing, or an idea. A **proper noun** names a particular person, place, thing, or idea.

When you call yourself a student, you are giving yourself a name that you share with all the other boys and girls in your school. This name is common to a whole group of people. Many other nouns are also common to whole groups of people, places, or things. Some examples are *photographer, picture, camera,* and *event.* These are called **common nouns.**

Some nouns name particular persons, places, or things. Names like *Ansel Adams, Washington, D.C.,* and *Lincoln Memorial* are called **proper nouns.** Proper nouns are always capitalized. Look at these examples of common nouns and proper nouns.

Writing
TIP

Use proper nouns to make your writing more precise. Do not say *teacher* when you mean *Mr. Engel.*

Common Nouns	Proper Nouns
children	Sara Curtis, Bob Curtis
photographer	Margaret Bourke-White
town	Columbus
magazine	*National Geographic*
river	Hudson River
building	United Nations
continent	Asia
park	Glacier National Park
road	Jefferson Road
lake	Lake Superior
monument	Gateway Arch
boy	Alex Bautista
girl	Sarah Lenz
school	Washington Junior High
store	Oak Street Photo
clerk	Emilia Flores

Practice Your Skills

A. CONCEPT CHECK

Common and Proper Nouns   Write the nouns from the following sentences. Identify each as a *Common* or *Proper* noun.

1. Dorothea Lange was a great photographer.
2. Her reputation was established during the Great Depression.
3. Lange roamed the states in the Dust Bowl.
4. There she took her most famous picture, *Migrant Mother.*
5. She later recalled, "I saw and approached the hungry and desperate mother, as if drawn by a magnet."
6. When Lange returned to her home, she sent the photo to a newspaper in San Francisco.
7. Soon afterward, the government of the United States rushed food to hungry workers.
8. Lange's photos captured the lives and feelings of poor people.
9. John Steinbeck said her work inspired his greatest novel.
10. His book, *The Grapes of Wrath,* won a Pulitzer Prize.

B. DRAFTING SKILL

Using Proper Nouns Effectively   Complete each of the following sentences by adding proper nouns.

> EXAMPLE   Many reporters cover news in _____ .
> Many reporters cover news in Washington, D.C.

11. Many photographers work for our newspaper, the _____ .
12. These photographers cover local news in our town of _____ .
13. They also travel to the state capital, _____ .
14. They often take pictures of _____, our governor.
15. At times, even national leaders like _____ may visit.
16. Sports photographers cover games at the high schools, including _____ .
17. They travel all over the state of _____ to shoot events.
18. Photographers take photos of entertainment stars like_____ .
19. I wish that _____, _____, and other celebrities would visit our town.
20. If I were a photographer, I would take pictures of _____ .

Migrant Mother (1936), Dorothea Lange.

FOR MORE PRACTICE
See page 388.

Understanding Nouns   **379**

Writing Theme
Favorite Moments
on Trips

A. APPLICATION IN LITERATURE

Write each underlined noun. Identify it as a *Common* or *Proper Noun.* Tell if it names a *Person,* a *Place,* a *Thing,* or an *Idea.*

EXAMPLE   After years in China, the family came home.
years, Common Noun, Thing
China, Proper Noun, Place
family, Common Noun, Person

¹The morning we were due to arrive in San Francisco, all the passengers came on deck early, but I was the first. **²**I skipped breakfast and went to the very front of the ship where the railing comes to a point. **³**That morning I would be the "eyes" of the *President Taft,* searching the horizon for the first speck of land. **⁴**My private ceremony of greeting, however, would not come until we were closer, until we were sailing through the Golden Gate. **⁵**For years I had heard about the Golden Gate, a narrow stretch of water connecting the Pacific Ocean to San Francisco Bay. **⁶**And for years I had planned my entrance.
    ⁷Dressed in my navy skirt, white blouse, and silk stockings, I felt every bit as neat as Columbus or Balboa and every bit as heroic when I finally spotted America in the distance.
                    Jean Fritz, *Homesick: My Own Story*

B. Copy these sentences, capitalizing every proper noun.

 8. Last year my family went to washington, d.c.
 9. My brother peter kept a list of all the monuments we saw.
10. My favorite moment came when we visited the white house.
11. The president of the united states walked past us!
12. We saw congress in session at the capitol building.
13. My youngest sister, mandy, was only three years old.
14. Her favorite site was the lincoln memorial.
15. She liked the red velvet rope around the statue of lincoln.
16. Driving to the jefferson memorial, dad took a wrong turn.
17. We wound up across the potomac river in virginia.

A **singular noun** names one person, place, thing, or idea. A **plural noun** names more than one person, place, thing, or idea.

Some nouns name just one person, place, thing, or idea. *Girl,* for example, names one person. It a **singular noun**. Other nouns name more than one person. They are **plural nouns.** *Girls* is a plural noun.

Here are seven rules for forming the plurals of nouns.

1 **To form the plurals of most nouns, just add -s.**

streets   islands   languages   teachers

2 **When the singular noun ends in s, sh, ch, x, or z, add -es.**

buses   bushes   coaches   boxes   waltzes

3 **When the singular noun ends in y with a consonant before it, change the y to i and add -es.**

city—cities   country—countries

4 **For most nouns ending in f or fe, add -s. For some nouns ending in f or fe, however, change the f to v and add -es or -s.**

chief—chiefs	self—selves	loaf—loaves
roof—roofs	life—lives	knife—knives
belief—beliefs	leaf—leaves	wolf—wolves
reef—reefs	half—halves	shelf—shelves
cuff—cuffs	wife—wives	calf—calves

5 **When the singular noun ends in *o*, add *-s*.**

radios halos pianos rodeos
Exceptions: For the following nouns ending in *o,* add *-es.*
echoes heroes potatoes tomatoes

6 **In some cases, the plural noun is exactly the same as the singular noun.**

salmon bass deer news

7 **Some nouns form their plurals in special ways.**

child—children goose—geese mouse—mice

Always check a dictionary when you are unsure about how to form the plural of a word. If the plural form is not listed in the dictionary, just add *-s* to the singular form.

Practice Your Skills

A. CONCEPT CHECK

Singular and Plural Nouns Change each of the nouns in parentheses to its plural form. Write the plural form.

1. The Inuit of Canada and the Inupiat and Yupik of Alaska were once called (Eskimo).
2. In the past, their (life) depended solely on nature.
3. They hunted bears, musk (ox), and (deer) called caribou.
4. They spread (net) to catch fish from the sea.
5. During the summer, they also ate (root), stems, and (berry).
6. In those months, (family) lived in (tent) made of skins.
7. During winter, most Inuit lived in (house) made of sod.
8. Using (knife), some cut blocks of snow to build (snow-house).
9. Today, however, many Inuit live in modern (town) and (city).
10. Their (belief) and (way) of life have changed.

B. PROOFREADING SKILL

Correcting Plural Nouns   Proofread the following paragraphs for errors in grammar, punctuation, and spelling. Rewrite the paragraphs correctly. Watch especially for errors in the plural forms of nouns. (15 errors)

Kyoko and her sisters have lived in Hong Kong all their lifes. They go to school only in the morning schools are crowded, so students go in shiftes. They compete strongly among themselfs to get into the best schools. In they're free time, many childrens work in the family business.

This Sundae morning, Kyoko's whole family is going out to breakfast they are celebrating a job promotion for Kyoko's father. Him works in one of the many Hong Kong factorys that produce radioes, televisions, and other electronic devices. The restaurant serves dim sum, which are dumplings. Kyoko isn't sure what kind she will order, because there are more than sixty varietys of dim sum.

At home, Kyoko's mother often prepares wonderfull seafood dishs. There are more than 150 kinds of fish in the nearby waters, plus mussels, oysters, and other shellfish.

FOR MORE PRACTICE
See page 389.

C. APPLICATION IN WRITING

A Description   Imagine that you have a pen pal who lives in a distant part of the world and whose life is very different from yours. Write a description of some part of your everyday life that will help your pen pal better understand your world. Use the plural form of at least ten of the following nouns.

potato	food	deer
hobby	wish	people
man	woman	city
bus	student	trout
belief	class	street
radio	life	country

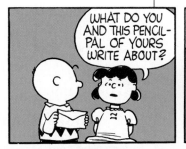

PEANUTS reprinted by permission of UFS, Inc.

Understanding
Nouns   **383**

> A **possessive noun** shows who or what owns something.

Everyone owns things, from clothes to toys to pets. When you wish to say that someone owns something, you use the **possessive form** of the noun.

> *China's* civilization is very ancient.
> (The possessive form of *China* is *China's.*)
> Local rulers constantly challenged the *emperor's* power.
> (The possessive form of *emperor* is *emperor's.*)

Making Singular Nouns Show Possession

To form the possessive of a singular noun, add an apostrophe and an *-s.*

Singular Noun	Possessive Form
ruler	ruler's
Confucius	Confucius's

Making Plural Nouns Show Possession

There are two rules to remember for forming the possessive of a plural noun.

1	If the plural noun ends in *s,* simply add an apostrophe to the end of the word.	
Plural Noun		**Possessive Form**
horses		horses'
invaders		invaders'
families		families'
riders		riders'
rulers		rulers'

	2 If the plural noun does not end in *s*, add an apostrophe and an *-s*.	
Plural Noun	**Possessive Form**
people	people's
women	women's
children	children's

When you form possessives, be careful to place the apostrophe in the correct position. Notice how changing the position of the apostrophe can change the meaning of a phrase. *The peasant's land* means the land belongs to one peasant. *The peasants' land* means the land belongs to two or more peasants. For more information about how to use apostrophes correctly, turn to Handbook 43, "Punctuation," pages 581–598.

Practice Your Skills

A. CONCEPT CHECK

Possessive Nouns   Rewrite the following sentences. Use the possessive form for each noun in italics.

Writing Theme
Ancient China

1. A youth who lived seven hundred years ago was one of *history* greatest travelers.
2. It was Marco Polo who described *Kublai Khan* empire, China.
3. *Marco Polo* diary told of all the wondrous sights he saw.
4. Polo reported seeing coconuts the size of a *man* head.
5. He noted that the *coconuts* insides were white and delicious.
6. The *explorer* description of a crocodile was amazing.
7. He told of a serpent ten paces long and said that this *reptile* jaws were wide enough to swallow a man.
8. In addition, some of the *cities* features amazed Polo.
9. Underground drainage systems showed the Chinese *people* engineering skills.
10. Beautiful gold-covered carvings demonstrated the native *artists* abilities.

B. PROOFREADING SKILL

Correcting Possessive Forms of Nouns   Proofread the following paragraph for errors. Then rewrite it correctly. Pay special attention to errors in the use of possessive forms of nouns. (18 errors)

No one knows whether Chinas scientists was the first to invent gunpowder, but they seem to have been the first to use it in fireworks. In fact, the chinese used gunpowder in fireworks, bombs, and rockets, but they're applications never included guns. The inventors skills became legendary. From the sixth century on, firecrackers were the peoples' delight in every Chinese religious parade and festival. By the time of Marco Polos visit in the thirteenth century, Chinese fireworks display's were quiet marvelous, in the Sixteenth Century, another european, Matteo Ricci, saw a fireworks display at a New Years festival in Nanjing. Riccis' diary reports that the Chinese were experts in "reproducing battles and in making rotating spheres of fire, fiery trees, fruit, and the like." On the occasion of the New Years' festival, Ricci wrote, "i calculated that they consumed enough powder to carry on a sizable war for a number of years.

To celebrate the Chinese New Year, dancers perform the Lion Dance, traditionally thought to bring good luck.

FOR MORE PRACTICE
See page 389.

C. APPLICATION IN WRITING

An Explanation   Choose one of these products, which were invented in China. Write one or more paragraphs to explain how the product is made, how it is used, or both. In your explanation, use at least five possessive nouns.

paper   rockets   compass   movable type

C H E C K ✔ P O I N T

MIXED REVIEW • PAGES 381–386

Write the following sentences. Correct all errors in the plural and possessive forms of nouns. If a sentence does not contain any errors, write *Correct.*

Writing Theme
Women
Mountaineers

1. The peak of Tibets Mount Everest is 29,108 foot above sea level.
2. Until a Japanese woman successfully climbed Everest in 1975, all the mountaineers' who reached the peak were man.
3. However, until September 1988, no female climbers from the United States reached Everests' peak.
4. That month, two U.S. groups with women members began their ascents of the mountain.
5. Members of one expedition hauled boxs and crates of equipment to a base camp high on the mountain's south side.
6. They carried more supplys to camps higher up that would be used by the climbers during their attempts to reach the top.
7. Small groupes of climbers then set off for the summit.
8. Stacy Allison's team included herself and two men.
9. At 28,000 feet, the three climber's oxygen supply ran short.
10. Without extra oxygen, the bloods' oxygen level drops.
11. If all three adventureres had continued, their energy and judgment could have suffered.
12. The team members held a lottery to decide who would go on.
13. The two mens' dreams of reaching the summit ended.
14. Allison took the remaining oxygen and climbed for three more houres before standing at the earth's highest point.
15. She stayed there for forty-five minutes, taking photoes of herself with the flag of the United States and with logos of companys that had sponsored the expedition.
16. Two daies later, another one of the expeditions' female mountaineers, Peggy Luce, reached the summit.
17. Luces' climb was nearly disastrous.
18. Because her goggle's had fogged up, Luce took them off; she was almost snow-blind when she reached the top alone.
19. Then, on her way down, her oxygen tanks supply ran out.
20. She survived, however, as one of the conquerors of Everest.

GRAMMAR
H A N D B O O K
35

Writing Theme
Animal
Communications

A. Finding Nouns   Write the nouns in each sentence.

1. Many chimpanzees live in the jungles of Africa.
2. These apes are like humans in many ways.
3. People wondered if these animals could learn to speak a language such as English.
4. Fifty years ago, Keith and Catherine Hayes tried to find out.
5. The couple brought a chimpanzee to live in their home.
6. The chimp, named Viki, soon settled into its new world.
7. Viki learned to say only four words.
8. Her voice was a hoarse whisper.
9. Since that time, scientists have learned that the vocal cords of chimps differ from the vocal cords of humans.
10. Once, the Hayeses asked Viki to sort some photographs.
11. Viki separated pictures of people from photos of animals.
12. The chimpanzee made only one mistake.
13. Viki put her own picture in the pile with photos of humans.
14. In a more recent experiment, a gorilla named Koko learned several hundred signs in sign language for words.
15. Koko even asked for a cat to be her pet.

B. Using Common and Proper Nouns   Write these sentences, capitalizing each proper noun.

16. Some scientists in the united states study how marine animals can learn languages.
17. One important study took place at a laboratory in hawaii.
18. Dr. louis herman, an animal researcher at the university of hawaii, worked with two dolphins.
19. Phoenix and akeakamai were captured in the gulf of mexico.
20. Their species of dolphin is common in the atlantic ocean.
21. Dr. herman worked in a laboratory near honolulu.
22. One dolphin, phoenix, learned to use whistles for words.
23. The other dolphin, akeakamai, learned sign language.
24. They learned about forty words, roughly what an eighteen-month-old baby learning to speak english would know.
25. Dolphins, which roam the oceans from norway to new zealand and south africa, seem to use their own language of whistles, squeaks, and other noises.

C. Using Plural Nouns Write the following sentences. Correct all errors in the use of the plural forms of nouns.

26. There are many formes of animal communications.
27. Cuckooes, salmon, wolves, and other animals send messages.
28. You probably know that gooses honk, coyotes howl, and sheeps bleat, and that crickets sing by rubbing their two front wings together.
29. Did you know that male deers bellow to scare off rivals?
30. You've probably seen fireflys flashing to attract mates.
31. Different kinds of these insects flash different patterns.
32. One day zookeeperes were watching an elephant named Siri.
33. Siri was making scratchs on the floor with a rock.
34. The zoo employees got Siri paper, paints, and brushs.
35. Siri created hundredes of pages of drawings.
36. Some observers said that her work looked as though it came from art studioes.
37. Vervet monkies use various signals to communicate.
38. They have three main enemys: eagles, snakes, and leopards.
39. To escape leopards, the monkeys go far out on tree branchs, but to escape eagles, they stay close to the tree trunks.
40. Vervets use three different calls to tell one another which enemy is near so they will know how to save their lifes.

D. Writing Possessive Forms Write the correct possessive form of each word in parentheses.

41. Humpback whales make (nature) most complex sounds.
42. The (humpbacks) sounds range from shrieks to groans.
43. Males sing songs during the (whales) mating season.
44. All humpbacks in each of the (ocean) regions sing one song.
45. The (group) song changes during the mating season.
46. Just as (people) taste in music changes, whales seem to get tired of singing the same song over and over.
47. Each (season) singing begins with last year's final song.
48. The songs seem to be a contest among a (region) males.
49. The (singers) breathing stops while they sing because whales cannot breathe and sing at the same time.
50. Most of the (performers) songs last ten to fifteen minutes.

GRAMMAR
HANDBOOK
35

Writing Theme
Tall Tales

A. Finding Common and Proper Nouns   Label two columns *Common Nouns* and *Proper Nouns.* Write each noun from this paragraph in the correct column. Capitalize proper nouns. If a noun is used more than once, you need to list it only once.

¹The story of paul bunyan is a famous tale that began in the united states. ²People all over america have told the stories of a giant lumberjack who could perform great deeds. ³The strength and abilities of this man were amazing! ⁴He could cut down ten trees at a time with a single swipe of his ax. ⁵Paul could drive the stumps into the ground with his bare fist. ⁶Our hero could even squeeze water out of boulders. ⁷paul dug the mississippi river and cleared the states of iowa and kansas for the farmers. ⁸With a blue ox named babe, paul cleared western pastures so cattle could graze. ⁹To give babe drinking water, the fantastic lumberjack scooped out the great lakes. ¹⁰The adventures of paul bunyan are still enjoyed by americans.

B. Writing Singular and Plural Nouns   Write the following sentences. Correct all errors in the plural forms of nouns.

11. Davy Crockett was one of many tall-tale heros.
12. He was real, but storys about him were bigger than life.
13. His strong opinions and the outrageous achievementes he claimed for himself made news everywhere.
14. Davy loved to exaggerate his adventures outrageously, and other people added more impossibilitys to his accounts.
15. The tales say he wasn't born like normal childs.
16. Davy was born on a meteor that crashed in the mountaines.
17. Many of the tales tell of fights Davy had, often with wild animals like mountain lions, wolfs, bears, and alligators.
18. Once he fought a huge mountain lion all night in the bushs, and by morning they had become lifelong friends.
19. All the raccoon knew that he was a great shot, so when they saw him they laid themselves down and gave up.
20. "When I was a baby," he claimed, "I could lick two grizzlys at once."

C. Writing Possessive Forms   Write the possessive form of each noun given in parentheses.

21. Back in the days of sailing ships, (sailors) lives were filled with hard work.
22. They often sang songs, or chanteys, while hoisting a (ship) sails, weighing anchor, or doing their other duties.
23. One of the (seafarers) favorite songs was "Old Stormalong."
24. The (chantey) hero was named Alfred Bulltop Stormalong.
25. Tales of (Stormy) adventures became popular.
26. This (hero) parents were unknown.
27. A tidal wave washed him onto (Cape Cod) coast, in New England, while he was still a baby.
28. Even then, Stormy was eighteen feet tall and drank milk by the barrel—to the (townsfolk) amazement.
29. When he grew up, many (ships) captains wanted him as a sailor.
30. He had numerous adventures on the seas and saved his fellow (crewmen) lives many times.

D. Proofreading   Write the following paragraph on your paper. Correct all errors in the use of proper nouns, plural forms, and possessive forms. (17 errors)

Of all this countries tall-tale heros, Mose was the first to come from a big city. He hailed from new york. People first heard about Mose in a broadway stage show called *A Glance at New York,* by B. A. Baker. From that time on, Mose' legend just grew and grew. Storys of his heroic deeds were told in newspapers and magazines.

Mose was a firefighter back when firefighters's dutys included pulling their wagones themselves. He was eight foot tall and was stronger than ten men. Once a horse-drawn trolley was caught in its track, blocking his fire trucks way. Mose unhooked the horses and picked up the trolley, with the trolleys' passengeres inside. He carried it across the street so that his team and their truck could get to the fire. Hearing a mothers crys, mose entered the burning building and soon carried out a baby—in his hat!

Observation and Description

A good way to learn about other cultures and customs is to describe them. (See Workshop 2.) When you revise this type of descriptive writing, look for ways to add vivid details. Using precise common and proper nouns will help you present information clearly.

Revise the following draft of a description by using the directions at the bottom of the page. Then proofread your work, looking especially for errors in the use of nouns. Also look for other errors in grammar, capitalization, punctuation, and spelling.

¹A tradition at many celebrations in mexico and other Countries of latin america is the breaking of a piñata. ²A piñata is a clay jug or a papier-mâché container covered with layer's of brightly colored paper. ³Many piñatas are made in the shapes of animals, such as burroes or birds. ⁴The piñata is dangled above the head's of guests. ⁵Each one is blindfolded. ⁶Each one gets three tries to break the piñata with a long stick. ⁷When someone succeeds, the piñatas contents come out. ⁸Everyone scurries to gather up the loot. ⁹The tradition of breaking piñatas started in spain. ¹⁰Today, it is carried on at celebrations for christmas, easter, and other ocasions throughout the year. ¹¹A piñata may also be an attraction at any party for childs.

1. In sentence 5, replace the vague pronoun "one" with the more precise noun "guest."

2. Combine sentences 5 and 6 to make a sentence with a compound verb.

3. In sentence 7, replace the vague verb "come" with the more expressive "tumble."

4. Add this missing information after sentence 7: "Sweets, toys, and other small presents fall to the ground."

5. Divide the passage into two paragraphs.

Sniglets

Have you ever searched for just the right word to describe something—and found that the word you wanted was one you had to make up yourself? If so, then you've invented a **sniglet,** a word that doesn't appear in the dictionary but probably should. What sniglets can you add to this list?

cinemuck *(si′ ne muk)* n. The combination of popcorn, soda, and melted chocolate that covers the floors of movie theaters.

glackett *(glak′ it)* n. The noisy ball inside a spray-paint can.

oatgap *(oht′ gap)* n. The empty space in a cereal box created by "settling during shipment."

pigslice *(pig′ slys)* n. The last unclaimed piece of pizza that everyone is secretly dying for.

profanitype *(pro fan′ i tipe)* n. The special symbols used by cartoonists to replace swear words (points, asterisks, stars, and so on).

snacktivity *(snak tiv′ ih tee)* n. Any amusing table pastime (i.e., putting olives on the ends of one's fingers, "biting faces" into a slice of bread, etc.)

spork *(spork)* n. The combination spoon/fork you find in fast-food restaurants.

wondracide *(wun′ druh side)* n. The act of murdering a piece of bread with a knife and cold butter.

Rich Hall and Friends

I wonder if the elephant
Is lonely in his stall
When all the boys and girls are gone
And there's no shout at all,
And there's no one to stamp before,
No one to note his might.
Does he hunch up, as I do,
Against the dark of night?

Gwendolyn Brooks
"PETE AT THE ZOO"

- Write a humorous description of what you think animals do when no one is around.
- Write about what you like to do when no one else is around.

Understanding Verbs

The people on this safari hope to shoot photos that will show all the activity of African wildlife: *running, grazing, stalking, playing, stampeding*—even *lounging* like these cheetahs. The photos will bring the African landscape to life for all who see them.

You can use verbs to make your writing come to life. Verbs are the engines that drive your sentences. They describe the action, tell that something exists, or link ideas.

In this handbook, you will learn ways to use verbs to capture the true spirit of the ideas you want to communicate.

KINDS OF VERBS

> **Verbs** are words that tell about action or state that something *is*.

You use two kinds of verbs when you speak or write. These are **action verbs** and **state-of-being** or **linking verbs.**

Action Verbs

Some verbs tell about action you can see.

The young boy *saddled* his pony.
The two *galloped* across the field.

Other verbs tell about action you cannot see. That is, there is no physical movement.

The boy *wished* for a long ride.
He *enjoyed* the time with his pony.

State-of-Being or Linking Verbs

Some verbs do not show action. They tell what something is, or they link the subject with a word or words in the predicate. Such verbs are called **state-of-being verbs** or **linking verbs.** Since state-of-being verbs and linking verbs are very similar, we will refer to both of them as linking verbs from this point on. These are the most common linking verbs.

am	are	were	being
is	was	be	been

FRANK & ERNEST® by Bob Thaves

FRANK & ERNEST reprinted by permission of NEA, Inc.

Look at the linking verbs in the following sentences.

The pony *is* a reddish color.
He *was* a year old last month.
His movements *are* graceful.

These are some other familiar linking verbs.

| look | appear | become | taste | seem |
| feel | sound | remain | smell | |

The clip-clop of the pony's hooves *sounds* hollow.
The pony *seems* relaxed now.
The pony *becomes* nervous around strangers.

Practice Your Skills

A. CONCEPT CHECK

Verbs   Write the verb from each of the following sentences.

Writing Theme
John Steinbeck

1. Salinas, California, was John Steinbeck's home.
2. John wandered freely through the valley as a boy.
3. His family seemed warm and happy.
4. At age four, he received a Shetland pony.
5. Young John felt proud of this new responsibility.
6. Family friends traveled to the Pacific Ocean in summer.
7. John's family often made the trip by train.
8. The salty spray smelled wonderful to him.
9. Long hikes were a daily activity at the beach.
10. Starfish beckoned from tide pools.
11. Magnificent shells glittered in the sun.
12. The young children went for swims as often as possible.
13. John remained at the beach only part of the summer.
14. His uncle invited him to his ranch near King City.
15. The ranch appeared very different from the ocean.
16. The sun beat harshly on the hills and fields.
17. John searched for special places in the hills.
18. These places inspired special thoughts and feelings.
19. John used the ranch as the setting for his story "The Red Pony."
20. In the story, Jody seems much like young John.

B. APPLICATION IN LITERATURE

Identifying Verbs   Write the verbs in italics from the following passage. Label each verb *Action* or *Linking.* Notice how the writer mixes the use of action and linking verbs.

21Jody *was* glad when [the boys] had gone. **22**He *took* brush and currycomb from the wall, took down the barrier of the box stall and *stepped* cautiously in. **23**The pony's eyes *glittered,* and he edged around into kicking position. **24**But Jody *touched* him on the shoulder and *rubbed* his high arched neck. . . . **25**The pony gradually *relaxed* his tenseness. **26**Jody curried and *brushed* until a pile of dead hair lay in the stall and until the pony's coat had taken on a deep red shine. **27**Each time he finished he *thought* it might have been done better. **28**He *braided* the mane into a dozen little pigtails, and he braided the forelock, and then he undid them and brushed the hair out straight again.

29Jody did not hear his mother *enter* the barn. **30**She *was* angry when she came, but when she looked in at the pony and at Jody working over him, she *felt* a curious pride rise up in her.

John Steinbeck, "The Red Pony"

C. APPLICATION IN WRITING

Description   In the sentence "The girl went down the beach," *went* is a dull action verb. Notice how the sentence becomes livelier with a specific action verb that tells you just how the girl moved:

The girl *raced* down the beach.

Write a description of someone doing an activity, such as a friend playing with a pet or a family member enjoying a nice day. Use as many specific action verbs as you can.

FOR MORE PRACTICE
See page 423.

MAIN VERBS AND HELPING VERBS

A verb may be a single word or a group of words.

You know that many verbs are single words. Read these sentences.

Dawn *makes* lunch.
Dave *mixes* the salad.

Often, however, a verb is made up of two or more words.

Dawn *is making* lunch.
Dave *was mixing* the salad.
Dawn *has been making* lunch.
Dave *might have mixed* the salad.

When there are two or more words in the verb, the last word is the **main verb.** Other words are **helping verbs.**

Helping Verbs	Main Verbs	Verb
is	making	is making
has been	making	has been making
was	mixing	was mixing
might have	mixed	might have mixed

Forms of the verbs *be, have,* and *do* are the most commonly used helping verbs.

be—be, am, is, are, was, were
have—have, has, had
do—do, does, did

Forms of *be, have,* and *do* can also be used as main verbs.

Used as Helping Verb	Used as Main Verb
Eric *is* cooking.	Eric *is* the cook.
Laura *has* finished.	Laura *has* the cookbook.
Kevin *did* stumble.	Kevin *did* his homework.

Several other helping verbs can be used with main verbs.

be	must	will	should
being	can	would	may
been	could	shall	might

Separated Parts of the Verb

The main verb and its helping verbs are not always together. They may be separated by other parts of the sentence.

The children *are* not *eating* their dinner.
Sherry *has* never *liked* snacks.
Did the kindergartners *make* popcorn today?
We *could*n't *find* the recipe.

Notice that *not* and the ending *n't* in the contraction are not verbs. Also notice that in questions, one or more words often come between the helping verb and the main verb.

Practice Your Skills

A. CONCEPT CHECK

Main Verbs and Helping Verbs   Write the main verbs and helping verbs from each sentence. Underline the helping verbs.

1. Can you imagine a world without French fries or corn on the cob?
2. Before Columbus's voyages, Europeans hadn't even heard of potatoes and corn.
3. People in the Americas, however, were growing potatoes and corn long before anyone else.
4. Crops had been cultivated for centuries.
5. These vegetables were quickly adopted by the Europeans.
6. What other American foods were the Europeans enjoying?
7. Tomatoes have become popular around the world.
8. At first, the tomato was considered an exotic food.
9. Only after many years did most Europeans like tomatoes.
10. Chocolate may be the most popular food native to the Americas.

B. DRAFTING SKILL

Using Helping Verbs   Write the following sentences. Add one or two helping verbs to each sentence. Choose from the lists on pages 399–400.

EXAMPLE   I ___ made pancakes for breakfast.
I have made pancakes for breakfast.

11. Somewhere in the world today, someone ___ eat a pancake.
12. Pancakes ___ have different shapes, sizes, and names.
13. In France, people ___ eating pancakes for ages.
14. French pancakes ___ called crêpes.
15. Crêpes ___ filled with meat, cheese, or even fruit.
16. ___ you ever eaten a crêpe with chocolate sauce?
17. You ___ probably love it!
18. Many Mexican families ___ not eat a meal without tortillas.
19. First made centuries ago, these corn pancakes ___ still enjoyed today.
20. In the United States, people ___ eating tortillas in tacos, enchiladas, and burritos.
21. Chinese people ___ made pancakes for centuries too.
22. Chinese pancakes ___ made of flour and water.
23. People ___ wrap them around meat, vegetables, and sauces.
24. Then they ___ fold them into long, thin tubes.
25. These tubes ___ eaten just like a sandwich.

C. APPLICATION IN WRITING

Paragraph   People write about food to describe how to cook, to describe what types of food people in other cultures eat, and for many other reasons. Write a paragraph about food. Use helping verbs and main verbs, such as the following:

Main Verbs

cook	simmer	make
fry	chop	enjoy

Helping Verbs

any form of *be*	any form of *do*	any form of *have*
will	should	can

FOR MORE PRACTICE
See page 423.

Writing Theme
Lunar Energy

Write the verb from each sentence. Underline the main verb twice. Underline each helping verb once, if there is one. Then write whether the main verb is *Action* or *Linking*.

1. Have you ever heard of solar power?
2. Do you know about lunar power?
3. Wolves howl at the full moon.
4. Sweethearts stroll hand in hand in the moonlight.
5. Perhaps someday people will be using the moon's forces for energy.
6. During the moon's orbits of the earth, the moon's gravity pulls on the earth.
7. Twice each day the moon is at its nearest point to the earth.
8. The pull becomes stronger at those times.
9. At other times, the distance of the moon from the earth weakens the force of the pull.
10. Scientists have explained the relationship between the rise and fall of the tides and the force of the moon's pull on the earth.
11. Many countries are seriously studying this force.
12. Tides may become a safe source of energy.
13. Some nations have built power plants on the ocean shore.
14. At high tide, water floods into the plant.
15. Machines convert the water's movement into energy.
16. This energy takes the form of electricity.
17. Tidal power is the name for the creation of energy from tidal movements.
18. One successful tidal power plant is located near St.-Malo, France.
19. Its giant machines run during high and low tides.
20. This plant can produce twice the power of other plants.
21. The tides, of course, follow the moon's cycle.
22. However, the sun's cycle, not the moon's, has always ruled human activities.
23. So, scientists must find ways of storing the energy.
24. All the problems must not seem too difficult, though.
25. The moon's future as an energy source looks bright!

DIRECT OBJECTS OF VERBS

A **direct object** is the noun or pronoun that receives the action of the verb.

In some sentences, the subject and verb alone express a complete thought.

Subject	Verb
The scientist	shouted.
Jemma	waved.
We	applauded

Other sentences, however, are not complete until a word or words are added after the verb.

Paul found *the bone.*
Erika recorded *the discovery.*
The archaeologist appreciated *our work.*

The noun or pronoun that receives the action of the verb is the **direct object** of the verb. *Bone* tells what Paul found. *Discovery* tells what Erika recorded. *Bone* and *discovery* are direct objects. Only action verbs, such as *found* and *recorded,* can have direct objects. Linking verbs do not have direct objects.

To find the direct object in a sentence, first find the verb. Then ask *whom* or *what* after the verb. The word in the sentence that answers *whom* or *what* is the direct object. If no word answers these questions, there is no direct object.

Jeff collects fossils.
Jeff collects *what? fossils*
The direct object is *fossils.*

Lamarr studies in the laboratory.
Lamarr studies *whom?* Lamarr studies *what?*
This sentence has no direct object.

Cave painting of a bison,
Altamira, Spain

A. CONCEPT CHECK

Direct Objects   Write each sentence. Underline the verb once and the direct object twice.

1. Paleontologists study fossils for many reasons.
2. Like detectives, they hunt clues to the past.
3. Fossils often contain the images of ancient animals.
4. Close study reveals the fossils' shapes.
5. However, scientists must know their age, as well.
6. Long ago, paleontologists made educated guesses.
7. In the 1940s, Willard F. Libby invented a better method.
8. Libby developed the process of radiocarbon dating.
9. Every living thing contains a small amount of radiocarbon, a radioactive form of carbon.
10. Living plants and animals constantly absorb atoms of radiocarbon from the air or from their food.
11. Dead organisms, however, slowly lose their radiocarbon.
12. Libby understood an important fact about radiocarbon.
13. Dead organisms lose radiocarbon atoms at a constant rate.
14. Now scientists can measure the number of radiocarbon atoms in a fossil.
15. This number gives exact information about the fossil's age.

B. CONCEPT CHECK

Identifying Direct Objects   Write the direct object from each sentence. If a sentence does not have a direct object, write *None*.

[16]Nine-year-old Maria de Sautuola wandered into a cave in northern Spain. [17]Nearby, her father was digging artifacts. [18]Suddenly, he heard screams. [19]He rushed to Maria. [20]Maria had seen animals on the cave ceiling! [21]The animals seemed very lifelike. [22]Maria had made an important discovery. [23]Experts soon were studying these fantastic paintings. [24]Ancient people created the drawings between 15,000 and 10,000 B.C. [25]The caves in Altamira are fine examples of prehistoric art.

FOR MORE PRACTICE
See page 424.

LINKING VERBS

> A **linking verb** connects, or links, the subject of a sentence with a word in the predicate that describes or renames the subject.

Linking verbs connect a word in the predicate with the subject. The word in the predicate says something about the subject.

> The ocean *is* huge.   Many islands *are* small.

Linking verbs connect *ocean* with *huge* and *islands* with *small*. The words *huge* and *small* tell about the subjects. They are linked to the subjects by the linking verbs *is* and *are*.

The words *am, is, are, was, were, be, been,* and *become* are used as linking verbs. The words *seem, look, appear, smell, taste, feel,* and *sound* can also be linking verbs. (See pages 396–397 for a more complete list of linking verbs.)

The words that follow linking verbs and tell something about the subject can be adjectives, nouns, or pronouns. These words are called **predicate words** because they follow the verb and are part of the predicate.

> The guests *feel* lucky. (*Lucky* is an adjective.)
>
> The coconuts *taste* sweet. (*Sweet* is an adjective.)
>
> Fish *became* their favorite food. (*Food* is a noun.)
>
> The best cook *is* she. (*She* is a pronoun.)

Do not confuse predicate words with direct objects. Predicate words describe or rename the subject. In the above examples, *food* renames *fish* and *she* renames *cook.* To identify a linking verb, decide if the word following the verb either describes or renames the subject. If it does, the verb is a linking verb.

Practice Your Skills

A. CONCEPT CHECK

Linking Verbs Write the linking verb in each sentence.

Writing Theme
Polynesia

1. The origin of the Polynesian people remains a mystery.
2. They were not Asian or South American.
3. Historians feel certain about these facts.
4. Centuries ago, the Polynesians became masters of the ocean.
5. They were brave ocean travelers.
6. Their main form of transportation was travel by canoe.
7. Their slender dugout canoes with elaborate decorations look too fragile for dangerous ocean trips.
8. Nevertheless, these vessels were efficient.
9. Polynesian navigators seemed sure of their skills.
10. The navigators were familiar with the ocean currents, the stars, and the winds.
11. On the sea, Polynesian sailors felt free and independent.
12. The sea also became an important source of food.
13. Fishing remains an important industry in Polynesia today.
14. However, tourism appears a likely growth industry.
15. Thousands of tourists are visitors to Polynesia every year.

B. CONCEPT CHECK

Identifying Linking Verbs and Predicate Words Make three columns: *Subject, Linking Verb,* and *Predicate Word.* Find these parts in each sentence and write them in the proper columns. Include helping verbs in the *Linking Verb* column.

16. Life on a Pacific island may seem ideal.
17. Islanders feel grateful for their kinship with people on other islands.
18. Village leaders are often chiefs.
19. The chiefs' sons usually become chiefs too.
20. Skilled problem solvers are they.
21. However, some problems appear unsolvable.
22. Work in the villages is frequently scarce.
23. Life in the cities sounds good to the villagers.
24. Villagers are quickly becoming city dwellers.
25. Traditional cultures may one day be nonexistent.

FOR MORE PRACTICE
See page 424.

Write the verb from each sentence. Then write the direct object or the predicate word. Write *DO* next to each direct object and *PW* next to each predicate word. If a sentence has no direct object or predicate word, write *None.*

1. Today, many women become doctors.
2. In the 1800s, people felt uneasy about women doctors.
3. The very idea of female physicians seemed outrageous.
4. Elizabeth Blackwell broke the barriers of prejudice with her leadership and determination.
5. As a young child, Blackwell lived in England.
6. In 1832, her family moved to the United States.
7. Even as a child, Blackwell wanted a career in medicine.
8. Later, she wrote applications to thirty medical schools.
9. Twenty-nine schools rejected her.
10. Finally, the thirtieth school, Geneva College, accepted her application.
11. Blackwell's training was difficult.
12. The future often looked bleak to her.
13. Nevertheless, she persevered in her studies.
14. In 1849, she finished her work at the college.
15. She became the first woman to receive a medical degree in the United States.
16. Her success, though, tasted bittersweet.
17. Hospitals closed their doors to her.
18. She couldn't even enter the wards of patients.
19. Fortunately, a persistent fighter was she.
20. For several years, she treated patients in Europe.
21. After a while, she returned to the United States.
22. However, prejudice appeared strong as ever.
23. In 1857, she opened a hospital with help from her sister.
24. The hospital served poor women in New York City.
25. It also included a medical school for women.

Elizabeth Blackwell (1821–1910), first woman physician in the United States.

Different forms of a verb are used to show time. These forms are called **tenses.**

Verbs do more than tell of an action or a state of being. They also tell about time. By changing their forms, verbs tell whether the action or state of being is past, present, or future.

The **present tense** tells about an action or a state of being that is happening now.

I *am* a jeweler.   I *polish* gems.   I *can work.*

The **past tense** tells about an action or a state of being that was completed in the past.

I *was* tired yesterday.   I *polished* fifty gems.

The **future tense** tells about an action or a state of being that will happen in the future.

I *will receive* rubies tomorrow.   I *will be* busy.

Notice that verb tense changes are made in three ways:

1. By a change in ending: *own, owned*
2. By a change in spelling: *see, saw*
3. By a change in helping verbs: *did work, will work*

A jeweler sorting diamonds.

Forming the Present Tense

When the subject is plural, use the base form of the verb. The base form of the verb has no endings or changes. Use the base form of the verb with the pronouns *I* and *you*. Add *-s* or *-es* to the base form when the subject is singular.

We *look.*   They *look.*   I *look.*
You *look.*   He *looks.*

Forming the Past Tense

Form the past tense of most verbs by adding *-d* or *-ed* to the base form of the verb. All verbs that form the past tense by adding *-d* or *-ed* to the base form of the verb are called **regular verbs.**

file	file*d*	wash	wash*ed*

Other verbs, called **irregular verbs,** undergo a change in their spelling to show the past tense. It's a good idea to memorize the past tense of irregular verbs.

go	*went*	wear	*wore*
choose	*chose*	do	*did*

There is another way that you can show a change in tense from the present form. You can use a helping verb along with the main verb.

rule	had ruled	cut	had cut

Forming the Future Tense

Form the future tense by using the helping verbs *will* or *shall* with the present tense.

shine	will shine	choose	will choose

Using Verb Tenses

Whenever you write, remember to keep your verbs in the same tense. Avoid switching from past to present or from present to past.

Incorrect	The opal gleamed. It glows and glitters.
Correct	The opal gleamed. It glowed and glittered.

Also, do not change the verb tense in the middle of a sentence.

Incorrect	I *slip* on the ring and *wore* it proudly.
Correct	I *slipped* on the ring and *wore* it proudly.

Writing **TIP**

You will need to change the ending of some regular verbs before adding *-ed* to form the past tense. For help with spelling past tense forms see Improving Your Spelling, pages 610–611.

Writing **TIP**

Notice how the use of verb tenses helps a reader understand the time order in these sentences.

Yesterday, I *fixed* the lock on the safe. Lady Markham *needs* a secure place to store her jewels. She *will bring* them tomorrow.

Understanding Verbs **409**

Practice Your Skills

Writing Theme
Precious Stones

A. CONCEPT CHECK

Verb Tenses   Write the verb in each sentence. Then label the verb tense *Past, Present,* or *Future.*

1. Will the legends about the Kohinoor diamond come true?
2. *Kohinoor* means "the mountain of light" in Persian.
3. Two legends surround this fabulous gem.
4. First, its owner will someday rule the world.
5. Second, a man will never safely wear the stone.
6. The Kohinoor diamond sparkled through the destruction of two empires.
7. Long ago, it belonged to Emperor Mohammed Mogul.
8. His empire fell to the Shah of Persia.
9. The diamond's new owner, the Shah, soon died in a palace revolt.
10. At present, the diamond glitters in the collection of the Queen of England.

B. DRAFTING SKILL

Using Tenses Accurately   Write the verb form given in parentheses.

11. Gems (past of *fascinate*) people of long ago in many unusual ways.
12. People even (past of *invent*) superstitions about gems and jewels.
13. Supposedly, diamonds (present of *give*) people strength in battle.
14. A sapphire (present of *bring*) wonderful happiness.
15. Rubies supposedly (future of *fill*) your life with love and joy.
16. An emerald under your tongue (future of *predict*) the future for you.
17. In other legends, amethysts (future of *increase*) your wisdom.
18. Turquoise supposedly (past of *prevent*) falls from horses and other accidents.
19. Of course, few (present of *believe*) these stories.
20. However, most people (future of *find*) the stories interesting.

C. PROOFREADING SKILL

Correcting Verb Tenses   Write the following paragraph, correcting errors in verb tenses. Also correct errors in spelling, capitalization, and punctuation. (10 errors)

Jade is a semiprecious stone, and it came in too kinds— jadeite and nephrite. Today, jadeite will be the more valuable of the two. Both kinds of jade are used for jewlery. In 1990, a huge boulder of nephrite jade was found in northeastern china. The boulder will weigh 291 tons. and it was 23 feet long by 20 feet high. can you imagine wearing that around you're neck.

C H E C K

C H E C K   ✔   P O I N T
MIXED REVIEW • PAGES 408–411

FOR MORE PRACTICE
See page 425.

Write the following sentences using the verb form given in parentheses.

1. I (past of *attend*) a horse show last Friday.
2. My friend Amy (past of *show*) her horse Gypsy.
3. Gypsy (present of *perform*) many beautiful movements for the appreciative crowd.
4. Amy (past of *work*) with Gypsy for a month preparing for Friday's show.
5. He (present of *bow*) and (present of *prance*) gracefully in front of the reviewing stand.
6. Before every show, Amy (future of *braid*) his tail.
7. Gypsy (present of *seem*) like a member of her family.
8. Some riders (future of *decorate*) their horses' manes with colorful satin ribbons.
9. Amy (past of *shudder*) when she learned about prehistoric people.
10. They (past of *hunt*) wild horses and ate the meat.
11. No one ever (future of *turn*) Gypsy into a ponyburger!
12. Almost any horse (future of *learn*) to obey commands.
13. Amy (present of *train*) Gypsy every day.
14. Sometimes Gypsy (present of *disobey*) her commands.
15. Amy simply (present of *repeat*) the command patiently.

Writing Theme
Horses

All verb tenses are made from the three **principal parts** of a verb: present, past, and past participle.

You have seen that every verb has many different forms. All of these different forms are made from just three **principal parts.** Look at the principal parts of the verbs below.

Present	Past	Past Participle
call	called	(have) called
halt	halted	(have) halted
print	printed	(have) printed
watch	watched	(have) watched
review	reviewed	(have) reviewed
carry	carried	(have) carried

The **present** part of the verb is its present tense. Add *-s* to form the singular. The present part used with *will* or *shall* forms the future tense.

The **past** part of the verb is its past tense. The spelling of the past tense of a verb may change if its present form ends in *y* or a consonant such as *-h, -d, -p,* or *-t.* For example, the past of *worry* is *worried;* the past of *snap* is *snapped.*

The **past participle** is always used with a helping verb such as *have.* Look at these other examples.

is called	has called	was being called
was called	have called	has been called
were called	had called	will have called
		will be called
		should have been called

Notice that with regular verbs, the past participle is the same as the past form. This is not always true of irregular verbs. You will learn more about the principal parts of irregular verbs later in this handbook.

Practice Your Skills

A. CONCEPT CHECK

Principal Parts of Verbs   Make three columns: *Present, Past,* and *Past Participle.* Write each of the following words in the *Present* column. Then write the past and past participle forms in their columns. Choose helping verbs to include with the past participles.

1. try	**6.** record	**11.** flub
2. produce	**7.** plan	**12.** vary
3. hurry	**8.** play	**13.** pick
4. act	**9.** edit	**14.** rehearse
5. learn	**10.** accept	**15.** shop

B. DRAFTING SKILL

Using the Principal Parts of Verbs   Write each sentence using the verb form given in parentheses.

16. Movies (past participle of *enjoy,* with *are*) by millions of people everywhere.
17. Movie making (present of *involve*) hundreds of people, from actors to costume designers to electricians.
18. Of course, no film ever (past of *start*) without a "property," or idea for a story.
19. The screenwriter's job never (present of *end*).
20. Scripts (past participle of *change,* with *must be*) often.
21. The director (present of *plan*) every detail.
22. His orders (past participle of *carry,* with *are*) out by the cast and crew.
23. For example, stunts (past participle of *practice,* with *should be*) many times for safety's sake.
24. In the past, stunt performers often (past of *injure*) themselves.
25. Today, safety equipment and procedures (present of *protect*) most stunt performers from harm during filming.

FOR MORE PRACTICE
See page 425.

> For some verbs, the past tense is formed by changing the spelling of the present form. These verbs are called **irregular verbs.**

You have already learned that the past form of all regular verbs is made by adding either *-d* or *-ed* to the present form of the verbs.

race   rac*ed*   jump   jump*ed*   dip   dipp*ed*

Some verbs, however, have past forms that are made by changing the spelling of the present form. These verbs are **irregular verbs.** Here are some examples.

run   *ran*   sing   *sang*   go   *went*

Sometimes, the past participle of an irregular verb is the same as the past form.

said   *(has) said*   taught   *(have) taught*

However, many irregular verbs have past participle forms that are different from the past forms.

threw   *(were) thrown*   swam   *(have) swum*

Remember these rules whenever you use regular or irregular verbs.

1. The past form of a verb is always used alone without a helping verb.

    The athlete *drank* the entire container of water.

2. The past participle must always be used with a helping verb.

    The athlete *had drunk* the entire container of water during the time out.

Here is a list of the principal parts of the most common irregular verbs. Refer to it whenever you are unsure about the proper form of an irregular verb. In addition, dictionaries list the principal parts of irregular verbs after the present form.

Principal Parts of Common Irregular Verbs

Present	Past	Past Participle
begin	began	(have) begun
break	broke	(have) broken
bring	brought	(have) brought
choose	chose	(have) chosen
come	came	(have) come
do	did	(have) done
drink	drank	(have) drunk
eat	ate	(have) eaten
fall	fell	(have) fallen
fly	flew	(have) flown
freeze	froze	(have) frozen
give	gave	(have) given
go	went	(have) gone
grow	grew	(have) grown
know	knew	(have) known
lay	laid	(have) laid
lie	lay	(have) lain
ride	rode	(have) ridden
rise	rose	(have) risen
run	ran	(have) run
say	said	(have) said
see	saw	(have) seen
sing	sang	(have) sung
sit	sat	(have) sat
speak	spoke	(have) spoken
steal	stole	(have) stolen
swim	swam	(have) swum
take	took	(have) taken
teach	taught	(have) taught
wear	wore	(have) worn
write	wrote	(have) written

Practice Your Skills

A. CONCEPT CHECK

Irregular Verbs   Write the correct form of the verb given in parentheses.

1. How many athletes have (past participle of *do*) what was thought to be impossible?
2. How many have (past participle of *say*), "I can do it"?
3. Sarah Covington-Fulcher (past of *choose*) a challenge that many believed impossible.
4. She (past of *run*) perhaps the longest distance ever.
5. She (past of *go*) 11,134 miles through 35 states.
6. Earlier records had now been (past participle of *break*).
7. This runner (past of *teach*) a lesson in endurance.
8. Her race (past of *begin*) on July 21, 1987.
9. It (past of *come*) to an end on October 2, 1988.
10. Twenty-six pairs of shoes were (past participle of *wear*) out during her run.
11. Could she have (past participle of *know*) the hazards?
12. Hazards, indeed, (past of *lie*) in wait along the route.
13. Once, the temperature (past of *fall*) way below zero!
14. In the desert, it (past of *rise*) to 124 degrees!
15. She must have (past participle of *drink*) lots of water!

B. PROOFREADING SKILL

Using Irregular Verbs Correctly   Write the paragraph. Correct all errors, especially those in the use of irregular verbs. (18 errors)

In 1926, gertrude ederle stealed the worlds' heart. She gave her best effort to a daunting task. At age ninteen, she swum the English Channel. Her time breaked all previous records, The feat taked fourteen hours and thirty-nine minutes. Other Swimmers had nearly frozen in the cold water. Gertrude, however, weared a heavy coat of greese for warmth. Reporters had flew in from all over the world for the event. Some rided next to her in rowboats. In they're articles, the reporters wrote about Gertrude's victory. And singed her praises for the Olympic meddals she had won earlier.

FOR MORE PRACTICE
See page 426.

C H E C K ✔ P O I N T
MIXED REVIEW • PAGES 412–416

Write the correct form of the regular or irregular verb given in parentheses.

1. Have you ever (saw, seen) Niagara Falls?
2. Each year, millions (visit, visited) the falls.
3. The water (runs, ran) violently over a rocky cliff.
4. Over time, the falls actually have (grew, grown) smaller.
5. Water (worn, wears) away part of the cliff.
6. This erosion (stolen, steals) an average of three inches from the cliff each year.
7. Still, water has (rush, rushed) over the cliff since the end of the Ice Age.
8. Visitors have (tell, told) of many amazing sights at Niagara.
9. Several times, for example, the falls have (freeze, frozen) in extremely cold weather.
10. Daredevils have also (try, tried) spectacular stunts.
11. Some have (went, gone) over the falls in barrels.
12. Most of them (fell, fallen) to disastrous ends.
13. A few, however, have (swam, swum) to safety.
14. In the 1800s, a famous French tightrope artist (gave, given) his greatest performance at Niagara.
15. People (came, come) from all over to see Blondin's performance.
16. Blondin (crossed, cross) above the falls on a thin wire several times.
17. During one crossing, he (wore, worn) a blindfold.
18. Another time, he (carried, carry) a man on his back.
19. At one point, he (sat, sit) calmly on the wire and (eat, ate) an omelet!
20. Officials have since (pass, passed) laws against such stunts.

Several pairs of verbs are often confused. These include **can** and **may, let** and **leave,** and **lie** and **lay.**

Look at the correct way to use these confusing verbs.

Can and May

1. *Can* means "to be able."
2. *May* means "to be allowed to," "to be permitted to," or "to have the possibility of."

> Can you walk a tightrope?
> You may go to the circus.

Let and Leave

1. *Let* means "to allow" or "to permit."
2. *Leave* means "to depart" or "to let stay or let be."

Principal Parts   let, let, let
                       leave, left, left

> *Let* me see your ticket.
> What time do you *leave* for the show?
> Do not *leave* your ticket behind.

Lie and Lay

1. *Lie* means "to rest" or "to recline."
2. *Lay* means "to put or place something."

Principal Parts   lie, lay, lain
                       lay, laid, laid

> The elephant *lies* down upon command.
> The clown *lays* a red carpet in the ring.

Lay also means "to produce eggs": A hen *lays* eggs.

Practice Your Skills

A. CONCEPT CHECK

Confusing Verbs   Write the correct verb from those given in parentheses.

Writing Theme
The Circus

1. I had just (laid, lain) down on the sofa for a nap.
2. Children's cries outside did not (let, leave) me sleep.
3. "(Can, May) I go to the circus?" cried a boy.
4. A girl cried, "(Leave, Let) me go too!"
5. I (can, may) imagine these same cries in ancient Rome.
6. The Romans (laid, lay) the foundations for the circus.
7. The circus's past also (lies, lays) in fairs and markets.
8. In the markets, vendors (lain, laid) out their goods.
9. I (can, may) picture the people shopping.
10. Vendors rarely (let, left) their stands.
11. Other people, though, would (lie, lay) down their purchases and watch jugglers, magicians, and minstrels.
12. Later, the idea of a market as a fair was (left, let) behind.
13. Fairs became separate celebrations that (left, let) people have fun.
14. People would (lie, lay) their troubles aside and laugh.
15. I (can, may) see why the children want to go to the circus!

B. REVISION SKILL

Using Verbs Correctly   For each sentence, if a verb is incorrect, write the correct verb. If a verb is correct, write *Correct*.

16. Have you ever laid down with a ball on your nose?
17. Graduates of National Circus Project workshops claim they may juggle and perform other circus stunts.
18. Many schools let project members work with students.
19. The circus performers arrive and lie out the equipment.
20. They do not let students alone while learning.
21. Instead, they let students learn tricks and stunts.
22. Some find they may juggle balls easily after only one lesson.
23. For others, many balls still fall and lay on the floor.
24. By the time instructors leave, students feel confident.
25. Sometimes, schools may invite promising students back.

FOR MORE PRACTICE
See page 426.

Other verb pairs that are often confused are these: **teach** and **learn, rise** and **raise,** and **sit** and **set.**

Here are some other pairs of verbs that are often confused and used incorrectly.

Teach and Learn

1. *Teach* means to "to show how" or "to explain."
2. *Learn* means "to understand" or "to gain knowledge."

Principal Parts   teach, taught, taught
                       learn, learned, learned

Can you *teach* an old dog new tricks?
My dog will not *learn* any tricks at all.

Rise and Raise

1. *Rise* means "to move upward" or "to get up."
2. *Raise* means "to move something upward" or "to lift."

Principal Parts   rise, rose, risen
                       raise, raised, raised

The lazy dog *rises* from the cushion.
Raise your paw for a handshake.

Sit and Set

1. *Sit* means "to be in a seat" or "to rest."
2. *Set* means "to put or place something."

Principal Parts   sit, sat, sat
                       set, set, set

The puppy *sits* on his blanket.
Set his bowl on the floor.

Practice Your Skills

A. CONCEPT CHECK

Confusing Verb Pairs   Write the correct verb from those given in parentheses.

Writing Theme
Training Animals

1. Almost any dog can be (learned, taught) new tricks.
2. Your skill level, too, will (rise, raise) with each trick.
3. (Set, Sit) reasonable goals for yourself and your pet.
4. A reward will (rise, raise) your dog's rate of success.
5. I (learned, taught) my dog several simple tricks.
6. Now she (rises, raises) her paw to shake hands.
7. At my command, she (sets, sits) and waits for me.
8. Also on command, she (raises, rises) up on her hind legs.
9. Eventually, she (learned, taught) to find toys and bring them to me.
10. Yesterday, she (set, sat) her favorite toy on my lap.
11. When she did that, my hopes (rose, raised).
12. I tried to (teach, learn) her to fetch my slippers.
13. However, she stubbornly (set, sat) on one slipper and chewed the other.
14. I guess I had (sat, set) my sights too high.
15. I (learned, taught) that some tricks might be too hard.

B. REVISION SKILL

Using Verbs Correctly   Write the sentences and correct any errors in the verbs. If a sentence is correct, write *Correct.*

16. Special trainers rise guide dogs to help blind people.
17. These trainers learn the dogs valuable skills.
18. First, a family rises a dog for about a year.
19. The family sits typical goals for basic obedience.
20. Then, an intense training program learns the dog other skills.
21. A guide dog even learns when to disobey commands.
22. A dog is learned to stop at busy intersections.
23. When cars are approaching, the dog will set still and refuse to move rather than endanger its owner.
24. Time is also sat aside for dog and owner to work together.
25. A well-trained dog will raise to almost any occasion.

FOR MORE PRACTICE
See page 426.

Writing Theme
Young Napoleon
Bonaparte

Write the correct verb from those given in parentheses.

1. How many great world leaders (can, may) you name?
2. Their deeds have (raised, risen) above the ordinary.
3. Some leaders (rose, raised) themselves to fame.
4. The stories of others (lay, lie) hidden in history.
5. We all (can, may) benefit from studying great leaders.
6. You (can, may) choose to learn about their childhoods.
7. Did they (sit, set) in school and not pay attention?
8. Did they (let, leave) diaries behind for us to read?
9. (Let, Leave) us examine the young Napoleon Bonaparte.
10. The Bonapartes did not (raise, rise) their son for a career in the army.
11. Bonaparte children were (learned, taught) to be priests, lawyers, or public officials.
12. Napoleon, though, (sat, set) his mind on military glory.
13. He would (lay, lie) a trap for his six younger brothers and sisters and then give them orders.
14. You (may, can) want to consider him bossy.
15. His orders often (raised, rose) a family ruckus.
16. What (can, may) you expect from a boy nicknamed "the little wolf"?
17. Only his older brother Joseph would (set, sit) quietly.
18. Usually, Napoleon (raised, rose) to the occasion and restored the family peace.
19. Napoleon's parents would (leave, let) him discover his own strengths and weaknesses.
20. He easily (learned, taught) science and mathematics.
21. In boarding school, the other students would not (leave, let) young Napoleon alone.
22. However, the boy preferred to (lay, lie) in bed and dream of glory.
23. He would (sit, set) goals for himself.
24. In time, he would (rise, raise) to fame and power.
25. In fact, "the little wolf" later (sat, set) on a throne as the Emperor of France.

A. Finding Action Verbs and Linking Verbs Write the main verb from each sentence. Then write whether it is an *Action Verb* or a *Linking Verb.*

1. Does exploration interest you?
2. Unexplored areas fascinated President Thomas Jefferson.
3. In the eastern United States, people knew little about the land west of the Mississippi River.
4. Little information was available to mapmakers in 1800.
5. An exploration party seemed the best solution.
6. In 1804, Jefferson organized a grand expedition.
7. He chose Meriwether Lewis as the leader.
8. William Clark became the second in command.
9. Clark was an excellent mapmaker and leader.
10. Forty-five men joined the dangerous expedition.
11. Lewis described the trip in his journal.
12. Grizzly bears attacked the men on the journey west.
13. Lewis felt happy and excited near the Rocky Mountains.
14. The men traveled about 7,700 miles to the Pacific Ocean.
15. Lewis published his journal in 1814.

Writing Theme
Great Expeditions

B. Identifying Main Verbs and Helping Verbs Write the verb from each sentence. Underline the helping verb(s) once and the main verb twice.

16. Can you name any women explorers?
17. Many women explorers have been ignored by history.
18. These valiant adventurers did not become famous.
19. By the time of her death, Louise Boyd had led seven expeditions to Greenland.
20. Delia J. Akeley is known for her African explorations and knowledge of Pygmy culture.
21. In 1929, Akeley was living in a Pygmy village.
22. Her greatest contribution may have been her open approach to different cultures.
23. Friendliness had always served her well with strangers.
24. Have other women undertaken dangerous expeditions?
25. Even in her fifties, Annie Smith Peck was scaling mountains in Peru!

C. Recognizing Direct Objects   Write the verb in each sentence. Then write the direct object. If a sentence has no direct object, write *None.*

26. Antonio and Margarita Serra loved their son Miguel.
27. Their bright little boy received an excellent education.
28. Young Miguel became a priest of the Franciscan order.
29. The world knows Miguel as Father Junípero Serra.
30. He had chosen the name of Junípero, a friend of St. Francis of Assisi.
31. The Franciscan order sent the priest to the Americas.
32. In Mexico, during the 1700s, Father Junípero learned many skills for survival in the wilderness.
33. Father Junípero joined an expedition to California.
34. He worked hard in the region known as Upper California.
35. He earned the respect of the native peoples there.
36. Together, they built the California missions.
37. Father Junípero defended the rights of the native peoples.
38. The first mission was established in San Diego in 1769.
39. Some missions are still standing.
40. In time, the original settlements became cities.

D. Identifying Linking Verbs and Predicate Words   Write the verb from each of the following sentences. If the verb is a linking verb, write the predicate word. If the verb is not a linking verb, write *NLV.*

41. In the 1900s, most expeditions were scientific.
42. Adventure remained an important part of them, though.
43. Roy Chapman Andrews's work seems an excellent example.
44. In time, he became director of the American Museum of Natural History.
45. The museum sponsored his expeditions.
46. At first, he was famous for adventures in faraway places.
47. Andrews's life sounded glamorous to many people.
48. One year, he traveled to Outer Mongolia.
49. There he found the first known dinosaur eggs.
50. Undoubtedly, he felt proud of this discovery.

E. Recognizing Verb Tenses   Write the tense of each verb in italics. Write *Present, Past,* or *Future.*

51. Millions of people *admire* Admiral Richard E. Byrd.
52. Few explorers ever *will rival* his daring or his vision.
53. Byrd *gained* fame as an aviator for the United States Navy.
54. In 1926, he *was* on the first flight over the North Pole.
55. We *remember* him mostly for his work at the South Pole.
56. Byrd *explored* the Antarctic for more than thirty years.
57. He *opened* the Antarctic to exploration by aircraft.
58. Byrd also *established* bases for scientific studies.
59. In a book, he *describes* one lonely winter at a base.
60. Because of his work, people someday *will understand* the mysterious and icy continent of Antarctica.

F. Identifying Principal Parts of Verbs   Write the verb from each sentence. Then tell whether the main verb is in the *Present, Past,* or *Past Participle* form.

61. In 1937, Amelia Earhart started her last expedition.
62. She and her navigator had planned a flight around the world.
63. Earhart had first gained fame as a pilot in the 1920s.
64. Over the years, she recorded many aviation firsts.
65. She also established many long-distance flying records.
66. Some of her achievements still stand in the record books.
67. By 1937, she had prepared for the ultimate flight.
68. Many people can recall the excitement of the flight's early stages.
69. Then, over the Pacific Ocean, Earhart, her navigator, and the plane all disappeared.
70. Since then, many expeditions have combed the area in search of her.
71. In fact, people still search for traces of the flight.
72. Investigators have advanced many theories.
73. The mystery of her tragic flight has never been solved.
74. It remains one of the great mysteries of this century.
75. The legend of Amelia Earhart lives on long after her death.

G. Using Irregular Verbs

Write the verb form given in parentheses.

76. Expeditions to the South Pole have (past participle of *bring*) some people fame and glory.
77. Others (past of *eat*) humble pie after their failure.
78. In 1911, Englishman Robert Scott (past of *take*) an expedition to the Antarctic.
79. By the time Scott and his companions reached the pole, they had (past participle of *see*) only icy misery.
80. In the end, Scott (past of *freeze*) to death.
81. Norwegian explorer Roald Amundsen also (past of *go*) to Antarctica in 1911.
82. Many writers have (past participle of *tell*) of the race between Scott and Amundsen to the South Pole.
83. Amundsen's group (past of *ride*) dog sleds and walked.
84. Their journey to the South Pole and back had (past participle of *go*) fairly smoothly.
85. British adventurer Robert Swan (past of *choose*) two dangerous expeditions.
86. Swan (past of *begin*) a walk to the South Pole in 1986.
87. Seventy days later, he (past of *sit*) down at the pole.
88. By 1989, he had (past participle of *come*) back from a walk to the North Pole.
89. Why have people (past participle of *do*) such daring and dangerous feats?

H. Choosing the Right Verb

Write the correct verb from those given in parentheses.

90. Armchair adventurers (sit, set) back and relax.
91. These people (lie, lay) around and dream.
92. Others have (risen, raised) flags in distant lands.
93. Real adventurers do not (lie, lay) aside their dreams.
94. They (can, may) put their dreams into practice.
95. Their exploits (learn, teach) them courage.
96. Their mistakes (let, leave) them grow and learn.
97. Has the spirit of adventure (raised, risen) in you?
98. Perhaps one day you (can, may) enter the record books.

A. Kinds of Verbs   Write the verb from each sentence. Then, tell whether it is an *Action Verb* or a *Linking Verb.* If the verb is an action verb, write the direct object. If the verb is a linking verb, write the predicate word.

1. A year without a summer seems impossible.
2. In 1816, people in New England experienced the coldest summer on record.
3. Snowstorms struck the Northeast in June.
4. Frost nipped noses in July and August.
5. The weather remained cool during that entire spring and summer.
6. This scientific oddity sounds unbelievable.
7. In 1815, the Mount Tambora volcano in Indonesia shot tiny particles of sulfur into the atmosphere.
8. These sulfur particles reflected much sunlight away from the earth.
9. In 1816, summer became winter in upstate New York and New England.
10. One single volcanic eruption cooled the globe!

Writing Theme
The Weather

B. Main Verbs and Helping Verbs   Write each of the following sentences. Underline the helping verb or verbs once. Underline the main verb twice.

11. Volcanoes have not been the only causes of strange weather around the world.
12. Many parts of the world are affected by an area of unusually warm sea water in the Pacific Ocean.
13. This stream of water is called El Niño.
14. Scientists haven't discovered the causes of El Niño.
15. They are still studying this oddity of nature.
16. However, they do know its effects.
17. In the past, El Niño has set off jet streams of warm, moist air.
18. These jet streams have created heavy rainstorms and other severe weather patterns.
19. How can people prepare for the effects of El Niño?
20. They should listen to the most recent weather forecast!

C. Verb Tenses   Write the following sentences. Use the tense of the verb given in parentheses.

21. A fishing net in the Mississippi River (past of *snag*) a foot-long mud puppy.
22. Then, the unhappy lizard (past of *travel*) to a laboratory in Colorado.
23. The mud puppy (future of *help*) scientists in their research on taste buds!
24. According to the scientists, mud puppies someday (future of *improve*) the taste of our foods.
25. For years, scientists (past of *study*) the lizard's large taste cells.
26. Research (present of *reveal*) new information about the sense of taste.
27. This complex sense (present of *fascinate*) scientists involved in taste research.
28. Their discoveries (past of *change*) some of their beliefs.
29. As a result, scientists (future of *create*) new taste sensations.
30. If so, we (future of *owe*) a lot to the large taste cells of the mud puppy!

D. Principal Parts of Verbs   Write the main verb from each of the following sentences. Then write whether it is in the *Present, Past,* or *Past Participle* form.

31. Entomologists have studied thousands of the world's insects.
32. Robber flies rank among the most interesting.
33. These unusual insects have been spotted in many different parts of the world.
34. Scientists investigated the fly's behavior.
35. These insect pirates robbed other insects of food.
36. Many robber flies, for example, love pollen.
37. However, no robber fly has ever gathered its own pollen.
38. Instead, it waits near a beehive for the return of the worker bees.
39. Usually, the worker bees are loaded with pollen.
40. The fly simply gobbles up a bee!

E. Irregular Verbs   For each sentence, write the form of the verb given in parentheses.

41. Between five and six P.M., the light (past of *grow*) dim.
42. Cecily (past of *fall*) over a skate on the sidewalk.
43. Cecily could never have (past participle of *see*) it.
44. Poor night vision has (past participle of *give*) doctors cause for concern.
45. Doctors (past of *know*) about the problem but not about its seriousness.
46. It has (past participle of *take*) years to recognize the extent of the problem.
47. Researchers have (past participle of *begin*) to study problems of contrast and lighting.
48. In fact, traffic accidents (past of *bring*) the problems to their attention.
49. Have you (past participle of *ride*) in a car at night?
50. One doctor (past of *say*) that dim light may cause about 80 percent of all accidents at night.

F. Confusing Pairs of Verbs   Write the correct verb from those given in parentheses.

51. You (can, may) use weight equipment to strengthen your muscles.
52. Now, computer programs will (rise, raise) your level of brainpower!
53. You (can, may) think brain exercises are useless.
54. Have you (let, left) your mental powers weaken?
55. Better brainpower (lays, lies) within your grasp.
56. For starters, you (set, sit) at the computer.
57. A mental workout program (lays, lies) mind-expanding puzzles and brain teasers before you.
58. For example, a picture of a brick (raises, rises) onto the screen.
59. How many different uses for it (can, may) you think of?
60. The program (sits, sets) up dozens of problems for you to solve during each workout session.

Informative Writing: Reports

Writing a family history allows you to explore your own past. (See Workshop 7.) When you revise a family history, make sure that your facts are correct and that you have presented them in the right order. Also check to see that you do not switch back and forth between the past and present tense.

Revise the following draft of a family history by using the directions at the bottom of the page. Then proofread your work, paying special attention to the use of verbs. Also look for other grammatical errors and mistakes in capitalization, punctuation, and spelling.

¹My grandfather told me this story about how his family came to the United States from Poland. ²His father, Anton, was just a boy of twelve at the time. ³He came by ship with his father sister and mother. ⁴When there ship arrives at New York, she was ill. ⁵The immigration officials examine her. ⁶The immigration officials put a cross on her jacket with chalk. ⁷Anton looks around and realizes that the poeple with crosses were being separated from the others. ⁸The immigation officials would not leave these people come into the United States. ⁹Anton set next to his mother and put his arm around her. ¹⁰When no one were looking, he wipes away the cross. ¹¹Thanks to his cleverness, his mother is not sent back like the others.

1. Make sentence 1 more complete by adding the information that the family came from Poland one hundred years ago.

2. In sentence 3, replace the weak verb "came" with the stronger "traveled."

3. In sentence 4, replace the unclear pronoun "she" with "his mother."

4. Combine sentences 5 and 6 to make one sentence with a compound verb.

5. Show Anton's quick thinking in sentence 9 by beginning the sentence with the adverb "Immediately."

on the LIGHT side

Crazy English

Why do we say the alarm clock is going off when it goes on? How can a building burn up and burn down at the same time? Why is a boxing ring square? It's a crazy language, you say? You're right! As Richard Lederer explains, the English language is very strange indeed.

In the crazy English language, there is no butter in buttermilk, no egg in an eggplant, and no ham in a hamburger. . . .

To add to this insanity, blackboards can be green, hot dogs can be cold, darkrooms can be lit, nightmares can take place in broad daylight ("That test was a real nightmare"), tablecloths can be made of paper, and silverware (especially in fast-food eateries) can be made of plastic. . . .

A writer is someone who writes, and a stinger is something that stings. But fingers don't *fing,* grocers don't *groce,* hammers don't *ham,* and humdingers don't *humding.*

If you wrote a letter, why don't we also say that you *bote* your tongue? If the teacher taught, why isn't it also true that the preacher *praught?* If you conceive a conception and receive at a reception, why don't you grieve a *greption* and believe a *beleption?*

Yes, English is a crazy language.

Skills

Directions   One or more of the underlined sections in the following sentences may contain an error in grammar, punctuation, spelling, or capitalization. Write the letter of each incorrect section. Then rewrite the section correctly. If there is no error in an item, write *D*.

> **Example**   Some <u>weasel's</u> coats turn white in the <u>winter</u>. These
>   **A**   **B**
> <u>weasels</u> are called ermines. <u>No error</u>
> **C**   **D**
>
> **Answer**   A—weasels'

1. Blue laws forbid certain <u>activities</u>, such as dancing, on <u>sundays</u>. At one
                         A   **B**
time, mothers could not kiss their <u>children</u> on this day. <u>No error</u>
                             C   **D**

2. Have you ever <u>ate</u> 480 oysters in an <u>hour?</u> <u>Thats</u> the oyster-eating record.
               A   **B**   **C**
<u>No error</u>
 D

3. President Ulysses <u>s.</u> Grant got a speeding ticket in <u>Washington, D.C.</u>
                 A   **B**
He <u>ridden</u> his horse over the speed limit of twenty miles per hour. <u>No error</u>
     C   **D**

4. It is sometimes possible to see five <u>states.</u> <u>From</u> the top of the
                                     A
<u>Empire State Building</u> in <u>New York</u>. <u>No error</u>
          B   **C**   **D**

5. Do people who were born in a leap year have <u>fewer</u> <u>Birthday</u> <u>partys</u> than
                                            A   **B**   **C**
other people do? <u>No error</u>
                D

6. Not all <u>Sedimentary</u> rocks are made of particles of <u>rock.</u> <u>Some</u> have been
           A   **B**
formed from fossils of animals and <u>leafs</u>. <u>No error</u>
                             C   **D**

7. The <u>Falkland Islands</u> <u>lay</u> about three hundred miles to the <u>East</u> of
　　　　　　 A　　　　　　 **B**　　　　　　　　　　　　　　　　 **C**
Argentina.　<u>No error</u>
　　　　　　 D

8. A woman in <u>Leeds, England,</u> is named <u>Ann Chovy can</u> you imagine having
　　　　　　　 A　　　　　　　　　　 **B**
the name of a pizza <u>topping.</u>　<u>No error</u>
　　　　　　　　　 C　　　 **D**

9. The tallest sea mountain <u>raises</u> 28,500 feet above the <u>ocean</u> floor. Yet its
　　　　　　　　　　　　 A　　　　　　　　　　 **B**
peak is still 1,200 feet below the <u>water's</u> surface.　<u>No error</u>
　　　　　　　　　　　　　 C　　　　　　 **D**

10. Shakespeare <u>wrote</u> *<u>The Merry Wives of Windsor</u>* in <u>fourteen</u> days.　<u>No error</u>
　　　　　　　 A　　　　 **B**　　　　　　 **C**　　　　　 **D**

11. <u>Knifes</u> have been around much longer than <u>forks before</u> the invention
　　 A　　　　　　　　　　　　　　 **B**
of these tools, people ate with <u>their</u> fingers.　<u>No error</u>
　　　　　　　　　　　 C　　　　　 **D**

12. You probably don't think of <u>tomatoes</u> and <u>potatos</u> as foreign foods, but
　　　　　　　　　　　 A　　　 **B**
originally the natives of South America <u>grown</u> them.　<u>No error</u>
　　　　　　　　　　　　　　 C　　　　 **D**

13. Famous authors have <u>wrote</u> many books on <u>typewriters, but</u> Mark Twain
　　　　　　　　 A　　　　　　 **B**
was the first. <u>he</u> typed *The Adventures of Tom Sawyer* himself.　<u>No error</u>
　　　　　 C　　　　　　　　　　　　　　　　　 **D**

14. We <u>seen</u> several camels in the <u>zoo's</u> Asian exhibit. One <u>drunk</u> a whole
　　 A　　　　　　　 **B**　　　　　　　 **C**
bucket of water while we watched.　<u>No error</u>
　　　　　　　　　　　 D

15. Don't <u>raise</u> the curtain yet. <u>Niether</u> of the <u>pianoes</u> is working.　<u>No error</u>
　　 A　　　　　　 **B**　　　 **C**　　　　　　 **D**

- You're in a baseball stadium when the home team scores the winning run. What happens? How does the crowd react?

- Tell about a time you were in a crowded place. It might have been a stadium, a theater, an elevator—anyplace where people are close together. Describe what you and the people around you were doing.

Understanding Pronouns

- **Pronouns and Antecedents**

- **Using Subject Pronouns**

- **Using Object Pronouns**

- **Possessive Pronouns**

- **Indefinite Pronouns**

A good team needs more than just starting players. It also needs substitute players on the bench who can come in to give the starters a rest. Nouns and pronouns work like a team too. You can use pronouns in your sentences as substitutes for nouns.

This handbook explains how pronouns can take the place of nouns and make your writing smoother and less repetitious.

A **pronoun** is a word used in place of a noun. An **antecedent** is the word or words a pronoun stands for.

Read these sentences:

> Leo made *Leo's* own flip book so *Leo* could play with the book.
> Leo made *his* own flip book so *he* could play with *it*.

The second sentence is less awkward than the first because some nouns have been replaced with pronouns. *His, he,* and *it* are **pronouns.** Pronouns take their meaning from the words they replace. *His* and *he* refer to *Leo*. *It* refers to *book*.

The word a pronoun stands for is the **antecedent** of the pronoun. In the examples above, *Leo* is the antecedent of both the pronouns *his* and *he. Book* is the antecedent of *it*.

Two nouns may also serve as the antecedent of a pronoun.

> *Leo* and *Iris* made many flip books for *their* friends.
> (*Leo* and *Iris* are both antecedents of *their.*)

Note that when a pronoun refers to the person speaking, there may not be a stated antecedent.

> *I* flip the pages to make the characters move.

In most sentences, a pronoun appears after its antecedent. However, sometimes a pronoun and its antecedent may appear in separate sentences.

> The *artists* arrived. *They* displayed *their* work.
> (*Artists* is the antecedent of *They* and *their.*)

Sometimes the antecedent of a pronoun is another pronoun.

> Did *you* watch Leo's cartoon in *your* room?
> (*You* is the antecedent of the pronoun *your.*)

Pronouns can be either singular or plural. Pronouns may be used to refer to yourself, to someone you are addressing, or to other persons, places, or things.

Singular Pronouns			
Person speaking	I	my, mine	me
Person spoken to	you	your, yours	you
Persons, places, and	he	his	him
things spoken about	she	her, hers	her
	it	its	it
Plural Pronouns			
Person speaking	we	our, ours	us
Person spoken to	you	your, yours	you
Persons, places, and things spoken about	they	their, theirs	them

Pronoun and Antecedent Agreement

Use a singular pronoun when the antecedent is singular. Use a plural pronoun when the antecedent is plural. This is called making the pronoun **agree** with its antecedent in number.

The *cartoon* (singular) began. *It* (singular) was funny. *People* (plural) laughed. *They* (plural) were amused.

Practice Your Skills

A. CONCEPT CHECK

Pronouns   Write each pronoun in the following sentences. After the pronoun, write its antecedent if one is given.

EXAMPLE   Cartoons and their creation interest me.
their, Cartoons; me

1. I enjoy cartoons, but my friends think they are silly.
2. A cartoon may look simple, yet it is complicated to make.
3. At some time in your life, you have probably made your own flip book.

As this work of the animator Arthur Babbitt illustrates, many drawings are necessary to create a simple walking sequence.

FOR MORE PRACTICE
See page 452.

4. We flip the pages and see figures move before our eyes.
5. Animators make their cartoons in a similar way.
6. Shamus Culhane is an animator. He is also an author.
7. He explains animation to us in his book *Animation from Script to Screen.*
8. Artists make many sketches for a simple movement, and they draw them on special sheets.
9. An artist draws his or her ideas on a transparent sheet, called a cel, that has holes along its top.
10. The holes fit on pegs, and they hold each drawing in the same place as the one before it.
11. The drawing table has a light under it, so the artist can see what he or she has drawn before.
12. The animators only draw key movements on their cels.
13. Assistant animators get the cels next, and they draw other movements on them.
14. Artists work closely with a writer, since his or her opinion of their drawings is important.
15. The writer invents characters, and the artists bring them to life.

B. REVISION SKILL

Substituting Pronouns for Nouns   Rewrite the following paragraph. Use pronouns in place of the words in italics to make the sentences flow smoothly.

Tom spends *Tom's* free time in an animation studio. *Tom* is learning the skill of painting animation cels with opaque paint. This skill requires patience. *This skill* also requires careful attention to detail. The painter puts the opaque paint in the center of the area to be colored. Then *the painter* pushes *the opaque paint* toward the outside of the area *the painter* is coloring. *The painter's* hand must be very steady, and the strokes must be smooth. If *the strokes* are not even, light can show through and ruin the cel. The work is sometimes very boring. To make *the work* more fun, the artists often play practical jokes. *Artists* must be alert for upside-down paint jars on *the artists'* desks or glue on *the artists'* brushes.

CHECK  POINT

MIXED REVIEW · PAGES 436–438

APPLICATION IN LITERATURE

Write each pronoun in the following sentences. Write the antecedent of each pronoun if there is one.

Writing Theme
Writers on Writing

1. "First you tell a diary all your secrets, then you publish it!"
   Richard Selzer

2. "Writing is more fun than ever. The longer I write, the easier it gets."
   Isaac Asimov

3. "You must write every single day of your life."
   Ray Bradbury

4. "Keeping a journal helps you get in touch with your own feelings."
   May Sarton

5. "I think writers—especially young writers—should want to read all the books they can get their hands on."
   Raymond Carver

6. "When we write, we make a contract: *My words are addressed to the outside world . . .* "
   Donald Hall

7. "People want to know why I do this, why I write such gross stuff. I like to tell them I have the heart of a small boy—and I keep it in a jar on my desk."
   Stephen King

8. "A writer doesn't so much choose a story as a story chooses him."
   Robert Penn Warren

9. "You were provided with an imagination. Use it. . . . For every new writer, every new year remains unexplored until he or she explores it."
   Irving Wallace

10. "I shoot the moment, capture feelings with my poems."
    Nikki Giovanni

11. "I don't tell; I don't explain. I show; I let my characters talk for me."
    Leo Tolstoy

12. "Sometimes young poets make the mistake of writing about things they think they ought to care about—they write about 'friendship' and 'peace' and the 'avenues of life' instead of about a certain friend, a certain day, a certain street. . . . The simple and particular way you talk with your friends is most likely the way you can best say what you want to."
    Kenneth Koch and Kate Farrell

The **subject pronouns** are *I, you, he, she, it, we,* and *they.* Use these pronouns as subjects of sentences and after linking verbs.

"So, then . . . Would that be 'us the people' or 'we the people'?"

Pronouns as Subjects

Use only subject pronouns as the subject of a verb.

While on vacation, Emma bought souvenirs. *She* bought them for friends.

In the first sentence, *Emma* is the subject. In the second sentence, *She* is the subject. Only the pronouns *I, you, he, she, it, we,* or *they* can be used as the subject of a verb. For example, you would never say, "*Her* bought them for friends."

Pronouns in Compound Subjects

You probably have no trouble choosing the correct pronoun when it appears by itself as the subject. Sometimes, however, one or more pronouns appear in a compound subject.

Shawn and (he, him) argued in the car.

The pronoun is part of the compound subject in this sentence. Therefore, you would use the subject pronoun *he.* If you are unsure about what pronoun to use, try dividing the compound subject into two parts. Then try each part as the subject.

Shawn argued in the car.   *He* argued in the car.

Put the parts together, using the same pronoun you used when it was alone in the sentence.

Shawn and *he* argued in the car.

Writing
═ TIP ═

Subject pronouns can serve as a link between two sentences as shown in this example:
My friends are from Iowa. *They* lived in Des Moines.

Follow the same steps to choose pronouns for the following example sentence.

> (She, Her) and (I, me) took snapshots.
> *She* took snapshots. *I* took snapshots.
> *She* and *I* took snapshots.

Sometimes a pronoun is followed by a noun in the subject of a sentence. To help you decide which pronoun to use in the sentence, try leaving out the noun.

> (We, Us) girls hiked up Mount Victoria.
> *We* hiked up Mount Victoria.
> *Us* hiked up Mount Victoria.
> *We girls* hiked up Mount Victoria.

Pronouns After Linking Verbs

Use subject pronouns after linking verbs. Look at these sentences:

> *He* is a good driver. A good driver is *he*.

Both sentences make sense, even though the subject and the pronoun are reversed. The pronoun following the linking verb *is* renames, or identifies, the subject. Therefore, you would use the subject pronoun *he*.

Practice Your Skills

A. CONCEPT CHECK

Subject Pronouns   Write the correct pronoun for each sentence.

1. Why do (we, us) think family trips are fun?
2. My family and (I, me) have had many adventures.
3. (We, Us) travelers have been lost in ten states.
4. Dad never asks directions. (He, Him) relies on the road map.
5. Emil and my other brother always fight. Emil and (he, him) have a talent for getting on Mother's nerves.
6. An impatient traveler is (she, her).

Writing Theme
Family Travel

7. Dad and (she, her) always bring travel games.
8. (We, Us) kids have to play dumb games and be quiet.
9. Emil and (I, me) have counted a trillion license plates.
10. (We, Us) passengers have also named all the state capitals.
11. What more can (they, them) expect of us?
12. My brothers and (I, me) think family trips are dull!

B. REVISION SKILL

Using Subject Pronouns   Write the second sentence of each pair. Replace the repeated words with a subject pronoun.

13. My family and I went to Australia. My family and I saw a strange sight near Scone.
14. Scone is north of Sydney. Scone is a small town.
15. Near Scone, a fire burns in a mountain. The fire never goes out.
16. Explorers first thought the fire was a volcano. The explorers were wrong.
17. A scientist learned that the fire is caused by a burning seam of coal. The scientist found the coal to be five hundred feet below the surface of the mountain.
18. The native people feared the place. These people thought a god lived there.
19. The people called the god Turramulan. The god "speaks from smoke."
20. My sister wondered how long the fire has burned. In the encyclopedia, my sister found the answer.
21. The mountain has been smoldering for centuries. The mountain is called "Burning Mountain" or Mt. Wingen.
22. One idea explains the fire. The idea suggests that lightning started the fire.

C. APPLICATION IN WRITING

Speech   Have you ever been on a trip and had something exciting, funny, or very annoying happen? Write a short speech about your trip. Include details about who was on the trip with you. Then use subject pronouns to link sentences and make your speech concise.

FOR MORE PRACTICE
See page 452.

C H E C K ✔ P O I N T

MIXED REVIEW • PAGES 440–442

Write the following sentences, correcting errors in the use of subject pronouns. If a sentence has no errors, write *Correct.*

Writing Theme
Partners in Invention

1. My friend and me found an old diary in a steamer trunk.
2. It was my great-grandmother's diary.
3. In Oakland, California, her and others saw the test flight of an airship invented by George and Lizzie Heaton.
4. They made it around 1905.
5. She and him worked as partners to make the engine.
6. An unusual pair were them.
7. I will tell you what my great-grandmother wrote.
8. "Us spectators watched the airship rise with Mrs. Heaton aboard."
9. "It was held down by cables and was supposed to rise only to the treetops."
10. "Mr. Heaton and us were horrified when the cables snapped and Mrs. Heaton was launched in the ship."
11. "She rose in the air with frightening speed."
12. "Apparently, Mrs. Heaton was very brave and smart. She bit a hole in the airship's gas bag."
13. "It released the gas and allowed the airship to go down."
14. "At first, the airship and her dropped like a flash."
15. "My beau and me were much relieved to see it land safely."
16. "Him and I rushed to interview Mrs. Heaton."
17. Both the airship and she were safe.
18. A courageous pilot was her.
19. Now, my friend and me want to make an airship.
20. Our classmates and us may have found a winning project for the science fair!

At the conclusion of the 1903 Paris Exposition, line handlers move the *Lebaudy I,* the first practical airship.

Understanding
Pronouns   **443**

The **object pronouns** are *me, you, him, her, it, us,* and *them.* Use these pronouns as the objects of verbs or prepositions.

Pronouns After Action Verbs

Nouns do not change their forms when they are used as the objects of verbs. Pronouns, however, have special object forms.

The object pronouns are *me, you, him, her, it, us,* and *them. You* and *it* can be used as both subject and object pronouns. Look at the object pronoun in this sentence:

The expert told *us* about the new computer.

Pronouns are sometimes part of a compound object.

Did the expert help (he, him) and (she, her)?

If you are unsure about what pronoun to use, try dividing the compound object into two parts. Then try each part as the object.

Did the expert help (he, him)?
Did the expert help (she, her)?
Did the expert help *him* and *her?*

Pronouns After Prepositions

A **preposition** usually has a noun or pronoun after it and shows a relationship between that noun or pronoun and the rest of the sentence. The noun or pronoun that follows a preposition is called the **object of the preposition.** Object pronouns are used as objects of prepositions.

He spoke to *Lee* and *Beth.* He spoke to *them.*

You will learn more about prepositions in Grammar Handbook 40. A list of common prepositions is on page 504.

Practice Your Skills

A. CONCEPT CHECK

Object Pronouns   Write the correct pronoun given in parentheses for each sentence.

1. Computers can be programmed for people with special
   needs, such as my friends and (I, me).
2. Some help blind people by speaking to (they, them).
3. We can talk to the computer, and it "hears" (we, us) kids.
4. Jay and Ann can ask a computer a question and it answers
   (he, him) and (she, her).
5. The new programs are good. People like (them, they).
6. A program can tell the difference between Jay and (I, me).
7. The computer knows Jay's voice belongs to (he, him).
8. One program amazes Ann and (us, we). It understands
   thirty thousand words.
9. When Ann spoke to the computer, it answered (her, she).
10. The computer gave (she, her) a printed reply in Braille.

B. DRAFTING SKILL

Using Object Pronouns in Sentences   Complete the
following sentences using correct object pronouns.

11. My neighbors Bill and Maggie have inspired ____.
12. Bill's customers like ____ very much.
13. He is always cheerful and polite to ____.
14. His customers know they can rely on ____.
15. Bill contacts ____ through his computer.
16. Maggie's boss, Al, is very happy with ____.
17. She does his record keeping for ____.
18. He has praised ____ very highly.
19. Bill and Maggie are blind, but computers help ____ work.
20. Computers are the key to success for both ____ and ____.
21. A special computer helps my co-workers and ____ make
    phone calls.
22. We type a message on ____ and a voice talks to the listener.
23. It is very useful to ____ because we cannot talk.
24. One computer finishes our words for ____.
25. It predicts the word and shows ____ on the screen.

Writing Theme
Special Computer
Programs

FOR MORE PRACTICE
See page 454.

POSSESSIVE PRONOUNS

Possessive pronouns show ownership or relationship.

Possessive pronouns are used to show ownership or relationship. The possessive pronouns are *my, mine, his, her, hers, its, our, ours, their, theirs, your,* and *yours.*

> *My* interview is with *your* cousin Amy.
> *His* report about *her* job was interesting.

In the first sentence, the pronouns *my* and *your* tell whom the interview and the cousin belong to. In the second sentence, *his* and *her* point to the owners of the report and the job.

To make a noun show possession, you add an apostrophe and an *s.* Pronouns, however, have special possessive forms. Possessive pronouns never use apostrophes.

Possessive pronouns may be confused with contractions that are spelled similarly. Look at the difference in these pairs of italicized words.

Possessive Pronoun	The factory opened *its* doors.
Contraction	*It's* a computer business. (It is)
Possessive Pronoun	*Their* jobs sound interesting.
Contraction	*They're* programmers. (They are)
Possessive Pronoun	*Your* interview is in the paper.
Contraction	*You're* a celebrity! (You are)

Practice Your Skills

A. CONCEPT CHECK

Possessive Pronouns and Contractions   Write the correct possessive pronoun or contraction from the words given in parentheses. Then label the word *Pronoun* or *Contraction.*

1. Security officers spend (their, they're) time on guard.
2. In a hotel, (their, they're) workday may begin at 4 P.M.

3. (Your, You're) probably wondering what these important employees do.
4. "Most of the time, (you're, your) helping guests."
5. "(Their, They're) always losing the room keys."
6. "You also have to stay on (your, you're) toes."
7. "(Its, It's) important to watch for troublemakers."
8. (Their, They're) job includes assisting hotel guests and having safety drills.
9. The hotel has a responsibility to protect (its, it's) guests in emergencies.
10. "I love to talk to kids. (Their, They're) fascinated by my walkie-talkie," says Sharona Lewis, an officer.

B. PROOFREADING SKILL

Correcting Pronoun Errors   Rewrite the following paragraph, correcting all errors in grammar, punctuation, capitalization, and spelling. Pay special attention to errors in possessive pronouns. (15 errors)

Ivan is a speechwriter for sevral important people. Its not easy writing speeches for them. They're speeches may last only fifteen minites apiece, but Ivan spends about thirty-two hours writing each one. He follows standard writing steps. Your familiar with them. Their the ones you use in you're classes. He gathers information. Writes a draft, and then rerites it. Ivan doesnt rest until its perfect. He spends his day talking with clients, holding interviews, and doing research at librarys in boston. "Your probably not going to believe this," he says. "Research is the most important step, and its the one that takes the longest."

C. APPLICATION IN WRITING

Report   Who is the most interesting person in the world to you? Write a report about a typical day in the life of this person. He or she may be an actual person or a character from fiction. Include some actual or imaginary quotations from the person. Use possessive pronouns to make your writing clear and concise.

FOR MORE PRACTICE
See page 453.

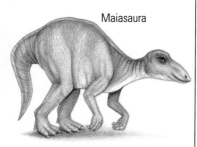

Maiasaura

Deinosuchus

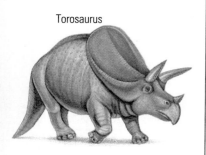

Tyrannosaurus

Torosaurus

Writing Theme
Dinosaur Quiz

Fill in the blanks in the following sentences with the correct object pronoun, possessive pronoun, or contraction. You may wish to refer to lists on page 444 and page 446. Using each set of descriptions, see if you can identify each dinosaur in the margin.

1. My head is larger than that of any other dinosaur, and ____ body is very large too.
2. Three horns protect ____ from ____ predators.
3. You don't need to worry. ____ safe around ____ because I eat plants.
4. If ____ guess is Triceratops, ____ wrong! Who am I?
5. Everyone's name has meaning, and ____ name means "the good mother lizard."
6. I lay eggs in a nest to keep ____ warm.
7. The eggs are hidden; ____ covered with sand or plants.
8. After the babies hatch, I bring them ____ food.
9. ____ hard work being a mother. Who am I?
10. ____ probably thinking that I look like a crocodile, and ____ right.
11. Other dinosaurs are afraid of ____ because I eat ____.
12. My victims don't see ____ hiding in the swamps, but I see ____.
13. The good mother lizard better watch ____ step as she passes by because I might devour ____! Who am I?
14. Scientists call ____ "tyrant lizard."
15. Around me, every plant eater fears for ____ or ____ life.
16. My razor-sharp teeth can cut ____ or ____ to shreds.
17. Skeletons of other dinosaurs and ____ are in museums.
18. You have seen many of ____ awesome creatures on ____ field trips.
19. One museum in the Smithsonian Institution is especially famous for ____ dinosaur skeletons.
20. Scientists differ in ____ opinions about me. ____ not sure if I am a scavenger or a great hunter. Only I know. Who am I?

INDEFINITE PRONOUNS

> An **indefinite pronoun** is a pronoun that does not refer to a specific person or a specific thing.

Pronouns such as *anyone* or *everybody* do not refer to any definite person or thing. These pronouns are called **indefinite pronouns.** Indefinite pronouns often do not have clear antecedents because the persons or things they refer to are unknown. This chart lists singular and plural indefinite pronouns.

Indefinite Pronouns

Singular			Plural
another	either	nobody	both
anybody	everybody	no one	many
anyone	everyone	one	few
anything	everything	somebody	several
each	neither	someone	

Use the singular possessive pronouns *his, her,* and *its* with singular indefinite pronouns.

> Someone left *her* purse on the boat.

> Another of the tourists lost *his* hat.

When the person referred to could be either male or female, *his or her* may be used.

> Everyone should bring *his or her* camera.

Use the plural possessive pronoun *their* with plural indefinite pronouns.

> Both enjoyed *their* visit. Many bring *their* children.

Refer to page 536 for information on making indefinite pronouns agree with verbs.

Practice Your Skills

A. CONCEPT CHECK

Indefinite Pronouns   Write the possessive pronoun that agrees in number with each indefinite pronoun.

Writing Theme
Hannibal, Missouri

1. Everyone has (his or her, their) reasons for visiting Hannibal, Missouri.
2. Many of the visitors carry (his or her, their) copies of *The Adventures of Tom Sawyer* by Mark Twain.
3. Everything looks like the 1800s because of (its, their) decor.
4. Someone tries (his or her, their) hand at the whitewash contest.
5. Everybody grabs (his or her, their) brush and bucket of paint.
6. Several of the contestants accidentally splatter paint on (his or her, their) clothes.
7. A few even get paint in (his or her, their) hair.
8. One of the girls is declared the winner and claims (her, their) prize.
9. Somebody still paints (his, their) part of the fence.
10. Nobody has it in (his or her, their) heart to stop him.

B. PROOFREADING SKILL

Making Indefinite and Possessive Pronouns Agree   Rewrite the paragraph, correcting all errors in grammar, capitalization, punctuation, and spelling. Pay special attention to errors in pronoun agreement. (15 errors)

One of Hannibal's yearly events is it's summer festival called National Tom Sawyer Days. Anyone in the seventh grade can have their chance to play tom sawyer or becky thatcher. Many compeet to spend his or her summer on a paddle wheeler named the *Mark Twain.* Judges choose three pares of students to take turns greeting the passengers. Neither of the new greeters is nervous their first time. Both do his or her best to make riders feel welcome. Anybody would have the time of its life on the boat ride. One of the girls shows their tour group Inspiration Point, a high lookout over the mississippi river.

FOR MORE PRACTICE
See page 453.

C H E C K   P O I N T
MIXED REVIEW · PAGES 449–450

Write the possessive pronoun in parentheses that agrees with each indefinite pronoun.

1. Does anybody you know spend (his or her, their) time watching bats?
2. Many of the visitors come to see (his or her, their) favorite creatures living at Volo Bog near Chicago, Illinois.
3. Almost every one of the bats here makes (its, their) home in an old dairy barn.
4. Several of the visitors plan (his or her, their) evenings to see the bats fly from the dairy barn.
5. Everyone takes (his or her, their) place at sunset.
6. Many set up (his or her, their) cameras to take pictures.
7. Somebody raises (his or her, their) binoculars to get a closer look.
8. Several of the spectators clap (his or her, their) hands and cheer for the furry creatures.
9. Afterward, both of the tour guides give (his or her, their) daily speech about bats.
10. Neither misses (his or her, their) chance to praise bats.
11. Either explains bats' helpfulness in (his or her, their) talk.
12. Very few of the visitors discuss (his or her, their) fear of bats.
13. Nearly everybody shares (his or her, their) belief that bats are not creepy or dangerous.
14. Someone in the group enjoys (his or her, their) job taking care of bats at a nearby zoo.
15. Another has bats in (his or her, their) attic.

Understanding
Pronouns   **451**

GRAMMAR
H A N D B O O K
37

Writing Theme
Water

A. Recognizing Pronouns   Write each pronoun—and its antecedent if there is one—in the following sentences.

1. I went hiking in the desert with my friends.
2. We lost our way in a large canyon.
3. By nightfall, only Shinae had water in her canteen.
4. Tim used his knife to cut scrub for a fire.
5. It was a wonderful fire.
6. Luckily, some wranglers saw our fire and found us.
7. The wranglers always carry extra water with them.
8. "You need a gallon of water for each day of your hike."
9. I only had two quarts of water with me, and it was gone.
10. We learned a lesson about water and its importance.

B. Using Subject Pronouns   Write the correct pronoun given in parentheses.

11. You and (I, me) may never know the secret of an ancient mummy called Otze.
12. (He, him) was found by a German couple.
13. Hiking in the Alps, (they, them) spotted him in a glacier.
14. "(She, Her) and (I, me) saw a human form in the ice."
15. Scientists and (they, them) were puzzled.
16. A frozen mystery was (he, him).
17. (He, Him) died suddenly, but (we, us) don't know why.
18. His tools and (he, him) are being studied.
19. Otze and (they, them) were buried for five thousand years.
20. "(We, Us) scientists are amazed at this discovery."

C. Using Object Pronouns   Write the correct pronoun given in parentheses.

21. Hard water affects (we, us) in many ways.
22. Water does not feel hard to you and (I, me).
23. It has mineral ions. Softeners remove (they, them).
24. Minerals make cloth feel stiff to you and (I, me).
25. These elements also stick to pipes and clog (they, them).
26. In the 1920s, an inventor gave a friend some zeolite and asked (he, him) to filter water through it.

27. He did, and it impressed his wife and (he, him).
28. It occurred to (they, them) to wash diapers in it.
29. The diapers felt softer to (she, her) and (he, him).
30. Today, many of (we, us) have soft water in our homes.

D. Using Possessive Pronouns Write the sentences, correcting errors in possessive pronouns and contractions. If a sentence has no errors, write *Correct*.

31. Without water, its certain that you're going to die.
32. You're body needs water to turn food into energy.
33. Certain life forms do not have you're problem.
34. They're able to go long periods without water.
35. They're bodies shrivel up and look dead.
36. Add water and they regain their shape.
37. Their in a state of cryptobiosis.
38. Its a word that means "hidden life."
39. A life form's ability to "play dead" helps it's survival.
40. It's puzzling to scientists how cryptobiosis works.

E. Using Indefinite Pronouns Write the correct possessive pronoun from those in parentheses.

41. Everyone is concerned about (his or her, their) future.
42. Many want (his or her, their) environment free of pollution.
43. Nobody wants (his or her, their) planet destroyed.
44. Several of the factories still dump (its, their) garbage.
45. A few of the local farmers spray (his or her, their) crops with poisonous bug spray.
46. Both of these practices have (its, their) dangerous effects on animals and humans.
47. For example, no one wants (his or her, their) drinking water to cause diseases.
48. Anybody worried about (his or her, their) health should try to solve this problem.
49. Someone wrote (his or her, their) solutions in a letter to the editor.
50. Almost everybody has (his or her, their) opinions about how to prevent water pollution.

GRAMMAR
HANDBOOK
37

Writing Theme
Mapmaking

A. Finding Pronouns   Write the pronouns from the sentences. Then write each pronoun's antecedent if there is one.

1. Do you remember Magellan from your history lessons?
2. Well, a new *Magellan* has taken his place.
3. Modern-day *Magellan* is not a man. It is a satellite.
4. Scientists use it to make their maps of Venus.
5. In 1726, Francesco Bianchini drew the first map of Venus, but he was unable to make an accurate drawing.
6. The planet is hidden by clouds that block our view.
7. However, *Magellan's* radar makes images of Venus, and we can study them.
8. In eight months, it recorded 84 percent of the surface.
9. Now scientists can't make up their minds.
10. We don't know if Venus's crust is thick or if it is thin.

B. Using Subject and Object Pronouns   Write the correct pronoun from those given in parentheses.

11. The sea floor is hidden from you and (I, me).
12. (We, Us) creatures of the land need to make maps of it.
13. Sailors mapped the ocean floor. (They, Them) lowered lead weights over the side of the ship.
14. Then mapmakers and (they, them) recorded the depths.
15. Later, the echo sounder gave (we, us) more information.
16. It allowed scientists and (we, us) to measure depths.
17. A mapmaker uses data that are valuable to (he, him) or (she, her).
18. With computers, (he, him) or (she, her) draws maps.
19. You and (I, me) can study the three-dimensional maps.
20. The maps allow (we, us) to see trenches and volcanoes.
21. Better technology is available to mapmakers and (we, us).
22. For example, a sonar device named *Gloria* has helped scientists and (they, them.)
23. A technician lowers this sensitive machine, and it sends (he, him) acoustic, or sound, pictures.
24. *Gloria* and (he, him) receive accurate "snapshots."
25. *Gloria's* pulses of sound fan out to both sides. Each sound wave bounces back to (we, us) from the ocean floor.

26. With computers, a picture appears before you and (I, me).
27. Line by line, the ocean floor is visible to (we, us).
28. Besides you and (I, me), other people also thought the ocean floor was flat.
29. However, *Gloria's* pictures show (they, them) and (we, us) mountains, trenches, and volcanoes.
30. (We, Us) land beings can now see the ocean bottom.

C. Using Possessive Pronouns and Contractions Write the correct possessive pronoun or contraction for each sentence.

31. (Your, You're) not going to believe this.
32. Some people still cling to (their, they're) belief in a flat earth.
33. (Their, They're) known as the Flat Earth Society.
34. (Its, It's) leaders scorn all satellite pictures.
35. (Their, They're) sure the pictures are fakes.
36. They also scorn the moon landing and question (its, it's) truth.
37. According to them, (its, it's) a Hollywood trick.
38. Are you going to change (your, you're) mind?
39. Will you start (your, you're) subscription to the *Flat Earth News*?
40. (Your, You're) sure the earth is a sphere, right?

D. Using Indefinite Pronouns Write the following sentences and correct all errors in agreement. If a sentence has no errors, write *Correct.*

41. Almost everyone checks their maps before a trip.
42. Many will even plot his or her route carefully.
43. If no one had their maps, would anyone travel?
44. Somebody had to take his or her chances and explore the unknown.
45. Each of the early explorers made maps for their country.
46. Several made their observations with instruments.
47. Not everybody knew how to use his or her tools well.
48. A few relied only on his compass and surveyor's chain.
49. Either of these instruments proved their value on expeditions.
50. However, neither was known for their accuracy.

51. Another was the astrolabe. Its purpose was to help explorers navigate at sea.
52. One could calculate his or her position by measuring the angles of stars above the horizon.
53. Anything used as a tool is given their own name.
54. Many of these tools, such as Gunter's chain, get its names from its inventors.
55. Anyone can learn to use their tools for mapping.

E. Proofreading   Rewrite the following sentences and correct all errors in the use of pronouns. If a sentence has no errors, write *Correct.*

56The chances of discovering buried treasure in you're back yard are slim. **57**You and me find secret maps and treasure only in adventure stories. **58**Yet treasure can really be ours.

59All that us treasure hunters have to do is bury some valuable-looking objects. **60**Marcus, Jen, and me have done this for fun. **61**They had the idea first. **62**Marcus and her found an antique watch and rhinestone costume jewelry. **63**Everybody searched their neighborhood for an old object that we could use as a treasure chest. **64**Someone had thrown away their old silverware, bowls, and other kitchen things. **65**Among them, we found an airtight container that was just the right size.

66Jen and me were in charge of figuring out distances. **67**Her and I used a yardstick to measure the length and width of our back yard. **68**Its not very big. **69**This part of our plan was easy for she and me to do. **70**Then we made a scale for our map: one inch equaled one foot. **71**Next, Jen and Marcus drew a grid on they're graph paper. **72**Jen and him added symbols to represent things in the back yard, such as the elm tree, the rosebushes, and the toolshed. **73**They're grid and map symbols looked pretty good. **74**It was up to Jen and he to pick the burial spot. **75**No one will guess it in their whole lifetime. **76**Their really excited about our secret burial ceremony!

WRITING CONNECTIONS

Elaboration, Revision, and Proofreading

Revise the following draft of a friendly letter by using the directions below. Then proofread the letter for errors in the use of pronouns. Also correct any other errors in grammar, capitalization, punctuation, and spelling.

Dear Martin,

¹We had a great time on our vacation in arizona. ²My favrite place was Canyon de Chelly National Monument. ³First we drove along the rim of the canyon and looked at the scenery. ⁴Then Chuck and me went down a trail into the canyon. ⁵It cut back and fourth for about a mile, finally, we reached a stream at the bottom. ⁶Taking off our shoes and socks, we waded through the stream. ⁷On the other side, we saw the ruins of a village. ⁸Parts of the village were built into the cliff. ⁹There are other cliff dwellings at Mesa Verde National Park in Colorado. ¹⁰Some of the buildings still have all they're walls. ¹¹Even now the ruins look beatiful. ¹²Chuck and me wish you could have been there with us to see it.

Your freind,
Rick

1. In sentence 4, replace the weak verb "went" with the more precise verb "hiked."

2. Replace the vague pronoun "it" in sentence 5 with the more precise noun "the trail."

3. Add details to sentence 6 by describing the stream as "cool and clear."

4. Add this information after sentence 7: "The Anasazi Indians built the village about one thousand years ago."

5. Delete the sentence that doesn't belong.

Personal and Expressive Writing

Writing a friendly letter is a good way to share your feelings and experiences with others. (See Workshop 1.) When you revise a letter you have written, make sure you present all of the details your reader will want to know. By using pronouns effectively, you can make your writing flow smoothly and present information clearly.

Understanding
Pronouns   **457**

- Imagine you see this creature walking down the street. Write a vivid description so your readers will be able to see it too.

Chock (1972),
Alexander Calder.

- Tell a tall tale about someone or something that is unusually big or small.

- Imagine that like Alice in Wonderland or Gulliver in the land of Lilliput, you have suddenly arrived in a place where you are much bigger or much smaller than all the things and people around you. Briefly describe your experience.

Understanding Adjectives

- **What Are Adjectives?**

- **Kinds of Adjectives**

- **Articles and Demonstrative Adjectives**

- **Predicate Adjectives**

- **Making Comparisons with Adjectives**

Click! A photographer captures an image on film. The color, the texture, the size, the detail—all make whatever the camera records seem very real. Yet a writer can do even more. A writer can capture and share the way something feels, sounds, tastes, and smells.

Adjectives help writers create clear, detailed, lively images. In this handbook you will learn how to recognize adjectives and use them to add color and precision to your writing and speaking.

Understanding
Adjectives   **459**

> An **adjective** is a word that modifies, or describes, a noun or a pronoun.

Look at these sentences:

A bull charged around the arena.
An angry bull charged around the hot, dusty arena.

What words in the second sentence tell you more about the bull and the arena? *Angry* describes *bull. Hot* and *dusty* tell about the *arena.* Each word adds more specific information to the sentence.

These words are **adjectives.** Adjectives describe, or modify, nouns and pronouns.

Adjectives may be placed before or after a noun or pronoun. Two or more adjectives modifying the same word sometimes need to be separated with commas. Use a comma after each adjective except the last one.

The *young, startled* cowpoke tumbled from the saddle.

Adjectives may also follow the word they modify.

This rider, *aching* and *bruised,* limped from the arena.

Proper Adjectives

Some adjectives, such as *Texan,* are made by adding endings to proper nouns. These are called **proper adjectives.**

Always begin a proper adjective with a capital letter. Common adjectives, those not formed from proper nouns, are not capitalized.

Africa + *-n* = African   China + *-ese* = Chinese

Other proper adjectives do not have special endings.

Wyoming rodeo   *Independence Day* celebration

Writing
TIP

If a noun is used as a describer, it becomes an adjective. In the sentence "I need *ham* for my *ham* sandwich," the word *ham* is used first as a noun and then as an adjective.

Practice Your Skills

A. CONCEPT CHECK

Adjectives   For the following sentences, write each adjective and the word it modifies. Label each adjective *Common* or *Proper*. You should find a total of twenty-one adjectives.

Writing Theme
Cowpokes & Rodeos

1. Cowhands in the brush country of the Southwestern hills are often called vaqueros.
2. Once, the term referred only to Spanish and Mexican cowpunchers.
3. Quickly, however, it came to mean any ranch hands.
4. South American historical records mention cowhands too.
5. For example, an Argentinian cowpoke was a gaucho.
6. Gauchos were good singers and storytellers.
7. Home was often a rough shack made of mud and twigs.
8. A gaucho wore loose white pants, a wool shawl at the waist, a shirt of bright color, and leather boots.
9. The gaucho, strong and brave, no longer exists.
10. Barbed wire ended the reign of this colorful figure.

B. REVISION SKILL

Using Lively Adjectives   Careful choice of adjectives can make your writing more interesting. Write the following sentences. Replace each of the underlined overused or vague adjectives with one that is more lively or precise. If a (P) follows the sentence, use a proper adjective.

11. The rodeo, which originated among working cowboys, is a U.S. tradition and a <u>nice</u> contest of skills.
12. Year-round, <u>big</u> crowds file into arenas throughout the United States.
13. Competing can be dangerous, so rodeos attract <u>good</u> riders.
14. Bronc riding and steer wrestling are two <u>good</u> events.
15. Bulls, mean and <u>mad</u>, also provide a challenge for riders.
16. Riding a bucking bull can result in a <u>bad</u> fall.
17. <u>Our</u> rodeos are not the only ones; Canada also has them. (P)
18. <u>Those</u> riders, our neighbors to the north, are also skilled. (P)
19. Cowboys in Mexico have <u>some</u> rodeos, or *charreadas*. (P)
20. Australia has ranches too, and <u>its</u> rodeos are popular. (P)

FOR MORE PRACTICE
See page 475.

Understanding
Adjectives   **461**

Writing TIP

Notice in "Yomarhi Purnima," pages 62–63, how the author Elizabeth Murphy-Melas uses adjectives to help the reader picture both Nepal and the thanksgiving festival she is describing.

> An **adjective** modifies a word by telling *what kind, how many,* or *which one.*

Every adjective has one of three functions. It tells *what kind, how many,* or *which one.*

Some Adjectives Tell *What Kind*

Some adjectives describe by telling *what kind.*

> The *gold medal* winners waved to the *cheering* crowd from a *twenty-foot-long* float.

Many adjectives that tell *what kind* are formed by adding an adjective ending to a noun.

rain*y*	adventur*ous*
fear*less*	color*ful*
comfort*able*	gold*en*

Some Adjectives Tell *How Many*

Some adjectives limit by telling *how many.*

> There are *two* astronauts who orbited the moon *ten* times.

Some Adjectives Tell *Which One*

Some adjectives point out specific members of groups by telling *which one* or *which ones.* Remember that possessive pronouns can be used as adjectives. A complete list of possessive pronouns appears on page 446.

Adjectives that tell *which one* or *how many* almost always come before the words they modify.

> *That* woman riding in the *third* car is *our* senator.

I designed *those three red robot* masks in the *second* row.

Practice Your Skills

A. APPLICATION IN LITERATURE

Recognizing Adjectives   Read this passage about the two-time Olympic gold medal winner Jim Thorpe. Divide your paper into three columns. Label the columns *What Kind, How Many,* and *Which One.* Find all the adjectives in each sentence and write them in the correct columns. You should find a total of nineteen adjectives.

1 It was July 6, 1912. . . at the fifth Olympic games.
2 Around the cinder track marched hundreds of athletes.
3 They came from twenty-six different countries, from every part of the world. **4** They strode along to the cheers of 30,000 people who had come to watch. **5** The athletes went proudly past the royal box of King Gustav and Queen Victoria of Sweden. . . .

6 The American athletes were just coming past the box. **7** In the fourth row marched a tall, powerful-looking American Indian. **8** He had a shock of black hair. **9** His big square jaw was set firmly. **10** His half-closed eyes stared straight ahead.

Guernsey Van Riper, Jr.,
Jim Thorpe: Native American Athlete

B. DRAFTING SKILL

Using Adjectives   Act as screenwriter and add adjectives that complete the following stage directions for a historical film. Number your paper from 11 to 20 and write the kinds of adjective asked for in parentheses.

EXAMPLE   _____ actors stand beside a flag. (how many)
             Two actors stand beside a flag.

11. A(n) _____ spacecraft can be seen on the right. (what kind)
12. _____ craters dot the rocky landscape. (how many)
13. Some of _____ craters are several feet wide. (which ones)
14. The door on _____ spacecraft begins to open. (which one)
15. _____ figures dressed in spacesuits come slowly through the door. (how many)

Grammar
── **TIP** ──

Remember, when two or more adjectives modify the same noun, you will often add commas after all but the last adjective. However, adjectives that tell number, size, shape, color, and age often do not require commas.

16. One of the actors holds a(n) _____ flag. (what kind)

17. He raises _____ hand and plunges the flagpole into the soil. (which one)

18. The camera frames the image of the earth in the _____ sky behind the figures. (what kind)

19. The scene shifts to a(n) _____ TV studio. (what kind)

20. A(n) _____ commentator reports this historic event. (what kind)

FOR MORE PRACTICE
See page 475.

Writing Theme
Hiccups

C H E C K ✓ P O I N T

MIXED REVIEW · PAGES 460–464

Write each adjective in the following sentences. Then write whether the adjective tells *What Kind, How Many,* or *Which One.* Identify each *Proper Adjective.* Ignore *a, an,* and *the.*

1. People have imagined many different causes for hiccups.
2. They have also invented numerous unusual cures.
3. According to some people, you get severe hiccups when someone talks about you.
4. If you guess who this person is, your hiccups will leave.
5. An ancient Greek tickled his nose so that he would sneeze.
6. Greek doctors believed that a sneeze chased away hiccups.
7. Many people still claim that this cure works.
8. The Aymara, a Native American people of Bolivia and Peru, say hiccups are caused by eating sugary sweets.
9. They say sweets make a small worm grow in your stomach.
10. Whenever this worm moves, you hiccup.
11. One popular cure today is to get someone to scare you.
12. A good fright almost always cures hiccups.
13. There are many folk remedies for hiccups.
14. Try drinking water from the opposite side of a glass.
15. Breathe into a brown paper bag for a few minutes.
16. Hold your breath and take several drinks of water.
17. Stand on one leg and say a tricky phrase quickly.
18. For bad hiccups, suck on a lemon.
19. Everyone seems to have a favorite cure for hiccups.
20. What is your secret for getting rid of the worst hiccups?

ARTICLES AND
DEMONSTRATIVE ADJECTIVES

A, an, and *the* are special adjectives called **articles.** *This, that, these,* and *those* are **demonstrative adjectives.**

Articles

The words *a, an,* and *the* are **articles.** Because these words always modify nouns, they are also adjectives.

Use *a* before words beginning with consonant sounds.

> a firefly   a lamp   a bulb   a candle

Use *an* before words beginning with vowel sounds.

> an afterglow   an intense light   an orange sunset

When you pronounce words that begin with a silent *h,* you do not say the *h* sound. Instead, you begin the word with the vowel sound after the *h.* Follow the rule for using *an.*

> an hour   an honor   an heir

A and *an* are used with singular nouns. *The* may be used before either a singular or a plural noun. *The* is used when you want to refer to a specific person, place, thing, or idea. *A* and *an* are used when you want to be less specific.

> *The* lantern shines brightly. (one specific lantern)
> Brian turned on *a* light. (any light)

Demonstrative Adjectives

This, that, these, and *those* are **demonstrative adjectives.** They point out specific things. Use *this* and *that* with singular nouns. Use *these* and *those* with plural nouns.

> *This* candle will burn longer than *that* one.
> *These* candles are brighter than *those* candles.

Demonstrative adjectives can show whether an object you are pointing out is nearer or farther away.

Near: this, these   *Far:* that, those

Demonstrative adjectives are often paired with the nouns *kind* and *sort.* Both *kind* and *sort* are singular words. Therefore, say *this kind* and *that sort.* Use *these* and *those* only with the plurals: *these kinds* or *those sorts.*

This kind of flashlight is called a penlight.
Those sorts of light bulbs use the least electricity.

Adjectives or Pronouns?

Demonstrative words can be adjectives or pronouns. A demonstrative word is an adjective if it answers the question *which one?* about a noun. A demonstrative word is a pronoun if it takes the place of a noun. Look at these examples.

Adjective	*This* bulb is burnt out. (*This* tells which bulb.)
Pronoun	*This* doesn't work.
Adjective	*These* candles are new. (*These* tells which candles.)
Pronoun	*These* are new.
Adjective	*That* light is too bright. (*That* tells which light.)
Pronoun	*That* is too bright.
Adjective	Do you see *those* stars? (*Those* tells which stars.)
Pronoun	Do you see *those?*

Them is always a pronoun. It is never used as an adjective. The pronoun *them* is always used as an object, never as the subject of a sentence.

Incorrect	*Them* candles cannot be blown out.
Incorrect	*Them* are trick birthday candles.
Correct	*Those* candles are for Sarah's cake. I chose *them* myself. (*Them* is a pronoun functioning as a direct object. It replaces the noun *candles.*)

Practice Your Skills

A. CONCEPT CHECK

Articles and Demonstrative Adjectives   Number your paper
from 1 to 15. Write the correct word from the parentheses.

Writing Theme
Sources of Light

1. Do you see (those, them) floodlights on the playing field?
2. (A, The) development of the modern electric lamp made such lighting possible.
3. (These, Those) lights near us are incandescent.
4. Inside these (kind, kinds) of bulbs, wires are heated.
5. (Them, Those) heated wires produce light.
6. (A, An) fluorescent bulb, however, does not rely on wires.
7. Your school probably uses (this, these) kind of light.
8. (These, Them) tubes contain gases called argon and mercury vapor.
9. Currents run through (these, them) gases; light is produced.
10. (This, That) colorful tube over there contains neon gas.
11. (Those, Them) neon bulbs are used in signs for stores.
12. (A, An) advertisement in neon lights gets attention.
13. Look at (this, that) huge spotlight next to me.
14. (These, This) kind of bulb lights up when electricity leaps between two rods inside the bulb.
15. Spotlights produce (a, an) hot and very bright light.

The Ghost of Rock and Roll (1987),
Lili Lakich.

B. DRAFTING SKILL

Using Adjectives Correctly   You and a friend are in a park
collecting fireflies, or lightning bugs, for a science project. The
following situations describe what you see. Use these situations
as starting points. Write five sentences using articles and
demonstrative adjectives to describe what you see.

> Two fireflies are close to you.
> Your friend chases a firefly a long way.
> There are two jars of fireflies—one nearby and one across the park.

FOR MORE PRACTICE
See page 475.

PREDICATE ADJECTIVES

> A **predicate adjective** is an adjective that follows a linking verb. It describes the subject of the sentence.

When an adjective follows a linking verb, it is part of the predicate. Therefore, it is called a **predicate adjective.** A predicate adjective modifies the subject. Notice that one predicate adjective may modify a compound subject and two predicate adjectives may be joined to describe the same subject.

> The cat and dog seem gentle. (*Gentle* describes *cat* and *dog.*)
> The lion looks fierce and dangerous. (*Fierce* and *dangerous* describe *lion.*)

A predicate adjective differs from other adjectives you have studied. Unlike most other adjectives, a predicate adjective comes after the word it modifies. Also, it is separated from the word it modifies by a linking verb.

Here are some linking verbs that often come before predicate adjectives. For more about linking verbs, see pages 405–406.

am	was	become	look	taste
are	were	feel	seem	sound
is	appear	grow	smell	remain

Practice Your Skills

A. CONCEPT CHECK

Predicate Adjectives   Copy the following sentences. Draw one line under the predicate adjective in each sentence and two lines under the word or words it modifies. Remember that more than one predicate adjective can follow a verb.

1. To you, do frogs and toads look identical?
2. Both creatures are cold-blooded and amphibious.

Writing **TIP**

To eliminate wordiness, try combining sentences to form a predicate adjective.

Writing Theme
Comparison and Contrast

3. They are comfortable both on land and in water.
4. Yet the skin and shape of frogs and toads seem different.
5. Frogs feel smooth and slippery.
6. In contrast, toads appear dry and bumpy.
7. However, frogs and toads are similar as babies, or tadpoles.
8. Tadpoles of both animals appear fishlike.
9. Their tails are long and powerful.
10. Tadpoles can grow big in a short time.
11. After the tadpole stage, frogs become long and graceful.
12. Toads remain squat and pudgy.
13. People seem needlessly fearful about handling toads.
14. The rumor about toads and warts is untrue.
15. Somehow, toads look uglier to people than frogs do.

B. CONCEPT CHECK

Recognizing Predicate Adjectives   Write the predicate adjectives in the following sentences. If a sentence does not contain a predicate adjective, write *None.*

> [16]Some scientists feel comfortable about the classification of giant pandas as bears; others group pandas with raccoons. [17]In many ways, giant pandas and bears are similar. [18]Their body shape and size look alike. [19]Both grow quite large. [20]The movements of both appear slow and clumsy. [21]Bears and pandas can stand erect on their hind legs. [22]Differences are apparent too. [23]The panda's coloring is black and white. [24]To a panda, only bamboo shoots taste good. [25]To a bear, honey is perfect.

C. APPLICATION IN WRITING

Comparison and Contrast   Write a brief paragraph comparing and contrasting two animals. Think about pets you've owned or animals you've seen at the zoo or in your back yard. Use at least five of the following linking verbs with predicate adjectives.

was	appear	seem	look	smell
are	become	grow	feel	

FOR MORE PRACTICE
See page 476.

Understanding
Adjectives   **469**

A. Write the correct word from those given in parentheses.

1. Have you ever played with (a, an) yo-yo?
2. You can get hooked playing with these (kind, kinds) of toys.
3. (A, The) yo-yo came to us from the Philippines.
4. (These, Them) yo-yos will do hundreds of tricks.
5. Grab one of (these, those) yo-yos over there.
6. Now throw (that, those) yo-yo to the end of its string.
7. When you can keep the yo-yo spinning down there at (this, that) end of the string, it is said to be "sleeping."
8. As you hold onto (this, that) end of the string, give a slight tug and the yo-yo will climb back up to your hand.
9. Once you master "sleeping," (this, these) yo-yo will do other tricks.
10. In (a, an) expert's hand, a yo-yo seems almost magical.

B. Write and label each Linking Verb and Predicate Adjective in the following sentences.

11. If yo-yos seem modern to you, you have a surprise coming.
12. Thousands of years ago, the Chinese were clever with yo-yos.
13. The ancient Greeks also became familiar with this toy.
14. In 1600, people in the Philippines grew serious about yo-yos.
15. To Filipinos, yo-yos appeared useful as hunting weapons.
16. Their yo-yos felt very heavy.
17. Made of rock, with twenty-foot-long strings, they looked awesome.
18. Filipino hunters became quite skillful with these yo-yos.
19. A repeat throw was easy after the return of the yo-yo on an unsuccessful attempt.
20. Today, after all these years, the yo-yo remains popular.

MAKING COMPARISONS
WITH ADJECTIVES

Use the **comparative form** of an adjective to compare two things. Use the **superlative form** of an adjective to compare three or more things.

A ruby is hard.   A diamond is hard.   An emerald is hard.

All of these gems are hard, but they do not all have the same degree of hardness. You can show the differences in hardness by using special forms of adjectives.

Use the **comparative form** to compare two things, two groups of things, or one thing with a group. *Harder* is the comparative form of *hard.*

A ruby is *harder* than an emerald. Rubies are *harder* than pearls. That gem is *harder* than the others.

Use the **superlative form** to compare three or more things. *Hardest* is the superlative form of *hard.*

The diamond is the *hardest* of all gems.

Follow these rules to make the comparative and superlative forms of adjectives.

1. **Use the comparative form to compare two things.** To make the comparative form of most short adjectives, add *-er.*
2. **Use the superlative form to compare three or more things.** To make the superlative form of most short adjectives, add *-est.*

Adjective	Comparative Form	Superlative Form
big	bigger	biggest
hard	harder	hardest
rare	rarer	rarest
lovely	lovelier	loveliest

Notice that when an adjective ends in a single consonant following a single vowel, such as *big,* you must double the final consonant before adding the ending. When the adjective ends in silent *e,* such as *rare,* simply add an *r.* When the adjective ends in a *y* following a consonant, such as *lovely,* change the *y* to *i* before adding *-er* or *-est.*

Using *More* and *Most*

The comparative and superlative forms of some adjectives are not made by adding *-er* or *-est.* For adjectives of more than two syllables, the word *more* is usually used before the adjective to make the comparative form. Use the word *most* before the adjective to make the superlative form.

Adjective	Comparative Form	Superlative Form
remarkable	more remarkable	most remarkable
colorful	more colorful	most colorful
brilliant	more brilliant	most brilliant

Never use the *-er* ending with the word *more.* Never use the *-est* ending with the word *most.*

Incorrect	This emerald seems *more greener* than that one.
Correct	This emerald seems *greener* than that one.

Irregular Adjectives

The comparative and superlative forms of some adjectives are completely different words. Here are some of those forms.

Adjective	Comparative Form	Superlative Form
good	better	best
bad	worse	worst
little	less	least
much	more	most
many	more	most
far	farther	farthest

Practice Your Skills

A. CONCEPT CHECK

Comparisons with Adjectives   Choose the correct form of the adjective from the parentheses.

1. Diamonds are the (more, most) popular of all gems.
2. Those that are clear and that sparkle with light are (more, most) valuable than others.
3. The Cullinan diamond was the (larger, largest) ever found.
4. It weighed 1⅓ pounds before being cut into smaller but (more, most) valuable stones.
5. The (best, goodest) gem cutters split the Cullinan into 105 gems.
6. The (most big, biggest) of them weighs one-fourth of a pound.
7. The Hope diamond is (smaller, more small) than the Cullinan.
8. Nevertheless, it is the (more, most) famous of the two.
9. This is not because the Hope diamond is (more pretty, prettier) but because some people claim it is cursed.
10. Thomas Hope was a British banker, and he was one of the (wealthiest, most wealthiest) people in England.
11. After he bought the diamond, however, his luck became (worse, more worse) than before.
12. (More late, Later) owners of the gem also had misfortunes.

B. DRAFTING SKILL

Making Comparisons   Write each sentence. Use the comparative or superlative form of the adjective in parentheses.

13. Without a doubt, diamonds are the (hard) of all gems.
14. They are also the (appreciated).
15. However, an emerald (large) than a diamond might cost more.
16. Sapphires are rare, but rubies are even (uncommon).
17. For that reason, rubies are (valuable).
18. How do experts judge which is the (good) of two sapphires?
19. They know that the (good) sapphires are a deep blue.
20. The (expensive) opals of all are the black ones.
21. In contrast, the (white) of two pearls would cost more.
22. It is often (important) for a gem to be flawless than large.

The world's largest cut diamond is the 530-carat Star of Africa. Set in the British royal scepter, this jewel can be removed and worn as a brooch.

Understanding
Adjectives   **473**

C. PROOFREADING SKILL

Correcting Errors in Comparisons Proofread the following paragraphs. Rewrite them correctly. Pay special attention to the correct use of adjectives in comparisons. (15 errors)

Ancient peoples beleived that precious jewels had great power and magic. The most precious gems of all had the greater powers. Sometimes people didn't agree on weather a gems magic was good or bad. Some thought opals were lucky. Others said opals brought the worse luck of all.

Gems were once used as medicine they were crushed into powder and then swallowed. Red jewells, such as rubies, were thought to controll or stop bleeding. Green ones, such as emeralds, were supposed to cure ailmants of the eye. Of all the colors, people thought green was the better because it was most restful to the eye than a brighter color In chosing between two gems, people claimed the costlier one produced more stronger medicine than the cheapest one.

FOR MORE PRACTICE
See page 476.

Writing Theme
Rivers

C H E C K ✔ P O I N T
MIXED REVIEW • PAGES 471–474

Write the following sentences, using the correct comparative or superlative form of each adjective given in parentheses.

1. Which river is (long), the Mississippi or the Missouri?
2. Many people think the Mississippi flows for (much) miles.
3. The Missouri is actually North America's (lengthy) river.
4. The Mississippi carries the (great) volume of water of any North American river because it is so wide.
5. By comparison, the Colorado is much (small) than the mighty Mississippi.
6. However, it has slowly carved the (gigantic) canyon in North America.
7. There is not a canyon (spectacular) than the Grand Canyon.
8. It is the (famous) canyon anywhere in the world.
9. The Snake River created Hell's Canyon, which is even (deep) than the Grand Canyon but not as wide.
10. Of these rivers, the Colorado carries the (little) water.

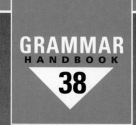

A. Identifying Adjectives Label three columns on your paper *What Kind, How Many,* and *Which One.* Write the adjectives in each sentence in the correct columns. Ignore articles.

1. Before 1600, people didn't have cloth or paper napkins.
2. In those days, even the king went without any napkin at all.
3. However, a wealthy family would own one fine tablecloth.
4. These tablecloths were imported from Damascus in Syria.
5. The famous weavers in Damascus made wonderful tablecloths with marvelous flower and animal patterns.
6. The white cloth had red borders and gold fringe.
7. These expensive tablecloths were part of the royal treasure.
8. Few households could afford them.
9. Picture a gorgeous tablecloth spread on a feast table.
10. In those days, people ate with their fingers.
11. They wiped their greasy hands on the tablecloth.
12. After a few feasts, the lovely tablecloth was a mess.
13. Finally, someone decided to protect these tablecloths.
14. A towel was given to each guest.
15. These towels were the first napkins.

Writing Theme
Inventions

B. Using Articles and Demonstrative Adjectives Write the correct word from the ones given in parentheses.

16. Have you heard (a, the) warning "Don't eat with your fingers"?
17. (This, These) kind of warning would have seemed foolish when people ate everything with their fingers.
18. The use of (a, an) fork for eating began in Asia.
19. (This, These) custom spread to Europe very slowly.
20. By 1500 (these, them) utensils were common in Italy.
21. The English thought the Italians were too dainty and made fun of (those, them).
22. The English had (a, an) humble view that fingers were made to eat with.
23. (This kind, These kinds) of utensil caught on slowly in England and America.
24. A fork was (a, an) unusual item in most homes before 1800.
25. Until then, (a, an) person who used a fork was laughed at.

C. Identifying Predicate Adjectives Write the following sentences. Draw one line under the predicate adjective or adjectives and two lines under the word that is modified.

26. Straight pins are very old.
27. Ice Age people were fond of fish-bone pins.
28. During the Bronze Age, people were happier with metal pins similar to today's safety pins.
29. Somehow through the years, the idea behind the efficient Bronze Age safety pin became unclear or lost.
30. Until 1849, straight pins remained popular.
31. That year, Walter Hunt became famous for his "invention," the safety pin.
32. Hunt's future looked bright.
33. However, his bank account remained small.
34. Furthermore, a friend of Hunt's was growing impatient about Hunt's unpaid fifteen-dollar loan.
35. The invention certainly appeared useful and practical.
36. The solution seemed obvious.
37. The friend would become rich from the ownership of the new invention.
38. Hunt would no longer be uncomfortable about his debt.
39. Furthermore, credit for the accomplishment would remain his.
40. Today, anyone with a missing button or a broken zipper is grateful to Walter Hunt.

D. Making Comparisons with Adjectives Write the correct form of the adjective shown in parentheses.

41. The (earliest, most early) houses did not have windows.
42. Even great castles of the (powerfullest, most powerful) kings had only a hole in the roof of the kitchen to let out smoke from the cooking fire.
43. A window is much (better, best) than a smoke hole.
44. The first windows let some rain in and were (worse, worst) about letting in cold.
45. In later times, they were stuffed with straw or covered with canvas so homes would be (comfortabler, more comfortable) in bad weather.

A. Identifying Adjectives Write the adjectives that modify each italicized noun in the sentences below. Include articles.

1. How would you like having a creepy *insect* living by your *bed*?
2. Strangely enough, many *people* enjoy having certain *kinds* of insects nearby.
3. These *bugs* that sing are often kept as pets.
4. Crickets and cicadas are two good *examples*.
5. They make wonderful *music*.
6. Chinese, Japanese, and Spanish *people* sometimes keep them.
7. These *owners* love their pets and give them special *care*.
8. Tiny *cages* are made for the *animals*.
9. An *owner* might keep several cricket *cages* near his or her *bed*.
10. The musical *crickets* then sing their *owner* to sleep.

Writing Theme
Unusual Pets

B. Using Adjectives Correctly Write the correct adjective from those given in parentheses.

11. Imagine waking up to (a, an) alarming cry—"*To-kay!*"
12. Your eyes open and you see a monster straight out of your (worse, worst) nightmare.
13. It's a gray, golden-eyed lizard with red dots, and it stretches a foot long—although right now it looks much (longer, more long).
14. It's staring down at you from (a, the) ceiling over your bed!
15. (Faster, More fast) than lightning, you leap from your bed.
16. But wait—now you remember. (This, That) monster up there is your new pet!
17. It's a tokay gecko, one of the (more common, more commoner) pets in Asia.
18. Some people in the United States like (these, them) unusual animals too.
19. Geckos have the (beautifullest, most beautiful) eyes.
20. They are also (more, most) useful than many other pets.
21. They're (better, more good) hunters than most lizards.
22. Nighttime, when they busily seek insects, finds them (more, most) active than daytime.
23. Most geckos are gentle, but the tokay doesn't like being handled and has the (worse, worst) bite of all.

Understanding
Adjectives   **477**

24. The tokay is also the (largest, most large) gecko.
25. Because they have thousands of fine hairlike structures on the pads of their feet, (them, these) animals can walk up walls and across ceilings.
26. They can even walk across mirrors, as (this, that) one on the wall over there is doing.
27. Geckos are the (unusualest, most unusual) lizards because they are the only ones that talk.
28. The tokay, in its (loudest, most loud) voice, cries, *"To-kay!"*
29. (A, An) few geckos bark or quack, and some say *"Gecko!"*
30. Can you guess how (those, them) lizards got their name?

C. Correcting Errors with Adjectives   Write each of the following sentences, correcting errors in the use of adjectives. If a sentence does not have an error, write *Correct.*

31. What would be the better animal of all to have as a pet?
32. Of all pets, dogs and cats are the more typical.
33. However, some people prefer more unusual animals.
34. If you're one of them people, you're in good company.
35. Some United States presidents chose stranger pets than you'd expect.
36. Perhaps the odder was the alligator John Quincy Adams kept in the White House.
37. Them Adamses also kept silkworms.
38. Silk was one of the costliest fabrics known, and Mrs. Adams's silkworms spun enough silk for her to make a dress.
39. Of all the presidents, Theodore Roosevelt may have had the larger assortment of creatures.
40. Parrots, snakes, lizards, pigeons, pigs, and rats—his children kept all them animals.
41. One of the better stories of all involves the snakes.
42. His son carried four of his most new snakes into a meeting.
43. Senators burst from the room, each trying to run more faster than the others.
44. The Kennedy children also had a collection of pets. Theirs were least unusual than those in the Roosevelts' zoo.
45. The Kennedys' more remarkable pets were rabbits and hamsters.

WRITING CONNECTIONS

Elaboration, Revision, and Proofreading

Revise the following draft of a description, using the directions at the bottom of the page. Then proofread the description, paying special attention to the use of adjectives. Also look for errors in grammar, capitalization, punctuation, and spelling.

¹Every year the recreation center is turned into a Haunted House for Halloween. ²As we approached the building this year, we heard sounds coming from inside. ³We walked to the door and timidly stepped into the dark and gloomy house. ⁴Ahead of us was a zigzag path that led us passed all sorts of creepy things. ⁵Arms reached out and grabed for us as we walked by. ⁶A Monster jumped in our path and then vanished. ⁷Compared to the monster, the swirling ghosts that swooped down from the rafters were definitately creepiest. ⁸A witch zoomed by on a broomstick. ⁹We reached the end. ¹⁰We all agreed this years' haunted house was more better than last years'.

1. Add one or more adjectives to tell what kind of "sounds" in sentence 2.

2. In sentence 5, add two adjectives that tell how the arms looked and felt.

3. In sentence 6, use adjectives to describe what the monster looked like.

4. Make the order of events clearer by adding a transition word to sentences that signal the next event.

5. Add "finally" to the beginning of sentence 9 to indicate the end of the description.

Observation and Description

Descriptive writing provides a chance to create a picture with words. (See Workshop 2.) When you revise descriptive writing, look for ways to use a variety of words that appeal to the senses. Using precise adjectives is one way to make your descriptions come alive.

"Well, then," I said, "either I am a lunatic or something just as awful has happened. Now tell me, honest and true, where am I?"

"IN KING ARTHUR'S COURT."

I waited a minute, to let that idea shudder its way home, and then said:

"And according to your notions, what year is it now?"

"528— nineteenth of June."

Mark Twain

A CONNECTICUT YANKEE IN KING ARTHUR'S COURT

- What if you woke up one day and you were living in the past? It could be the time of King Arthur's court or the Roman Empire or any other time in history or legend. Write about how you would act, where you would go, and what you would do and see during your first day.

- Imagine you are a newspaper reporter witnessing an important event. Write a brief account for tomorrow's newspaper. Remember to include the five *w*'s—*who, what, when, where,* and *why.*

- How would you compare yourself to your best friend? What do you do better? What does your friend do better?

Understanding Adverbs

- **What Are Adverbs?**
- **Making Comparisons with Adverbs**
- **Adjective or Adverb?**
- **Double Negatives**

Camelot. The wizard Merlin. Sir Lancelot. Queen Guinevere. You are probably familiar with the legends of King Arthur and the knights of the Round Table. To retell rich tales such as these, you need to use rich language. By using adverbs, you can include details about how, when, and where actions take place.

In this handbook you will study ways you can use adverbs to make your writing precise and lively.

> An **adverb** modifies a verb, an adjective, or another adverb.

Adjectives add excitement and clarity to your sentences. Adverbs can help you be more precise.

An **adjective** modifies a noun or pronoun.

An **adverb** modifies a verb, an adjective, or another adverb.

> Mail moved *slowly*. (*Slowly* modifies the verb *moved*.)
> Postage was *extremely* expensive. (*Extremely* modifies the adjective *expensive*.)
> Settlers waited *very* impatiently for news. (*Very* modifies the adverb *impatiently*.)

An **adverb** tells *how, when, where,* or *to what extent* about the word it modifies.

> Bill Cody rode *swiftly*. (*Swiftly* tells *how* Bill rode.)
> He arrived *yesterday*. (*Yesterday* tells *when* he arrived.)
> The coach went *west*. (*West* tells *where* the coach went.)
> The rider was *completely* exhausted. (*Completely* tells *to what extent* the rider was exhausted.)

An adverb that modifies an adjective or another adverb often comes before the word it modifies.

> *extremely* steep   *very* carefully

An adverb that modifies a verb may be found in one of several positions.

> She wrote *often*.   She *often* wrote.   *Often,* she wrote.

Many common adverbs are formed by adding the ending *-ly* to adjectives. For example, the adjectives *quick* and *usual* become the adverbs *quickly* and *usually*.

Other adverbs include *there, now, never, almost,* and *too*.

Writing
TIP

Adverbs can help make a story you're writing more specific. Use adverbs to tell more about the time, place, and extent of the action. See how adverbs add to this sentence.

Bob saddled his horse.
Bob *hurriedly* saddled his horse.

Practice Your Skills

A. CONCEPT CHECK

Adverbs   Write each adverb and tell whether it answers *How,
When, Where,* or *To what extent.* Then write the word it modifies.

EXAMPLE   The stagecoach sped wildly downhill.
wildly, How, sped; downhill, Where, sped

1. In the Old West, mail service was unbelievably slow.
2. Until 1858, California had very irregular mail service.
3. It often took two to three months for a letter to arrive.
4. Finally, the Butterfield Overland Mail Service began.
5. Stagecoaches carried passengers and mail east and west.
6. Now, imagine a trip to California in 1858.
7. You eagerly board the train in St. Louis.
8. After nearly 150 miles, you transfer to a stagecoach.
9. Hold on tight, because the ride is really rough.
10. You and the mail travel almost constantly day and night.
11. Sleep is practically impossible.
12. The coach eventually jolts to a stop in San Francisco.
13. Shakily you climb down.
14. You're totally exhausted.
15. Just think, your trip took only twenty-four days!

B. REVISION SKILL

Using Precise Adverbs   Sometimes you can make a sentence
more precise or change the meaning by changing an adverb.
Write each sentence. Replace each adverb in italics with another
adverb that answers the same question of *how, when, where,* or
to what extent.

EXAMPLE   The rider galloped *fearlessly* into the night.
The rider galloped bravely into the night.

16. A Pony Express rider comes *quickly* into view.
17. A fresh rider and a horse stand *nearby.*
18. The first rider brings his horse *sharply* to a halt.
19. *Then* the new rider grabs the mail, leaps onto a waiting
    horse, and is off at top speed.

Understanding
Adverbs   **483**

20. Riders carried mail 1,966 miles from St. Joseph, Missouri, to Sacramento, California, and then brought mail *back.*

21. Pony Express riders *always* rode as fast as possible.

22. They galloped *tirelessly* across the driest deserts.

23. They *scarcely* slowed down for steep mountain trails.

24. In deep snow, they *continually* urged their horses on.

25. Bad weather and rough trails *never* stopped them.

FOR MORE PRACTICE
See page 495.

Writing Theme
Bullfighting

C H E C K ✔ P O I N T
MIXED REVIEW • PAGES 482–484

Application in Literature   Write ten adverbs from this paragraph and the word each modifies. If a sentence has no adverbs, write *None.* There are fourteen adverbs in all.

[1]Juan . . . slowly, arrogantly, lifted the lure in both hands and let the animal charge under it. [2]Back came the bull, and again, with quiet assurance, the boy controlled the animal's speed and direction. [3]Without looking back, Juan walked towards Manolo. [4]The animal seemed to have been nailed to the sand by the last pass, but suddenly it charged fast, too fast for Manolo to warn Juan. [5]It happened in an instant. [6]The boy was tossed up in the air and landed with a thud on the ground. [7]The bull stomped the earth and moved his horns toward Juan, who had both arms thrown over his head. [8]But Manolo . . . acted automatically with no thought of what he was doing. [9]He picked up the muleta and waved it in front of the horns, and the horns charged the red cloth. [10]Manolo ran backwards, taking the bull away from Juan.

Maia Wojciechowska, *Shadow of a Bull*

MAKING COMPARISONS
WITH ADVERBS

> Use the **comparative form** of an adverb when you compare two actions. Use the **superlative form** of an adverb when you compare three or more actions.

Since adverbs, like adjectives, are words that describe, they can be changed to the comparative or superlative form.

Use the **comparative form** when you compare one action with another.

> Killer bees will attack *faster* than ordinary honeybees.

Use the **superlative form** when you compare three or more actions.

> Of the three insects, yellow jackets, bumblebees, and wasps, yellow jackets will usually attack the *fastest*.

The comparative and superlative forms of adverbs are formed in three different ways.

1. **Some short adverbs add *-er* to form the comparative. They add *-est* to form the superlative.**

Adverb	Comparative	Superlative
high	higher	highest
loud	louder	loudest
early	earlier	earliest

2. **Most adverbs that end in *-ly* form the comparative with the word *more*. They form the superlative with *most*.**

Adverb	Comparative	Superlative
angrily	more angrily	most angrily
dangerously	more dangerously	most dangerously
painfully	more painfully	most painfully

Grammar
═══**TIP**═══

Don't be confused by phrases such as "many other." Such phrases may signal that something is being compared to a group. Use the comparative form. Jeff runs *faster* than many other players.

3. Some adverbs change completely to form the comparative and superlative.

Adverb	Comparative	Superlative
well	better	best
badly	worse	worst
much	more	most
little	less	least

Practice Your Skills

A. CONCEPT CHECK

Comparisons with Adverbs   Write the adverb in each sentence that is used in comparison. Then write whether the adverb is used in the *Comparative* or *Superlative* form.

1. Killer bees are spreading more rapidly than we thought!
2. Of all honeybees, killer bees attack most viciously.
3. These bees are more accurately called Africanized bees.
4. They become angry the quickest and attack in swarms.
5. The common European honeybees behave best of all bees.
6. These bees don't behave more agreeably by chance.
7. Beekeepers sought wild bees they could manage most easily.
8. They worried most about finding bees that produced a great deal of honey.
9. They bred bees that could be handled more safely than those in the wild.
10. These bees produced honey successfully in Europe, Asia, and North America, but they performed less productively in tropical areas.
11. Then a scientist, who should have known better, imported African honeybees into Brazil.
12. He thought beekeepers could produce honey more profitably with this kind of bee.
13. The bees escaped and have been spreading through South America and into North America faster than anyone imagined.
14. Scientists predict that the bees will survive better in areas below 34 degrees north latitude than in northern regions.
15. That means that people in the southern United States should worry more about this threat than people to the north.

B. DRAFTING SKILL

Using Adverbs in Comparisons   Rewrite these sentences. Write the correct form of each adverb in parentheses.

16. Driven by a ceaseless hunger, army ants may hunt the (savagely) of all the inhabitants in a tropical forest.
17. You rarely find just a few army ants or even small swarms; they are (commonly) found in swarms of millions.
18. Nothing attacks (ferociously) than a swarm that has found some food.
19. These ants bite (viciously) than almost any other animal.
20. These ants tear the (efficiently) of all forest creatures.
21. An army ant can bite through a grasshopper's leg (easily) than you can bite through a stick of celery.
22. They don't run the (fast), but what they do catch, they eat.
23. Ants don't like to take on a big animal when it is alert, so they attack big animals (much) often when the animals are in pens or asleep.
24. The victims are eaten (rapidly) than you can imagine.
25. Of all insects, army ants scare me (bad).

C. PROOFREADING SKILL

Correcting the Use of Adverbs   Rewrite the following paragraph, correcting all errors in grammar, capitalization, punctuation, and spelling. Pay special attention to the use of adverbs to make comparisons. (10 errors)

People fear scorpions worse than most other animals, and with good reason. Some scorpions inject a very harmful Poison. Even tarantulas, bumblebees, and hornets are not as great a threat poisons of these animals kill prey least effectivly than the poisons some scorpions inject. Have also adapted and survived longest than many other creatures. In fact, they have existed on earth more longer than all other creatures except perhaps the Cockroach. There are more than a thousand species of scorpions. They look like miniature lobsters. However, scorpions are most closely related to spiders than to lobster's.

FOR MORE PRACTICE
See page 495.

Understanding
Adverbs   **487**

ADJECTIVE OR ADVERB?

An **adjective** describes a noun or pronoun. An **adverb** modifies a verb, an adjective, or another adverb.

Look at these lists of words.

Adjective	Adverb
cautious	cautiously
angry	angrily
slow	slowly
easy	easily
quick	quickly
beautiful	beautifully
sad	sadly

Grammar
TIP

To decide whether an adjective or adverb should follow verbs such as *look* or *feel,* ask yourself whether the verb is functioning as an action verb or linking verb. Use an adverb only if the verb is an action verb.

Adjectives and adverbs are both modifiers. Because adverbs are often formed from adjectives, they look very much alike. For these reasons, it is sometimes difficult to know when to use each type of word.

To decide whether to use an adjective or an adverb in a sentence, ask yourself what word is being modified.

Read this example.

The petals moved (gentle, gently) in the breeze.

Which word is correct? In this case, the verb *moved* is being modified. Since adverbs modify verbs and *moved* is a verb, choose the adverb *gently*.

Now look at this sentence.

Little Shop of Horrors is a (real, really) good play.

Which word is correct? Here, the adjective *good* is being modified. Therefore, the adverb *really* is the correct choice.

> **Remember these rules:**
>
> **Adjectives** tell *which one, what kind,* or *how many* about nouns and pronouns.
>
> **Adverbs** tell *how, when, where,* or *to what extent* about verbs, adjectives, and other adverbs.

Using *Good* and *Well,* or *Bad* and *Badly*

Choosing between *good* and *well* or *bad* and *badly* can be confusing. *Good* and *bad* are adjectives. They tell *what kind.*

> Those flowers smell *good.* (*Smell* is used as a linking verb here. Therefore, *good* is a predicate adjective that modifies *flowers.*)
>
> You shouldn't feel *bad* about picking them; picking them makes them grow. (*Feel* is a linking verb. *Bad* is a predicate adjective.)

The words *well* and *badly* are adverbs. Use them to modify verbs. *Well* and *badly* tell *how* something is done.

> Violets grow *well* in shade. (*Well* tells *how* they grow.)
>
> Seymour behaved *badly.* (*Badly* tells *how* he behaved.)

Note that *well* is an adjective when it describes a noun or pronoun and means "healthy," as in *Seymour does not feel well.*

Practice Your Skills

A. CONCEPT CHECK

Adjective or Adverb?   Choose the correct modifier from those given in parentheses.

Writing Theme
Unusual Plants

1. To Seymour, an assistant in a run-down florist shop, the plant seemed (pitiful, pitifully).
2. It looked small and (weak, weakly).
3. He knew (quick, quickly) that it was special.
4. Seymour nursed it (slow, slowly) to health.
5. It didn't do very (good, well), and he didn't know why.

6. Then one day, he (accidental, accidentally) cut his finger.
7. The plant moved (sudden, suddenly); it wanted blood!
8. The plant looked so (miserable, miserably) that Seymour fed it his blood.
9. Soon, the plant had grown (gigantic, gigantically).
10. Its appetite became (enormous, enormously).
11. To the plant, only human blood seemed (satisfactory, satisfactorily).
12. Because of the plant, Seymour behaved (bad, badly).
13. Who would guess he was capable of doing such (real, really) terrible things?
14. When you see the movie or play called *Little Shop of Horrors,* you can decide for yourself if it ends (good, well).
15. Remember, act (careful, carefully) around plants.

B. REVISION SKILL

FOR MORE PRACTICE
See page 495.

Using Adjectives and Adverbs Correctly   Revise the following paragraph to correct errors in the use of adjectives and adverbs.

Have you ever careful observed a carnivorous plant such as the Venus's-flytrap? These plants grow especially good in damp and boggy areas. White blossoms rise bright from the flower's leaves. The shape of the flytrap's hinged leaves appears strangely. A fly buzzes unsuspecting over the flower stalk. To the fly, the red centers of the leaves look attractively. Tiny hairs on the leaves are extreme sensitive. Buzzing closer, the fly lightly touches a hair. The leaves of the flytrap instant clamp shut. The flytrap's digestive juices gradual set to work. Soon the fly does not feel too good.

C H E C K ✔ P O I N T

Write the correct modifier from those given in parentheses.

Writing Theme
Lacrosse

1. Lacrosse has been played (longer, longest) than many other team sports.
2. It is (true, truly) an American game.
3. Native Americans, the inventors, were (real, really) skilled players.
4. Various groups played the game (different, differently).
5. All of them used a stick, or crosse, that was bent (sharp, sharply) at one end with a pouch for holding the ball.
6. Compared to a baseball, a lacrosse ball is (smaller, smallest).
7. Players catch the ball and pass it (quick, quickly).
8. Today's teams have ten players, but Native American teams had (more, most) players—usually about seventy.
9. At times, however, the number was (remarkable, remarkably), with as many as a thousand men on a team.
10. Native Americans played very (serious, seriously).
11. They would prepare (careful, carefully) for weeks.
12. When a team member played (bad, badly), he often suffered painful injuries.
13. Of all the players, the ones who ran the fastest were injured (less, least).
14. If a young brave played (good, well), he was considered ready for battle.
15. Often the team that was the (better, best) of the two was the one that severely hurt the largest number of the opposition's players.
16. Often winning players didn't feel too (good, well) either.
17. The Cherokee name for the game, little brother of war, is (sure, surely) appropriate.
18. French settlers in Canada learned the game (slow, slowly).
19. In 1867, Parliament declared it Canada's national game, and today Canadians point (more, most) proudly to their lacrosse players than to their football players.
20. Native Americans on reservations in both Canada and the United States still field excellent teams (regular, regularly).

Understanding
Adverbs   **491**

DOUBLE NEGATIVES

Never use a **double negative** when you write or speak.

The word *not* is an adverb that often causes problems. It is a negative. A negative is a word that says "no."

You remember that many contractions end in *-n't.* The *-n't* ending is a shortened form of *not.* Therefore, contractions that use *-n't* are negatives. Look at this list of negatives.

was + not = wasn't	would + not = wouldn't
have + not = haven't	can + not = can't
will + not = won't	does + not = doesn't

Not all negatives are contractions. Look at these examples of negatives. They are easy to remember because most of them contain the word *no.*

no	no one	nothing	not
none	nobody	nowhere	never

When two negatives appear in one sentence, they result in a **double negative.** Avoid double negatives in both your writing and speaking.

Incorrect	The captain *couldn't* do *nothing* to save the ship.
Correct	The captain *couldn't* do anything to save the ship.
Correct	The captain could do *nothing* to save the ship.

Practice Your Skills

A. CONCEPT CHECK

Double Negatives   Write the correct word from those given in parentheses.

1. Clearly, Christopher Columbus's last voyage (was, wasn't) no success story.
2. For a year, he searched for a route to the Indian Ocean but didn't find (anything, nothing).

3. Heat and humidity took their toll; there wasn't food without maggots (anywhere, nowhere).
4. At one point, his ships were anchored in a bay off Panama; Columbus didn't (never, ever) know he was one day's march away from the Pacific Ocean.
5. By then, his ships weren't very seaworthy (any, no) longer.
6. Worms didn't like (nothing, anything) better than ships.
7. Two ships were sinking and not fit for (no one, anyone) to sail.
8. There wasn't (anything, nothing) to do but set out across the Gulf of Mexico in the two remaining ships.
9. The ships never got (any, no) closer to home than Jamaica.
10. Marooned, Columbus didn't go (anywhere, nowhere) for a year.
11. Jamaica's governor hadn't (never, ever) liked Columbus.
12. The governor wouldn't use (any, none) of his ships or men to help Columbus.
13. On a chartered ship, Columbus made it back to Spain without (any, none) of the riches he had hoped for.

B. REVISION SKILL

Correcting Double Negatives Revise each of the following sentences to eliminate a double negative. Some sentences can be corrected in more than one way.

14. In 1912, no ships weren't better built than the *Titanic*.
15. Everyone said there wasn't nothing that could sink the ship.
16. However, the *Titanic* didn't never complete its only voyage.
17. On April 14, the crew sighted an iceberg that was so close that there wasn't nothing they could do to avoid hitting it.
18. The *Titanic* didn't take no more than three hours to sink.
19. Many passengers couldn't find no way to escape the ship.
20. The lifeboats couldn't hold no more than half of the people.
21. Today, ocean liners aren't never without strict safety rules and the help of the International Ice Patrol.
22. For years, people couldn't find the sunken *Titanic* nowhere.
23. In 1985, explorers found the sunken ship, but it is in such deep water it hasn't never been explored except with robots.

FOR MORE PRACTICE
See page 496.

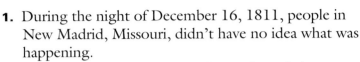

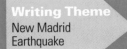

Writing Theme
New Madrid
Earthquake

Write each sentence and correct all errors in the use of adverbs. If a sentence has no errors, write *Correct*.

1. During the night of December 16, 1811, people in New Madrid, Missouri, didn't have no idea what was happening.
2. They hadn't never expected the earth to shake so violently.
3. It was late at night, but nobody could get no sleep.
4. People couldn't do nothing but leave their houses.
5. Some probably thought this was the worse earthquake ever.
6. Scientists back then didn't have any of the equipment we have today for measuring the intensity of earthquakes.
7. Today's scientists know that there haven't been many quakes nowhere that were stronger.
8. Log cabins, they know, don't never fall down easily.
9. Most of New Madrid's cabins weren't nothing but rubble.
10. Nothing less than thirty-thousand square miles of land sank abruptly by five to fifteen feet.
11. In Tennessee, twenty-square-mile Reelfoot Lake formed rapidly when the land wasn't no longer high enough for the water to drain off.
12. Huge cracks in the earth opened sudden all over the region.
13. The Mississippi River became violently with massive waves.
14. The Mississippi actually ran backwards for a short time.
15. The quake didn't shake nothing less than a million square miles.
16. No one in New Orleans could ignore the shocks.
17. The earth shook so bad that it made a church bell in Charleston, South Carolina, ring.
18. It seemed as if the aftershocks wouldn't never end.
19. For a year, strong shocks occurred unexpected.
20. Two aftershocks weren't no weaker than the first tremors.

An engraving of inhabitants fleeing their homes in New Madrid, Missouri, during the great earthquake of 1811.

GRAMMAR
H A N D B O O K
39

Writing Theme
Speed

A. Finding Adverbs   Find every adverb in these sentences.
Write the adverb and the word it modifies.

1. In the 1700s, bicycles were pretty crude and slow.
2. There were bikes then, but you'd barely recognize them.
3. In 1791, a French count invented a two-wheeled device that people rather playfully called a *célérifère,* which means "swift-footed."
4. It more or less resembled a bicycle.
5. It was designed strangely; it had two wheels but no pedals.
6. The rider actually ran while he or she sat on the thing.
7. The count also somehow left off any steering mechanism.
8. For a change in direction, a rider picked the célérifère up to move it.
9. The machine's wood wheels produced an extremely rough ride.
10. Célérifères were somewhat clumsy, but they were much faster than walking.

B. Using Adverbs Correctly   For each sentence, write the
correct form of the adverb in parentheses.

11. Each year, engineering improvements create race cars that travel (more, most) rapidly than the previous year's models.
12. Certainly, early race cars traveled (more slowly, most slowly) than today's cars.
13. At the first automobile race, held in France in 1894, people were (more curious, most curious) about which cars would finish than about which car was fastest.
14. Of the twenty cars in the race, a car powered by a steam engine performed (more reliably, most reliably).
15. Not only was it reliable, but it ran the (faster, fastest).
16. Of the cars that finished, the winner puttered (more quickly, most quickly), averaging almost twelve miles per hour.
17. The other cars did (worse, worst), and most didn't finish.
18. The cars traveled (less, least) than seventy-five miles.
19. In 1895, the cars raced (farther, farthest) than they had the year before.
20. The car that ran (best, better) averaged fifteen miles per hour!

Understanding
Adverbs   **495**

C. Choosing the Right Modifier   Write the correct modifier, the word it modifies, and whether it is an *Adjective* or *Adverb*.

> EXAMPLE   Trains can travel (safe, safely) at 120 mph.
> safely, travel, Adverb

21. Until recently, people didn't travel very (swift, swiftly).
22. If someone was in a hurry, horses were pretty (well, good).
23. Then trains made it possible for people to travel (real, really) fast.
24. To some people, early trains appeared (frightening, frighteningly).
25. An 1825 train seemed like a (real, really) blur at 7 mph.
26. Trains improved (rapid, rapidly), however.
27. By 1850, trains broke 60 miles per hour (easy, easily).
28. It may sound (unbelievable, unbelievably), but in 1955 a French train set a record by traveling 205 miles per hour.
29. At 160 mph, a Japanese train doesn't do so (bad, badly).
30. It seems (incredible, incredibly), but a United States rocket train that tests spacecraft parts reaches a rate of 3,090 mph.

D. Using Negatives Correctly   Write the following sentences, correcting all double negatives.

31. No one had never circled the world until Magellan did so in 1521.
32. His ships didn't make it in nothing less than two years.
33. We haven't never quit trying to circle the globe faster.
34. The next noteworthy trip wasn't made by nobody else but Nellie Bly, a reporter who in 1889 went around the world in about seventy-two days.
35. That record wasn't nothing after people started flying.
36. In 1924, one plane never had no trouble circling the earth in fifteen days.
37. Not even that record wasn't safe, though.
38. Wiley Post and Harold Gatty didn't take no time at all to break the record, taking less than eight days in 1931.
39. By 1957, the record wasn't no more than two days.
40. None of these records means nothing to space vehicles.

Writing Theme
Bears

A. Identifying Adverbs   Write each adverb below. Also write whether the adverb tells *How, When, Where,* or *To what extent.*

1. A newborn bear is usually only seven or eight inches long.
2. The tiny cub ordinarily weighs less than a pound.
3. It is completely blind and lacks both teeth and hair.
4. It grows quickly, though, and very soon it is not helpless.
5. In only a few years, it may weigh 300 to 1,500 pounds.
6. Alaskan brown bears are the tallest—sometimes nearly nine feet high when standing up on two legs.
7. They are powerful and dangerously unpredictable animals.
8. Some bears can run faster than a horse for short distances.
9. Bears once lived everywhere in the United States.
10. Now, many black bears and a few grizzlies still live here.

B. Making Comparisons   Write the correct form of each adverb given in parentheses.

11. Of all Americans who have worked with animals, James Capen Adams may be the (well) known animal trainer.
12. People know him (well) as Grizzly Adams.
13. Adams had many jobs; the one he probably liked (little) was his first one as a shoemaker in Massachusetts.
14. In 1849, he joined the California Gold Rush, thinking he couldn't do (badly) as a prospector than he had done as a shoemaker.
15. He wanted (desperately) of all to work with animals.
16. He quit mining and traveled even (deep) into the mountains.
17. He caught and trained many animals; one, a bear he named Lady Washington, he trained the (carefully) of all.
18. Lady Washington fought back (hard) than a cub would have.
19. In time, Lady grew (much) gentle and they became friends.
20. Later, Grizzly captured a grizzly cub, which he named Benjamin Franklin; it was (easily) trained than Lady.
21. Ben had lived (briefly) as a wild animal than Lady.
22. Lady and Ben served Grizzly the (loyally) of all his animals.

Understanding
Adverbs   **497**

C. Using the Correct Modifier   Write the following sentences, correcting all errors in the use of adjectives and adverbs. If a sentence has no error, write *Correct.*

23. At one time, the sight of a grizzly bear was not unusual in North America.
24. These creatures survived very good everywhere west of Ohio and Kentucky.
25. Native Americans lived uneasy with them from the beginning.
26. Some groups would hunt the grizzly only if they needed food bad.
27. They respected the animal and felt badly when they killed one.
28. Others worshipped the awesome grizzly and never hunted it.
29. They were real sure that their ancestors had become bears.
30. Bears appear frequent in their legends and stories.
31. No doubt, this extremely deadly bear deserved its reputation.
32. When angry, it could overtake a rider on horseback easy.
33. It could knock down both the rider and the horse with one remarkable powerful swipe.
34. Early pioneers never felt too safely with grizzlies near.
35. The settlers killed bears rather regular.
36. Most grizzlies south of Canada have been gradually destroyed.

D. Using Negatives   For each sentence, write the correct word from those given in parentheses.

37. None of our presidents did (no, any) more to protect wilderness areas and wild animals than Theodore Roosevelt.
38. There wasn't (no one, anyone) who loved the outdoors more.
39. However, he wasn't in (any, no) way against hunting.
40. He didn't like (anything, nothing) much better than a bear hunt; but one time in Mississippi an old bear was caught.
41. Teddy didn't think (anybody, nobody) ought to shoot it.
42. He wouldn't (ever, never) shoot a helpless creature.
43. There wasn't (anybody, nobody) who ignored that story.
44. A toy maker (could, couldn't) not let the opportunity pass.
45. Nothing would sell (any, no) better than "Teddy" bears.
46. T.R. himself didn't have (any, no) objection to the toys.

WRITING CONNECTIONS

Elaboration, Revision, and Proofreading

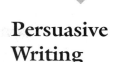

Revise the following draft of an opinion paper by using the directions at the bottom of the page. Then proofread your paper, paying special attention to the use of adverbs. Also look for other grammatical errors and errors in capitalization, punctuation, and spelling.

¹Squirt guns don't seem like something for no one to get concerned about. ²They are just a way for kids to have some good, clean (and wet) fun. ³However, some people want to ban squirt guns. ⁴My cousin has a squirt gun. ⁵Why should all the kids who play safely with these toys be punished because a few kids act irresponsibly? ⁶The gun that people are worried about is a new, high-powered squirt gun. ⁷This gun holds more water. ⁸It shoots it more forceful. ⁹Critics say that if these guns are missused, they can be dangrous a few kids have been injurd. ¹⁰Yet any toy is dangrous if it is missused. ¹¹Some toys are too expensive. ¹²When these squirt guns are used properly, theyre a blast. And they are not unsafe.

1. Remove the two sentences that do not support the main idea.

2. Strengthen the argument by adding an example to sentence 10. "Even a tricycle can be dangerous if a child rides too fast or out into a street."

3. Improve the flow of sentences by combining 7 and 8 to make a sentence with a compound verb.

4. Replace the informal words *a blast* in sentence 12 with a more formal expression.

5. Make the conclusion of the paragraph stronger by placing sentence 5 after sentence 12.

Persuasive Writing

Stating your opinion allows you to share ideas on issues you feel strongly about. (See Workshop 5.) When you revise an opinion paper, look to see that you have stated your position clearly and supported it. Use adverbs to add details that tell *how, when, where,* and *to what extent.*

Directions   One or more of the underlined sections in the following sentences may contain an error in grammar, punctuation, spelling, or capitalization. Write the letter of each incorrect section. Then rewrite the section correctly. If there is no error in an item, write *D.*

> **Example**   I watched the magician very <u>close</u>, but I don't understand.
> **A**
>
> How did <u>him</u> and his assistant make the rabbit <u>disappear</u>?
> **B**   **C**
>
> <u>No error</u>
> **D**
>
> **Answer**   A—closely; B—he

1. Big animals <u>arent</u> always parents of big <u>babies</u>. Kangaroos are about an
    A   **B**
inch long when <u>their</u> born. <u>No error</u>
                C   **D**

2. If a bus is going <u>real</u> fast and stops <u>suddenly</u>, it is the force of inertia that
                    A   **B**
pushes <u>your</u> body forward. <u>No error</u>
        C   **D**

3. A <u>bloodhound's</u> nose works really <u>good</u>. Some of these dogs can follow
        A   **B**
a trail <u>that's</u> ten days old. <u>No error</u>
        C   **D**

4. The song <u>"Happy Birthday"</u> was a gold mine for Mildred Hill. It was <u>written</u>
                A   **B**
by <u>she</u> and her sister Patty and has earned millions of dollars. <u>No error</u>
    C   **D**

5. If a salamander loses <u>it's</u> tail, <u>it</u> just <u>grows</u> a new one. <u>No error</u>
                        A   **B**   **C**   **D**

6. <u>There</u> are a great many people named John and Jim. Muhammad, however,
    A
is the <u>most popularest</u> name in the <u>world</u>. <u>No error</u>
        B   **C**   **D**

7. Neither <u>John F. Kennedy</u> nor Warren G. Harding outlived <u>their</u> <u>father</u>.
               A   **B**   **C**
<u>No error</u>
D

8. <u>Rubies</u>, not diamonds, are currently the <u>more precious</u> stones on this
   A   **B**
<u>planet</u>. <u>No error</u>
C   **D**

9. <u>Them</u> stingers on a queen bee won't hurt <u>nobody</u>. <u>They</u> are only used
   A   **B**   **C**
as weapons against other queen bees. <u>No error</u>
                                   D

10. July and <u>august</u> have something in common. Each got <u>their name</u> from
          A   **B**
a <u>Roman</u> emperor named Caesar—a Julius and an Augustus. <u>No error</u>
    C   **D**

11. My brother and <u>I</u> are twins, but <u>him</u> and my cousin <u>look</u> more alike than
               A   **B**   **C**
he and I do. <u>No error</u>
               D

12. <u>These</u> kind of penguin <u>grows</u> four feet tall and can weigh <u>nearly</u> one
    A   **B**   **C**
hundred pounds. <u>No error</u>
                    D

13. Watch <u>out!</u> <u>Those</u> chili peppers are much <u>hotter</u> than bell peppers.
          A   **B**   **C**
<u>No error</u>
D

14. Two-thirds of all adult <u>Americans</u> see <u>poor</u> enough to need eyeglasses.
                         A   **B**
That leaves one third that don't <u>never</u> need to wear them. <u>No error</u>
                           C   **D**

15. Has everyone in the <u>string</u> section tuned <u>his or her</u> <u>instrument</u>? <u>No error</u>
                      A   **B**   **C**   **D**

Sketch Book

Extravaganza Televisione (1984), Kenny Scharf.

- This television gives new meaning to the question, What's on TV? Write a description of this television set. Use words that help you tell your readers exactly where things are located.

- Write about what happened in a recent episode of a television show you often watch.

- Imagine that you and a friend are going to meet at your home or some other specific place. Write directions to tell your friend how to get there.

Prepositions and Conjunctions

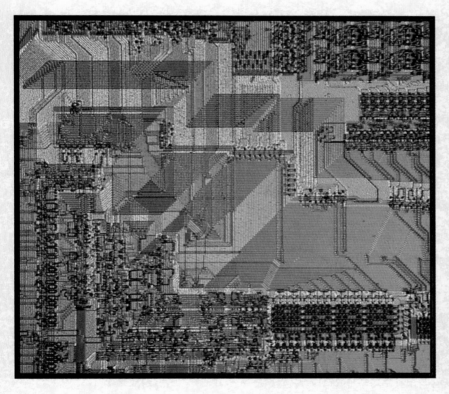

Circuits like this one provide the electrical connections that make a picture appear on your television set. When you write, you often need to provide connections between words and sentences.

In this handbook you will learn ways to use prepositions and conjunctions to show your readers how your ideas are connected and to add details to your writing.

A **preposition** shows how a noun or a pronoun relates to another word in a sentence. The noun or pronoun that follows a preposition is the **object of the preposition.**

The girl is *on* the table.

The girl is *above* the table.

Writing
TIP

Choose prepositions carefully to make your meaning clear. Often, by changing prepositions, you can change the relationship between words in a sentence.

Prepositions help to show relationships. For example, *on* and *above* show the relationship between the girl and the table. The noun or pronoun following a preposition is called the **object of the preposition.** Which word is the object in the captions below the pictures?

Commonly Used Prepositions

about	before	down	of	to
above	behind	during	off	toward
across	below	for	on	under
after	beneath	from	onto	underneath
against	beside	in	out	until
along	between	inside	outside	up
among	beyond	into	over	upon
around	but (except)	like	past	with
at	by	near	through	without

Practice Your Skills

A. CONCEPT CHECK

Prepositions Write the prepositions in the following sentences. Beside each preposition, write its object. Some sentences have more than one preposition and object.

Writing Theme
Science and Magic

1. Some magic tricks rely on appearances.
2. The laws of science are behind others.
3. Place a deck of cards on a table and cut the deck in half.
4. Look at the top card, show it to your audience, and then replace it.
5. Conceal a saltshaker in your pocket.
6. Reach inside that pocket.
7. Secretly coat the tip of your finger with salt and tap the top card with your finger.
8. Be sure you leave some salt on the surface of the top card.
9. Place one stack beneath the other.
10. The selected card seems lost in the middle of the deck.
11. Take a saltshaker from your pocket.
12. Sprinkle a little salt over the deck.
13. Also gently tap against the side of the deck with the shaker.
14. As if by magic, the deck will separate at the point where the selected card is.
15. Grains of salt on that card act like ball bearings, making the cards separate there.

B. DRAFTING SKILL

Using Prepositions Write prepositions that logically complete the following sentences.

[16]Stick a piece ____ double-sided sticky tape ____ the front edge of a table. [17]Show a six-inch piece of thread ____ your audience, then attach one end ____ the tape. [18]Take a comb ____ your pocket. [19]Run the comb ____ your hair. [20]Say, "Rope, rise ____ the air." [21]Hold the comb ____ the free end of the thread. [22]Draw the comb up ____ the air, and the thread mysteriously rises. [23]This trick is done ____ static electricity caused by rubbing the comb ____ your hair.

FOR MORE PRACTICE
See page 521.

Prepositions and
Conjunctions **505**

A **prepositional phrase** is a group of words that begins with a preposition and ends with its object.

Look at the italicized prepositional phrases in the sentences below. Notice each preposition and its object.

            Preposition   Object of Preposition

The Pueblo people live *in the Southwest.*

            Preposition   Object of Preposition

They have lived there *for many centuries.*

In a prepositional phrase, one or more words that describe the object may come between the preposition and its object. The preposition, the object, and all the words that describe the object form the **prepositional phrase.**

Sentences often contain more than one prepositional phrase.

> The ancestors *of the Pueblos,* the Anasazi, made their homes *in high cliffs.*

A preposition may have a **compound object** made up of two or more nouns or pronouns joined by *and* or *or.*

        Object   Object   Object   Object

They settled *in New Mexico, Arizona, Utah, and Colorado.*

You can often make your writing smoother by reducing a sentence to a prepositional phrase and combining it with another sentence.

> The Pueblos later built more elaborate homes. They built them *of stone and adobe.*
> The Pueblos later built more elaborate homes *of stone and adobe.*

Always be sure to place the prepositional phrase close to the word or words it describes.

Practice Your Skills

A. APPLICATION IN LITERATURE

Prepositional Phrases   Notice how this writer uses prepositional phrases to add detail to her narrative. Write the prepositional phrases in these sentences. If a sentence contains no prepositional phrases, write *None.*

¹The house of Tassai was the last one in the little town, on the very edge of the mesa top. **²**She ran into the door and did not notice that the little white girl who had followed her had stopped suddenly just outside the doorway. **³**The child was watching, with wide, frightened eyes, a snake that lifted its head. . . . **⁴**It was a rattlesnake, and it moved its flat, ugly head closer and closer to the little girl. **⁵**She gave one sharp cry as Tassai came out . . . with the jar in her arms. **⁶**Tassai had thrown aside the blanket and held the jar unwrapped in her arms. . . .

⁷Tassai did the only thing she could do. **⁸**With all her strength she threw the jar at the snake. **⁹**It broke into many pieces on the rock, and the snake lay flat and still.

Grace P. Moon, "The Jar of Tassai"

Prepositions and
Conjunctions   **507**

B. DRAFTING SKILL

Using Prepositional Phrases   Rewrite each of the following pairs of sentences by reducing one sentence to a prepositional phrase and combining it with the other sentence.

EXAMPLE   *Separate*   At the heart of the community was a kiva. It was used *for meetings and ceremonies.*

Combined   At the heart of the community was a kiva *for meetings and ceremonies.*

10. The kiva was a large underground space. It lay beneath the community's living quarters.
11. The kiva was carefully built. It was built in a circle or a rectangle.
12. The kiva had a deep pit. The pit was in the middle.
13. The Anasazi built fires in this pit. The fires were for their most important ceremonies.
14. There was often a roof over the pit. It was made of timbers.
15. A ladder led to the kiva. It came from the buildings above.
16. Members entered easily. They came through a hatchway.
17. The Anasazi created hundreds of communities. They were in the area of Chaco Canyon.
18. Pueblo Bonito is a remarkable example. It is in the famous Chaco Culture National Historical Park.
19. This city was four stories high. It was built with almost 650 rooms and 32 kivas.
20. Nearly a thousand people lived there. They lived there about nine hundred years ago.
21. The largest of the kivas is two stories deep. It was dug to a diameter of over fifty feet.

C. APPLICATION IN WRITING

Using Prepositions in Directions   Prepositions and prepositional phrases are especially useful in giving directions. Write a set of directions. Tell a friend how to get somewhere—for example, how to get from the airport to your house—or how to do something, like fold a paper airplane.

FOR MORE PRACTICE
See page 521.

CHECK ✔ POINT
MIXED REVIEW • PAGES 504–508

Writing Theme
Cameras

Write the prepositional phrases in the following sentences. Draw a line under the object of each preposition.

1. A pinhole camera can easily be made from any box with a tight-fitting lid.
2. A pinhole will perform the job of a lens in the camera.
3. First, take a small square of aluminum foil about an inch on each side.
4. Lay the foil on a flat, hard surface.
5. Press the point of a needle through the foil.
6. The pinhole should be round and free of ragged edges.
7. Select a box and paint the inside with black paint.
8. Cut a hole in one side of the box.
9. Tape the aluminum foil over the hole in the box.
10. Be sure that the pinhole is in the center of the foil.
11. Take a piece of nontransparent tape and cover the pinhole.
12. Load the pinhole camera with a sheet of light-sensitive photographic paper.
13. Loading must be done in a darkroom with a safelight.
14. Center the photographic paper on the opposite side of the box from the pinhole.
15. Replace the lid of the box.
16. Take the pinhole camera outdoors and place it on a firm support.
17. Remove the tape from the pinhole for two minutes.
18. If the day is cloudy, open the pinhole for eight minutes.
19. Remove the exposed photographic paper and develop it in the darkroom.
20. A negative image will form on the paper.
21. If your negative is too dark, repeat the procedure and shorten the time of exposure.
22. Lengthen the time of exposure if your negative is too light.
23. You can make several pinhole cameras for multiple shots of various scenes.
24. Try making a pinhole camera from an oatmeal box.
25. Making a camera of this kind is fun and inexpensive.

> When a pronoun is the object of a preposition, the object form of the pronoun must be used.

Object forms of pronouns must be used as objects of prepositions. Here are the object forms:

> me   you   him   her   it   us   them

Notice the pronouns in these sentences.

> The pioneers are an inspiration for *us* today.
> They traveled west, taking all their possessions with *them*.

Sometimes a pronoun is part of a **compound object of a preposition.** When a pronoun is part of a compound object, you must use an object pronoun.

Simple Object	**Compound Object**
The girl rode with *me*.	The girl rode with *Hank and me*.
She held the reins for *me*.	She held the reins for *him and me*.

If you are unsure which form of pronoun to use in a compound object, say the sentence with just the pronoun following the preposition. Then write the sentence with the complete prepositional phrase.

> Everyone was ready but the Cranes and (we, us).
> Everyone was ready but *us*.
> Everyone was ready but the Cranes and *us*.

For more information on using object pronouns, see Handbook 37, "Understanding Pronouns," pages 434–457.

Pioneer families in canvas-covered wagons formed wagon trains and journeyed west.

Practice Your Skills

A. CONCEPT CHECK

Pronouns After Prepositions   Write the correct pronoun.

1. Your letter was a treat for Tina and (I, me).
2. It came to (we, us) just before our wagon train left St. Louis.
3. To Mom, Tina, and (I, me), that seems like years ago.
4. Imagine all these families taking everything they own with (they, them).
5. One of the drivers stands guard near (we, us) all night.
6. His rifle shots are an alarm clock for my family and (I, me).
7. To get ready for the day's journey, Pa gathers the oxen and puts harnesses on (they, them).
8. The oxen are always shoving against (he, him) because they don't like to be harnessed.
9. This morning Mom made pancakes and split the extra ones between Tina and (he, him).
10. Pa takes a lot of teasing from Tina and (she, her) about his healthy appetite.

B. PROOFREADING SKILL

Using the Correct Pronoun Forms   Proofread the following paragraph. Then write the paragraph, correcting all errors in grammar, capitalization, punctuation, and spelling. Make sure that the correct pronoun forms are used. (10 errors)

Women preformed many important tasks in a pioneer community. A woman prepared meals. And washed clothes for she and her family. Women also drove wagons gathered fuel and food, and cared for the sick. Recording the births, deaths, and other events in a families life were part of a womans' role. Even when women's families were settled, life was just as hard for they and their husbands as it had been on the trail. Together they cleared the land, planted crops, and herded animals. Often, stores, mills, and even mines were started by they and their husbands. Sometimes because of death. or other misfortune, women had to run these businesses by themselves.

Writing Theme
Life as a Pioneer

FOR MORE PRACTICE
See page 521.

Prepositions and
Conjunctions   **511**

Some prepositions need special attention.

Several words that are used as prepositions are also used as adverbs. Some examples are *up, down, around, in,* and *out.*

> Josh looked *up.* (adverb)
> Josh looked *up* the street. (preposition)

> The cat dashed *around.* (adverb)
> The cat dashed *around* the room. (preposition)

To determine if a word is an adverb or a preposition, look at how it is used. If it is used alone, it is probably an adverb. If it begins a phrase, it is probably a preposition.

For more information on adverbs, see Handbook 39, "Understanding Adverbs," pages 480–499.

Using *Between* and *Among*

You may hear the prepositions *between* and *among* used as though there were no difference between them. However, there is a difference.

Usually, *among* is used to refer to three or more persons, objects, or groups.

> Chris was *among* the many guests at Ann's party.
> Joan's present was hidden *among* all the others.

Between is usually used to refer to two persons, objects, or groups.

> Jenna sat between Ben and Chloe.

Between may also be used to refer to more than two items when you wish to show that each is related to the others.

> A treaty *between* France, Germany, and Italy was drafted.

Writing
TIP

Avoid using unnecessary prepositions.
  Unnecessary
    Where is the package *at?*
  Improved
    Where is the package?

Practice Your Skills

A. CONCEPT CHECK

Adverbs and Prepositions   Write each italicized word. Label it *Adverb* or *Preposition*.

Writing Theme
Celebrations Around the World

1. People *around* the world celebrate birthdays in many ways.
2. Have you ever seen birthday candles blown *out?*
3. Blowing out candles first became popular *in* Germany.
4. *Over* the years, the custom has spread to other countries.
5. *In* Korea a baby's first birthday may be used to tell the child's future.
6. The baby sits at a table covered *with* a variety of objects.
7. The baby reaches *among* the objects.
8. The first object the baby picks *up* foretells his or her future.
9. In China people associate long noodles *with* long life.
10. On birthdays, bowls *of* long noodles are exchanged between friends.
11. The noodles mean "Long life *to* you."
12. In England prizes are hidden in a tub of sawdust and guests dig *in* to find them.
13. In Mexico piñatas are hung *up* for birthdays and other celebrations.
14. A piñata is filled *with* candies, fruits, and gifts.
15. Blindfolded guests swing sticks *around,* hoping to hit the piñata.
16. When it breaks, the prizes spill *down* onto the guests.

B. REVISION SKILL

Using Prepositions Correctly   Revise the sentences in which *between* or *among* is used incorrectly. If a sentence contains no error, write *Correct*.

17. The arrival of a new year has been a special day between people for ages.
18. Thousands of years ago, the Egyptians celebrated the new year among May and July, when the Nile overflowed.
19. From between their various gods, the ancient Romans chose Janus as the god of the new year.
20. Janus had two faces and so did not have to choose among looking forward and looking backward.
21. January was named for Janus, and on the first day of January, good-luck gifts were exchanged between friends.
22. In contrast, ancient Persians shared new year's eggs among family members.
23. Celtic priests in what is now England gave out branches of mistletoe between their followers.
24. Between some Native Americans, the new year meant new possessions.
25. The Creeks, between July and September, threw out old things and got new clothes, furniture, and even new toys.

Bahamian drummers welcome the New Year as they perform in the Junkanoo Parade. This event may be named after John Canoe, a local folk hero.

C. APPLICATION IN WRITING

Think of the funniest or most unusual party you ever attended. Did people wear costumes? Describe the party in a few sentences. Use at least two of these words as adverbs: *up, down, around, through,* and *in.* Use at least three of these words as prepositions: *for, from, with, out, behind,* and *of.*

FOR MORE PRACTICE
See page 522.

CHECK  POINT
MIXED REVIEW • PAGES 510–514

Choose and write the correct word from the two given in parentheses.

1. (Between, Among) barnstorming and air shows, many early pilots gained experience and skill.
2. Many of these pilots pleased large crowds by performing daring tricks for (they, them).
3. Many of their stunts would be thrilling even for (we, us) today.
4. The planes were flimsy, but the pilots did amazing stunts with (they, them).
5. One pilot, "Linc" Beachey, stood out; there was a difference between (he, him) and the other fliers.
6. For one trick this fearless daredevil would zoom (between, among) the doors of airplane hangars—in one side and out the other.
7. With six thousand feet between (he, him) and the crowd below, he would begin his "dive of death."
8. Gasps and cries could be heard (between, among) the amazed spectators as he turned off his engine and headed straight for them.
9. Just in time, he pulled out of the dive and landed safely (between, among) them.
10. Another important name (among, between) early pilots was Bessica Raiche.
11. For (she, her) and her husband, building a plane in their living room was no small accomplishment.
12. (Between, Among) the various materials available, they chose bamboo, silk, and piano wire.
13. (Between, Among) the aircraft builders of her day, Raiche became a pioneer.
14. After poor health forced her out of flying, she decided medicine was the career for (she, her), so she became a doctor.
15. Credit for the first solo flight by a U.S. woman is shared by (she, her) and Blanche Scott.

Prepositions and
Conjunctions   **515**

> A **conjunction** joins words or groups of words.

A conjunction can be used to join sentence parts or whole sentences. The words *and, but,* and *or* are conjunctions. In the following sentences, the conjunctions join sentence parts.

> Glenna *and* her dogs sped across the ice. (*And* joins subjects.)
> The team was tired *but* raced on. (*But* joins predicates.)
> By nightfall they might reach McGrath *or* Takotna. (*Or* joins direct objects.)

You have learned that *compound* means "having more than one part." In the examples above, conjunctions were used to join compound sentence parts. Conjunctions may also be used to join whole sentences that are closely related.

> The team came to a stop. Glenna unhitched the dogs.
> The team came to a stop, *and* Glenna unhitched the dogs.

Notice that a comma is used at the end of the first sentence, before the conjunction *and.* A comma is not used, however, when two sentence parts are joined. Also, you may omit the comma when the two sentences you join are very short.

Practice Your Skills

A. CONCEPT CHECK

Compound Constructions   Write the compound part in each of the following sentences and label it *Subject, Verb, Object,* or *Sentence.*

1. For many years dogs and dog sleds provided the main form of winter transportation in Alaska.
2. Sleds carried goods and people across the countryside.

3. In 1925, dog-sled teams proved their strength and value.
4. That year a diphtheria epidemic broke out in Nome, but the town was not prepared.
5. More serum was needed, or the town would face disaster.
6. Dog sleds and railroads combined their efforts.
7. Trains took the serum part of the way, and sleds carried it on to Nome.
8. Nineteen drivers and teams worked in a relay for a week.
9. Nome's residents cheered and celebrated the team's arrival.
10. Now every March the Iditarod Trail Sled Dog Race duplicates and honors that event.

B. DRAFTING SKILL

Sentence Combining   Combine each of the following sentence pairs into a single sentence. Choose a conjunction and use a comma if necessary. Omit words in italics.

11. Susan Butcher is a dog-sled racer. *She is* a four-time winner of the Iditarod race.
12. This famous race covers over 1,100 miles. *It* lasts many days.
13. Sled dogs in the race must be strong. They could not survive.
14. Early in one race, Butcher's sled got stuck in an icy creek. *The sled* broke in four places.
15. Her sled no longer steered properly. She continued anyway.
16. Later, a brutal snowstorm came up. *There were* fierce winds.
17. Butcher could wait out the storm. She could go on.
18. Two opponents were close. They were forced to stop.
19. She trusted her dogs. They trusted her.
20. She drove all night through the storm. *She* beat the second-place dog-sled by fourteen hours.

The four-time Iditarod winner Susan Butcher poses with a hard-working friend.

FOR MORE PRACTICE
See page 522.

Prepositions and
Conjunctions   **517**

USING WORDS AS DIFFERENT PARTS OF SPEECH

Some words may be used as more than one part of speech. How a word is used in a sentence determines what part of speech it is.

On page 512 of this handbook, you learned that words like *up, down, around, in,* and *out* can be used either as prepositions or as adverbs. Many other words can function as more than one part of speech. Before you can determine what part of speech a word is, you must decide how the word is used in a sentence. Look at how the word *farm* is used in the following sentences.

As a noun
Josh and Jenna live on a *farm.*

As a verb
Their family first *farmed* that land a hundred years ago.

As an adjective
Josh and his father take care of the family's *farm* machinery.

Remember the rules for each part of speech when using words in different ways. For example, when you use *farm* as a noun, you add *-s* to form the plural *farms.* When you use *farm* as a verb, you add *-ed* to form the past tense *farmed.* To use *farm* in some tenses, you may need to add a helping verb such as *did* or *will.*

There is only one sure way to tell what part of speech a word is. Look at the sentence in which the word is used.

Practice Your Skills

A. CONCEPT CHECK

Parts of Speech   Identify the part of speech of each word in italics. Write *Noun, Verb, Adjective, Adverb,* or *Preposition.*

Writing Theme
Weather and
Almanacs

1. Are you a good *weather* forecaster?
2. Certain signs have been used as *warning* signs of future weather for centuries.
3. Generally, *rain* is not likely if the wind is from the north.
4. In contrast, it will often *rain* or snow shortly after a south wind.
5. A *red* sky at sunrise can also be a warning of coming rain.
6. Red skies in the evening *promise* clear weather.
7. Trees with curling leaves are a *promise* of a coming storm.
8. If bees stay *inside* the hive, a storm is on the way.
9. Just before a storm, ordinary *daily* sounds are often louder.
10. With these tips you can predict the weather *daily.*

B. DRAFTING SKILL

Using Words as Different Parts of Speech   For each sentence, write your own sentence, using the word in italics. Use the italicized word as the part of speech shown in parentheses.

11. Many people *turn* to an almanac for information about the weather and other topics. (Noun)
12. Almanacs have been *around* for ages. (Preposition)
13. *In* fact, almanacs are among the earliest published works. (Adverb)
14. An almanac from ancient Egypt has *lists* of religious festivals and lucky and unlucky days. (Verb)
15. Later almanacs even forecasted the *weather.* (Adjective)
16. These forecasts helped guide explorers like Christopher Columbus *across* the seas. (Adverb)
17. The oldest almanac published in this *country* first appeared in 1792. (Adjective)
18. It offered numerous tips *on* planting. (Adverb)
19. Most almanacs *forecast* the weather months in advance. (Noun)
20. These *forecasts* are right eight times out of ten. (Verb)

FOR MORE PRACTICE
See page 522.

A. In each of the following sentences, write and label the compound part as *Subject, Verb, Object,* or *Sentence.* For a compound object of a preposition, use the label *Object P.*

1. Apparently a monster was attacking and sinking ships.
2. Ned Land and a French professor tried unsuccessfully to destroy the monster.
3. An explosion sent them overboard, but they were rescued.
4. They had come up against Captain Nemo and the *Nautilus.*
5. The underwater ship had oxygen, electricity, and fuel.
6. Food and clothing came from the sea.
7. With special equipment they walked and hunted on the ocean floor.
8. For months they sailed around the world, and they experienced many adventures.
9. They woke up one morning on an island, with no sign of Nemo or the ship.
10. Jules Verne published the story *Twenty Thousand Leagues Under the Sea* in 1870, before submarines or atomic power.

B. Write the italicized words in the following sentences and identify the part of speech of each.

11. Armed with a treasure map, Jim Hawkins, Squire Trelawney, and Dr. Livesey *sail* off to find gold.
12. Long John Silver, the ship's cook, is really a *pirate,* however.
13. Several of his *pirate* friends are part of the crew.
14. They *plan* to take over the ship.
15. Jim, however, overhears their *plan*.
16. Shortly after going ashore, Jim looks back to see a skull-and-crossbones flag flying above the *sail.*
17. On the island, the pirates find a chest, but nothing is *inside.*
18. Ben Gunn, a pirate marooned on the island for three years, has already found the *treasure.*
19. Eventually Jim and his friends get the *gold.*
20. Long John Silver escapes with a bag of *gold* coins.

Writing Theme
Rain Forests

A. Recognizing Prepositions and Prepositional Phrases
Write the prepositional phrases in the following sentences.
Underline the object or objects of each preposition.

1. Imagine a huge forest growing in a hot, steamy environment.
2. In a tropical rain forest, the tallest trees rise nearly two hundred feet above the ground.
3. Direct sunlight reaches only the highest of their branches.
4. Only dim light filters through the leaves to the ground.
5. Thundershowers occur often throughout the year.
6. However, few raindrops fall directly to the ground.
7. Water drips down tree trunks or falls from leaves.
8. The place teems with wildlife.
9. Many animals spend their entire lives in the trees.
10. Frogs, toads, lizards, and snakes dwell among the branches.
11. Flying squirrels and flying lemurs glide from tree to tree.
12. Monkeys scamper along branches or swing from vines.
13. Bats, gibbons, monkeys, squirrels, and toucans eat nuts and fruits from the highest branches.
14. Few low-growing plants can live in the dim light of the forest floor.
15. You could easily walk through most parts of such a forest, among the fallen leaves.

B. Using Pronouns as Objects of Prepositions   Write the correct form of the pronoun in parentheses.

16. One writer found an African rain forest quite useful to (he, him) as a setting for adventure stories.
17. Edgar Rice Burroughs wrote many books, but the most famous of (they, them) is *Tarzan of the Apes.*
18. The Tarzan stories are still familiar to (we, us) today.
19. The son of an English nobleman, Tarzan is lost as an infant in the jungle—where death waits for most people, but not for (he, him).
20. Instead, he is raised by a tribe of great apes, and an incredible series of exciting events unfold for Tarzan and (they, them).
21. It is easy for (he, him) to communicate with the animals.

Prepositions and
Conjunctions   **521**

22. Eventually Tarzan meets Jane and falls in love with (she, her).

23. The stories about (he, him) and (she, her) are widely read.

24. In the film version of the story, a chimpanzee named Cheeta lives in the jungle with Jane and (he, him).

25. Today, all this might seem unlikely to you and (I, me).

C. *Among* and *Between*   Choose and write the correct preposition from the two given in parentheses.

26. (Among, Between) the world's tropical rain forests, the Amazon rain forest is the largest.

27. It lies (among, between) the Andes and the Atlantic.

28. It will be hard to keep a balance (between, among) protecting the environment and using the resources.

29. Scientists estimate that (between, among) 40 million and 60 million acres of rain forest are destroyed yearly.

30. Governments will have to choose (among, between) several different approaches to the problem.

D. Using Conjunctions   Write each sentence pair as a single sentence, using *and, but,* or *or.* Add commas where needed.

31. The natives of the Amazon forest are highly inventive. They also value generosity.

32. Some are farmers. Most are hunters and gatherers.

33. They invented the hammock. They also created blowguns.

34. These forest dwellers have an interesting history. Their future is uncertain.

35. They could survive in many places. They could disappear.

E. Identifying Parts of Speech   Write each italicized word and identify its part of speech.

36. The *outside* world knows little of life *inside* the forest.

37. The Amazon flows *past* the little villages as it did in the *past.*

38. However, times are changing *along* this river, and the forest people may have no choice but to go *along* with the changes.

39. The life they have lived *over* centuries may be almost *over.*

40. *On* the other hand, perhaps their traditions will live *on.*

Writing Theme
Stone-Age Man

A. Prepositional Phrases Write the prepositional phrases in the following sentences. Underline the object or objects of each preposition.

1. In 1991, two hikers made a strange discovery in the Alps.
2. They were walking along a snow-covered mountain ridge.
3. They spotted part of a skull in a melting glacier.
4. To their surprise, the skull was part of a mummified body.
5. Scientists were soon at work on this cold, lonely site.
6. In a short while, a startling discovery was made.
7. The body was that of a prehistoric man who had died, and whose body had lain there for over 5,000 years.
8. Around the body were many of his belongings.
9. Among them were leather clothes, a bow, arrows, and an ax.
10. Without a doubt, this was one of the most important discoveries of its kind in recent years.

B. Pronouns and Prepositions Write the correct pronoun or preposition given from the two in parentheses.

11. (Among, Between) the prehistoric man's belongings was a pair of shoes.
12. His shoes were different from those used by (we, us) today.
13. Scientists think that for (he, him) and others of his time, shoemaking may have been part of daily life.
14. Each shoe has a bottom sole and an upper flap, both of (them, they) made of leather.
15. (Among, Between) these parts is a socklike net sewn onto the sole.
16. Roswitha Goedecker-Ciolek is (among, between) the experts studying the shoes.
17. According to (she, her) and others on the team, the man stuffed grass into the nets so that the shoes would fit snugly.
18. It would have been easy for (he, him) to replace the grass when it became dirty or matted.
19. It seems clear to (she, her) that the man didn't remove his shoes often; they were too delicate.
20. These shoes may seem crude to you or (I, me), but they offered warmth and protection.

C. Conjunctions and Compound Constructions Combine each of the following pairs of sentences to form a single sentence. Add conjunctions and commas where needed. Omit italicized words.

21. Scientists do not know where this Stone Age man lived. *They also do not know* why he was in the mountains.
22. A snowstorm probably killed him. *It might have been* an avalanche.
23. The man was 5 feet 4 inches tall. *He was* twenty-five to thirty-five years old.
24. Scientists may not be sure of the man's home. They believe he was a herdsman or hunter from a nearby village.
25. There were many such villages. Scientists know little about them.
26. Most of the man's tools were made of copper. *Some were of* flint.
27. He carried a small box filled with leaves wrapped around pieces of charcoal. We can only guess about their use.
28. The man probably carried glowing charcoal from his last fire. *He* used it to start a fire at the next camp.

D. Words as Different Parts of Speech. Write each word in italics. Identify its part of speech by writing *Noun, Verb, Adjective,* or *Preposition.*

29. Scientists believe the man died *about* 3000 B.C.
30. However, there *remain* many mysteries about this man.
31. For one thing, why was he walking *about* on this mountain?
32. Maybe he was part of a *search* party looking for copper.
33. Perhaps he was on a *search* for lost sheep or goats.
34. The man's bow is unfinished; clearly he did not *use* it.
35. An unfinished bow is of little *use* to anyone.
36. Possibly he was looking *around* for some materials to finish his bow.
37. As scientists study the man's *remains,* they may find the answers to their questions.
38. *Around* these mountains, they will also seek other clues to the ancient past.

WRITING CONNECTIONS

Elaboration, Revision, and Proofreading

On a separate sheet of paper, revise the following set of directions for assembling a pizza. Use the instructions given at the bottom of the page. Then proofread the directions for errors in grammar, capitalization, punctuation, and spelling. Notice the use of prepositions and conjunctions.

¹Use a mix to prepare pizza dough and sauce or make them from scratch. ²Then follow these directions to assemble the pizza. ³Sprinkle flour on a cutting board. ⁴Put the pizza dough on the cutting board. ⁵Flatten the dough. ⁶Use a rolling pin. ⁷Push the rolling pin in all directions to make the pizza as round as possible. ⁸Add more flour as necesary to prevent the dough from sticking. ⁹Sprinkle the shreded Cheese on top of the sauce. ¹⁰Spoon the pizza sauce on the dough and spread it evenly. ¹¹Finally, add your toppings. ¹²Now your ready to put the pizza in the oven. ¹³Bake it in an oven heeted to 425 degrees for ten to fifteen minutes. ¹⁴You will know you're pizza is done when the crust turns golden brown.

1. Combine sentences 3 and 4, using the conjunction *and*.

2. Add the information in sentence 6 to sentence 5 as a prepositional phrase beginning with *with*.

3. Make sentence 8 clearer by adding the phrase "to the cutting board" at the end.

4. Add *next* to the beginning of sentence 10 to tell your readers you are moving on to a new step.

5. Switch the order of sentences 9 and 10 so that these steps are in the proper order.

Informative Writing: Explaining *How*

Writing directions involves giving step-by-step instructions. (See Workshop 4.) When you revise directions, look to see that you have included all the steps and have presented them in a clear order. Use prepositions and conjunctions to lead your readers clearly through the steps.

Prepositions and Conjunctions

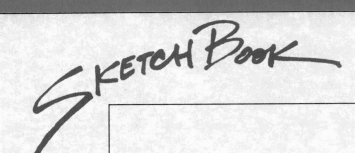

Sketch Book

Dying planet
sends SOS to Earth

WOLF BITE TURNS TEEN GIRL INTO *WEREWOLF!*

Boy addicted to wood eats baseball bats!

- How would you complete these headlines? Be as outrageous as you please.

    Aliens from Outer Space _____

    Escaped Gorilla _____

    Dog with Two Heads _____

- Try creating some weird and wacky headlines of your own.

- What is the strangest thing you ever saw? Describe what happened.

Subject-Verb Agreement

WORLD TABLOID

Vol. 21, No. 4

Prehistoric crustacean terrorizes honeymoon cruise

Pet iguana rescues girl from burning building

Elvis spotted at Omaha drycleaner

Woman finds diamond bracelet in breakfast cereal

EXCLUSIVE

"What a crab!"
Cleveland couple cries.

- **Subject and Verb Agreement**
- **Agreement with Special Verbs**
- **Special Agreement Problems**
- **Agreement with Pronouns**

You may not agree with the outrageous claims of these headlines. Yet the headlines are in agreement—their subjects and verbs work together. When you match singular subjects with singular verbs and plural subjects with plural verbs, your sentences are in agreement.

This handbook shows you how to avoid confusion in your sentences by making sure your subjects and verbs agree.

Subjects and verbs in sentences must agree in number.

A singular noun stands for one person, place, thing, or idea.

man   county   box   invention

A plural noun stands for more than one person, place, thing, or idea.

men   counties   boxes   inventions

Verbs can also be singular or plural. A verb must **agree in number** with its subject. A subject and verb agree in number when they are both singular or both plural.

Singular	**Plural**
One *dog barks* at the bike.	Two *dogs bark* at the bike.
The *rider falls* off.	The *riders fall* off.

Singular verbs in the present tense usually end in *s* or *es*. In the sentences above, the verbs *barks* and *falls* are singular. They are used with the singular nouns *dog* and *rider.*

When the subject is plural, the verb must be plural too. Plural verbs in the present tense do not usually end in *s.* The noun *dogs* is plural. Therefore, the plural verb *bark* does not have an *s.* The noun *riders* is plural, so *fall* does not end in *s.*

Not all singular verbs are formed by adding -*s.* Here are some examples.

Singular	Plural
match*es*	mat*ch*
scurr*ies*	scurr*y*
miss*es*	mi*ss*
do*es*	d*o*

Practice Your Skills

A. CONCEPT CHECK

Subject and Verb Agreement   Write the verb in parentheses that agrees with the subject.

1. Some problems (present, presents) unusual challenges.
2. Often an unusual solution (solve, solves) them.
3. Snoring (result, results) from a blocked air passage.
4. Experts (think, thinks) thirty million Americans snore.
5. Inventors (design, designs) anti-snoring aids.
6. Muzzles (hold, holds) snorers' mouths closed.
7. One invention (keep, keeps) sleepers from turning over.
8. Another device (strap, straps) the forearm to the chin.
9. One plan (remove, removes) salt from the snorer's diet.
10. Some people (try, tries) hypnotism to stop snoring.
11. Snorers (seek, seeks) surgery to enlarge nasal passages.
12. Earplugs (resolve, resolves) the problem for people sleeping near snorers.

B. DRAFTING SKILL

Making Subjects and Verbs Agree   Write the following sentences, changing the verb in parentheses to the present tense. Make sure the verb agrees in number with the subject.

13. Inventions (helped) solve many practical problems.
14. A special book (presented) some fascinating inventions.
15. The book's title (attracted) readers: *Feminine Ingenuity: Women and Inventions in America.*
16. The book (showed) cyclists with a problem.
17. Some dogs (chased) bicycles recklessly.
18. A clever invention (repelled) the dogs.
19. Pepper boxes (attached) to the handlebars.
20. The rider (squeezed) a bulb on the box.
21. One squeeze (released) a cloud of pepper.
22. The sharp, spicy pepper (made) the dogs' eyes smart.
23. Also, the dogs (sneezed).
24. Just one dose (stopped) the dogs from chasing the bikes.
25. This unusual procedure (succeeded) in solving the problem.

Writing Theme
Unusual Solutions

FOR MORE PRACTICE
See page 539.

Subect-Verb
Agreement   **529**

Some verbs have special forms. Follow the rules of agreement for these verbs.

Special Forms of Certain Verbs

A few verbs have special forms. Make sure you choose the verb form that agrees in number with your subject.

Is, Was, Are, Were   The verb forms *is* and *was* are singular. The forms *are* and *were* are plural.

Singular	Lily *is* a detective. Lily *was* a detective.
Plural	The clues *are* here. The clues *were* here.

Has, Have   The verb form *has* is singular. *Have* is plural.

Singular	The investigator *has* no answer.
Plural	The investigators *have* no answer.

Does, Do   The verb form *does* is singular. *Do* is plural.

Singular	Lewis *does*n't like mysteries.
Plural	They *do*n't like mysteries.

There Is, Where Is, Here Is

Many sentences begin with *There, Where,* or *Here.* These words are never subjects of sentences. To decide whether to use a singular or plural form of a verb in such a sentence, first find the subject by asking *who* or *what* before the verb.

There (is, are) the planes.

Who or *what* is *there?* The planes are.

The word *planes* is the subject, and the word *planes* is plural.

Use the plural verb *are.*

Writing
TIP

Remember to find the subject of the sentence when you use contractions.
Wrong
  Here's the answers.
Correct
  Here are the answers.

Practice Your Skills

A. CONCEPT CHECK

Agreement with Special Verbs Write the verb form in parentheses that agrees with the subject of each sentence.

1. The state of Vermont (has, have) many scenic mountains.
2. The Green Mountains (is, are) famous for their beauty.
3. However, the forests (has, have) a mysterious secret.
4. The mystery (is, are) more than forty years old.
5. There (was, were) six strange disappearances on a hiking trail called the Long Trail.
6. Authorities (does, do) not know what happened.
7. Two of the people (was, were) experienced hikers.
8. Here (is, are) another puzzling fact.
9. Only one person's body (was, were) ever found.
10. Mysteriously, the body (was, were) in an open spot in the woods.
11. Where (is, are) the other people?
12. Searchers (has, have) never found clues.
13. (Was, Were) the hikers victims of foul play?
14. (Doesn't, Don't) the mystery intrigue you?

B. DRAFTING SKILL

Making Subjects and Verbs Agree Write the present tense of each verb in parentheses in these sentences. Make sure the verb agrees in number with the subject.

15. There (be) strange tales about the Bermuda Triangle.
16. The Triangle (be) an area of the ocean near Florida.
17. Sometimes, vessels (have) difficulty there.
18. In fact, there (be) reports of vessels disappearing and strange radio signals.
19. Often, wreckage (do) not even appear.
20. Where (have) these vessels gone?
21. Here (be) one explanation.
22. The vessels (be) thrown off course by violent storms.
23. (Have) any investigator found definite evidence?
24. The many theories (do) not explain the mystery.

FOR MORE PRACTICE
See page 539.

Writing Theme
Help Yourself

Clarence Saunders, inventor of the first self-service grocery store, developed a patented automated grocery machine for his store called the Keedoozle (adapted from the phrase "key does all").

If a sentence has an error in agreement, write the sentence correctly. If a sentence is correct, write *Correct.*

1. Does most people like self-service in cafeterias?
2. Customers enjoys choosing their own food.
3. There's stories about the history of cafeterias.
4. The first cafeterias was for hungry factory workers.
5. In the 1890s, a quick meal was important to them.
6. There was many diners pleased with the low prices too.
7. Where was the first cafeterias located?
8. Kansas City was one of the first places.
9. Today, almost every person have eaten in a cafeteria.
10. The grocery store is another self-service business.
11. Before 1920, though, stores was not self-service.
12. Don't every shopper know about the first self-service market?
13. The inventor was Clarence Saunders.
14. His store designs has a patent.
15. The diagram look like a giant maze.
16. "Where are the canned soups?" ask a customer.
17. "Here's the soups, ma'am, in aisle two," answers a clerk.
18. Originally the stores was unusual to shoppers.
19. Now, however, most grocery stores uses self-service.
20. There's a model of Saunders's first store in Memphis.
21. Visitors has a unique chance to step back in time.
22. The museum's exhibit try to recapture the era.
23. Old brands lines the shelves.
24. There's old price stickers too.
25. Does shoppers believe a price of thirty-seven cents for pancake mix?

Watch for compound subjects and prepositional phrases when making subjects and verbs agree.

Compound Subjects

When two or more parts of a compound subject are joined by the conjunction *and,* use the plural form of the verb.

> The hiker and the guide *are* amazed.
> Water and steam *shoot* into the air.
> Geysers and hot springs *do* not *behave* in exactly the same way.

When the parts are joined by *or, either/or,* or *neither/nor,* use the form of the verb that agrees with the subject closest to the verb.

> Clint or Ross *is* reading about geysers.
> Either these books or that article *has* good pictures.
> Neither a picture nor videotapes *show* the force of water.

Prepositional Phrases After the Subject

Be careful with prepositional phrases that come between the subject and the verb. Do not confuse the subject of the verb with the object of the preposition. Look at this example.

> The explanation for geysers is simple.

> What is the sentence about? *Explanation*
> *Explanation* is the subject of the sentence.

Explanation is singular, so you use the singular verb *is.*
For geysers is a prepositional phrase. *Geysers* is the object of the preposition *for;* it is not the subject of the sentence.

For more information about prepositional phrases, see Grammar Handbook 40, pages 506–509.

Writing TIP

Casual conversation contains many errors. To make subjects and verbs agree, do not rely on what "sounds right." Follow the rules.

Practice Your Skills

A. CONCEPT CHECK

Special Agreement Problems   Write the verb form in parentheses that agrees with the subject of each sentence.

1. Jubilee Grotto and Crystal Cone (erupts, erupt) regularly and spectacularly.
2. Neither lava nor rocks (comes, come) out, however.
3. Instead, plumes of steam (shoots, shoot) skyward.
4. The Valley of the Geysers (is, are) their home.
5. Geysers (is, are) the rarest wonders of the world.
6. Reports and studies about the region (mentions, mention) only twenty-three geysers.
7. However, shouts of delight (was, were) heard recently.
8. Visitors to the region (has, have) counted two hundred!
9. Few people on earth (has, have) seen them.
10. Only Russian scientists or officials (was, were) there.
11. Now these Russian frontiers on the Kamchatka Peninsula (is, are) open to outsiders.
12. Either earthquakes or temperature changes (causes, cause) less frequent eruptions.
13. Changes in geyser activity (happens, happen) often.
14. Heat or underground forces (affects, affect) eruption.
15. Drilling and other human activities (does, do) damage.
16. This valley of springs and steam (is, are) unspoiled.

17. Steep trails and harsh terrain (hinders, hinder) visitors.
18. The possibility of tourism (is, are) being considered.
19. The valley and the geysers (needs, need) protection, however.
20. Neither tourists nor the weekend visitor (has, have) easy access to this incredible region—for now.

B. DRAFTING SKILL

Using Verbs That Agree with Subjects   Write the sentences, using the present-tense form of the verb in parentheses.

21. Hot water or cold water (spout) from the earth.
22. Some spouts in Utah (be) called "soda-pop geysers."
23. Soda pop and other fizzy drinks (have) carbonation.
24. Dissolved carbon dioxide gas in underground pockets (make) these fake geysers erupt.
25. A well or other drilling operations (cause) them.
26. These wells of ice-cold water (erupt) like geysers.
27. Hot-water plumes or steam (be) necessary for true geysers.
28. Rest periods and activity periods (be) needed too.
29. Four phases of activity (occur) in true geysers.
30. Neither hot springs nor a "soda-pop geyser" (qualify).

C. PROOFREADING

Finding Errors in Agreement   Rewrite the following paragraph, correcting any errors in subject-verb agreement. Also correct errors in grammar, spelling, capitalization, and punctuation. (15 errors)

Each year, millions of tourists flock to yellowstone national park. Here, minrals and the earth's inner heat creates unbeleivable effects. Lakes of colored mud bubbles furiously, springs and geysers burst from cracks in the ground. Hot water jets and vapor sprays high into the air. Tiny plants of brilliant color fills steaming pools. Hot water in the center of the pools stay blue. Because the water is so hot in the center, neither yellow algae nor brown algae grow there. Tiny red mushrooms or thick moss are found near the edges of the pools. A bordwalk for spectators go right to the water's edge.

FOR MORE PRACTICE
See page 540.

> Follow special rules of agreement with the pronouns *I* and *you* and with indefinite pronouns.

I and *You*

The pronoun *I* stands for a single person. However, the only singular verb forms used with it are *am* and *was*. Otherwise, the plural form of the verb is always used.

> I *am* a fussy eater. I *was* a young gourmet.
> I *do* the cooking. I *have* an award. I *enjoy* winning.

Although *you* can be singular or plural, always use a plural verb with this pronoun.

> "You *were* messy," the judge said to the contestant.
> "You *were* messy," the judge said to the contestants.

Indefinite Pronouns

The indefinite pronouns below are singular. They use singular verbs.

either	each	everyone	anyone
neither	one	everybody	nobody

> Either *likes* rice.
> Neither *eats* with chopsticks.

In the sentences above, a singular verb follows a singular subject. When a prepositional phrase follows one of these pronouns, the verb must still agree with the pronoun subject.

> Either of the boys *likes* rice.
> Neither of the girls *eats* with chopsticks.

For more information about indefinite pronouns, see Grammar Handbook 37, pages 449–451.

Practice Your Skills

A. CONCEPT CHECK

Agreement with Pronouns   Write the correct verb.

1. Everybody (has, have) a favorite food or snack.
2. Each of the world's nations (is, are) known for a particular kind of food.
3. If you (is, are) French, you (has, have) probably eaten escargots.
4. I (knows, know) that *escargots* is French for "snails."
5. Someday, I (am, is, are) going to try frog legs.
6. Each of these French dishes (is, are) cooked in butter.
7. Neither (is, are) prepared without garlic.
8. Anyone from Greek towns (talks, talk) about octopus.
9. One (cuts, cut) dried octopus into chunks and broils it.
10. (Has, Have) you ever tasted sushi?
11. Almost everyone in Japan (likes, like) this dish.
12. Nobody in the restaurants (turns, turn) down raw fish.

B. DRAFTING SKILL

Using Verbs with Pronouns   Write each sentence, changing the verb in parentheses to its present-tense form.

13. Everyone in Asian countries (eat) rice daily.
14. You (do) not like rice as much as I (do).
15. (Have) you read that rice is a kind of grass?
16. Anyone (use) chopsticks or fingers to eat rice.
17. I (have) learned of other uses for rice, though.
18. Anybody with cows or pigs (feed) them rice bran.
19. Another of the uses (be) for oil.
20. Nobody (throw) away the rice hulls or stalks.
21. Almost everybody in industry (use) the byproducts.
22. Each of the uses (be) clever.
23. I (know) it's used for fuel, fertilizer, and clothes!
24. One of the varieties of rice (be) called miracle rice.
25. Someone (have) tried to solve world hunger.
26. Everyone (do) not have faith in miracle rice.
27. No one among the growers (be) discouraged, though.

Write the following sentences and correct all errors in subject and verb agreement. If a sentence is correct, write *Correct.*

1. Everyone have heard of famous collaborators.
2. Hasn't you read stories by Ellery Queen?
3. Frederic Dannay and Manfred B. Lee was Ellery Queen.
4. Dannay and Lee was cousins and friends.
5. Neither of them were trained as a detective.
6. Each of them were famous only as a collaborator.
7. One team of inventors have not become famous.
8. Anybody with a knowledge of inventions remember Samuel Morse, the inventor of the telegraph.
9. Neither you nor I knows his partners' names today.
10. Neither of Morse's partners were able to get money for work on the telegraph.
11. Morse, without his partners, were given congressional help for an experiment.

The animators William Hanna and Joseph Barbera with a few of their cartoon characters.

12. Anyone from Baltimore or Washington remember the location of the first experimental telegraph line.
13. The Morse code and the telegraph is what we remember Samuel Morse for.
14. Fortunately for us, teams or partners often succeed.
15. William Hanna and Joseph Barbera is familiar to us.
16. Nobody denies their success in the cartoon world.
17. Everyone love the Tom and Jerry characters.
18. Each of the characters by this team are lovable and funny.
19. Yogi Bear and Huckleberry Hound are my favorites.
20. One of the hardest tasks are collaboration, I think.

A. Using the Right Verb Form Write the form of the verb that agrees with the subject in each sentence.

GRAMMAR
H A N D B O O K
41

Writing Theme
Processes

1. People (takes, take) gears for granted.
2. Gears (makes, make) many things work.
3. Gears (connects, connect) in many different ways.
4. Usually, one gear (turns, turn) faster or slower than its partner.
5. Car ads (talks, talk) about rack-and-pinion steering.
6. A rack-and-pinion system (works, work) quite simply.
7. The driver (spins, spin) the steering wheel.
8. The pinion (rotates, rotate) like a wheel.
9. Its teeth (fits, fit) into the teeth of the rack.
10. The rack (slides, slide) back and forth.
11. Both elements (moves, move) in the same direction.
12. In this way, movement (becomes, become) easy.
13. Gears (comes, come) in a great variety of sizes and types.
14. Their names (reflects, reflect) their appearance.
15. A worm gear (looks, look) like a worm!
16. Cowboy spurs (inspires, inspire) the name "spur gear."
17. Planetary gears (resembles, resemble) planets moving around a sun.
18. Automatic transmissions (uses, use) planetary gears.
19. Books (tells, tell) about the different kinds of gears.
20. Remember, wheels (forms, form) part of most gears.

B. Writing the Correct Verb Form Write the form of the verb in parentheses that agrees with the subject.

21. (Was, Were) pens always ballpoints?
22. (Doesn't, Don't) people know how they work?
23. The process (is, are) called capillary action.
24. Capillaries (is, are) tubes, like veins in the body.
25. Where (does, do) the ink go?
26. (Here's, Here are) the answer!
27. Inside the ink tube, pressure (does, do) all the work.
28. There (is, are) pressure on the ballpoint.
29. Higher pressure (has, have) the job of releasing ink.
30. Low pressures (has, have) the job of holding in the ink.

Subject-Verb
Agreement   **539**

C. Choosing the Right Verb Form   Write the sentences, correcting errors in subject-verb agreement.

31. Thelma, Ina, and Carl washes their hair every day.
32. Mostly, Ina or Carl fight over using the hair drier.
33. Neither the sisters nor the brother know anything about driers.
34. Currents of electricity flows into the drier.
35. Wire coils inside the drier heats up.
36. The blades of a small fan blows the hot air out.
37. Heat and jets of air makes water evaporate.
38. Soon the tangled locks of Ina's hair is dry.
39. At times, either the coil or other elements gets too hot.
40. Burns and the hazards of fire is possible.
41. A thermostat inside the components sense the heat.
42. The power to the elements shut off.
43. The heating units inside the drier cools down.
44. Before long more wet heads requires the hair drier again.
45. Isn't science and technology wonderful?

D. Making Verbs Agree with Pronouns   Write the correct present-tense form of the verb for each sentence.

46. I (be) fascinated with photocopiers.
47. (Have) you ever made copies at the library?
48. (Do) either of us know about the inventor of copy machines?
49. Everyone who makes copies (thank) Chet Carlson.
50. One of the photocopying processes (be) completely dry.
51. Each of the other processes (require) liquid developers.
52. Everyone (learn) that Carlson invented the dry process.
53. One of his contributions (be) the process of xerography.
54. Anyone at his mother-in-law's beauty parlor (know) of him.
55. Everybody (remember) that is where he invented it.
56. Each of the uses of xerography (save) time and work.
57. Neither of these savings (be) trivial.
58. Everybody in offices (use) copy machines.
59. (Do) you recognize the corporation name that is based on the word *xerography?*
60. I (see) it: the Xerox Corporation!

Writing Theme
Diaries

A. Making Subjects and Verbs Agree   Write the verb that agrees with the subject in number.

1. Diaries (preserves, preserve) thoughts and feelings.
2. Many people (keeps, keep) diaries and journals.
3. Famous people (has, have) published theirs.
4. Where else (does, do) people share their hopes and dreams and disappointments?
5. Where else (has, have) a reader become acquainted with a queen?
6. There (is, are) important lessons to be learned from diaries.
7. Here (is, are) one example from Queen Victoria's diary.
8. Even English queens (likes, like) parties.
9. One entry (tells, tell) about her dancing until 3 A.M.!
10. Other entries (reveals, reveal) her crush on Prince Albert.
11. (Does, Do) a queen get nervous before her wedding?
12. Queen Victoria (was, were) nervous and happy.
13. "The ceremony (was, were) very imposing," she wrote.
14. Other diaries (has, have) fascinating insights too.
15. Readers (shares, share) Davy Crockett's last days.
16. There (is, are) an account of the battle at the Alamo.
17. Provisions (was, were) running out.
18. The diary (shows, show) Crockett's great courage and determination.
19. Many paragraphs (describes, describe) the battle.
20. "Shells (has, have) been falling into the fort. . . ."
21. Another paragraph (states, state) a wish for freedom.
22. His diary (recounts, recount) his last day.
23. Crockett's last entry (was, were) "Liberty and independence forever!"
24. Here (is, are) stirring pieces of eyewitness accounts.
25. Without a doubt, diaries (makes, make) fascinating reading.

B. Using the Correct Verb   Write the correct present-tense form of the verb in parentheses.

26. Fame and money (be) only trifles to Thomas Edison.
27. Problems with dandruff (bother) him in July.
28. "Powerful itching of my head" (be) what he wrote.

Subject-Verb
Agreement   **541**

29. Entries in Edison's diary (tell) us about the man.
30. The person behind the inventions (come) through in his plain, direct style.
31. Neither complaints nor embarrassing events (be) kept out of the diary.
32. Two keys on his piano (be) out of tune.
33. A clerk in a drugstore (do) not have peroxide.
34. A demon with eyes four hundred feet apart (haunt) his dreams.
35. Edison's comments and logic (be) keen.
36. Either nonfiction or novels (fill) part of every day for him.
37. This self-taught man of strong opinions (love) reading.
38. Lack of lessons or school (have) not discouraged or stopped him.
39. The walls of his office (do) not have diplomas.
40. He wonders if perhaps encyclopedia articles or the dictionary (have) facts about dandruff!

C. Making Verbs and Pronouns Agree   Write the correct verb.

41. I (is, am, are) the famous fly on the wall—a diary!
42. (Does, Do) you know of me?
43. I (saves, save) the thoughts of John Quincy Adams, our sixth president.
44. Nobody in Congress (escapes, escape) his sharp comments.
45. Each of Thomas Jefferson's tales (is, are) retold and made fun of.
46. Everyone (knows, know) about Jefferson's tendency to exaggerate.
47. One of Adams's dislikes (is, are) newspaper editors and their stories.
48. Everybody in Congress (has, have) the same dislike, he believes.
49. Anyone from Washington also (understand, understands) Adams's notes about summer heat.
50. Neither of his two sons (wish, wishes) to swim in the Potomac River to cool off, however.

WRITING CONNECTIONS

Elaboration, Revision, and Proofreading

Revise the following draft of a personal narrative by using the directions at the bottom of the page. Then proofread the narrative, making sure that all subjects and verbs agree in number. Also look for other errors in grammar, capitalization, punctuation, and spelling.

¹When we started our band, we had a problem. ²Bob's mom said we couldnt use there garage after just one session. ³Because we was too loud. ⁴None of the other parents even let us try. ⁵Then one day Keith said, "I found a great studio for us." ⁶He give us directions. ⁷He told us to meat him there the next afternoon. ⁸When Bob and I arrived, we was shocked. ⁹Our "studio" was the parking lot of an old gas station. ¹⁰"Don't worry," Keith said, "bands practices here all the time." ¹¹Then he pulled out his horn and blowed. ¹²"That really sound great," Bob said. ¹³"I like the way the sound echoes off the walls of the old building." ¹⁴In addition, there were no one living nearby to complane. ¹⁵We unpacked all of our gear. ¹⁶We begun to play to our audience of passing cars.

1. After sentence 1, add information to explain the problem the band had: finding a place to practice without disturbing the neighbors.

2. Combine sentences 6 and 7 to make one sentence with a compound verb.

3. Make sentence 14 more complete by adding the phrase "about the noise" to the end.

4. Add "anxiously" to the beginning of sentence 15 to show how the band members prepared to play.

5. Divide the passage into paragraphs.

Narrative and Literary Writing

Writing a personal narrative is a chance to share your experiences with others. (See Workshop 3.) When you revise a narrative, make sure you have presented events in the order in which they occurred. Also make sure your subjects and verbs agree so that your readers can easily follow your story.

Skills

Directions One or more of the underlined sections in the following sentences may contain an error in grammar, punctuation, spelling, or capitalization. Write the letter of each incorrect section. Then rewrite the section correctly. If there is no error in an item, write *D*.

> **Example** Palindromes <u>is</u> words or sentences that read the
> **A**
>
> same forward and backward. <u>"Madam</u>, I'm Adam" is one
> **B**
>
> of the <u>most famous</u>. <u>No error</u>
> **C** **D**
>
> **Answer** A—are

1. Sometimes a flock of geese <u>flies</u> as high as <u>26,000</u> feet. That is almost five
   A **B**
   <u>miles</u> above the earth! <u>No error</u>
   C **D**

2. Which shoes <u>fit</u> <u>looser,</u> <u>these</u> kind or that kind? <u>No error</u>
   A **B** **C** **D**

3. <u>There's</u> only one irregular verb in the <u>Turkish</u> language. That verb
   A **B**
   is *imek,* and it means "to be." In English there <u>are</u> sixty-eight irregular
   C
   verbs. <u>No error</u>
   D

4. Where <u>are</u> the <u>science fiction</u> books shelved in this <u>library?</u> <u>No error</u>
   A **B** **C** **D**

5. Neither of these spices <u>make</u> rice <u>yellow, it</u> is saffron that turns rice
   A **B**
   <u>golden</u>. <u>No error</u>
   C **D**

6. Either our <u>neighbors</u> next door or my <u>Aunt</u> <u>feeds</u> our hamster when we
   A **B** **C**
   are away. <u>No error</u>
   D

7. Bud Abbott and Lou Costello <u>is</u> in the <u>Baseball Hall of Fame</u>, but neither

                    A   **B**
of them ever played professional <u>baseball. They</u> are honored for their

                                                     C
"Who's on First?" comedy routine. <u>No error</u>

                                              D

8. The <u>principle</u> said, "If it snows hard enough, everybody at John Wood

       A
<u>middle school</u> <u>goes</u> home early." <u>No error</u>

      B   **C**   **D**

9. A fjord is a <u>long, narrow</u>, deep inlet of the sea. A fjord <u>lays</u> between

                    A   **B**
steep <u>cliffs</u>. <u>No error</u>

      C   **D**

10. <u>Neither</u> the <u>brushes</u> nor the paint for our project <u>have</u> arrived. <u>No error</u>

      A   **B**   **C**   **D**

11. <u>Bubbles</u> in <u>soda pop</u> <u>forms</u> where carbon dioxide gas is present. <u>No error</u>

      A   **B**   **C**   **D**

12. Only two presidents of the United States <u>have</u> entered the <u>White House</u>

                                       A   **B**
as bachelors—Grover <u>Cleveland, and</u> James Buchanan. <u>No error</u>

                      C   **D**

13. <u>There's</u> some <u>childrens'</u> television shows that are <u>really</u> educational. <u>No error</u>

      A   **B**   **C**   **D**

14. Cream is <u>thicker</u> than milk and has more fat and <u>calories when</u> you weigh

            A   **B**
each, however, milk is <u>heavier</u> than cream. <u>No error</u>

                    C   **D**

15. Each of these computer <u>disks</u> <u>are</u> full. You <u>need</u> to get another disk.

                          A **B**   **C**
<u>No error</u>

 D

- Imagine you've been asked to develop a theme park like Safari Funland. Write a brief description of the park. What would it be called? What types of rides would the park have and what would you name them?

- Which movies or books do you like the best? Who do you think deserves to be called "great"? Make lists of movies, people, books, songs, products, or other items that are in your Top Ten.

Capitalization

- **Proper Nouns and Proper Adjectives**
- **More Proper Nouns**
- **First Words**
- **Outlines and Titles**

Amusement park rides like the Zipper that spin 'round and 'round can make you really dizzy. Trying to remember all the rules for capitalization can make you really dizzy, too!

These rules, however, are important because capital letters are an important part of writing. Writers use them to name specific people, places, and things. This handbook will show you how to use capitalization in your writing.

PROPER NOUNS

AND PROPER ADJECTIVES

Capitalize proper nouns and proper adjectives.

A **common noun** is a general name for a person, a place, a thing, or an idea. A **proper noun** names a particular person, place, thing, or idea. A **proper adjective** is made from a proper noun. All proper nouns and proper adjectives are capitalized.

Common Noun	Proper Noun	Proper Adjective
peninsula	Arabia	Arabian
country	Ireland	Irish

A proper noun may be made up of one or more words. Capitalize all important words in a proper noun.

Rocky **M**ountains   **L**incoln **P**ark **Z**oo   **P**eter the **G**reat

Proper adjectives are often used with common nouns. Do not capitalize the common noun.

Irish wolfhound   **B**urmese cat   **A**merican saddle horse

There are many kinds of proper nouns. These rules will help you recognize words that need to be capitalized.

Capitalize the names of people and pets.

Begin every word in a name with a capital letter. An initial stands for a name. Write initials as capital letters. Put a period after each initial.

Ken **G**riffey, **J**r.   **E**. **B**. **W**hite   **L**assie

Often, a word for a family relation is used in place of the name of a particular person, or as part of the name. *Dad* and *Aunt Jane* are two examples. Capitalize a word used in this way.

Capitalize a personal title used with a person's name.

A **personal title** is a term of respect used in front of a name. Many titles have short forms called **abbreviations.** Capitalize abbreviations of personal titles. Follow an abbreviation with a period.

>   **M**ister—**M**r.   **M**istress—**M**rs.   **D**octor—**D**r.

The title *Miss* has no abbreviated form. Do not use a period after this title. *Ms.* has no long form.

>   **M**rs. **C**asey saw **C**aptain **G**etz and **D**r. **Y**ung at the zoo.

Do not capitalize a title that is used alone or that follows a person's name.

>   The mayor met Joy Ortiz, the ambassador to China.

Capitalize the following titles when used before names, or when used alone to refer to the current holders of the positions.

>   the **P**resident (of the United States)   **Q**ueen Elizabeth II
>   the **V**ice-**P**resident (of the United States)   the **P**ope

Capitalize the word *I*.

>   Clarice and **I** took our dogs to obedience classes.

Practice Your Skills

A. CONCEPT CHECK

Proper Nouns and Adjectives   Write the following sentences, using capital letters where necessary.

1. Yesterday i asked dad who he thought was the most popular fictional animal in the world.
2. He suggested garfield, the cartoon cat, but i think it is charlie brown's dog, snoopy.
3. The cartoonist charles m. schulz first drew this funny beagle over forty years ago, basing him on his own childhood dog, spike.

4. Later mr. schulz named snoopy's brother spike.
5. Charlie brown once wrote about his pet, "He's kind of crazy."
6. This dog has been to france, the sahara, and the moon.
7. He fought the red baron, a german pilot, in a very popular series of cartoons that appeared in the late 1960s.
8. An american pop hit was "snoopy Versus the red baron."
9. In 1969, the apollo 10 astronauts named their command module charlie brown and their lunar module snoopy.
10. Snoopy sent personal get-well wishes to president reagan when the president was shot in 1981.
11. Fans from japan, finland, and chile follow the dog's story.
12. But snoopy is not always known by the same name—in swedish he is called snobben, and in norwegian he is sniff!

B. PROOFREADING SKILL

Capitalizing for Clarity   Proofread the paragraph. Then write it, correcting mistakes in capitalization and other errors. (35 errors)

My Mother claims that her siamese cat, albie, warned the family about a fire in the house. Such stories are not unnusual, i have found. A british man, ray wakelin, fell on ice. His german Shepherds, rommel and zeus, lay on mr wakelin to keep him warm. A pig named priscilla saved a texas boy from drowning. Priscilla recieved the stillman Award from the american Humane Association. the award is Named for dr. william o. stillman, a past President of the association. The Quaker Oats company also gives awards to brave animals. One went to a dog named jet that alerted neighbors when its Owner went into a diabetic coma. "i know i would have died without jet's help," said candy sangster.

C. APPLICATION IN WRITING

Report   Investigate a real or fictional animal and write a one- or two-paragraph report about it. Possibilities include Benji, Kermit the Frog, Flipper, Black Beauty, and Sounder. Make your writing more precise by using proper nouns and adjectives. Be sure to capitalize words correctly.

CHECK ✓ POINT

Write the sentences. Capitalize proper nouns and adjectives, and correct improperly capitalized common nouns.

Writing Theme
The Moran Tugboats

1. In 1860, the irish immigrant michael moran came to new york city.
2. He became part Owner of a tugboat called the *ida miller*.
3. From his office on south street, facing the east river, he sold towing services to boats using new york harbor.
4. Here began the moran transportation and towing company.
5. Michael's son, eugene f. moran, worked on a tug too.
6. He said, "i was born practically on the Sea, and i have lived on and off it ever since."
7. Moran tugboats took part in major new york harbor events.
8. They were there when the brooklyn bridge opened in 1883.
9. With other american vessels, Moran's boats paraded with italian, french, and spanish Ships on the 400th anniversary of columbus's arrival in america.
10. Moran's tugs welcomed president theodore roosevelt home in 1910.
11. They have played an interesting role in american History.
12. They handled army transport in the spanish-american war.
13. In fact, the first commercial american boat to enter havana harbor after the war was the tugboat *m. moran*.
14. mr. moran advised assistant secretary of the navy franklin d. roosevelt on equipping Patrol Boats for world war I.
15. During world war II, moran boats worked on both the atlantic ocean and the pacific ocean.
16. The *edmond j. moran*, under capt. hugo kroll, had many adventures dodging german Submarines.
17. A moran tug hauled a german submarine to lake ontario.
18. The Sub is now at chicago's museum of science and industry.
19. In peacetime the tugboats have docked many famous ocean liners, including the queen mary and the queen elizabeth.
20. There is even a walt disney cartoon, named *Little toot*, about a moran tug.

MORE PROPER NOUNS

Capitalize the names of places, races, languages, religions, days, months, holidays, and historical events.

Capitalize the names of particular places and things.

1. Capitalize names of cities, states, and countries.

We stopped in **C**hicago, **I**llinois, on our way to **C**anada.

2. Capitalize names of streets, bridges, parks, and buildings.

We took **L**ake **S**hore **D**rive to **G**rant **P**ark and crossed the **M**ichigan **A**venue **B**ridge near the **W**rigley **B**uilding.

3. Capitalize geographical names. Do not capitalize *north, south, east,* and *west* when they refer to directions. Capitalize them only when they refer to particular areas or are parts of geographical names.

The highway runs east and west along **L**ake **O**ntario.
Many cities in the **E**ast lie along rivers and lakes.

Capitalize the names of months, days, holidays, and historical events.

Do not capitalize the names of the four seasons: *spring, summer, autumn,* and *winter.*

In **S**eptember, **L**abor **D**ay and the first day of autumn make me think of school and colorful leaves.
Last spring we studied the causes of **W**orld **W**ar II.

Capitalize the names of races, religions, nationalities, and languages.

Native **H**awaiians belong to the **P**olynesian race.
Both **H**induism and **B**uddhism began in **I**ndia.
Brazilian people speak **P**ortuguese.

Capitalize words referring to God and to religious scriptures.

the **D**eity	the **B**ible	the **G**ospels
the **L**ord	the **T**almud	the **B**ook of **P**salms
Allah	the **K**oran	the **O**ld **T**estament

Capitalize the names of clubs, organizations, and business firms.

The **S**ierra **C**lub has fought for one hundred years to protect the environment.
Clara **B**arton founded the **A**merican **R**ed **C**ross in 1881.
In 1972, **S**tandard **O**il of **N**ew **J**ersey became **E**xxon.

Practice Your Skills

A. CONCEPT CHECK

Capitalization of Proper Nouns Write the following sentences, using capital letters where necessary.

Writing Theme
Cultures Around the World

1. North America's first immigrants were asian nomads.
2. They came from siberia thousands of years ago.
3. The inuits and other native peoples of north, central, and south america are descended from these immigrants.
4. The first europeans to reach north america were the Vikings.
5. They landed on the eastern coast of what is now canada about a thousand years ago.
6. About five hundred years later, john cabot, an italian sailing for king henry VII of england, explored the area.
7. Later, french ships sailed west up the st. lawrence river.
8. During the winter of 1535 to 1536, french explorers camped at what is now cartier-brébeuf park in quebec city.
9. Members of the society of jesus and other french missionaries brought stories from the bible to the native people.
10. Both britain and france claimed canada as a colony, and for more than one hundred years, the french, the algonquins, and the hurons fought the british and the iroquois.
11. In 1763, after the seven years' war—called the french and indian war in the united states—the french surrendered.

12. From 1763 until 1870, much of canada was controlled by the hudson's bay company, a fur-trading organization.
13. On july 1, 1867, three canadian colonies formed the dominion of canada, which grew and became independent in 1931.
14. Every summer, on july 1, canadians celebrate canada day, the country's biggest national holiday.
15. Today canada has two official languages, french and english, and most canadians are either roman catholics or members of protestant denominations.

B. PROOFREADING SKILL

Focus on Capitalization   Write these paragraphs, correcting the errors in capitalization, grammar, and punctuation. (35 errors)

The Taj Mahal is one of the world's most beautiful tombs. It was built between 1630 and 1650 in memory of Mumtaz Mahal, the wife of the Indian ruler Shah Jahan.

India, located on the continent of asia, is the seventh largest country in the world. India stretches from the indian ocean to the himalayas. Its largest cities are bombay, delhi, and calcutta. Bombay lies on the west coast, between the arabian sea and the mountains called the western ghats. To the north, delhi lies along the jumna river. Calcutta lies in the east, near the border with bangladesh. The most famous building in india is the taj mahal, at agra in the north.

The majority of indians believe in the hindu religion. Many others are muslims, who worship allah and base their faith on the sacred book called the koran. Fourteen major languages, including hindi and urdu, are recognized by the indian government. Each winter, on january 26, indians join to celebrate republic day. This holiday honors the birth of india as an independent, democratic country in 1950. In new delhi, the capital, the celebrations are held on a wide avenue called the rajpath.

C. APPLICATION IN WRITING

Report   Imagine that a time machine has taken you to a strange place. In two or three paragraphs, describe the place. Tell about the land, the people, their language, religion, and any other interesting facts. Be sure to capitalize correctly.

C H E C K ✔ P O I N T

MIXED REVIEW • PAGES 552–554

Write the following sentences, adding capital letters where necessary. If a sentence has no errors, write *Correct*.

Writing Theme
Marian Anderson,
Singer

1. Marian anderson believed that her voice was a gift from god and that god expected her to develop and share that gift.
2. She was born in philadelphia on february 17, 1902.
3. At age six, she joined the choir at the union baptist church.
4. In 1923, ms. anderson became the first african-american singer to win a vocal contest sponsored by the Philharmonic Society of Philadelphia.
5. She learned to sing in german, french, and italian.
6. In 1925, she won a competition to sing in new york city with the new york philharmonic orchestra at lewisohn stadium.
7. Then she went on several concert tours in Europe.
8. She was cheered by the scandinavians, the french, and the swiss.
9. In december of 1935, she returned to the united states.
10. Marian anderson's 1935 concert at manhattan's town hall was a success, and she became a top concert singer.
11. However, some americans were not as accepting as the europeans.
12. Particularly in the south, some people rejected anderson on the basis of her color.
13. Because of her race, anderson was denied permission to perform at constitution hall in washington, d.c., in 1939.
14. This unjust act angered many people, including president Roosevelt's wife, eleanor.
15. Mrs. Roosevelt arranged for Anderson to sing at the Lincoln Memorial that year; over 75,000 people attended the concert.
16. In 1955, marian anderson became the first african-american singer to perform at new york's metropolitan opera.
17. In 1958, president eisenhower made her a delegate to the united nations.
18. Her final concert was at carnegie hall on easter sunday, 1965.
19. Anderson retired to marianna farm near danbury, connecticut.
20. Yet she continued to work for charitable causes, including the american red cross and the eleanor roosevelt foundation.

Capitalize the first words of sentences and lines of poetry.

Capitalize the first word of every sentence.

My brother likes to read Shel Silverstein's poems.
Have you read any of Eve Merriam's poems?
What an unusual title that poem has!

Capitalize the first words in some lines of poetry.

In poetry, the first words of lines are often capitalized, even when they do not begin new sentences.

Sunset through the Golden
Gate Bridge, San Francisco

> **I** went to San Francisco.
> **I** saw the bridges high
> **S**pun across the water
> **L**ike cobwebs in the sky.
> **Langston Hughes, "Trip: San Francisco"**

Sometimes, especially in modern poetry, the lines of a poem may not begin with capital letters.

> STOP LOOK LISTEN
> as gate stripes swing down,
> count the cars hauling distance
> upgrade through town:
> warning whistle, bellclang,
> engine eating steam,
> engineer waving,
> a fast-freight dream . . .
> **Phillip Booth, "Crossing"**

Practice Your Skills

Writing Theme
Poets and Poetry

A. CONCEPT CHECK

First Words   Write each sentence, capitalizing letters where necessary. If a sentence is correct, write *Correct.*

1. listen, my children, and you shall hear
   of the midnight ride of paul revere
   on the eighteenth of april, in 'Seventy-five;
   hardly a man is now alive
   who remembers that famous day and year.
2. these are the opening lines of "Paul Revere's Ride."
3. The poem honors Revere's role in the American Revolution.
4. it first appeared in a book called *Tales of a Wayside Inn.*
5. The book is a collection of tales in verse that are supposed to have been told by people at an inn in massachusetts.
6. did you know they were written by henry wadsworth longfellow, a famous american poet of the 1800s?
7. the tales are set in america, in spain, and elsewhere.
8. Longfellow is best known for his long narrative poems.
9. a famous one is *Evangeline,* which is set in north america.
10. It tells about french immigrants to nova scotia who were forced to move south during the french and indian war.

B. PROOFREADING SKILL

Capitalizing Correctly   Write this passage, correcting errors in capitalization, punctuation, and grammar. (15 errors)

The american Poet emily Dickinson was a very private Person. she did not write her Poetry for publication. Only a few of her poems was published during her Lifetime. After her death in 1886, her Sister found many of emily's poems and had them published. Dickinsons poems was usually short they often had unusual rhythms they explored everyday experiences of Life.

> Capitalize the first words of entries in outlines. In a title, capitalize the first and last words and all other words except articles, coordinating conjunctions, and prepositions of four or fewer letters.

Capitalize the first word of each line of an outline.

Roman numerals (I, II) mark the major divisions of an outline. Capital letters (A, B) identify the next rank of items, and Arabic numerals mark the rank after that.

The **W**riting **P**rocess
I.   **P**rewriting activities
    A. **C**hoosing a topic
      1. **B**rainstorming
      2. **R**eviewing journal notes and past writing
    B. **R**esearching the topic
II. **W**riting techniques

Capitalize the first and last words of a title and all other words except articles, coordinating conjunctions, and prepositions of four or fewer letters.

Do not capitalize articles (*the, a, an*), coordinating conjunctions (*and, but, or, nor*), or prepositions of four or fewer letters (*of, with, in*) except as the first or last word of a title.

***A**nne of **G**reen **G**ables* (book)
"**W**here **D**o **T**hese **W**ords **C**ome **F**rom?" (poem)
***T**he **P**hantom of the **O**pera* (movie, musical play)
"**T**he **M**an **W**ho **L**iked **D**ickens" (short story)
***L**os **A**ngeles **T**imes* (newspaper)
***N**ational **G**eographic **W**orld* (magazine)
"**S**urefire **S**teps to **S**trong **P**lots" (magazine article)
Bill of **R**ights (document)

Writing
TIP

Some titles are underlined, and others are enclosed in quotation marks. Look on page 590 for rules on writing titles correctly.

Practice Your Skills

CONCEPT CHECK

Titles and Outlines   Write each item, using capital letters where needed. If the item is correct, write *Correct*.

1. what is your favorite type of story or poem?
2. Is it short stories like O. Henry's "hearts and hands"?
3. Do you prefer novels such as Cleary's *the luckiest girl?*
4. Do you like poems like David McCord's "rollercoaster"?
5. These authors share something with the writer of the *Iliad* of ancient Greece and reporters for today's *New York Times.*
6. Whether they write for a textbook or for *sesame street*, most writers use a similar writing process.
7. Imagine that you are a reviewer for the *Chicago tribune.*
8. you are to write an article titled "my favorite movie."
9. you want to explain why *the wizard of oz* is your favorite.
10. first, you might brainstorm about the movie, then write your ideas in a draft you could title "working draft."
11. you might organize your article this way:
12. I. elements of the movie *the wizard of oz*
    A. plot, action, and special effects
    b. performances
       1. main characters
       2. minor characters
    II. my reaction to the movie
13. reread your draft and revise it so that it expresses just what you want to say about *the wizard of oz.*
14. You could research facts in a book like *The Oscar Movies.*
15. You might add a comparison with a film like *star wars.*
16. You could write about the contribution "somewhere over the rainbow" and other songs make to the film.
17. After revising and proofreading, you would prepare a final draft of "my favorite movie" for publication.
18. Authors use this process whether writing an article for *Newsweek,* a school report, or a legal document.
19. for example, Thomas Jefferson revised the declaration of independence many times before it was finally approved.
20. Now you can write a report titled "the writing process."

A. Write the sentences, using capital letters where necessary. If a sentence is correct, write *Correct*.

1. should Eloise Greenfield be called a poet or a novelist or a biographer—or simply a writer?
2. If you had read the *hartford times* back in 1963, you would have enjoyed her first published poem, "to a violin."
3. since then, she has had many other poems published, including a book of poems entitled *honey, i love.*
4. Her poems use words and rhythms to put the reader in the middle of a scene, as in "*rope rhyme.*"
5. It begins this way:
   get set, ready now, jump right in
   bounce and kick and giggle and spin. . . .
6. But Greenfield has also written novels, such as *sister.*
7. She has written biographies of famous African Americans too.
8. With her mother, Greenfield wrote the children's book *i can do it by myself.*
9. In addition to poems and books, she has written articles for magazines, including *ebony, Jr.*
10. Greenfield hopes her writing encourages young people to be proud of themselves, their heritage, and their abilities.

The poet, novelist, and biographer Eloise Greenfield.

B. Application in Literature   Write this paragraph, using capital letters where necessary.

i fell in love with langston terrace the very first time i saw it. our family had been living in two rooms of a three-story house when mama and daddy saw the newspaper article telling of the plans to build it. it was going to be a low-rent housing project in northeast washington, and it would be named in honor of john mercer langston, the famous black lawyer, educator, and congressman.

Eloise Greenfield and Lessie Jones Little, "Childtimes"

Writing Theme
Moviemakers

A. Capitalizing Proper Nouns and Adjectives   Write the following sentences, using capital letters where necessary.

1. Steven spielberg once said, "Like peter pan, i never wanted to grow up."
2. Audiences from north america to asia are glad he didn't.
3. spielberg was born in december 1947 to a jewish family.
4. His family moved from cincinnati, Ohio, east to new jersey, then west to Phoenix, and eventually to california.
5. Mr. and mrs. spielberg encouraged Steven's interest in movies.
6. He made a short film to earn a merit badge in the boy scouts.
7. By 1969, spielberg was a director at universal studios.
8. His first big american film was *Jaws* in 1975.
9. spielberg then wrote and directed the 1977 science fiction blockbuster *Close Encounters of the Third Kind*.
10. *Raiders of the Lost Ark*, in the summer of 1981, was the first of three films about the archaeologist indiana jones.
11. It takes place in the middle east just before world war II.
12. The lost ark is a box that contained the ten commandments written in stone as handed down from god to moses.
13. Indiana hopes to find it in a temple called the well of souls in the sahara desert.
14. Another film, *e.t.: The Extra-Terrestrial,* from 1982, may be spielberg's best-known movie.
15. People from austria to zaire love the tale of e.t. and elliot.

B. Capitalizing First Words   Write the following sentences, capitalizing where necessary.

16. can you name the first full-length animated film?
17. it was *Snow White and the Seven Dwarfs.*
18. producer walt Disney introduced this classic in 1937.
19. later, disney produced other animated films of children's stories, including *Pinocchio* and *alice in Wonderland.*
20. eventually Disney combined live action with animation.
21. the movie *Mary Poppins* used this technique.
22. usually disney's composers wrote new song lyrics and music.
23. in *Alice in Wonderland,* however, one song used these lines from the poem "Jabberwocky" in lewis carroll's book:

24. 'twas brillig, and the slithy toves
    did gyre and gimble in the wabe;
all mimsy were the borogoves,
    and the mome raths outgrabe.

25. however, that lovable rodent mickey mouse was Disney's first great animated success!

C. Capitalizing in Outlines and Titles   Write the following items, adding capital letters where needed.

26. the following outline shows some sources of popular movies:

27.   I. existing literature
       A. books
          1. children's books like *the wonderful wizard of oz*
          2. novels like *gone with the wind*
       b. fairy tales, legends, and other traditional stories
       c. stage plays, musicals, and operas
     II. original screenplays

28. many children's books, such as *heidi, treasure island,* and *sounder,* have been turned into movies starring child actors.

29. Others—for example, *the wind in the willows* and *aladdin*—were put on screen with animated characters.

30. films based on novels, such as *around the World in 80 days* and *Dances with wolves,* have won Oscars for best picture.

31. The animated film *cinderella* was based on the fairy tale.

32. another fairy tale, "beauty and the beast," has been made into two feature films, one with actors and the other animated.

33. the movie *oliver!* was the film version of the musical stage play *oliver!,* which was based on the book *oliver twist.*

34. its stars sang such songs as "who will buy?" and "consider yourself."

35. The movie (and musical) *annie* was based on a comic strip!

36. Most of the classic comedies, such as Laurel and Hardy's short film *the music box*, were original movie scripts.

37. *citizen kane* was loosely based on William Randolph Hearst.

38. He published the *san francisco examiner* and *harper's bazaar.*

39. *gandhi* was a more factual account of its subject's life.

40. whatever their source, movies are great entertainment!

GRAMMAR
HANDBOOK
42

Writing Theme
Symbols of Patriotism

A. Using Capitalization   Write the sentences, capitalizing where necessary. If a sentence is correct, write *Correct.*

1. Early flags of American colonies often showed a rattlesnake.
2. The first flag for all the colonies joined thirteen red and white stripes with the british flag, called the Union Jack.
3. During the revolutionary war, patriots wanted a new flag.
4. Legend says Betsy Ross, a quaker seamstress, made the first u.s. flag in a house on arch street in philadelphia in 1776.
5. In her honor, the site is called the betsy ross house.
6. The new design replaced the union jack with thirteen white stars on a blue rectangle.
7. Records show that the continental congress adopted this flag on june 14, 1777, when it passed the Flag Resolution.
8. the new flag, the stars and stripes, was first used in a land battle on august 16, 1777, at the battle of bennington.
9. It was first flown at sea on november 1, 1777, on a ship commanded by captain john paul jones.
10. The Flag Act of 1818 set the number of stripes at thirteen, with the number of stars matching the number of states.
11. From 1791 till 1959, when a star was added for hawaii, the flag of the united states changed twenty-six times!
12. The flag that flew over fort mcHenry during the war of 1812 had fifteen stripes and fifteen stars.
13. this flag inspired francis scott key to write a poem.
14. Key was an american lawyer held on a british ship in chesapeake bay on tuesday, september 13, 1814.
15. He watched into the night as british ships shelled baltimore.
16. The next morning, overjoyed that the U.S. flag still flew over the fort, Key wrote some words that would soon be set to music:
17. "oh! say, can you see, by the dawn's early light, what so proudly we hailed at the twilight's last gleaming?"
18. The title "The star-Spangled banner" comes from a line in the song: "oh! say, does that star-spangled banner yet wave."
19. On march 3, 1931, president herbert hoover signed a bill adopting the song as the united states' national anthem.
20. the very flag that inspired the song can be seen at the smithsonian institution in washington, d.c.

B. Mastering Capitalization　For each sentence and outline item, write correctly only the words lacking correct capitalization.

21samuel francis smith was a student at andover theological seminary in massachusetts. **22**he studied the bible and other religious subjects. **23**in 1831, lowell mason gave smith some german song books. **24**mason wanted smith to write songs for children, using melodies from the song books. **25**On a dreary winter day in february 1832, smith chose a melody and wrote these words:

> **26**my country! 'tis of thee, sweet land of liberty,
> of thee i sing. . .

27His patriotic song was introduced to the public on independence day in 1832. **28**four years later, the song was published in a book called *the boston academy* under the title "america, national hymn." **29**dr. smith eventually became the pastor of the first baptist church in newton, west of boston. **30**His song, "america," was being sung throughout the united states. **31**during the civil war, it was very popular among citizens of the North. **32**they sang it at rallies, in army camps, and at meetings.

33this patriotic song is still popular. **34**Some are surprised to learn that it has the same melody as the british national anthem. **35**Smith himself did not know he had chosen the melody of "god save the king." **36**the song from which he took the tune had german lyrics. **37**The result is that the melody appeals to the patriotism of people in two nations—the united kingdom and the united states.

38In 1914, Smith's son donated the original manuscript of "America" to the library at harvard university. **39**This manuscript is considered one of the treasures of the united states.

40The song "america"—a history
   I.　Origin of the song "america"
      a.　basic facts
         1.　who, when, where
         2.　what happened
      b.　excerpt—first three lines
  II.　the song's growth in popularity

WRITING CONNECTIONS

Elaboration, Revision, and Proofreading

Revise the following draft of a personal response to literature by using the directions at the bottom of the page. Then proofread your work, paying special attention to using capitalization correctly. Also look for errors in grammar, punctuation, and spelling.

[1]Reading The diary of a young girl by Anne frank made me think about my reactions to writing in my own journal. [2]Like anne, i sometimes wonders what the point is. [3]Why would anyone want to read the scribblings of someone like me. [4]On the one hand, her Dairy is a fascinating record of a terible time. [5]It tells about all the things she endured with her Parents and her Sister. [6]It also provide a chilling picture of what europe was like during world war II. [7]Anne's writing shows me the value of just getting my thoughs out. [8]Even if no one ever reads it, my thoughts have value for me. [9]Writing is a way to relese my emotions. [10]It is a way to figure out what I am thinking. [11]It is a way to figure out what I am feeling.

1. Add the following information after sentence 3 to introduce the sentences that follow. "Anne's diary gives two very powerful answers to that question."

2. Add emphasis to sentence 7 by beginning it with the phrase "more importantly, however."

3. Make sentence 8 clearer by replacing the vague pronoun "it" with the more precise "my journal."

4. Eliminate repetition by combining sentences 10 and 11 to make one sentence.

5. Divide the passage into three paragraphs.

Responding to Literature

Writing a personal response to literature allows you to share your thoughts and opinions about the things you read. (See Workshop 6.) When you revise this type of writing, make sure you present your reactions clearly and support them with specific details. Also check for errors in capitalization that could detract from your message.

Sketch Book

- Imagine you just arrived in another world. Write the conversation you have with the first alien you meet.

- What is the biggest difference between this new world and the earth? Write a letter to your best friend, telling him or her about the wonders you've seen.

Punctuation

No matter how you get your message across—with your voice, with your hands, or with your writing—you need to use signals. Punctuation marks are the signals you use when you write. They point out stops and starts. They add emphasis, join together words, or show how ideas are related.

In this handbook, you will learn ways you can use punctuation to clearly signal your meaning to your readers.

Use a period after declarative sentences, after most imperative sentences, and after abbreviations, initials, and numbers and letters in lists.

Use a period at the end of declarative sentences and most imperative sentences.

A **declarative sentence** makes a statement.

Louis Pasteur developed the first rabies vaccine.

An **imperative sentence** states a command or a request.

Pour the solution into the beaker slowly.

Use a period after an abbreviation.

When taking notes or doing other kinds of informal writing, people often use shortened forms of words, or **abbreviations.** Notice how periods are used in these abbreviations:

P.O. (Post Office)	Co. (Company)
tsp. (teaspoon)	oz. (ounce)
Jan. (January)	Mon. (Monday)

Some abbreviations are written without periods.

FM (frequency modulation)	L (liter)
UPC (Universal Product Code)	m (meter)

The two-letter postal abbreviations of state names, such as *MA, AL,* and *CA,* are written with capital letters and no periods.

Dictionaries, newspapers, and magazines do not always punctuate abbreviations the same way. When deciding whether to use a period with an abbreviation, see what your teacher prefers or follow what your class dictionary says. Except for such abbreviations as *Mr., Mrs., Ms., Dr., A.M.,* and *P.M.,* avoid using abbreviations in formal writing.

Use a period after an initial.

An **initial** is the first letter of a person's name. It is used alone to stand for the name.

R. L. Carson—Rachel Louise Carson
Albert B. Sabin—Albert Bruce Sabin

Use a period after each number or letter in an outline. Use a period after each number in a list.

Astronomy
I. Galaxies and stars
   A. Types of galaxies
      1. Spiral
      2. Elliptical
      3. Irregular
   B. Types of stars
      1. Dwarf
      2. Giant
II. Solar system

Scientific Measurements
1. Volume
2. Mass and weight
3. Density
4. Temperature
5. Length

For information about the use of capital letters in outlines, see page 608.

Do not use periods when abbreviating metric units of measurement. For example, use *g* for "gram" and *mm* for "millimeter."

Writing
TIP

Practice Your Skills

A. CONCEPT CHECK

Periods Copy each word, abbreviation, letter, or number that should be followed by a period. Then add the period.

1. Everyone in Mr Ramos's class had to do a science project
2. This chart shows the growth of plants for one project

Date	With Fertilizer	Without Fertilizer
Mon, Sept 21	7 cm	8 cm
Fri, Nov 20	12 cm	9.5 cm

3. T L Fabbri, M L Gibbons, and J T Ortez recorded the data
4. Dr Sharon Adams of Biotech Ltd was their advisor
5. Tom, Mary Lou, and J T gave both their plants the same amount of water and light but gave only one plant fertilizer

Writing Theme
Science World

6. These are the measurements they used:
  1 Water—50 ml per day
  2 Sunlight—6 hr 30 min daily
  3 Fertilizer—1 tsp per week
7. For two months they carefully observed the plants' growth
8. They wrote a project report based on this outline:
  I What we thought would happen—our hypothesis
  II Our procedures
    A Daily watering and sunlight for both plants
    B Organic fertilizer for only one plant
  III Results and conclusions
9. Organic fertilizer caused one plant to grow taller
10. Use organic fertilizer if you want big, healthy plants

B. REVISION SKILL

Using Periods for Clarity   All needed periods are missing from these notes. Copy each word, abbreviation, letter, or number that should be followed by a period, adding the period.

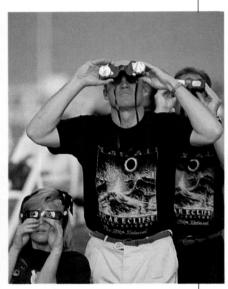

[11]The Science Club met Tues, Sept 6, at 7:00 PM [12]We were at 45 E Main St [13]I was asked to write to this address for a catalog:

  Science Equipment Co, Inc
  4652 Main St
  Beloit, WI 53511

[14]Dr Robert Alvin and Mrs B J Craig showed slides of their trip to Hawaii to see a solar eclipse [15]Clouds and ashes from the Mt Pinatubo eruption the previous June made viewing difficult [16]Yet B J Craig took fascinating pictures of the eclipse [17]She described safe ways to view a solar eclipse:

  1 Do not look directly at the sun
  2 Look through a special filter or use a pinhole projector

[18]Our next trip is to the Adler Planetarium, Chicago, IL [19]Alicia made arrangements with Corren Bus Co, Inc, for Mon and Tues, Oct 3 and 4 [20]The baggage weight limit for each person is 40 lb [21]We'll stay at the Hillcrest Hotel on Michigan Ave

[22]The meeting ended at 9:30 PM

FOR MORE PRACTICE
See page 592.

THE QUESTION MARK AND
THE EXCLAMATION POINT

Use a question mark after an interrogative sentence. Use an exclamation point after an exclamatory sentence, after an imperative sentence that is exclamatory, and after an interjection.

Use a question mark after an interrogative sentence.

An **interrogative sentence** asks a question.

> When does the game start?   Who is the new pitcher?

Use an exclamation point at the end of an exclamatory sentence that expresses excitement or another strong feeling.

> It's a home run!   We're number one!

Use an exclamation point at the end of an imperative sentence that makes a strong command.

> Run! Get that ball! Throw it!

Use an exclamation point after an interjection, a word or group of words used to express surprise or another strong feeling.

> Wow! What a catch! Unbelievable!

Practice Your Skills

A. CONCEPT CHECK

Question Marks and Exclamation Points   Copy this conversation. Add needed periods, question marks, and exclamation points. Try not to overuse exclamation points.

1. ED: We've won We've won
2. AL: What a fantastic game That's the way to play ball

Writing
TIP

Exclamations express strong feelings, but too many exclamations in your writing can make the feelings seem less important.

Writing Theme
Sports Fans

3. ED: Can you believe it We beat the Cougars by nine runs

4. MIA: Hurry They're showing replays

5. AL: Didn't you think that ball was out of the park

6. MIA: Yes, but Jackson's one-handed catch saved the day

7. ED: Right What an unbelievable catch

8. MIA: I was so afraid the Cougars would score in the ninth

9. AL: So was I, but we really held on

10. ED: Weren't you impressed with Garcia today

11. AL: That's for sure He was incredible

12. MIA: Can you imagine how it felt to hit three homers

13. ED: Great It had to feel just great

14. AL: Do you think the Cougars regret trading him away

15. ED: Who knows I'm just glad he's on our team now

B. PROOFREADING SKILL

Using Question Marks and Exclamation Points Write this script for a television advertisement. Correct the errors in punctuation and spelling. Use exclamation points in ways you think are correct for an advertisement. (24 errors)

ACTOR 1: Wow. What a stunning performance

ACTOR 2: There's her score. Its a ten A perfect ten

ACTOR 1: Outstanding T A Bukro is the new world champion. Listen to this crowd roar

ACTOR 3: Are you a gymnastics fan Do you enjoy watching track-and-feild events. Or is soccer your favorite sport

ACTOR 4: Do you know where you can see these and other exciteing sports events

ACTOR 3: You can see them on Super Sports Station. Super Sports offers you the best in sports all day long, every day?

ACTOR 4: You don't want to miss the most thrilling sports events shown on television, do you.

ACTOR 3: Of course not Just call this number, and we'll add Super Sports to your cable pakage.

ACTOR 4: Hurry! Order today and get one month free Thats' right Absolutely free

ACTOR 3: Call today What sports fan could turn down this offer.

FOR MORE PRACTICE
See page 592.

Write the following phrases and sentences, adding periods, question marks, and exclamation points where necessary.

Writing Theme
Circus

1. Come one, come all See the Greatest Show on Earth
2. Under those huge words on the sign were several lines in smaller type
3. The other lines gave important information:
   —Ringling Bros and Barnum & Bailey Combined Shows, Inc
   —Opening in St Louis on Sun, Oct 15
4. Sara Hird, T J Hart, and I went to the circus that Sunday
5. Mr and Mrs Hart sat with us
6. The show was fantastic Truly fantastic
7. I couldn't believe my eyes
8. The show began at 7:00 PM with the grand entrance
9. Suddenly, things started happening in all three rings
10. Have you ever seen anyone let go of a trapeze and do four somersaults before being caught by a partner
11. Wow What a stunt
12. The high-wire performers were amazing
13. Can you imagine riding a bicycle on a thin wire high above ground with someone standing on your shoulders
14. What an awesome sight
15. Here's a list of my favorite acts:
    1 The tightrope walkers
    2 The trapeze artists
    3 The clowns
16. I also liked the animals, especially the elephants and the seals
17. Now, those are really smart animals
18. I decided to write a report about the circus
19. This is part of my outline:
    I Great circus owners
      A James A Bailey and P T Barnum
      B Ringling Brothers
    II Outstanding circus performers
20. I can hardly wait until the circus comes back next year

"Lorenzo and Lorenzo" of San Francisco's Pickle Family Circus.

Use commas to separate items in a series. Use a comma when you use *and, but,* or *or* to join two sentences. Use a comma to avoid confusion.

Commas tell readers to pause. This pause keeps readers from running together words or ideas that should be kept separate.

Use commas to separate the items in a series. There are always three or more items in a series.

Roses, carnations, and other flowers were for sale.
Our class planned, advertised, and set up the art fair.
Sue, Cliff, Dave, and Shawna sold tickets on Friday, Saturday, and Sunday.

In a series, place a comma after each item except the last. Notice how the use of commas changes the meaning of this sentence.

At the food fest we tasted chicken, enchiladas, fruit, salad, cheese, ravioli, and bran muffins.
At the food fest we tasted chicken enchiladas, fruit salad, cheese ravioli, and bran muffins.

When you use *and, but,* and *or* to combine complete sentences, put commas before these words.

Sara enjoyed the art fair. She didn't buy anything.
Sara enjoyed the art fair, but she didn't buy anything.

Use a comma whenever the reader might be confused.

Some sentences can be very confusing without commas.

Confusing   Soon after opening the farmers' market ran out of corn.
Clear   Soon after opening, the farmers' market ran out of corn.

Writing
═ TIP ═

Remember, do not overuse commas. Too many commas may make a sentence harder to read instead of easier.

Practice Your Skills

A. CONCEPT CHECK

Commas That Separate Ideas   Write the following sentences, adding commas where necessary.

Writing Theme
Open-Air Markets

1. Growers sell food at markets or they sell it at roadside stands.
2. Farmers plant crops grow them and sell them in nearby towns.
3. Some supply fresh corn and others offer delicious tomatoes.
4. Yesterday, we went to a market and we looked for bargains.
5. We wanted to buy corn on the cob but it was sold out.
6. Instead, we bought tomatoes green beans and zucchini.
7. Dad said he would make bacon lettuce and tomato sandwiches.
8. As we ate Dad talked about the farm where he grew up.
9. Remembering the farm Dad always smiles.
10. His family grew apples and they shipped the apples out of state.

B. DRAFTING SKILL

Using Commas to Make Writing Concise   Combine the sentences in each group, adding commas where necessary.

EXAMPLE   The parking lot was crowded. The booths were crowded. The shops were crowded.
The parking lot, the booths, and the shops were crowded.

11. You may know them as flea markets. You may know them as swap meets. They are also known as outdoor marketplaces.
12. Today these events are popular throughout the United States. They are becoming even more widespread.
13. Flea markets are in parking lots. They are in stadiums.
14. Some attract just a few loyal fans. Others draw thousands.
15. Companies such as Sears may set up booths. J. C. Penney may set up booths. MCI Communications may set up booths.
16. People come to have fun. They are also looking for bargains.
17. Shoppers arrive early. They browse around. They make deals.
18. Browsers can find interesting items. They can find unusual items. They can find practical items.
19. They buy new cars. They buy antiques. They buy clothes.
20. Shoppers can enjoy just looking. They can buy treasures.

FOR MORE PRACTICE
See page 592.

Punctuation   **575**

Use commas to set off introductory phrases, the names of people spoken to, and appositives. Use commas to separate parts of dates and addresses.

Grammar
=== **TIP** ===

Remember to use a comma after a transition word such as *next, however,* or *therefore* at the beginning of a sentence.

Use a comma after *yes, no,* or *well* at the beginning of a sentence.

Yes, I'll take a bicycle tour.   Well, have a great time.

Use commas to set off the name of a person spoken to.

One comma is needed when the name starts or ends the sentence. A comma is needed both before and after a name in the middle of a sentence.

Inez, don't forget your helmet. Do you have yours, Ted? It's important, Lenore, to check the air in the tires.

Use commas to set off most appositives.

An **appositive** follows a noun and renames the noun. It is used to give more information.

Camille Morilla, a veteran cyclist, won the race.

Use commas to separate the parts of a date. Use a comma after the last part of a date in the middle of a sentence.

Our school will hold a bike rally on Monday, October 6. On May 31, 1868, the first recorded bike race was held.

Use a comma to separate the name of a city from the name of a state or country. Use a comma after the name of the state or country in the middle of a sentence.

The Tour de France bicycle race ends in Paris, France. The bike race in Bloomington, Indiana, drew a big crowd.

Practice Your Skills

A. CONCEPT CHECK

Commas and Special Elements   Write the following sentences. Add commas where needed.

1. TEACHER: Class our guest is Alex Doren a cycling fan.
2. SPEAKER: Thank you Ms. Farino.
3. Good morning students. Yes I do love to ride my bicycle.
4. I first rode a bicycle on June 7 1967 my fifth birthday.
5. I have toured all over Ohio my home state by bicycle.
6. Once I toured Toronto Canada with Barney my favorite bike.
7. Well my most recent tour began on Sunday April 18 1993.
8. Please dim the lights Ms. Farino so I can show my slides.
9. Friends and I started off from Hampton New Hampshire.
10. We cycled along the ocean to Newburyport Massachusetts.
11. Our scenic seaside tour ended on April 24 1993 at Hampton.
12. I also plan to cycle through Acadia a scenic national park in Maine.

B. REVISION SKILL

Using Commas for Clarity   The paragraphs below are missing some commas. Copy the paragraphs, adding commas where needed.

[13]Shelly did you know that the first bicycle was invented in the 1790s? [14]Well although it had two wheels, the *célérifère* wasn't much of a bike. [15]It could not be steered and a rider had to paddle his or her feet on the ground to make it move. [16]Baron Karl von Drais a German inventor added a steering bar to this kind of bike. [17]He displayed his improved bicycle in Paris France on April 6 1818.

[18]In 1866, Pierre Lallement a French immigrant and James Carroll of Ansonia Connecticut received the first bicycle patent in the United States. [19]Their bicycle the boneshaker had pedals on the front wheel. [20]The high-wheeler or penny-farthing was introduced in the 1860s. [21]Then the safety bicycle a bike more like bicycles of today came along in the 1870s. [22]Yes Shelly the bicycle has certainly come a long way since the *célérifère!*

Writing Theme
On the Bike

The English racer M.W. Wright stands beside his bicycle. Wright removed the brakes before each race and wore tightly fitted clothing in order to race as fast as possible.

FOR MORE PRACTICE
See page 592.

> Use commas to set off direct quotations. Use commas after the greeting and closing of a friendly letter.

Use commas to set off explanatory words from direct quotations.

Compare the positions of the commas in these sentences:

Lee asked, "Did you see the mystery on TV last night?"
"I saw somebody sneaking away," insisted the witness.

In the first sentence, the explanatory words *Lee asked* come before the quotation. Therefore, a comma is placed after the last explanatory word. In the second sentence, the explanatory words come after the quotation. A comma is placed inside the quotation marks after the last word of the quotation.

Explanatory words can separate a quotation into two parts.

"No one knows," said the detective, "when it happened."

One comma is used inside the quotation marks that end the first part of the quote. Another comma is used after the last explanatory word. You will learn more about punctuating quotations on pages 586–587.

Use a comma after the greeting of a friendly letter and after the closing of any letter.

Dear Anita,   Your friend,

Practice Your Skills

A. CONCEPT CHECK

Other Uses of Commas   Write the following sentences, adding commas where needed.

1. "I just read a book about the *Mary Celeste*" said Beth.
2. Curious, I asked "What is the *Mary Celeste?*"

3. "It was a ship" replied Beth "that left New York with eleven crew members and passengers on November 7, 1872."
4. "A month later" Beth continued "the crew of another ship saw the *Mary Celeste* on course, but swinging left and right."
5. "A few sailors investigated the ship" Beth went on.
6. "Well" I asked "what did they find?"
7. Beth whispered "They found everything just as it should be, but no one, not one single person, was on the *Mary Celeste*."
8. "They noticed that the lifeboat was missing" she added.
9. "The crew and passengers could have sailed away in it" I suggested.
10. "Could be" agreed Beth "but the lifeboat was never found."
11. "Also, no one from the ship was ever seen again" said Beth.
12. I concluded "Then their fate is a mystery of the sea."

B. REVISION SKILL

Using Commas in Friendly Letters   Copy this letter, adding commas where needed.

¹³Dear Mr. Sherlock Holmes

¹⁴I must congratulate you on your solution to the last strange case. ¹⁵Yes I know I should be used to your special abilities by now but I am still amazed. ¹⁶After all Holmes who else would have suspected the timid servant? ¹⁷As you questioned the witnesses the case became more puzzling to me. ¹⁸I became confused but you grew more certain of the guilty person's identity.

¹⁹One of the family members wondered "Why does Holmes ask us so many questions?"

²⁰"The solution" one brother suggested "must become clear soon if it is ever to be found."

²¹"I think Mr. Holmes is as stumped as the rest of us" said a family friend.

²²Well Holmes you showed them once more that you are the smartest quickest and greatest detective who ever lived. ²³It is an honor to work with you and I am proud to call you my friend.

²⁴Best regards
Dr. Watson

FOR MORE PRACTICE
See page 592.

CHECK ✔ POINT
MIXED REVIEW · PAGES 574–579

A. Write the sentences, adding commas where necessary. If a sentence is correct, write *Correct*.

1. The Second Continental Congress first met on May 10 1775.
2. Delegates attended meetings in Philadelphia Pennsylvania.
3. On June 7 1776 Richard H. Lee gave a speech.
4. Lee proclaimed "These United Colonies are, and of right ought to be, free and independent states."
5. Well, some delegates agreed with him, but others did not.
6. Meanwhile, Thomas Jefferson John Adams Benjamin Franklin and two others began working on the Declaration of Independence.
7. As Jefferson wrote the others suggested changes.
8. Finally, on July 2 1776 the congress voted for independence.
9. Members then discussed debated and passed the declaration.
10. John Hancock, president of the congress, signed it on July 4.

B. Write this friendly letter, adding commas where necessary.

11Dear Kristin

12Happy Fourth of July! **13**Today is July 4 1993 and we had a huge family picnic. **14**My grandparents from Phoenix Arizona came but my joke-loving grandmother from Green Bay Wisconsin couldn't come. **15**Without her things were quieter than last year.

16Yes we all ate delicious food played games and watched a fireworks show.

17My little brother asked "Why do we celebrate on the fourth of July Terry?"

18"Well that is the day" I answered "that some American leaders decided to make a new country."

19"David we celebrate because this day marks the beginning of our nation the United States of America" Mom explained.

20Write and tell me what your family did Kristin. **21**Did you go to a picnic like I did or did you celebrate at home?

22Your friend always
Terry

THE APOSTROPHE

AND THE HYPHEN

Use apostrophes to show possession and to form contractions. Use hyphens to divide words at the end of lines and to write compound numbers and fractions.

Use an apostrophe to show possession. To form the possessive of a singular noun, add an apostrophe and s.

musician + 's = musician's   Charles + 's = Charles's

To form the possessive of a plural noun that does not end in s, add an apostrophe and s.

children + 's = children's   women + 's = women's

To form the possessive of a plural noun that ends in s, add only an apostrophe.

composers + ' = composers'   violins + ' = violins'

Use an apostrophe in a contraction.

A **contraction** is two words written as one, with one or more letters left out. An apostrophe replaces the missing letter or letters.

can + not = can't   she + will = she'll
I + am = I'm   he + had = he'd

Use a hyphen after the first part of a word divided at the end of a line. Then write the second part on the next line.

Musicians in the orchestra watched closely as the conductor raised her baton.

Divide a word only between syllables. Never divide a word of one syllable, such as *count* or *score.* A dictionary shows how to divide a word into syllables.

Do not write a single letter at the end or the beginning of a line. These divisions would be wrong: *a- dapt, regga- e.*

Use hyphens in compound numbers from twenty-one through ninety-nine and in fractions.

eighty-eight piano keys   two-thirds of the audience

Practice Your Skills

CONCEPT CHECK

Apostrophes and Hyphens   Write the words that need apostrophes or hyphens in these sentences.

1. Originally, an orchestra was a group of musicians who ac companied opera performances.
2. Soon, audiences attention centered on the orchestras as much as on the opera singers.
3. If youve ever seen an orchestra play, then you know it has a leader, called a conductor.
4. A conductors baton and arm motions hold the musicians attention.
5. The conductors signals and gestures lead the orchestra.
6. Orchestra members wouldnt be able to play without direction.
7. Its important that the musicians play together as a group.
8. The orchestras success depends on each players skill and sense of cooperation.
9. More than one half of the musicians play stringed instru ments, such as violins, violas, double basses, and cellos.
10. For example, in an orchestra of one hundred members, about sixty five usually play stringed instruments.
11. About one fourth play brass instruments, such as trumpets, French horns, trombones, and tubas.
12. The rest of the musicians play either woodwinds—includ ing clarinets, oboes, and flutes—or percussion instruments.
13. The timpani, or big kettledrums, are a percussionists most important instruments.
14. Theyre large, hollow copper kettles covered with drumheads.
15. Listening to Sergey Prokofievs *Peter and the Wolf* often builds childrens interest in the orchestra.

FOR MORE PRACTICE
See page 592.

Use a colon after the greeting of a business letter and between hours and minutes in an expression of time. Use a semicolon to join two related sentences.

Use a colon after the greeting of a business letter.

Dear Mrs. DeMille: Dear Sir:

Use a colon between numerals representing hours and minutes. Also use a colon between chapter and verse in Biblical references.

10:14 A.M.   6:33 P.M.   Genesis 1:1–5

Remember to capitalize the letters and to use a period after each letter in the abbreviations A.M. and P.M.

Use a semicolon to combine two related sentences.

You can combine two related sentences into one by using a comma and a conjunction such as *and, but,* or *or* to connect the sentences.

We ran to the theater, but the show had already begun.

Another way to combine two related sentences is to use a semicolon (;). The semicolon takes the place of both the comma and the conjunction.

We ran to the theater; the show had already begun.
We ran to the theater; however, we were late.

You can use semicolons to avoid writing run-on sentences. For more about run-on sentences, see Handbook 34, pages 344–345.

Incorrect   The lights dimmed the movie began.
Correct   The lights dimmed; the movie began.

THOSE OF YOU WAITING TO BUY A TICKET, PLEASE FORM AN ORDERLY SENTENCE!

TALK TO THIS GUY. HE'LL MAKE SURE WE GET IT TOGETHER!

Practice Your Skills

A. CONCEPT CHECK

Colons and Semicolons   Write the following business letter, adding colons, semicolons, and commas where necessary.

[1]April 10 19—

[2]Dear Ms. Velez

[3]Please put this announcement in the school paper. [4]Mr. Wu's sixth-grade class has made a video it's called *On a Sunny Day.* [5]It's about summer sports hobbies and activities. [6]The video will be shown on Tuesday April 28 at 1100 A.M. and 200 P.M. [7]The movie is free however a donation for the Food Bank is welcome. [8]Cans of fruit vegetables and soup are needed. [9]We hope people come the class has worked hard.

[10]Sincerely yours

Andrea Giotti

B. DRAFTING SKILL

Sentence Combining   Combine each pair of sentences, using either a comma and a conjunction or a semicolon, as indicated in the parentheses.

11. Mr. Chandler's class made a video last fall. Now they are making another one. (semicolon)
12. They discussed story ideas. They chose one. (conjunction)
13. Anya wrote the script. Stacy helped her. (semicolon)
14. Class members are actors in the video. They handle the technical jobs. (conjunction)
15. Jaina hopes to borrow her family's video camera. Mr. Chandler may bring his camera. (conjunction)
16. Costumes are Sonya's job. She loves sewing. (semicolon)
17. Jason and Mike are collecting props. They don't know where they will find a pair of stilts! (conjunction)
18. The actors must rehearse. They must learn lines. (semicolon)
19. The first rehearsals have been a little shaky. Everyone is nervous. (conjunction)
20. By the end of the month, everything must be ready. It will be time to start filming. (semicolon)

FOR MORE PRACTICE
See page 593.

C H E C K  P O I N T

MIXED REVIEW · PAGES 581–584

Writing Theme
Mythical Animals

A. Write the following business letter, adding apostrophes, hyphens, colons, semicolons, and commas where necessary.

1Dear Dr. Wasser

2Yesterday morning, about 600 A.M., I was walking on the beach near some cliffs when I saw the most incredible crea ture! **3**It had an eagles head and wings and a lions tail and body. **4**Ive heard youre an expert on unusual animals thats why I decided to write to you. **5**You must be used to peoples imaginations running wild. **6**However please dont tell me that I was dreaming. **7**I was only twenty five feet away from this animal and I saw it clearly. **8**I tried to get even closer but it flew away then. **9**Please answer soon nobody else believes me!

10Sincerely
Alice Stein

B. Write the following reply. Add apostrophes, hyphens, colons, semicolons, and commas where necessary.

11Dear Ms. Stein

12Thank you for writing to me I enjoy hearing about peoples unusual experiences. **13**The animal you saw was a griffin but I have to tell you that its thought to be an imagi nary creature. **14**Legend says that griffins lived in western Persia and guarded the gods gold mines from greedy humans. **15**A griffin was supposed to be stronger than ninety nine eagles one could carry off and devour oxen elephants and even people. **16**Griffins claws were thought to contain an antidote to poison and it is said that the claws were made into drinking cups.

17Please come to see me Id like to hear more about your ex perience on the beach. **18**My office hours are 100 P.M. to 500 P.M. on Tuesdays and Fridays. **19**Its not necessary to make an appointment.

20Yours truly
Dr. Alvin Wasser

Use quotation marks at the beginning and the end of a direct quotation.

When you write what a person has said, you are writing a **quotation.** A **direct quotation** is a restatement of the person's exact words. If you do not write the exact words, you are writing an **indirect quotation.** Here are examples:

Direct Quotation	Jenny said, "I've met the mayor."
Indirect Quotation	Jenny said that she had met the mayor.

Put quotation marks before and after the words of a direct quotation.

In the first sentence above, Jenny's exact words are set apart by quotation marks. The second sentence tells what Jenny said without using her exact words.

Place a period inside the quotation marks if the quotation ends the sentence.

Jenny said, "He shook my hand."

Use a comma, exclamation point, or question mark to separate explanatory words from a direct quotation.

"I was surprised," said Jenny.
"I couldn't think of anything to say!" Jenny exclaimed.

Place question marks and exclamation points inside quotation marks if they belong to the quotation itself.

Rita asked, "What did the mayor say to you?"
"I can't remember!" answered Jenny.

In the first sentence, the question is quoted. Therefore, the question mark is placed inside the quotation marks. In the second sentence, the speaker is showing strong emotion. The exclamation point is also placed inside the quotation marks.

Place question marks and exclamation points outside quotation marks if they do not belong to the quotation.

Did Christopher say, "Sometime I would like to talk to the mayor myself"**?**

How amazing that Jenny said, "Maybe you can"**!**

Divided Quotations

Sometimes a quotation is divided. Explanatory words, like *he said* or *she asked,* are in the middle of the quotation.

"The interview,**"** said Jenny, **"** is scheduled for Friday.**"**

Notice that two sets of quotation marks are used for this quotation. This sentence has a comma after the explanatory words because the second part of the quotation does not begin a new sentence. Use a period after the explanatory words if the second part of the quotation is a new sentence.

"Today is Tuesday**,**" said Paul**.** "That gives me three days to get my questions ready."

In this sentence, the second part of the quotation begins with a capital letter because it is a new sentence.

Practice Your Skills

A. CONCEPT CHECK

Quotation Marks   Write the sentences, adding quotation marks and other punctuation where necessary. Write *Correct* if no additional punctuation is needed.

1. Our guests today announced the talk show host are two famous world leaders.
2. Ladies and gentlemen, please welcome Genghis Khan and Abraham Lincoln she said.
3. Mr. Lincoln she asked you are our sixteenth president. How do you lead people?
4. First of all, you must earn their respect Lincoln answered That's vital.
5. I disagree shouted Genghis You must show strength.

Use a variety of explanatory words when you write quotations. Some common explanatory words are *explained, shouted, asked, laughed,* and *replied.* Make sure the word you choose fits the situation.

Writing Theme
Interviews

Abraham Lincoln (1809–1865) and Genghis Khan

6. I conquered Asia Genghis boasted loudly by taking what I wanted.
7. He said that a leader must be able to command loyalty.
8. I agree said Lincoln but a leader must also trust the people.
9. Lincoln said that the people could make the right choices.
10. What was Lincoln's response when Genghis said My people trusted me to make the right choices?

B. REVISION SKILL

Using Quotation Marks for Livelier Writing   Change these indirect quotations to direct quotations. You may need to change some words in the sentences. Try to put the explanatory words in different positions in your sentences.

11. Andy asked how he should prepare to conduct an interview.
12. Kris said that she would try to learn about the person first.
13. Leon exclaimed that doing research was a good idea.
14. Janine said that she would think of a list of questions.
15. Kevin asked whether that would be hard to do.
16. Janine replied that the difficult part was thinking of open-ended questions.
17. José said that a reporter should ask questions that can't be answered just yes or no.
18. Mai declared that thinking up good questions is the most important part of a reporter's job.
19. Andy asked whether he should try writing some practice questions.
20. Mai said that it would probably help him if he did.

FOR MORE PRACTICE
See page 593.

C H E C K ✔ P O I N T

MIXED REVIEW · PAGES 586–588

Writing Theme
Moonstruck

A. Write the sentences, adding quotation marks and other punctuation where necessary.

1. The planetarium guide said People around the world see different pictures when they look at the moon.
2. She asked Have you heard of the man in the moon
3. Marie nodded, and Thomas shouted Sure
4. To many Europeans explained the guide the markings on the moon look like a man carrying a bundle of twigs
5. Many Native American people she said see a frog
6. People in Tibet and Mexico see a hare she continued.
7. Samoans see a woman the guide added So do the Maori of New Zealand
8. What image do you see in the moon she asked the children.
9. Marie said I see a sleeping cat.
10. Did Thomas really say I see a monkey

B. APPLICATION IN LITERATURE

Punctuating Quotations Write the following passage, adding quotation marks and other punctuation as needed.

11The Princess Lenore was awake, and she was glad to see the Court Jester but her face was very pale and her voice very weak.

12Have you brought the moon to me she asked.

13Not yet said the Court Jester but I will get it for you right away. **14**How big do you think it is

15It is just a little smaller than my thumbnail she said for when I hold my thumbnail up at the moon, it just covers it

16And how far away is it asked the Court Jester.

17It is not as high as the big tree outside my window said the Princess for sometimes it gets caught in the top branches

18It will be very easy to get the moon for you said the Court Jester **19**I will climb the tree tonight when it gets caught in the top branches and bring it to you

James Thurber, "Many Moons"

Use quotation marks to set off titles of short works. Underline the titles of longer works.

Put quotation marks around the titles of stories, poems, reports, articles, and chapters of a book.

In a sentence, a period or comma following the title is placed within the quotation marks. Place any other punctuation for the sentence outside the quotation marks.

> In this issue, read the article "Window to the Future."
> I enjoyed the story "Mars Morning"; it's imaginative.

Underline the titles of books, magazines, plays, movies, very long poems, and TV series. In print, these titles appear in italics.

> E.T.: The Extra-Terrestrial   *E.T.: The Extra-Terrestrial*

Underline the title of a painting or the name of a ship. These titles also appear in italics in printed materials.

> The Persistence of Memory (painting)
> Flying Dutchman (ship)

To review the guidelines for capitalizing words in titles, see Handbook 42, pages 546–565.

Practice Your Skills

A. CONCEPT CHECK

Titles   Use quotation marks or underlining for these titles.

1. Time Travel (article)
2. Amazing Stories (magazine)
3. A Martian Odyssey (story)
4. Star Trek (TV series)
5. The Monsters Are Due on Maple Street (play)
6. Star Wars (movie)
7. The Future Now (chapter)
8. The Time Machine (book)
9. The Raven (poem)
10. The Voyage (painting)

Writing Theme
Science Fiction

B. PROOFREADING SKILL

Punctuating Titles   Write the paragraph. Punctuate titles correctly and correct other errors in punctuation, capitalization, and spelling. (32 errors)

   Mary Shelley's Frankenstein, written in 1818, may have been the first science fiction novel? Some of Edgar allan Poe's stories, such as The Balloon-Hoax, are close to science fiction. Poe is best known, of corse, for horrer stories, such as The Tell-Tale Heart. Jules verne's first book, Five Weeks in a Balloon, resembles Poe's The Balloon-Hoax. With the sucess of his book Journey to the Center of the Earth, Verne became the first author to earn a living writing science fiction. However; isaac asimov, in an artecle called The Science Fiction Breakthrough, claimed that h. g. wells was the first writer to put science fiction first. My favrite Wells novel is The War of the Worlds. His alien's are not frendly beings like those in the movie E.T. In another article, Beyond Our Brain, asimov said that The War of the Worlds opened a new chapter in science fiction! This novel, along with The Time Machine and The Invisible Man, set the tone for science fiction ever sence.

CHECK POINT
MIXED REVIEW · PAGES 590–591

Write the sentences. Add needed quotation marks and underlining.

1. At the age of nineteen, Isaac Asimov sold his first science fiction tale, Marooned Off Vesta, to Amazing Stories magazine.
2. At twenty-one, he wrote one of his best stories, Nightfall.
3. His story The Fun They Had appears in many collections.
4. Asimov said that his favorite story was The Last Question.
5. His first book was Pebble in the Sky, published in 1950.
6. He won a Hugo award for science fiction for his books Foundation, Foundation and Empire, and Second Foundation.
7. Asimov's Caves of Steel is a science fiction detective novel.
8. His other science fiction books include Nemesis and I, Robot.
9. He wrote a popular book based on the movie Fantastic Voyage.
10. Asimov also wrote dozens of nonfiction science books, including Our World in Space and Understanding Physics.

Writing Theme
Eyewitness to
History

A. Using Commas and End Marks   Write the sentences, adding commas and end marks where they are needed.

1. John my nephew asked me if there was any day that I would always remember
2. "Well John I will never forget Sunday July 20 1969" I replied.
3. Why is that date so memorable
4. On that day, two American astronauts Neil A Armstrong and Edwin E Aldrin, Jr landed on the moon
5. At 9:56 PM Central Time, Armstrong stepped down from the *Eagle* the lunar landing module onto the moon's surface
6. "That's one small step for a man" he proclaimed "one giant leap for mankind."
7. I stared at the TV and shouted "Come quickly Mom Look"
8. Wow Incredible
9. It was hard to believe but a human was standing on the moon
10. What did the astronauts do on the moon
11. During their short stay on the moon, they did the following:
    1 Planted a U.S. flag
    2 Collected rock samples
    3 Set up scientific equipment
12. Have you ever seen the movies Armstrong and Aldrin took of each other bouncing across the lunar landscape
13. Also I remember that on July 24 1969 the first men to visit the moon returned to earth
14. What an extraordinary mission
15. I can't imagine a more thrilling exciting or inspiring event

B. Using Apostrophes and Hyphens   Write the following sentences. Make the words in italics contractions, make underlined words show possession, and add hyphens where needed.

16. On October 8, 1871, the watchman Mathias Schaffer *was not* surprised when he spotted a fire across the river.
17. There had been twenty seven fires in Chicago that week.
18. This, however, was to be one of the worst fires in <u>America</u> history.
19. Supposedly, it began when <u>Mrs. O'Leary</u> cow kicked over a lantern.

20. *It is* certain that the fire did begin in the O'Learys barn.
21. In 1871, most of Chicago buildings were made of wood.
22. Most people *could not* afford to build with brick and stone.
23. A strong wind blew fiery sparks from building to building, de spite firefighters heroic efforts.
24. The fire even traveled across the river to the city downtown.
25. It burned for twenty six hours, destroying 17,450 buildings and taking 250 people lives, before rain finally put it out.

C. Using Colons, Semicolons, and Commas   Write this letter. Add colons, semicolons, and commas where these punctuation marks are needed.

²⁶June 18 1849

²⁷Dear Mr. Hunt

   ²⁸Please forgive my late reply your letter was one of many I have received recently. ²⁹I appreciate your writing to Smith & Hardwick about your invention however, I do not think we would be interested in your "safety pin." ³⁰There are many stylish pin designs already on the market another one is not needed. ³¹Also, your pin is not good-looking enough to decorate hats coats or other clothing. ³²Not many people would use this pin and we could not expect to profit from making it. ³³We regret that we cannot use your pin however, you may have other clever inventions to show us. ³⁴If so, Mr. Smith and I can meet with you on Friday June 24 at 1030 A.M.

³⁵Yours sincerely

Davidson Hardwick

D. Punctuating Quotations   Write the sentences. Add quotation marks and other punctuation where necessary.

36. Can you imagine what it was like to see the Wright brothers' airplane fly at Kitty Hawk, North Carolina asked Jane.
37. It would have been so exciting she exclaimed.
38. David asked whether many people saw that famous flight.
39. I think so answered Jane Some local men were there.
40. She explained that they were from a nearby lifesaving station.

41. The Wrights had been trying to fly their plane for some weeks she continued before they finally succeeded.
42. Jane said that the Wrights took turns being the pilot
43. On December 17, 1903 she said they had more than one successful flight.
44. Who was piloting the plane on the first flight asked David.
45. Orville was Jane replied Wilbur, however, piloted the longest flight.
46. Just imagine she exclaimed They must have been so happy!
47. Did you know that they had worked on this project for seven years she asked.
48. Why did Jane smile when David said That's a long time?
49. Yes she agreed but they were really determined to be the first to fly.
50. Was David surprised when Jane said I wish I had been at Kitty Hawk that day?

E. Using Punctuation Marks   Copy the sentences. Add underlining, quotation marks, and other punctuation marks where necessary.

51. On August 19 a tornado destroyed Maystown Ohio
52. However the townspeople werent discouraged they immediately began rebuilding their houses schools and businesses
53. Junior-high students wrote about their tornado experiences in a school magazine they called Twister!
54. Simone wrote a poem called At Exactly 323 P.M.
55. Mr. Clybourns class wrote a play called Where Were You
56. Davids eyewitness report Its Not a Freight Train also appeared in the local newspaper
57. Keisha wrote an article called No Home in Maystown it told about people whose homes had been destroyed
58. Theo focused on the speed power and random nature of the tornado in his short story, Gone in Twenty two Seconds
59. Martin heard that his photographs of Maystown before and after the tornado might be used in a book, Forces of Nature
60. Did you see Sarahs home video of the tornado when it was shown on the TV series Eyewitness Video

A. End Marks and Commas   Write this friendly letter, adding punctuation where necessary.

Writing Theme
African Dream

¹Dear Alicia

²Wow What a surprise ³After your letter arrived, I ran home and shouted "Mama look Look! ⁴I have a letter from America" ⁵As I read Mama listened carefully and urged me to write to you soon

⁶Well I am Celia A Katanga from Zambia an African nation and I am happy to be your pen pal ⁷Zambia was once a British colony but it became independent on Saturday Oct 24 1964 ⁸My family lives in a cement house in Livingstone Zambia ⁹The city was named in honor of Dr David Livingstone the famous British explorer of Africa ¹⁰Would you be surprised to learn that we usually cook eat study and visit outdoors rather than in the house

¹¹Yes Alicia I like school very much ¹²Our classes begin at 7:30 AM and they are not over until 3:50 PM ¹³Is your school day longer or shorter ¹⁴These classes are my favorites:

1 Social studies
2 English
3 Home economics

Write soon and tell me more about yourself.

¹⁵Sincerely

Celia your new pen pal

B. Commas   Write the sentences, adding commas where necessary.

16. Ted asked "Raul have you heard of Ndoki a tropical region in northern Congo?"
17. "No I haven't Ted" I replied "but tell me about it."
18. "The Ndoki rain forest is a beautiful exotic and remote place, which very few people have seen" said Ted.
19. Ted said that Michael Fay a botanist with a wildlife conservation organization recently led an expedition there.
20. The expedition began in May of 1992 in Ouesso Congo.
21. The members of the expedition entered the forest several days later and they were often delighted by what they saw.

22. As they walked chimps would stare and screech at them.
23. A gorilla charged stopped and then walked away from them.
24. Conservationists hope that the forest will become a wildlife preserve but they fear it will soon be destroyed.
25. Ndoki must be saved or the world will lose a precious natural resource.

C. Apostrophes and Hyphens Write the sentences, adding apostrophes and hyphens where necessary.

26. Baobab trees grow only on Africas dry savannas.
27. Theyre unusual trees because their branches look like roots.
28. According to the Bushmen, thats a hyenas fault.
29. When the Great Spirit gave him the baobab to plant, he mis takenly planted it upside down!
30. A baobab may be thirty five feet across and fifty five feet tall.
31. But heres the most amazing fact—it can live 1,000 years!
32. Many animals food and shelter are provided by the baobab.
33. Birds nest in the hollows, baboons eat the fruit, bush ba bies drink the flowers nectar, and insects eat the wood.
34. What about the local peoples uses of the baobab?
35. They gather honey from the tree, use the bark to make bas kets and rope, and use the roots and leaves to make medicines.

D. Colons, Semicolons, and Commas Write this business letter, adding colons, semicolons, and commas where necessary.

[36]March 25 19—

[37]Dear Ms. Khouri

   [38]Thank you for asking about Ruckomechi the enclosed brochure should answer your questions. [39]Ruckomechi may be remote but it is worth the trip. [40]Our safari camp has the best location in Africa it is perfect for wildlife watching. [41]We have game drives every day at 600 A.M. and 200 P.M. [42]You will see elephants lions and hyenas. [43]You can also canoe fish and bird watch. [44]Our busiest time is September to December however, the camp is open from April 1 to January 1.

[45]Sincerely

Zena Gwelo, Manager

E. Quotation Marks Write the sentences, adding quotation marks where necessary. Write *Correct* if no quotation marks are needed.

46. The students said that they had enjoyed their safari in Zimbabwe, Africa.
47. I asked, What is your favorite memory of the safari?
48. I saw lions in the wild, said Hilton. That was very exciting!
49. We learned to track animals, said Doris, by studying the trails they left.
50. At night, Stuart said, we played games, sang songs, and put on plays.
51. I asked how they had felt on the last day of the safari.
52. I felt happy and sad at the same time, said Hilton.
53. Everyone nodded in agreement when Stuart exclaimed, It was wonderful!
54. Do you want to go on a safari again? I asked.
55. Would you be surprised to learn that everyone shouted, Yes?

F. Titles Write the sentences, adding either quotation marks or underlining for each title.

56. I need to find information for a report I'm writing, called The Influence of African Music on American Music: Blues, Jazz, and Rock.
57. First, I read the book The Music of Africa: An Introduction.
58. One chapter, The Music of Contemporary Africa, was helpful.
59. However, another book, African Music: A People's Art, dealt only with traditional African music.
60. More current was an article in Fortune magazine called Africa's Hot New Export: Music.
61. Another article, The Roots of the Blues, was also good.
62. It was one of a series of articles in Music magazine.
63. Now I'm looking for a book called A Celebration of African-American Music.
64. It is based on a program from a TV series, Music Travels.
65. I'm planning to begin my report with a quotation about African music from a poem called African Heaven.

Informative Writing: Reports

A report presents facts about a topic in a clear and organized way. (See Workshop 7.) When you revise a report, make sure your facts are presented accurately. Also make sure you have used punctuation correctly, especially in quotations and titles.

Revise this portion of a report, using the directions at the bottom of the page. Then proofread your writing, paying special attention to the use of punctuation. Also look for errors in grammar, capitalization, and spelling.

¹An unusual military strategy of Hannibal's army in the Second Punic War involved it's use of elephants. ²Elephants come from Africa and Asia. ³When Hannibal invaded Italy in 218 bc, his army included thirty seven elephants. ⁴According to the book "The ancient romans" by Chester Starr, the elephants were used as "walking tanks" against enamy foot soldiers. ⁵To reach Italy, Hannibals troups had to go over the Alps. ⁶They was attacked along the way by mountain tribes. ⁷The elephant's scared away some of the attacker's. ⁸The greek historian Polybius said "The enemy was so terrified of the animals' strange appearance that they dared not come anywhere near them".

1. Delete the sentence that does not belong.

2. Add this sentence after sentence 4 to introduce the information that follows: "Even before the army entered Italy, the elephants played an important role."

3. In sentence 5, replace the weak verb "go" with a more expressive verb.

4. Combine sentences 6 and 7 by using the conjunction "but."

5. Divide the passage into two paragraphs.

Silly Signs

Signs are everywhere—on street corners and on diner counter tops, in store windows and in hotel lobbies. But do signs always mean what they say? Look at the examples below and judge for yourself. These signs appear in *English Well Speeched Here* by Nino Lo Bello.

WARNING: DOOR IS ALARMED

We Take Your Bags and Send Them in All Directions.

PLEASE DO NOT FEED THE ANIMALS. IF YOU HAVE ANY SUITABLE FOOD, GIVE IT TO THE GUARD ON DUTY.

If You Consider Our Help Impolite, You Should See the Manager.

Authentic Tie Cuisine

The Parade Will Take Place in the Morning If It Rains in the Afternoon.

Courteous and Efficient Self-Service

Skills

Directions   One or more of the underlined sections in the following sentences may contain an error in grammar, punctuation, spelling, or capitalization. Write the letter of each incorrect section. Then rewrite the section correctly. If there is no error in an item, write *D*.

> **Example**   Sonja's <u>grandmother</u> came to the United States from
>   **A**   **B**
> Norway in <u>1932 mine</u> came from Ireland the same year. <u>No error</u>
>   **C**   **D**
>
> **Answer**   C—1932. Mine

1. Peter Pan fans all recognize the name <u>captain Hook</u>, but few know that
                                                A
<u>Hook's</u> first name was <u>James</u>. <u>No error</u>
  B   **C**   **D**

2. After we <u>ate the</u> electricity went off, so we couldn't watch <u>*nova*</u> on
            A   **B**
<u>public television</u>. <u>No error</u>
    C   **D**

3. The biggest city in the United States is <u>anchorage</u>, Alaska. It doesn't
                                         A
have the most <u>people but</u> it covers the <u>largest</u> area. <u>No error</u>
            B   **C**   **D**

4. "The bus leaves in two <u>hours,</u>" the guide said. <u>"don't</u> be late or you'll
                    A   **B**
be left <u>behind!"</u> <u>No error</u>
       C   **D**

5. The <u>woolly mammoth</u> had tusks sixteen feet long. <u>it</u> has been extinct since
      A   **B**
the <u>Ice Age</u>. <u>No error</u>
     C   **D**

6. The brochure says the <u>museum</u> closes at 8:00 <u>P.M. the</u> doors are locked
                  A   **B**
at <u>8 05</u>. <u>No error</u>
   C   **D**

7. The usher at the concert told Eric and <u>us</u> that <u>"There</u> might be a few seats
A **B**
near the <u>stage."</u> <u>No error</u>
C **D**

8. African elephants are larger and <u>more dangerous</u> than <u>asian</u> elephants.
A **B**
African elephants also <u>have</u> larger ears. <u>No error</u>
C **D**

9. Charles Dickens named one of the <u>worst</u> villains in his stories after his best
A
<u>friend</u>, Bob <u>Fagin. Fortunately</u>, Fagin had a sense of humor. <u>No error</u>
B **C** **D**

10. The <u>colorado river</u> is important to millions of <u>Americans. It</u> is the major
A **B**
source of water for all the states in the <u>Southwest</u>. <u>No error</u>
C **D**

11. Who <u>shouted, "Give</u> me <u>Liberty</u> or give me <u>death"?</u> <u>No error</u>
A **B** **C** **D**

12. On every U.S. coin <u>there</u> <u>is</u> the motto "In <u>god</u> we trust." <u>No error</u>
A **B** **C** **D**

13. One of my favorite short stories by <u>Ray Bradbury</u> <u>is</u>
A **B**
<u>"All summer in a Day."</u> <u>No error</u>
C **D**

14. Some bristlecone pine trees in <u>California</u> are four thousand years old.
A
<u>They're</u> believed to be the <u>oldest</u> living things in the world. <u>No error</u>
B **C** **D**

15. The planet Jupiter is so large that all the other <u>planet's</u> in our solar system
A
could be placed inside it if it were hollow. However, there wouldn't be
<u>no room</u> for all of the <u>planets'</u> moons. <u>No error</u>
B **C** **D**

Skills

Directions   One or more of the underlined sections in the following sentences may contain an error in grammar, punctuation, spelling, or capitalization. Write the letter of each incorrect section. Then rewrite the section correctly. If there is no error in an item, write *D*.

> **Example**   The statue of Crazy Horse in <u>south dakota</u> will be the largest
>   **A**
>
> sculpture in the world when it is <u>completed</u>. It is being carved out of a
>   **B**
>
> <u>mountain</u>. <u>No error</u>
>   **C**   **D**
>
> **Answer**   A—South Dakota

1. Christopher <u>Columbus's</u> younger brother Bartholomew helped the famous
                A
navigator plan his <u>voyages. Christopher</u> and <u>him</u> were very close. <u>No error</u>
                    B   **C**   **D**

2. Was the letter <u>addressed</u> to <u>Paris France</u> or Paris, <u>Ontario.</u> <u>No error</u>
              A   **B**   **C**   **D**

3. The instructions for operating this VCR <u>is</u> very <u>confusing can</u> you help
                               A   **B**
me <u>please?</u> <u>No error</u>
   C   **D**

4. At first, Samuel B. <u>Morse, the</u> inventor of the <u>telegraph was</u> <u>better</u> known
                   A   **B**   **C**
as a painter than as an inventor. <u>No error</u>
                           D

5. Was it Nathan Hale who <u>said,</u> "I regret that <u>I</u> have but one life to give
                    A   **B**
for my <u>country?"</u> <u>No error</u>
      C   **D**

6. My <u>Uncle</u> has two pet ferrets. One of them <u>like</u> to eat French fried
      A   **B**
<u>potatoes.</u> <u>No error</u>
  C   **D**

7. Somehow each of the ewes in that large flock of <u>sheep</u> <u>know</u> how to find
                                                                    A   **B**
<u>their</u> lambs. <u>No error</u>
  C   **D**

8. Mount Kenya <u>sets</u> right along the Equator, but because of <u>its</u> <u>height</u>—over
                    A   **B** **C**
17,000 feet—the top is covered with snow. <u>No error</u>
                                              D

9. Rural households in ancient <u>Greece</u> often kept snakes <u>indoors. To</u> control
                                    A   **B**
rats and <u>mouses</u>. <u>No error</u>
          C   **D**

10. Most metals conduct electricity <u>good</u>. On the other hand, <u>substances</u>
                                         A   **B**
made of nonmetal conduct electricity <u>poor</u>. <u>No error</u>
                                       C   **D**

11. Parts of Scotland <u>lay</u> as far <u>North</u> in latitude as southern Alaska, but warm
                           A   **B**
air from the <u>Gulf Stream</u> makes Scotland's climate quite mild. <u>No error</u>
              C   **D**

12. Stalactites <u>hung</u> all around <u>us</u>, and a bat flew at Tom and <u>I</u>. <u>No error</u>
                    A   **B**   **C** **D**

13. The triathlon participants had <u>swum</u> a <u>mile, but</u> they still had the
                                        A   **B**
<u>bycycling</u> and running events ahead of them. <u>No error</u>
  C   **D**

14. On <u>December 7, 1941,</u> millions of Americans turned on <u>their</u> <u>radios</u> and
           A   **B**   **C**
heard about the Japanese attack on Pearl Harbor. <u>No error</u>
                                                    D

15. Stevland Morris is a great musician. However, most people <u>wouldn't</u>
                                                                   A
recognize that <u>name. They</u> know <u>him</u> as Stevie Wonder. <u>No error</u>
                B   **C**   **D**

Colorful ceremonial masks, such as the ones shown here from (counter-clockwise from top) Indonesia, Nepal, and Hong Kong, are used in religious festivals to portray characters from mythology and legend.

ACCESS GUIDE

TECHNIQUES FOR PEER RESPONSE

Sharing your writing with others is a good way to get encouragement and new ideas. It is also a way to find out what things your readers like in your writing and what ideas may not be clear. Here are some techniques to help you get the responses you need to improve your writing.

Sharing

How to Use   Share your writing with your peer readers by asking them to read or listen to it. Hearing how your words sound may help you and your peer readers discover new ideas or places where more details are needed.

At this stage your peer readers serve as your friendly audience. They should not evaluate your writing.

When to Use   You may use this technique when you are exploring ideas. You may also use it to celebrate a finished piece of writing.

Pointing

How to Use   Ask your readers to tell you about the things they like best in your writing. Ask them to be specific and to avoid simply saying, "I like it."

Have readers point out the words and phrases that create an image or express an idea clearly.

When to Use   Use this technique when you want to find out what ideas are getting through to your readers. Also use it when you want encouragement and support for your writing.

Summarizing

How to Use   Ask readers to tell you the main idea in your writing. If readers stray from the main idea and start to talk about specific parts that they like or that confuse them, you might say, "For now, I want to know if I got my idea across to you."

Remind readers that at this stage you are not asking for an evaluation of your writing.

When to Use   Use this technique when you want to know if your main idea or goals are getting through to readers.

Telling

How to Use   Ask readers to tell you how they felt as they read your words. For example, did they feel sad or happy at any parts of your story? Did they get the characters mixed up? Did anything make them laugh?

As readers describe their feelings, ask them to point out the parts of the story that caused their reactions.

When to Use   Use this technique when you want to find out which words and phrases are creating the effect you want and which ones are confusing your readers.

Identifying

How to Use   Ask for feedback about things the readers don't understand, things they want to know more about, and questions that came to mind as they read.

Ask specific questions, such as these: What part was most interesting to you? Is there anything you'd like to know more about? Was anything confusing? How can I improve the organization? What are your views on this topic?

When to Use   Use this technique to identify strengths and weaknesses in your writing.

OUTLINING

An outline helps you plan your writing and take notes. In an outline main ideas are listed as headings. Details are shown as subpoints. A **sentence outline** uses complete sentences for the main ideas and details. A **topic outline** uses words or phrases, as in this model.

Sign Language

Thesis Statement: Sign language is a system of gestures and hand symbols developed to help hearing-impaired people communicate.

  I. Types of sign language (Main idea)
    A. American Sign Language (Subpoint for I)
      1. Based on ideas, not words (Detail for A)
      2. Expresses ideas in gestures
    B. American Manual Alphabet
      1. Based on the alphabet (Detail for B)
      2. Uses finger symbols for letters
      3. Combines finger symbols with gestures
 II. Uses of sign language
    A. By deaf people (Subpoint for II)
    B. By hearing-impaired people
    C. By non-hearing-impaired people

Correct Outline Form

1. Write the title at the top of the outline.
2. Arrange main ideas and details as shown in the model.
3. Indent each division of the outline.
4. Break down each heading into at least two details. For example, if there is a 1 under A, there must be a 2.
5. In a topic outline, use the same form for items of the same rank. If A is a noun, then B and C should be nouns.
6. Begin each item with a capital letter. Do not use end punctuation in a topic outline.

Business Letter

Heading 3148 Main Street
Downers Grove, IL 60516
September 22, 19—

American Assn. of Zoological Inside Address
Parks and Aquariums
4550 Montgomery Avenue
Suite 940N
Bethesda, MD 20814

Dear Sir or Madam: Salutation

Body I would like to learn about zoos that allow people to pay a small amount of money to "adopt" an animal. These zoos then use the money to buy food, improve habitats, and help support special programs for endangered animals. I understand that your association can send me information about adopt-an-animal programs.

Please send me information about programs in Illinois and Ohio. If you know of zoos that have unusual animals, such as cinnamon tarantulas, laughing thrushes, or pygmy hippos, please send me that information also.

Thank you for your help.

Sincerely, Closing

Laurie Douvris Signature
Laurie Douvris

Heading The heading contains your street address; your town or city, state, and ZIP code; and the date of the letter.

Inside Address Include the name of an individual if you know it and the name and address of the organization.

Salutation Begin the salutation two lines below the inside address and end with a colon. If you are writing to a specific person, include that person's name. If you do not know who will receive your letter, use a general greeting.

Body This section should be brief, courteous, and clear. State the purpose of your letter and indicate any items that you are requesting or have enclosed.

Closing This appears two lines below the body and is always formal. "Sincerely" and "Yours truly" are examples.

Signature Skip four spaces below the closing, print or type your name, and write your signature in the space.

Like hitting a fastball or mastering the backstroke, becoming a spelling whiz takes planning and practice. By following these tips and basic rules, you can become a better speller.

Spelling Tips

1. **Identify your own spelling demons.** Make a list of the words you have misspelled in your writing.

2. **Pronounce words carefully.** Sometimes people misspell words because they say them incorrectly. For example, if you say the word *schedule* correctly, you will not misspell it *s-c-h-e-d-u-e-l.*

3. **Make a habit of seeing the letters in a word.** Pay attention to every letter of a new or difficult word. For example, when you come upon a word like *library,* look at each letter to fix the spelling in your mind.

4. **Invent memory devices for problem words.** Here are some examples:

   princi**pal** (pal)   The princi**pal** is my **pal**.
   tra**ge**dy (age)   Every **age** has its tra**ge**dy.
   emba**rrass** (rr, ss)   I turned **r**eally **r**ed and felt **s**o **s**illy.

5. **Proofread what you write.** Reread your work word for word so that you don't miss incorrectly spelled words.

Steps for Mastering Difficult Words

1. Look at the word and say it one syllable at a time.
2. Look at the letters and say each one.
3. Picture the word in your mind as you write it.
4. Check to see that you have spelled the word correctly. If you misspelled the word, notice what the mistake was and repeat steps 1–3.

Words Ending in a Silent *e*

Before adding a suffix beginning with a vowel to a word ending in a silent *e*, drop the *e* (with some exceptions).

love + -able = lovable   improve + -ing = improving

Exceptions: dye + -ing = dyeing   mile + -age = mileage

When adding a suffix beginning with a consonant to a word ending in a silent *e*, keep the *e* (with some exceptions).

hate + -ful = hateful   excite + -ment = excitement

Exceptions: true + -ly = truly   argue + -ment = argument

Words Ending in *y*

When adding a suffix to a word that ends in a *y* preceded by a consonant, change the *y* to *i*.

noisy + -ly = noisily   nutty + -est = nuttiest

However, when adding *-ing,* do not change the *y.*

cry + -ing = crying   deny + -ing = denying

When a suffix is added to a word that ends in a *y* preceded by a vowel, the *y* usually does not change.

play + -ing = playing   enjoy + -ment = enjoyment

Words Ending in a Consonant

If a one-syllable word ends in one consonant preceded by one vowel, double the final consonant before adding a suffix beginning with a vowel, such as *-ing* or *-ed.* (Such a word is sometimes called a 1 + 1 + 1 word.)

sit + -ing = sitting   red + -est = reddest

The rule does not apply to words of one syllable that end in a consonant preceded by two vowels.

meet + -ing = meeting   dream + -er = dreamer

For a word of more than one syllable, double the final consonant (1) when the word ends in one consonant preceded by one vowel and (2) when the word is accented on the last syllable.

ad•mit′   be•gin′   pre•fer′

In these examples, note that after the suffix is added, the accent remains on the same syllable.

ad•mit′ + -ed = ad•mit′ ted
be•gin′ + -ing = be•gin′ ning

In this example, the accent does not remain on the same syllable; thus, the final consonant is not doubled.

pre•fer′ + -able = pref′ er•a•ble

Prefixes and Suffixes

When adding a prefix to a word, do not change the spelling of the base word.

un- + known = unknown   mis + spell = misspell

When adding -ly to a word ending in l, keep both l's. When adding -ness to a word ending in n, keep both n's.

practical + -ly = practically   mean + -ness = meanness

Special Spelling Problems

One English word ends in -sede: supersede. Three words end in -ceed: exceed, proceed, and succeed. All other words ending in the sound seed are spelled with -cede.

concede   precede   recede   secede

When choosing between ie and ei, if the sound is long e (ē), you should usually spell the word with ie except after c.

i before e   belief   shield   yield   niece   field
except after c   conceit   receive   ceiling deceive receipt

Exceptions: either   neither   weird   leisure   seize

The following words are commonly misused or misspelled. Some of these words are **homonyms**, or words that have similar sounds but are spelled differently and have different meanings. Study this section to make sure you are using words correctly in your writing.

accept, except   *Accept* means "to agree to" or "to receive willingly." *Except* usually means "not including."

> My brother will *accept* the job at the grocery store.
> Luis likes every flavor of yogurt *except* lemon.

a lot   *A lot* is informal. Do not use it in formal writing. *Alot* is incorrect.

borrow, lend   *Borrow* means "to receive on loan." *Lend* means "to give temporarily."

> I *borrowed* my sister's watch.
> Please *lend* me your eraser.

capital, capitol, the Capitol   *Capital* means "very serious" or "very important." It also means "seat of government." A *capitol* is a building in which a state legislature meets. The *Capitol* is the building in Washington, D.C., in which the U.S. Congress meets.

> The *capital* of Illinois is the city of Springfield.
> The Illinois *capitol* is a stately building in Springfield.
> The senator arrived at the *Capitol* in time to vote.

desert, dessert   *Des'ert* means "a dry, sandy, barren region." *De sert'* means "to abandon." *Des sert'* is a sweet food, such as pie.

> Tall cactus plants grow in the *desert*.
> The crane would not *desert* his injured mate.
> Jake loves ice cream for *dessert*.

good, well   *Good* is always an adjective. *Well* is usually an adverb that modifies an action verb. *Well* can also be an adjective meaning "in good health."

> That dress looks *good* on you.
> Anne performed her skating routine *well*.
> Nikki didn't feel *well* today.

hear, here   *Hear* means "to listen to." *Here* means "in this place."

> Every time I *hear* this song, I feel happy.
> The mayor's family has lived *here* for generations.

its, it's   *Its* is a possessive pronoun. *It's* is a contraction of *it is* or *it has*.

> The boat lost *its* sail during the storm.
> *It's* nearly midnight.

lay, lie   *Lay* is a verb that means "to place." It takes a direct object. *Lie* is a verb that means "to recline" or "to be in a certain place." *Lie* never takes a direct object.

> Don't *lay* your coat on the couch.
> The terrier likes to *lie* under the swing.
> The island *lies* in the path of the hurricane.

lead, led   *Lead* can be a noun that means "a heavy metal" or a verb that means "to show the way." *Led* is the past tense form of the verb.

> These pellets contain *lead*.
> The lieutenant *leads* her troops in the parade.
> He *led* a group of explorers out of the jungle.

learn, teach   *Learn* means "to gain knowledge." *Teach* means "to instruct."

> In social studies we are *learning* about frontier life.
> He is *teaching* us to use a computer.

like, as, as if   *Like* is a preposition. Use *as* or *as if* to introduce a clause.

He ran the pass pattern *as* he should.

loose, lose   *Loose* means "free" or "not fastened." *Lose* means "to mislay or suffer the loss of."

The rider kept the horse's reins *loose.*
If you *lose* your book, tell the librarian right away.

of   Use *have,* not *of,* in phrases such as *could have, should have,* and *must have.*

We should *have* invited her to our party.

peace, piece   *Peace* means "calm" or "quiet." *Piece* means "a section or part."

After two years of war came *peace.*
The statue was carved from a *piece* of jade.

principal, principle   *Principal* means "of chief or central importance" or "the head of a school." *Principle* means "basic truth," "standard," or "rule of behavior."

The *principal* export of Brazil is coffee.
The *principal* of our school organized a safety council.
One *principle* of science is that all matter occupies space.

quiet, quite   *Quiet* means "free from noise or disturbance." *Quite* means "truly" or "almost completely."

The library is *quiet* in the afternoon.
The aquarium tank is *quite* full.

raise, rise   *Raise* means "to lift" or "to cause to go up." It takes a direct object. *Rise* means "to go upward." It does not take a direct object.

Can you *raise* the sail by yourself?
The jury will *rise* when the judge enters the courtroom.

set, sit *Set* means "to place." It takes a direct object. *Sit* means "to occupy a seat or a place." It does not take a direct object.

> I *set* the bag of groceries inside the door.
> *Sit* still while we take your picture.

their, there, they're *Their* means "belonging to them." *There* means "in that place." *They're* is a contraction of *they are.*

> Our neighbors sold *their* house and moved to a farm.
> Please play with the squirt guns over *there.*
> My sisters don't swim, but *they're* eager to learn.

to, too, two *To* means "toward" or "in the direction of." *Too* means "also" or "very." *Two* is the number 2.

> The surgeon dashed *to* the emergency room.
> It was *too* hot to run a race.
> Only *two* of the six lifeboats reached shore.

weather, whether *Weather* refers to conditions such as temperature or cloudiness. *Whether* expresses a choice.

> The *weather* is perfect for a picnic.
> *Whether* we drive or take the train, we will arrive late.

whose, who's *Whose* is the possessive form of *who. Who's* is a contraction of *who is* or *who has.*

> *Whose* wallet is lying under the chair?
> *Who's* been chosen the student of the month?

your, you're *Your* is the possessive form of *you. You're* is a contraction of *you are.*

> Please bring *your* cameras to the assembly.
> *You're* doing much better this semester than last.

A sentence diagram is a drawing that shows how the parts of a sentence are related. Use the following models as guides.

Subjects and Verbs

To diagram a subject and a verb, first draw a horizontal line. On this line write the subject and the verb. Then draw a vertical line between them. Capitalize words capitalized in the sentence. Do not use punctuation marks except in abbreviations.

Cars collided.

| Cars | collided |

Questions, Exclamations, and Commands

In a sentence that asks a question, the subject often comes after the verb. When you diagram a question, put the subject before the verb.

Do dolphins communicate?

| dolphins | Do communicate |

In a command or an exclamation, the subject is usually understood to be you. In diagraming, put the understood subject you before the verb and enclose it in parentheses.

Look.

| (you) | Look |

Go!

| (you) | Go |

Compound Subjects and Verbs

To diagram a compound subject, split the subject line. Then write the conjunction on a dotted line between the subjects. Diagram compound verbs similarly.

Rose and Allan studied. *(Compound subject)*

Raul fields and throws. *(Compound verb)*

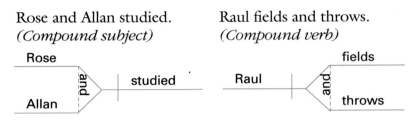

Direct Objects

Write a direct object after the verb. Then draw a short vertical line between the verb and the direct object.

Jody writes stories.

Predicate Words

Write a predicate word—noun, pronoun, or adjective—after the verb. Between the verb and the predicate word, draw a line slanting toward the subject.

Frogs feel slippery.

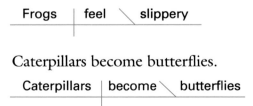

Caterpillars become butterflies.

Adjectives

Write an adjective on a slanted line below the word it modifies. Treat possessive nouns and pronouns as adjectives.

The explorers searched a secret cave.

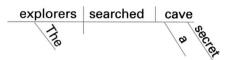

Adverbs

Write an adverb on a slanted line below the word it modifies.

Cats pounce silently.

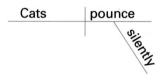

Prepositional Phrases

A prepositional phrase acts as an adjective or an adverb, so diagram it in a similar way. Draw an angled line below the word modified. Write the preposition on the slanted part and its object on the horizontal part. Put any modifiers on slanted lines below the object.

Fish darted through a coral tunnel.

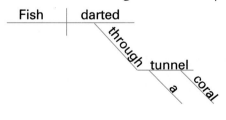

ADJECTIVE   a word that modifies a noun or pronoun: *one* day.

ADVERB   a word that modifies a verb, an adjective, or another adverb; in "She smiles often," *often* is an adverb modifying the verb *smiles.*

AUDIENCE   your readers or listeners.

BRAINSTORMING   a way of finding ideas that involves listing them without stopping to judge them.

CHRONOLOGICAL   arranged in order of occurrence.

CLICHÉ   an overused expression, such as "sly as a fox."

CLUSTER   a kind of map made up of circled groupings of related details.

COHERENCE   in paragraphs, logical flow from one sentence to the next; in compositions, logical ties between paragraphs.

CONJUNCTION   a word or pair of words that connects other words or groups of words: Glenna *and* Gary won.

DIALECT   a form of a language that has a distinctive pronunciation, vocabulary, and word order.

DIALOGUE   spoken conversation; the conversation in novels, stories, plays, poems, and essays.

ELABORATION   the support or development of a main idea with details, incidents, examples, or quotations.

FIGURATIVE LANGUAGE   the imaginative and poetic use of words; writing that contains such figures of speech as similes, metaphors, and personification.

FREEWRITING   a way of exploring ideas, thoughts, or feelings by writing down everything that comes to mind within a specific length of time.

GLEANING   a way of finding ideas for writing by jotting down things you see, hear, read, do, think, and feel as they catch your attention.

GRAPHIC DEVICE   a visual presentation of details; graphic devices include charts, graphs, outlines, clusters, and idea trees.

IDEA TREE   a graphic device in which main ideas are written on "branches" and details related to them are noted on "twigs."

INTERJECTION   a word or phrase used to express strong feeling.

JOURNAL   a personal notebook in which you can freewrite, collect ideas, and record thoughts, feelings, and experiences.

LEARNING LOG   a kind of journal in which you record and reflect on what you have learned and note problems and questions to which you want to find answers.

METAPHOR   a figure of speech in which a comparison is made without the word *like* or *as;* "life is a journey" is a metaphor.

NONSEXIST LANGUAGE   language that includes both men and women when referring to a role or group made up of people of both sexes; "A coach shares his or her skills and experience" and "Coaches share their skills and experience" are two nonsexist ways of expressing the same idea.

NOUN   a word that names a person, a place, a thing, or an idea.

PARAGRAPH   a group of related sentences that develop a single main idea or accomplish a single purpose.

PEER RESPONSE   suggestions and comments on a piece of writing, provided by peers, or classmates.

PERSONIFICATION   a figure of speech in which human qualities are given to nonhuman things.

PORTFOLIO   a container (usually a folder) for notes on work in progress, drafts and revisions, finished pieces, and peer responses.

PREPOSITION a word that relates its object to some other word in the sentence; in "Alec waited near the fence," *near* is a preposition.

PRONOUN a word that is used to take the place of a noun or another pronoun; in "He will help us," *he* and *us* are pronouns.

RUN-ON SENTENCE two or more sentences incorrectly written as one.

SENSORY DETAILS words that show the way something looks, sounds, smells, tastes, or feels.

SENTENCE FRAGMENT a group of words that does not express a complete idea.

SIMILE a figure of speech in which the word *like* or *as* is used to make a comparison; "hands like ice" is a simile.

SPATIAL ORDER organization in which details are arranged in the order they appear in space, such as from left to right, front to back, top to bottom, or inside to outside.

TOPIC SENTENCE a sentence that states the main idea of a paragraph.

TRANSITION a connecting word or phrase that clarifies relationships between details, sentences, or paragraphs.

UNITY in a paragraph, the working together of all the sentences to support the same main idea; in a composition, the working together of all the paragraphs to support the overall goal.

VERB a word that expresses an action, a condition, or a state of being; in "The clown painted his face," *painted* is a verb.

WRITING VOICE the personality of the writer as it comes across through word choice and sentence structure.

Reading and Writing Across the Curriculum

You probably already know and use many strategies for reading and studying, such as previewing your reading, reading actively, looking for main ideas and key terms, and reviewing your notes. (See Writing Handbooks 25 and 26, pages 294–301, if you wish to review these strategies.)

As you may recall, one especially useful strategy is the KWL method, which gives you a three-question approach:

K: What do I already **know** about the topic?
W: What do I **want** to find out about it?
L: What did I **learn** about the topic?

By answering these questions in a learning log, you can improve your recall and understanding of material you read.

In addition to these general strategies, you may find it helpful to try the following special tips and strategies for reading and writing about social studies, math, and science.

SOCIAL STUDIES

- When reading a chapter or studying for a test, create a time line to help you understand the chronological order of events.
- Ask "what-if" questions to explore the impact of historical events. For example, if Lincoln had not been assassinated, how might he have helped the nation recover from the Civil War?
- Use a Venn diagram to show the commonalities and differences between people, places, or events.
- Study the charts, photos, graphics, and maps found in a lesson. As you examine maps, consider the influence of geography upon historical events, such as the migration of a people or the conflicts between two countries.
- Think about connections between the events you are studying and other situations you have studied or observed. What events taking place today remind you of those you are reading about?

MATH

- Preview any exercises or activities at the end of a lesson.
- Think through any sample problems as you read. If you don't understand how the solution was reached, retrace the steps that led to the solution.
- Whenever possible, use manipulatives to help visualize relationships or problems.
- Discuss concepts and problem-solving tips in pairs or groups.
- Think about ways to apply math skills to real-life situations, for example, to calculate the quantity and cost of materials for building a birdhouse.
- Compile a portfolio to assess your mathematical progress.
- Explore ways to use technology as a tool for solving problems. For example, try using a graphing calculator to visualize mathematical relationships or spreadsheets to organize data.

SCIENCE

- Before reading a chapter, flip through the assigned pages to get an overview of the lesson.
- As you read, study pie charts, bar and line graphs, and data tables carefully. Draw diagrams, graphs, and flow charts to organize information and to help you understand processes not illustrated.
- Ask "what-if" questions to explore relationships between scientific events. For example, what would happen to the forest ecosystem if there were no owls or hawks to prey on rabbits?
- If your reading reminds you of something you have observed or read about, jot down similarities and differences.
- Scan any experiments in your text before performing the procedures, noting the purpose and the materials needed. When writing lab reports, identify the purpose of an experiment, list the materials and equipment required, state the problem, describe how you investigated it, and explain your conclusion.
- Get into the habit of thinking scientifically about your experiences, such as why a brown paper bag holding potato chips becomes discolored and soggy over time.

Working in Groups

TIP

The writing skills that you learned as you used this book will help you in all your classes. Use the Springboards on pages 44, 67, 89, 110, 137, 160, and 185 to get ideas for the kind of writing you do in various subject areas. See pages 326–333 for special help in the kind of writing you do on tests.

According to an old saying, "Two heads are better than one." Working in groups gives you an opportunity to brainstorm, exchange ideas, and share responsibilities. Group members usually have two key goals: (1) getting the task done and (2) helping the group to function effectively.

GETTING THE TASK DONE

Try making a chart that specifies each member's task. One group used the following chart to plan a videotape of a scene from a story.

TASK	PERSONS
Script writing	DeVona and Andrew
Costumes	Allen and Melissa
Lighting	Carmen
Camera operating	José
Sound effects	Jack and Paul
Acting	DeVona, Andrew, Allen, & Melissa

HELPING THE GROUP

Besides taking responsibility for a specific task, each group member should choose one of the following roles:

- Facilitator—Makes sure everyone stays "on task"
- Liaison—Takes questions to the teacher or other mentor and reports the answers back to the group
- Materials Manager—Locates the supplies for a project or assigns members to bring them from home
- Scribe—Takes notes during meetings and keeps a record of the group's comments and suggestions
- Presenter—Presents the results of the group's work to the class

Problem Solving

Whether working in groups or alone, you need to call upon many different skills to solve problems. Try some of the following techniques to solve problems that you encounter in your classes, with your friends, or at home.

- **Figure out what the problem is.** Sometimes that's more difficult than you may think! Describe or define the problem as clearly as you can. State your definition orally or in writing.

- **Think carefully about the problem.** What's causing it? Who's being affected? Where does your information about the problem come from?

- **Specify your goals.** Think about what you'd like your solution to accomplish. Consider how your solution can avoid causing new problems. Be aware that solving the problem may require time, money, changes in behavior, and real effort.

- **Identify several possible solutions.** Has anyone tried these solutions already? What happened? Will a different solution work?

- **Choose the best solution.** Will it meet your goals? If not, how might you improve it to get better results?

- **Evaluate the solution.** Decide how to test the solution. Agree on a time frame and on the standards you'll use to determine whether or not the solution is working.

- **Solve the problem!** Put your solution into practice. Is it solving part of the problem? Is it creating new problems? Do you need to try a different approach?

Using Electronic Resources

ACCESS GUIDE

TECHNOLOGY

Electronic resources provide you with a convenient and efficient way to gather information.

LIBRARY COMPUTER SERVICES

Many libraries offer computerized catalogs and a variety of other electronic resources.

Computerized Catalogs

As you know, you can search for a book in a library by typing the title, author, or subject into a computer terminal. Most libraries also have software programs that allow you to search by typing in "keywords," that is, any word or combination of words found in the title, the subject, or the author's or publisher's name. For example, if you want to find a particular book but know only the author's first or last name and one or more words in the title, you can type in these words in the keywords location bar. The computer screen will then display a list of titles, one of which may be the title you are looking for. By clicking on this title, you can call up complete information about the book, including whether or not it is on the shelf or checked out. When a particular book is not available at your library, you can ask a librarian to search the catalogs of other libraries to try to locate another copy.

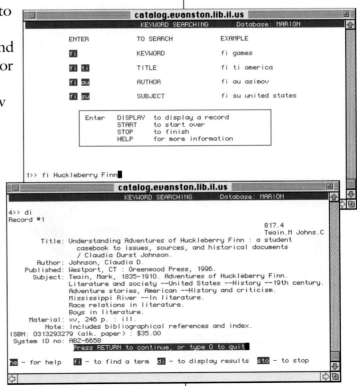

Other Electronic Resources

In addition to computerized catalogs, many libraries offer a variety of electronic indexes. For example, a newspaper index allows you to search the files of a particular newspaper, such as the *Chicago Tribune*, for recent articles on a topic of your choice. Another valuable electronic research tool is *InfoTrac*, which has three separate listings: a magazine index, a health reference index, and a business file. To use the magazine index, you type in the subject you are interested in. The screen then displays a list of articles from several magazines that deal with that subject, with the most recent articles listed first. For each article, the index provides either an abstract (a kind of summary) or an extended citation that tells you what the article is about. You can print this abstract or extended citation directly from the screen. Another useful index, called *SIRS*, lists magazine or newspaper articles that concern social topics, such as homelessness or the environment. Ask your librarian for assistance in using these indexes.

CD-ROM

A CD-ROM (compact disc–read-only memory) stores data that may include text, sound, photographs, and video. Almost any kind of information can be found on CD-ROMs, including

- encyclopedias, almanacs, and indexes
- other reference books on a variety of subjects
- news reports from newspapers, magazines, television, or radio
- museum art collections
- back issues of magazines
- literature collections

You can use CD-ROMS at the library or purchase them for home use.

ON-LINE RESOURCES

When you use your computer to communicate with another computer or with another computer user, you are working "on-line." On-line resources include commercial information services and resources available on the Internet.

Commercial Information Services

Various services to which computer users can subscribe offer access to the following:

- up-to-date news, weather, and sports reports
- encyclopedias, magazines, newspapers, dictionaries, almanacs, and databases (collections of information)
- electronic mail (e-mail) to and from other users
- forums, or ongoing electronic conversations among users interested in particular topics
- the Internet

COMPUSERVE

Internet

The Internet is a vast network of computers. The Internet provides computer users with the power to exchange information with millions of other computer users throughout the world. News services, libraries, universities, researchers, organizations, government agencies, schools, and individuals like you can use the Internet to communicate with people worldwide.

Finding and Exploring Sites One of the most popular resources on the Internet is the World Wide Web. The Web connects pages of text and graphics stored on computers throughout the world. If you have the necessary software, you can explore the Web, stopping to chat with others about your hobbies or even to send a message to the President of the United States. You can visit an exhibit of dinosaur fossils, take a virtual tour of the Grand Canyon, read a book, watch a video, listen to music or a speech. The possibilities for exploration are mind-boggling.

Each Web site has a specific location—somewhat like a postal address—known as its URL, short for Universal Resource Locator. For example, the URL address shown below belongs to the White House home page:

When you type in this URL address in the location field of your browser, your computer displays the White House home page on your computer screen.

Open Location

Open Location: http://www.whitehouse.gov

Cancel   Open

> ## What You'll Need
>
> - To access on-line resources, you can use a computer with a modem linked to a telephone line or a television set with an Internet-ready box. Your school computer lab or resource center may be linked to the Internet or to a commercial information service.
>
> - To use CD-ROMs, you need a computer system with a CD-ROM drive.

Following Links In a Web page, such as the White House home page shown below, you find icons, pictures, or underlined and colored words and phrases. These are called links. By clicking on a link, you immediately go to another Web page that contains related information. These links provide options, allowing you to explore subjects in more detail if you like and to visit Web pages in the order you choose.

Using a Search Engine If you want to find Web sites of interest to you, try using a search engine. A search engine serves as a navigational tool, or a means of finding other sites. A search engine is somewhat like an electronic card catalog. You search for sites by typing in a topic or key words.

link

One widely used search engine called *Yahoo* offers an excellent menu of topic headings. You can click on one of the links to call up a more specialized menu, and continue clicking on links until you identify sites you want to explore. For example, if you want to find sites that provide information about Mars, you can click successively on the links *Science, Astronomy, Solar System, Planets,* and *Mars.* Each time you click on a link, Yahoo scans thousands of databases, displaying the results on your computer screen.

Finding Newsgroups On the Internet you can visit thousands of "newsgroups." These serve as discussion groups, each centered on a common area of interest. For example, if you like professional basketball, you can visit a newsgroup that contains articles about it as well as postings from other fans throughout the world. You might even wish to add a posting of your own and chat electronically with others. Since computer users worldwide have access to newsgroups, it's a good idea to protect your privacy if you post something. Never provide personal information such as your full name, home address, or phone number.

link

Exploring Other Areas of the Internet Besides exploring Web sites, you can access other kinds of documents on the Internet by using such tools as Gopher and FTP (File Transfer Protocol).

Gopher and FTP, which were available before the World Wide Web was created, contain only pages of text with no graphics and no links to other pages. Gopher pages, which are run by colleges and universities, provide menus to conduct your searches. FTP servers store files that you can access, view, and copy, such as transcripts of White House speeches. Some computers have access only to Gopher or to FTP. Even if your computer is connected to the Web, you might want to use these tools because they may help you find information not currently available on the Web.

Using Information from the Internet

As you explore the Internet, you can print files or **download** them, that is, make an electronic copy to save on a computer. Usually, the procedure is similar to the one you use to save other files.

You must evaluate information that you find on the Internet with great care. Since anyone with a computer hooked up to the Internet can make information available to other computer users, the quality of the information varies greatly. Some information is excellent; other information may be misleading, out of context, or even inaccurate. Consider the source of the information carefully, asking yourself whether or not it is likely to be reliable. For example, national research centers such as the Library of Congress and the Smithsonian Institution have reputations for excellence. Home pages created by individuals probably are less reliable. Of course, it is a good practice to check and then double check all information gathered from electronic sources.

As when working with information from printed sources, avoid plagiarism, or using someone else's words or ideas as your own. Instead of copying information directly from your sources, get into the habit of paraphrasing ideas—that is, stating them in your own words. Then record the source of the information and the date you accessed it.

TECHNOLOGY
—— TIP ——

As you explore the Web, you can keep track of sites you have visited and may wish to revisit later. The browser that gives you access to the Internet probably contains a feature that lets you list visited sites for immediate access.

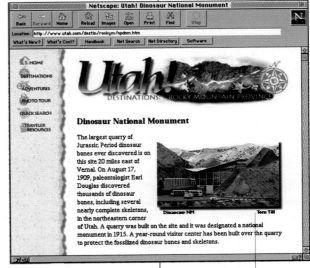

link

The Modern Language Association has not standardized the format for citing Internet sources. Generally, however, try to provide as much of the following information as you can.

- the author's name
- the title of the material, in quotation marks
- the title of the complete work (if applicable)
- the date of the material
- the database title (if applicable)
- the publication medium (online)
- the name of the computer service (if applicable)
- the date of access

Follow these models to credit electronic sources in a list of works cited:

- **Recording (LP, compact disc, audiocassette)**
  Guthrie, Woody. "Do-Re-Me." <u>Dust Bowl Ballads</u>. Rounder, 1988.

- **Television program**
  "A Desert Blooming." Writ. Marshall Riggan. <u>Living Wild</u>. Dir. Harry L. Gorden. Prod. Peter Argentine. PBS. WTTW, Chicago. 29 Apr. 1984.

- **CD-ROM**
  <u>Berlitz Think and Talk Spanish</u>. Vers. 1.0. CD-ROM. Knoxville: Hyperglot, 1992.

- **On-line information service**
  "The Great Depression." <u>Compton's Online Encyclopedia</u>. Online. America Online. 30 July 1992.

Publishing on the Internet

The Internet provides not only resources for gathering information but also opportunities for publishing your own work. If your school has a home page on the Web, you might consider publishing your writing or multimedia presentation on it. You might also choose to send completed pieces electronically to a Web site that showcases student writing, such as the McDougal Littell home page at the following address:

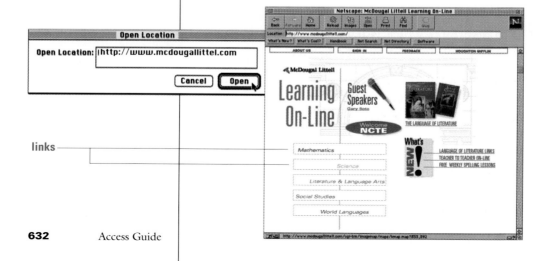

Writing with Computers

Word-processing programs allow you to draft, revise, edit, and format your writing and to produce neat, professional-looking papers. They also allow you to share your writing with others.

PREWRITING AND DRAFTING

A computer makes it easy to experiment with different ways of expressing and organizing your ideas. You can use it to keep an electronic journal or portfolio, to organize your notes in files, or to access templates for special writing formats. It also allows you to store multiple drafts of a paper and even to add graphics to clarify and enhance your message.

CREATING VISUALS

Charts, graphs, diagrams, and pictures often communicate information more effectively than words alone do. You can use visuals—graphs, tables, time lines, diagrams, and flow charts—to illustrate complex concepts and processes or to make a page look more interesting.

The visuals you choose will depend on the type of information you want to present to your readers. Take time to explore ways to display your data to determine which visual format best suits your purpose. Here are some options you might consider.

Tables, Graphs, and Charts Many word-processing programs have table and graphic functions you can access through the tool bar to help you create these kinds of graphics with ease.

- Use tables to arrange facts or numbers into rows and columns so that your readers can compare information more easily.
- Use a graph or chart to help communicate complex information in a clear visual image. Choose a different color or a different shade of gray for each part of a pie chart or graph.

COMPUTER TIP

Create a separate file to use as a writing notebook. Keep all of your story starters, ideas to research, and other writing ideas in this file.

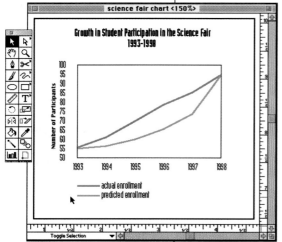

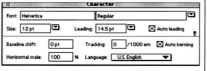

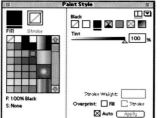

Other Visuals Art and design programs allow you to create visuals for your writing. Many programs include the following features:

- drawing tools that allow you to draw, color, and shade pictures like the one at the left
- clip art that you can copy into your document
- page borders that you can use to decorate title pages, invitations, or brochures
- text options that allow you to combine words with your illustrations
- tools for making geometric shapes in flow charts, time lines, and process diagrams

REVISING AND EDITING

Improving the quality of your writing becomes easier when you use a word-processing program to revise and edit.

Revising a Document

Most word-processing programs allow you to do more than just add and delete words in your draft. Writing electronically makes it easy to move text from one location in your document to another. You can try out different ideas and save them by making multiple drafts of the same work, saving each document with a new name. You can even merge parts of several documents to create a new document.

Peer Editing on a Computer

The writer and the reader can both benefit from the convenience of peer editing "on screen," or at the computer. Some programs, like Writing Coach, have a split-screen function that provides space for a peer reader or your teacher to comment on your writing. The reader might also type comments or suggestions in a different typeface or type style within your text.

If you use a computer, be sure to save your current draft and then copy it for each of your peer readers. Also, ask each reader who responds on-line to include his or her initials in the file name.

Peer Editing on a Printout

Some peer readers prefer to respond to a draft on paper rather than on the computer. If you type your document in a compact form, remember to respace it just before printing. It is common to double-space or triple-space your document and leave extra-wide margins to give peer readers room to note their reactions and suggestions. Provide a separate printout for each reader.

Editing a Document

Many word-processing programs have the following kinds of features to help you catch errors and polish your writing:

- The spell checker and grammar checker automatically find possible errors in your writing and suggest corrections. Evaluate each suggestion carefully to make sure it is appropriate before making changes in your text.
- The thesaurus suggests synonyms to improve your writing.
- The search-and-replace feature searches your document and corrects every occurrence of something you want to change.

TECHNOLOGY
—— TIP ——

Some word-processing programs or other software provide preset templates, or patterns, for writing outlines, memos, letters, or invitations. If you use one of these templates, you will not need to adjust the formatting.

FORMATTING AND PUBLISHING

Format refers to the layout and appearance of your writing on the page. You can use a computer to manipulate the type size, typeface, and position of your text to show the importance and organization of ideas. The screen at the right shows some of your options. Keep your format simple. Remember that your goal is to create an attractive document that is easy to read.

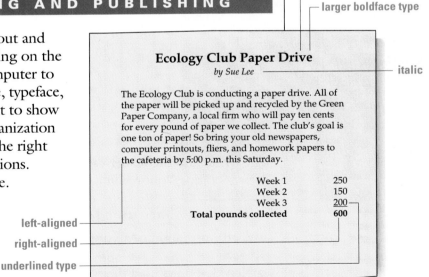

centered

larger boldface type

Ecology Club Paper Drive
by Sue Lee

italic

The Ecology Club is conducting a paper drive. All of the paper will be picked up and recycled by the Green Paper Company, a local firm who will pay ten cents for every pound of paper we collect. The club's goal is one ton of paper! So bring your old newspapers, computer printouts, fliers, and homework papers to the cafeteria by 5:00 p.m. this Saturday.

Week 1	250
Week 2	150
Week 3	200
Total pounds collected	**600**

left-aligned

right-aligned

underlined type

Creating a Multimedia Presentation

A multimedia presentation is a combination of text, sound, and visuals such as photographs, videos, and animation. You can combine these elements in an interactive presentation—one in which the user chooses a path to follow in exploring the information.

LEARNING ABOUT MULTIMEDIA

To start planning a multimedia presentation, you need to know the options available to you. Ask your school's technology adviser which of the following elements you could include.

Photos and Videos

Photographs and live-action video clips can make your subject come alive. Here are some examples of visuals that can be downloaded or scanned in:

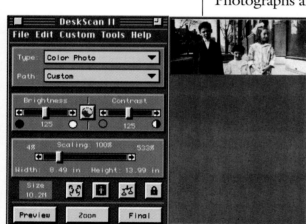

- video of news coverage of a historical event
- video of music, dance, or theater performances
- photos of an artist's work
- photos or video of a setting that is important to the text

Sound

Including sound in your presentation can help your audience understand information in your written text. For example, the user may be able to listen to and learn from

- the pronunciation of an unfamiliar or foreign word
- a speech
- a recorded news interview
- a musical selection
- a dramatic reading of a work of literature

Animation

Many graphics programs allow you to add animation, or movement, to the visuals in your presentation. Animated figures add to the user's enjoyment and understanding of what you present. You can use animation to illustrate

- the steps in a process
- changes in a chart, graph, or diagram
- ways your user can explore information in your presentation

PLANNING YOUR PRESENTATION

To plan a multimedia presentation, first choose your topic and decide what you want to include. For example, instead of writing a family history (see pages 180–184), Merrill might create a multimedia presentation about her grandfather's arrival in the United States. She could include the following items:

- introductory text describing her grandfather
- a videotaped interview with him
- a letter he wrote after his arrival in America
- a photo gallery with written captions
- a drawing of the family tree
- a poster ad from the early 1900s showing the kind of ship that carried immigrants from Europe to the United States

Next plan how you want your user to move through your presentation. You can choose one of the following ways to organize your presentation:

- step by step with only one path, or order, in which the user can see and hear the information.
- a branching path that allows users to make some choices about what they will see and hear, and in what order

If you choose the second way—an interactive presentation—you need to map out your presentation in a flow chart, or navigation map. This will help you plan the links among your screens so that your user can choose a path through your presentation. Each box in the navigation map on the following page represents a screen in Merrill's presentation.

TECHNOLOGY TIP

You can download many photos, sound clips, and video clips from Internet sources onto your computer. This process allows you to add elements to your multimedia presentation that would usually require complex editing equipment. There are also CD-ROMs with extensive collections of video and audio clips.

Writing TIP

If you want to copy materials, you usually need permission from the copyright owner. You do not need permission, however, if you are not making money from your presentation, if you use it only for educational purposes, and if you use only a small percentage of the original material.

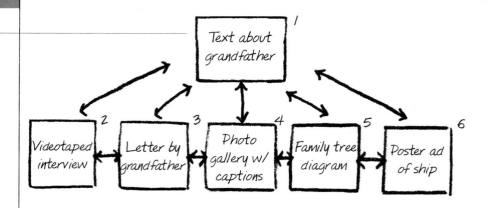

You could follow screens 1–6 in order, or you could keep returning to the contents, or menu, on the first screen. This would allow you to choose the order in which you follow the presentation.

CREATING YOUR PRESENTATION

As you create your multimedia presentation, use the navigation map as a guide.

When you have decided on the content of a screen, it is helpful to sketch the screen out. Remember to include in your sketch the links you will create to other screens in your presentation. Refer to the navigation map to see what links you need to add to each screen.

This example shows screen 1 from the navigation map above.

This screen includes a photograph that has been scanned in.

The user clicks on an underlined heading to move to a different screen.

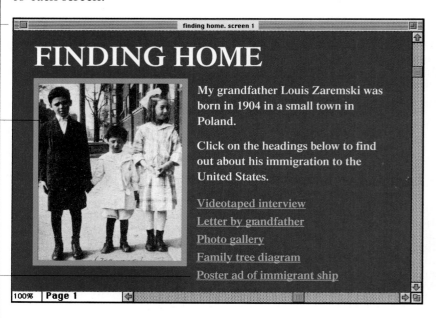

ACKNOWLEDGMENTS

Sources of Quoted Materials

28: G. P. Putnam's Sons: For an excerpt from *Homesick: My Own Story* by Jean Fritz. Copyright © 1982 by Jean Fritz. Reprinted by permission of G. P. Putnam's Sons. **30:** Crown Publishers, Inc.: For excerpts from *The Diary of Latoya Hunter* by Latoya Hunter. Copyright © 1992 by Latoya Hunter. Reprinted by permission from Crown Publishers, Inc. **40:** Macmillan Publishing Company: For "letter of February 11, 1945," from *Letters to Children* by C. S. Lewis, edited by Lyle W. Dorsett and Marjorie Lamp Mead. Copyright © 1985 by C. S. Lewis PTE Limited. Reprinted with the permission of Macmillan Publishing Company. **50:** Susan Bergholz Literary Services: For an excerpt from "The Monkey Garden," from *The House on Mango Street* by Sandra Cisneros. Copyright © 1989 by Sandra Cisneros. Published in the United States by Vintage Books, a division of Random House, Inc., New York and distributed in Canada by Random House of Canada Limited, Toronto. Originally published in somewhat different form by Arte Publico Press in 1984 and revised in 1989. Reprinted by permission of Susan Bergholz Literary Services, New York. **62:** Elizabeth Murphy-Melas: For an edited version of "Yomarhi Purnima" by Elizabeth Murphy-Melas, from *Cricket*, November 1992 issue. Reprinted by permission of the author and thanks to Nepal Embassy, Washington. **72:** G. P. Putnam's Sons: For an excerpt from "A Child of the Movement," from *Freedom's Children* by Ellen Levine. Copyright © 1992 by Ellen Levine. Reprinted by permission of G. P. Putnam's Sons. **84:** Curtis Brown, Ltd.: For "Rain" by Adrien Stoutenburg, from *The Things That Are*. Copyright © 1964 by Adrien Stoutenburg. Reprinted by permission of Curtis Brown, Ltd. **85:** HarperCollins Publishers: "Reggie," from *Honey, I Love* by Eloise Greenfield. Text copyright © 1978 by Eloise Greenfield. By permission of HarperCollins Publishers. The Touchstone Center, Inc.: For "Scrapyard" by Michael Benson, from *Miracles: Poems by Children of the English-speaking World*, collected by Richard Lewis. Copyright © 1992 by Richard Lewis and The Touchstone Center, Inc. **94:** Ed Ricciuti: For "Take Tracks Home" by Ed Ricciuti, from *Field & Stream*, November 1992 issue. Reprinted by permission of the author. **116:** *Chicago Tribune:* For an adapted version of "Video Web Weaves an Inadequate Tale" by Barbara Brotman, from *Chicago Tribune*, March 22, 1992. Copyright © 1992 by Chicago Tribune Company. All rights reserved, used with permission of *Chicago Tribune.* **143:** Francisco Jiménez: For

excerpts from "The Circuit" by Francisco Jiménez in *Arizona Quarterly*, Autumn 1973. Reprinted by permission of the author. **157:** GCT, Inc.: For "What Would We Do Without You?" by Jeff Hayden, from *Creative Kids*, March 1992 Vol. 10, No. 6. Reprinted with permission of *Creative Kids* magazine, Mobile, Alabama. **214:** Golden West Publishers: For excerpts from *Cowboy Slang* by Edgar R. "Frosty" Potter. Reprinted by permission from Golden West Publishers, Phoenix, Arizona. **264:** Marian Reiner, Literary Agent: For "The Sidewalk Racer," from *The Sidewalk Racer and Other Poems of Sports and Motion* by Lillian Morrison. Copyright © 1965, 1967, 1968, 1977 by Lillian Morrison. Reprinted by permission of Marian Reiner for the author. **393:** Macmillan Publishing Company: For six sniglets: "cinemuck," "glackett," "oatgap," "profanitype," "spork," and "wondracide," from *Sniglets* by Rich Hall and Friends. Copyright © 1984 by Not the Network Company, Inc. For one sniglet: "snacktivity," from *Angry Young Sniglets* by Rich Hall and Friends. Copyright © 1987 by Not the Network Company, Inc. For one sniglet: "pigslice," from *More Sniglets* by Rich Hall and Friends. Copyright © 1985 by Not the Network Company, Inc. Reprinted with the permission of Collier Books, an imprint of Macmillan Publishing Company. **394:** Gwendolyn Brooks: "Pete at the Zoo," from *Blacks* by Gwendolyn Brooks. Copyrighted by Gwendolyn Brooks, published by Third World Press, December 1991. By permission of the author. **431:** Weekly Reader Corporation: For excerpts from "English Is a Crazy Language" by Richard Lederer, from *Writing*, December 1986. Copyright © 1986 by Weekly Reader Corporation. Reprint permission granted by *Writing*, published by Weekly Reader Corporation.

The authors and editors have made every effort to trace the ownership of all copyrighted selections in this book and to make full acknowledgment for their use.

Illustration & Photography Credits

Commissioned Illustrations: Rondi Collette: **193, 295**; Pat Dypold: **106–107**; Joe Fournier: **278–279, 338**; Tyrone Geter: **84–85**; Mary Jones: **96–98, 100, 103, 105, 132, 215–216**; Linda Kelen: **247, 296, 321, 417, 504**; Keith Kraus: **87**; Jared D. Lee: **4, 6, 9, 305, 464, 513**; Rich Lo: **190**; Steven Mach: **94–95**; Eric Masi: **529**; Marlies Merk Najaka: **50–51**; Clinton Meyer: **526**; Richard Murdock: **307**; Kevin Pope: **222, 276**; Jesse Reisch: **142–145**; Douglas Schneider: **448**; Richard Shanks: *graphics* **166,**

374; Roni Shepard: **161, 214, 285, 393, 431**; Steve Skelton: **546, 583**; Kat Thacker: **28–29**; Russell Thurston: **180–181**; Meryl Treatner: **254**; Robert Voigts: **43, 109, 118, 194–196, 199, 202–203, 215–216, 235–236, 263, 299, 301, 309–312, 318, 527, 599**; Amy Wasserman: **120, 125, 127**; Don Wilson: **116–117**; Cheryl Winser *(hand-coloring)*: **167–168, 179, 207, 281, 325, 470, 532, 573**.

Assignment Photography: John Morrison: **14–15, 22–23, 26, 30–31, 41, 52–53, 67** *top*, **74–76, 78, 81, 89, 96–97, 110** *top*, **118–119, 128, 140, 146–147, 166–169, 174, 201, 292**; Art Wise: **ii**.

Art and Photography: 2: Courtesy Michelle Ryan; **15:** Reprinted by permission of Sterling Publishing Co., Inc., NY, NY, from *John Hedgecoe's Complete Guide to Photography* by John Hedgecoe, © 1990 by Collins & Brown, Text © by Collins & Brown and John Hedgecoe, Photographs © 1990 by John Hedgecoe; **23:** © Tony Freeman/PhotoEdit; **24:** Slide MS 33-2-3, Leland C. Wyman Collection, Museum of Northern Arizona; **28–29:** Courtesy Jean Fritz; **30–31:** Copyright © 1992 by Latoya Hunter. Reproduced by permission of Crown Publishers, Inc., NY; **34:** © Mary Kate Denny/PhotoEdit; **39:** © Skjold; **40–41:** © Carr Clifton; **44:** *top*, Utah State Historical Society; *bottom*, Pablo Picasso, *Three Musicians*, Fontainebleau, summer 1921. Oil on canvas, 6'7" x 7'3 3/4" (200.7 x 222.9 cm). The Museum of Modern Art, New York. Mrs. Simon Guggenheim Fund; **52:** Courtesy Alisa Monnier; **53:** © Dave Bartruff/FPG; **54:** © J. Kugler/FPG; **61:** © J. Kugler/FPG; **62:** © Bill Wassman; **63:** *top*, © Eric Reynolds/Adventure Photo; *bottom left*, © Paula Bronstein/Black Star; *bottom right*, © Bill Wassman; **64:** © Andy Selters/Viesti Associates, Inc.; **67:** *bottom*, © Campbell Laird; **70:** The Granger Collection, New York; **72–73:** © James H. Karales/Peter Arnold, Inc.; **75:** © David Perry; **81:** Photograph of W. B. Johns courtesy of Corrine Johns; **89:** *top*, NASA; *bottom*, Reproduced by permission of HarperCollins Publishers. Cover photograph © Frans Lanting; **92:** Negative # DOM.APP. 022/Trustees of the Science Museum, London; **110:** *bottom*, Illustration and Character Designs © 1988 Danielle Jones; **114:** Marc Chagall. *I and the Village*. 1911. Oil on canvas, 6'3 5/8" x 59 5/8". The Museum of Modern Art, New York. Mrs. Simon Guggenheim Fund; **117:** Shooting Star; **118:** Courtesy Dave Smith; **118–119:** Reprinted by permission of the *Sarasota Herald-Tribune*; **128–129:** © Joe Viesti/Viesti Associates, Inc.; **135:** Reproduced by courtesy of the Trustees of the British Museum; **137:** *top*, Courtesy Robert B.

Mayer Family Collection, Chicago; *bottom,* © Laurie Rubin/Tony Stone Images; **146:** Courtesy Vanessa Ramirez; **147:** © Melanie Carr/Viesti Associates, Inc.; **149:** © Bill Aron/PhotoEdit; **152:** © Spencer Grant/Photo Researchers, Inc.; **155:** © Mary Kate Denny/PhotoEdit; **156–157:** © 1990 Kristin Finnegan/Allstock; **158:** from *What Would We Do Without You?* copyright © 1990 by Kathy Henderson. Used with permission of Betterway Books, a division of F&W Publications, Inc.; **160:** *top left,* © Weinberg/Clark/The Image Bank; *bottom right,* © Michael Grecco/Sygma; **164:** © Jean-Francois Podevin/The Image Bank; **166:** *center,* Reprinted with permission of the Baltimore Sun Company; *bottom left,* UPI/Bettmann; *bottom right,* National Baseball Library, Cooperstown, NY; **167–168:** UPI/Bettmann; **170:** UPI/ Bettmann; **179:** UPI/ Bettmann; **180–181:** Zaremski Family photographs courtesy Merrill Wilk; Nieuw Amsterdam photograph from The Peabody & Essex Museum, Salem, Mass., Neg. #13704; **183:** Courtesy Holland America Line; **184:** The Granger Collection, New York; **185:** *top,* © Sterling FX/The Image Bank; *bottom,* India Office, London/The Bridgeman Art Library, London; **188:** Collection Chloe Sayer/Photography © David Lavender; **191:** © 1993 Cindy Lewis; **197:** Leonard McCombe, *LIFE* Magazine © Time Warner; **198:** Copyright © October 6, 1992, Chicago Tribune Company, all rights reserved, used with permission; **200:** Courtesy Beth & John Morrison; **203:** © Ken Merfeld; **205:** Shooting Star; **207:** UPI/Bettmann; **208:** © Tom McHugh/Allstock; **212:** © 1993 SIS/Jerry Werner; **218:** Baron Hugo Van Lawick, © National Geographic Society; **221:** Courtesy ACA Galleries, New York; **225:** © E. R. Degginger/Animals, Animals; **226:** © 1992 New World Computing. Spaceward Ho is a trademark of Delta Tao, Inc. under license to New World Computing. New World Computing is Registered trademark of New World Computing, Inc., Woodland Hills, CA; **229:** Chloe Sayer Collection/Photography © David Lavender; **230:** © The Detroit Institute of Arts, Museo Diego Rivera, Guanajuato (INBA); **234:** © Suzanne Murphy/FPG; **237:** Drawings copyright © 1989 by Chuck Jones Enterprises, Inc. Reproduced by permission. BUGS BUNNY, the character, name and all related indicia are property of Warner Bros. © 1993; **241:** © Chip Simons; **246:** © Steven E. Sutton/Duomo; **249:** © Fred Marcellino; **252:** © Norma Morrison/Hillstrom Stock Photo; **260:** Courtesy Pat Iversen; **264:** © 1993 The Estate of Keith Haring; **265:** © Walter Iooss Jr./ *Sports Illustrated;* **267:** © Francois Gohier/ Photo Researchers, Inc.; **269:** Annie Griffiths Belt; **270:** *top,* © Bob Krist; *bottom,* © Doug Wechsler; **271:** *top left,* © Tom Ives; *top right,* © Eddie Adams/ courtesy

1989 H. J. Heinz Annual Report; **272:** *top,* © Will van Overbeek; *center,* © C. B. Harding; *bottom,* © Linda Gebhardt; **273:** © Gerald Farber; **281:** Photograph courtesy Harry Shunk; **283:** Reprinted by permission: Tribune Media Services; **286:** Sygma; **289:** © Edgar Moench/Allstock; **292:** *The Way Things Work,* © 1988 Dorling Kindersley Limited, London. Published in the United States by Houghton Mifflin Company, *Incredible Cross-Sections,* © 1992 Dorling Kindersley Limited, London. Published in the United States by Alfred A. Knopf, Inc. Distributed by Random House, Inc., Cover from *Knights in Armor* by John D. Clare, copyright © 1992, 1991 by Random House (UK) Limited, reproduced by permission of Harcourt Brace & Company; **293:** © James Marsh; **319:** Margaret Bourke-White, *LIFE* Magazine © Time Warner Inc.; **325:** public domain; **329:** The Granger Collection, NY; **333:** © Wendy Shattil & Bob, Rozinski/Tom Stack & Associates; **334:** Photograph courtesy of Thos. K. Woodard American Antiques and Quilts; **339:** © Robert E. Daemmrich/Tony Stone Images; **343:** Courtesy Louis K. Meisel Gallery, New York, photo by Steve Lopez; **345:** © Martin Harvey/ The Wildlife Collection; **346:** © Peter Gridley/FPG; **351:** The Granger Collection, New York; **353:** © Travelpix/FPG; **357:** © Leon French; **358:** © Lee Balterman/FPG; **361:** © J. Carmichael, Jr./The Image Bank; **375:** © Mike Robins; **376:** © John Hanley; **379:** The Library of Congress; **386:** © Martha Cooper/Viesti Associates, Inc.; **395:** © Joe McDonald/ Natural Selection; **398:** © Robert Frerck/ Tony Stone Images; **404:** © Tom McHugh/ Photo Researchers, Inc.; **407:** Courtesy New York Downtown Hospital; **408:** © Jon Love/The Image Bank; **413:** © 1993 Galen Rowell; **420:** © Ron Kimball; **434:** © Patrick Tehan; **435:** © Andy Levin; **438:** Sketches by the great Arthur Babbitt courtesy Mrs. Arthur Babbitt, reprinted from *Animation— From Script to Screen,* by Shamus Culhane; **443:** Mary Evans Picture Library; **451:** © Merlin D. Tuttle/Bat Conservation International; **458:** Alexander Calder, *Chock,* 1972. 11 x 28 x 22 inches. (27.9cm x 71.9cm x 55.9cm). Collection of Whitney Museum of American Art. Gift of the artist 72.55a-b; **459:** © Gerard P. Byrne. Reprinted from the Parade/Kodak We the People photo contest winners; **461:** The Library of Congress; **462:** © Jurgen Schmitt/The Image Bank; **467:** © 1987 Lili Lakich; **470:** UPI/Bettmann; **473:** © Her Majesty's Stationery Office; **480:** Illustration copyright © 1988 by Trina Schart Hyman from *A Connecticut Yankee in King Arthur's Court.* Reprinted by permission of Morrow Junior Books, a division of William Morrow and Co., Inc.; **481:** Illustration from *The Legend of King Arthur* by Alan Baker, published by Kingfisher Books. Copyright © Grisewood & Dempsey 1993; **484:** © Jeff Hunter/The

Image Bank; **487:** © Joe DiStefano/ Photo Researchers, Inc.; **490:** © J.A.L. Cooke/Animals, Animals; **494:** State Historical Society of Missouri, Columbia; **502:** Courtesy Tony Shafrazi Gallery, New York, Photography by Tseng Kwong Chi; **503:** © Manfred Kage/Peter Arnold, Inc.; **507:** © Jack Parsons; **510:** Archive Photos/Wilgos; **514:** © Joe Viesti/Viesti Associates, Inc.; **517:** © William R. Sallaz/ Duomo; **518:** © Peter Miller/ Photo Researchers, Inc.; **527:** © Joe Baraban; **532:** AP/Wide World Photos; **534:** © Mark Newman/Tom Stack & Associates; **538:** © and TM 1993 Hanna-Barbera Productions Inc. All Rights Reserved; **547:** © Eric Meola/The Image Bank; **554:** © Brian Vikander/ West Light; **556:** © 1990 Mark Downey; **559:** *THE WIZARD OF OZ,* © 1939 Turner Entertainment Co. All Rights Reserved. Photo courtesy of MGM/UA Home Video, Inc.; **560:** Courtesy Eloise Greenfield; **566:** The Everett Collection, Inc.; **567:** © Russ Kinne/Comstock; **570:** © Tobias Everke/Gamma-Liaison; **573:** © Terry Lorant; **577:** Smithsonian Institution Photo No. 33184; **580:** © Mark Green/ Tony Stone Images; **588:** The Granger Collection, New York; **604:** *top,* © E. C. Stangler/Leo de Wys, Inc.;*bottom left,* © Robert Holmes; *bottom right,* © Ken Haas/Leo de Wys, Inc.; **626:** © Tony Freeman/Photoedit; **627:** Screens from Evanston (Illinois) Public Library, using system from Data Research Associates; **629:** *top* Prodigy Internet and the Prodigy Internet logo are trademarks of Prodigy Services Corporation. For subscription information, call 1-800-PRODIGY or visit our Web Site at www.prodigy.com; *center* Copyright © 1997 America On Line. Used by permission; *bottom* CompuServe logo courtesy of CompuServe, Incorporated; **630, 631, 632:** Copyright © 1996 Netscape Communications Corp. All rights reserved. This page may not be reprinted or copied without the express written permission of Netscape. Netscape Communication Corporation has not authorized, sponsored, or endorsed, or approved this publication and is not responsible for its content. Netscape and the Netscape Corporate logos are trademarks of their respective owners; **634:** Adobe and Adobe Illustrator are trademarks of Adobe Systems Incorporated; **636, 638:** *background* Used with permission of Hewlett Packard; **636** *inset,* **638:** Photo courtesy of Merrill Wilk.

Cover

Ryan Roessler
Greeting card copyright © 1989 Hallmark Cards, Inc. Used by permission. Tickets courtesy Ticketmaster, Inc. Article copyright © 1992 The Chicago Tribune Company. Used by permission.